A brilliantly executed and creative collaboration. The product is not just a contribution to discourses on politics and aesthetics, but a productive mobilisation of what Edkins and Kear call 'cross-talk'. The critical methodologies that emerge are used to explore core questions such as warfare and political protest.

Vivienne Jabri, *King's College London, UK*

International Politics and Performance

In recent years we have witnessed an increasing convergence of work in International Politics and Performance Studies around the troubled, and often troubling, relationship between politics and aesthetics. Whilst examination of political aesthetics, aesthetic politics and politics of aesthetic practice has been central to research in both disciplines for some time, the emergence of a distinctive 'performative turn' in International Politics and a critical return to the centrality of politics and the concept of 'the political' in Performance Studies highlights the importance of investigating the productivity of bringing the methods and approaches of the two fields of enquiry into dialogue and mutual relation.

Exploring a wide range of issues including rioting, youth-driven protests, border security practices and the significance of cultural awareness in war, this text provides an accessible and cutting-edge investigation of the intersection of international politics and performance examining issues surrounding the politics of appearance, image, event and place; and discusses the development and deployment of innovative critical and creative research methods, from auto-ethnography to site-specific theatre-making, from philosophical aesthetics to the aesthetic thought of new securities scenario-planning.

The book's focus throughout is on the materiality of performance practices—on the politics of making, spectating and participating in a variety of modes as political actors and audiences—whilst also seeking to explicate the performative dynamics of creative and critical thinking. Structured thematically and framed by a detailed introduction, the volume aims to produce a dialogue between contributors and to provide an essential reference point for this developing field.

This work is essential reading for students of politics and performance and will be of great interest to students and scholars of International Relations, performance studies and cultural studies.

Jenny Edkins is Professor of International Politics at Aberystwyth University.

Adrian Kear is Professor of Theatre and Performance at Aberystwyth University.

Interventions
Edited by:
Jenny Edkins, *Aberystwyth University* and Nick Vaughan-Williams, *University of Warwick*

> As Michel Foucault has famously stated, "knowledge is not made for understanding; it is made for cutting." In this spirit the Edkins–Vaughan-Williams Interventions series solicits cutting edge, critical works that challenge mainstream understandings in international relations. It is the best place to contribute post disciplinary works that think rather than merely recognize and affirm the world recycled in IR's traditional geopolitical imaginary.
>
> Michael J. Shapiro, *University of Hawai'i at Mānoa, USA*

The series aims to advance understanding of the key areas in which scholars working within broad critical poststructural and postcolonial traditions have chosen to make their interventions, and to present innovative analyses of important topics.

Titles in the series engage with critical thinkers in philosophy, sociology, politics and other disciplines and provide situated historical, empirical and textual studies in international politics.

Critical Theorists and International Relations
Edited by Jenny Edkins and Nick Vaughan-Williams

Ethics as Foreign Policy
Britain, the EU and the other
Dan Bulley

Universality, Ethics and International Relations
A grammatical reading
Véronique Pin-Fat

The Time of the City
Politics, philosophy, and genre
Michael J. Shapiro

Governing Sustainable Development
Partnership, protest and power at the world summit
Carl Death

Insuring Security
Biopolitics, security and risk
Luis Lobo-Guerrero

Foucault and International Relations
New critical engagements
Edited by Nicholas J. Kiersey and Doug Stokes

International Relations and Non-Western Thought
Imperialism, colonialism and investigations of global modernity
Edited by Robbie Shilliam

Autobiographical International Relations
I, IR
Edited by Naeem Inayatullah

War and Rape
Law, memory and justice
Nicola Henry

Madness in International Relations
Psychology, security and the global governance of mental health
Alison Howell

Spatiality, Sovereignty and Carl Schmitt
Geographies of the nomos
Edited by Stephen Legg

Politics of Urbanism
Seeing like a city
Warren Magnusson

Beyond Biopolitics
Theory, violence and horror in world politics
François Debrix and Alexander D. Barder

The Politics of Speed
Capitalism, the state and war in an accelerating world
Simon Glezos

Politics and the Art of Commemoration
Memorials to struggle in Latin America and Spain
Katherine Hite

Indian Foreign Policy
The politics of postcolonial identity
Priya Chacko

Politics of the Event
Time, movement, becoming
Tom Lundborg

Theorising Post-Conflict Reconciliation
Agonism, restitution and repair
Edited by Alexander Keller Hirsch

Europe's Encounter with Islam
The secular and the postsecular
Luca Mavelli

Re-Thinking International Relations Theory via Deconstruction
Badredine Arfi

The New Violent Cartography
Geo-analysis after the aesthetic turn
Edited by Sam Okoth Opondo and Michael J. Shapiro

Insuring War
Sovereignty, security and risk
Luis Lobo-Guerrero

International Relations, Meaning and Mimesis
Necati Polat

The Postcolonial Subject
Claiming politics/governing others in late modernity
Vivienne Jabri

Foucault and the Politics of Hearing
Lauri Siisiäinen

Volunteer Tourism in the Global South
Giving back in neoliberal times
Wanda Vrasti

Cosmopolitan Government in Europe
Citizens and entrepreneurs in postnational politics
Owen Parker

Studies in the Trans-Disciplinary Method
After the aesthetic turn
Michael J. Shapiro

Alternative Accountabilities in Global Politics
The scars of violence
Brent J. Steele

Celebrity Humanitarianism
The ideology of global charity
Ilan Kapoor

Deconstructing International Politics
Michael Dillon

The Politics of Exile
Elizabeth Dauphinee

Democratic Futures
Revisioning democracy promotion
Milja Kurki

Postcolonial Theory
A critical introduction
Edited by Sanjay Seth

More than Just War
Narratives of the just war and military life
Charles A. Jones

Deleuze & Fascism
Security: war: aesthetics
Edited by Brad Evans and Julian Reid

Feminist International Relations
'Exquisite corpse'
Marysia Zalewski

The Persistence of Nationalism
From imagined communities to urban encounters
Angharad Closs Stephens

Interpretive Approaches to Global Climate Governance
Reconstructing the greenhouse
Edited by Chris Methmann, Delf Rothe and Benjamin Stephan

Postcolonial Encounters with International Relations
The politics of transgression
Alina Sajed

Post-Tsunami Reconstruction in Indonesia
Negotiating normativity through gender mainstreaming initiatives in Aceh
Marjaana Jauhola

Leo Strauss and the Invasion of Iraq
Encountering the abyss
Aggie Hirst

Production of Postcolonial India and Pakistan
Meanings of partition
Ted Svensson

War, Identity and the Liberal State
Everyday experiences of the geopolitical in the armed forces
Victoria M. Basham

Writing Global Trade Governance
Discourse and the WTO
Michael Strange

Politics of Violence
Militancy, international politics, killing in the name
Charlotte Heath-Kelly

Ontology and World Politics
Void universalism I
Sergei Prozorov

Theory of the Political Subject
Void universalism II
Sergei Prozorov

Visual Politics and North Korea
Seeing is believing
David Shim

Globalization, Difference and Human Security
Edited by Mustapha Kamal Pasha

International Politics and Performance
Critical aesthetics and creative practice
Edited by Jenny Edkins and Adrian Kear

International Politics and Performance

Critical aesthetics and creative practice

**Edited by
Jenny Edkins and Adrian Kear**

LONDON AND NEW YORK

First published 2013
by Routledge
2 Park Square, Milton Park, Abingdon, Oxon OX14 4RN

and by Routledge
711 Third Avenue, New York, NY 10017

Routledge is an imprint of the Taylor & Francis Group, an informa business

© 2013 Selection and editorial matter Jenny Edkins and Adrian Kear; contributors, their contributions.

The right of **Jenny Edkins** and **Adrian Kear** to be identified as editors of this work has been asserted by them in accordance with the Copyright, Designs and Patent Act 1988.

All rights reserved. No part of this book may be reprinted or reproduced or utilised in any form or by any electronic, mechanical, or other means, now known or hereafter invented, including photocopying and recording, or in any information storage or retrieval system, without permission in writing from the publishers.

Trademark notice: Product or corporate names may be trademarks or registered trademarks, and are used only for identification and explanation without intent to infringe.

COVER IMAGE: *Coriolan/us*, directed by Mike Pearson and Mike Brookes, National Theatre Wales, RAF St Athan, August 2012. Credit: Simon Banham, courtesy of Simon Banham and National Theatre Wales.

British Library Cataloguing in Publication Data
A catalogue record for this book is available from the British Library

Library of Congress Cataloging in Publication Data
International politics and performance : critical aesthetics and creative practice / [edited by] Jenny Edkins, Adrian Kear.
　　p. cm. – (Interventions)
　Summary: 'The book's focus is on the politics of making, spectating and participating and the performative dynamics of creative and critical thinking'– Provided by publisher.
　Includes bibliographical references and index.
　1. International relations. 2. International relations–Philosophy. 3. Critical theory. 4. Performing arts–Political aspects. 5. Cultural awareness. I. Edkins, Jenny. II. Kear, Adrian, 1970-
　JZ1305.I56425 2013
　327.101–dc23
　　　　　　　　2013015731

ISBN: 978-0-415-70622-3 (hbk)
ISBN: 978-0-415-70623-0 (pbk)
ISBN: 978-1-315-88400-4 (ebk)

Typeset in Times New Roman
by Taylor & Francis Books

Contents

List of illustrations xiii
List of contributors xiv

Introduction 1
JENNY EDKINS AND ADRIAN KEAR

PART I
Logics of staging 17

1 Traces of presence 19
   ADRIAN KEAR

2 Facing and defacing 40
   JENNY EDKINS

PART II
Aesthetic thought and the politics of practice 61

3 Justice and the archives: 'the method of dramatization' 63
   MICHAEL J. SHAPIRO

4 The 'little cold breasts' of an English girl,
   or art and identity 78
   ALEXANDER GARCÍA DÜTTMANN

5 Animating politics 84
   DIANA TAYLOR

6 A golden surface: on virtuosity and cosmopolitics 96
   JOE KELLEHER

PART III
Ontological and ethnographic co-performance 111

7 Theatre as post-operative follow-up: The Bougainville
  Photoplay Project 113
  PAUL DWYER

8 Stagecraft/statecraft/mancraft: embodied envoys, 'objects'
  and the spectres of estrangement in Africa 130
  SAM OKOTH OPONDO

9 Impossibilities: generative misperformance and the
  movements of the teaching body 150
  NAEEM INAYATULLAH

PART IV
Bodies politic and performative 159

10 Performing audience: the politics of relation and
   participation in *Coriolan/us* 161
   PATRICK PRIMAVESI

11 Bellies, wounds, infections, animals, territories:
   the political bodies of Shakespeare's *Coriolanus* 179
   STUART ELDEN

PART V
Dramaturgies of scenario and security 201

12 Power, security and antiquities 203
   CHRISTINE SYLVESTER

13 Staging war as cultural encounter 221
   MAJA ZEHFUSS

14 Lines of sight: on the visualization of unknown futures 234
   LOUISE AMOORE

   Select bibliography 252
   Index 271

Illustrations

Figures

5.1	Plantón	86
5.2	AMLO	87
5.3	AMLO and Jesusa Rodriguez	90
5.4	Regina Orozco	91
7.1	Tearouki, Bougainville, 1962	116
7.2	Villagers of Pateaveave, Bougainville, 1962	120
7.3	Pateaveave, Bougainville, 1962	121
7.4	Tarlena, Bougainville, 1966	122
7.5	Mary and the Sisters at Chabai, 1966	123
7.6	Nuns at Chabai, 2004	123
7.7	Torokina, Bougainville, 1962(?)	126
10.1	Coriolan/us: Richard Lynch, John Rowley and Gerald Tyler	163
10.2	Coriolan/us: Matthew Thomas, Richard Lynch and Jonny Glynn	164
10.3	Coriolan/us: Richard Lynch and Jonny Glynn	173
10.4	Coriolan/us: Richard Harrington	175

Contributors

Louise Amoore is Professor of Political Geography at Durham University and RCUK Global Uncertainties Leadership Fellow. Her research focuses on three key areas: global geopolitics and the security practices of the border; the politics and practices of risk management and risk consulting as a technology of governing; and political and social theories of resistance and dissent. Her publications include: *The Politics of Possibility: Risk and Security Beyond Probability* (Duke University Press, 2013); *Gloablisation Contested: An International Political Economy of Work* (Manchester University Press, 2002); *Risk and the War on Terror* (co-edited with Marieke de Goede, Routledge, 2008); and *The Global Resistance Reader* (Routledge, 2005).

Alexander García Düttmann is Professor of Philosophy in the Department of Visual Cultures at Goldsmiths, and Visiting Professor in the Department of Photography at the Royal College of Art. His research has focused on the relationship between language and history in authors such as Adorno, Benjamin and Heidegger. He has also been interested in the question of political deconstruction, especially in the context of identity politics (AIDS activism, recognition and multiculturalism). In one of his latest publications he outlines the very idea of deconstruction. In 2011 he published *Participation: Consciousness of Semblance*, an attempt to make sense of the often used concept of participation, especially in relation to art and politics. His book *Naive Art: An Essay on Happiness* (2012), is a series of prose fragments set in San Francisco.

Paul Dwyer is Chair of the Department of Performance Studies at the University of Sydney. After almost a decade of professional theatre work, mostly as an actor, animateur, director or dramaturge in the field of youth/community theatre, he returned to university study in the mid-1990s. Dr Dwyer teaches courses that include performance and political life, and ethnographic approaches to performance. His critically acclaimed The Bougainville Photoplay Project has toured nationally and is based on journeys made by his father Dr Allan Dwyer, a world-renowned orthopaedic surgeon, who visited Bougainville during the 1960s. It takes the form of a performance lecture that uses storytelling and a multimedia installation. He is also currently undertaking an ARC Discovery research project that looks at ceremony, ritual and other kinds of performance practices designed to foster reconciliation.

Jenny Edkins is Professor of International Politics at Aberystwyth University. Prior to joining the Department as Leverhulme Special Research Fellow in 1997, she taught at the University of Manchester and the Open University. She is co-editor with Maja Zehfoss of the successful textbook *Global Politics: A New Introduction*, now in its second edition, and has published six other books, including most recently: *Missing: Persons and Politics* (Cornell, 2011); *Trauma and the Memory of Politics* (Cambridge, 2003); and *Whose Hunger? Concepts of Famine, Practices of Aid* (Minnesota, 2000).

Stuart Elden is Professor of Political Theory and Geography at the University of Warwick. His latest book, *The Birth of Territory* (University of Chicago Press 2013) was the product of a Leverhulme Major Research Fellowship. His other books include *Terror and Territory: The Spatial Extent of Sovereignty* (University of Minnesota Press, 2009) and studies of Martin Heidegger, Michel Foucault and Henri Lefebvre. He has won the Association of American Geographers Globe Book Award for Public Understanding of Geography, the AAG Political Geography Speciality Group Julian Minghi Outstanding Research Award, and the Royal Geographical Society's Murchison award. He edits the journal *Environment and Planning D: Society and Space*, and blogs at www.progressivegeographies.com

Naeem Inayatullah is Professor in the Department of Politics, Ithaca College, and was President of the Global Development Section, International Studies Association, 2007–08. He publishes on international political economy, international relations and autoethnography, among other things, and his recent publications include: *Savage Economics: Wealth, Poverty and the Temporal Walls of Capitalism* (with David Blaney, 2010); *Autoethnography and International Relations: I, IR* (Routledge, 2010); *Interrogating Imperialism: Conversations on Gender, Race and War* (co-editor with Robin Riley, Palgrave, 2006); and *International Relations and the Problem of Difference* (with David Blaney, Routledge, 2004).

Adrian Kear is Professor of Theatre and Performance at Aberystwyth University. His publications include: *Theatre and Event: Staging the European Century* (Palgrave, 2013); *On Appearance* (with Richard Gough, Routledge, 2008); *Psychoanalysis and Performance* (with Patrick Campbell, Routledge, 2001); and *Mourning Diana: Nation, Culture and the Performance of Grief* (with Deborah Lynn Steinberg, Routledge, 1999).

Joe Kelleher is Professor of Theatre and Performance and Head of Department for Drama, Theatre and Performance at Roehampton University. His research interests are largely in contemporary theatre and performance.

xvi *Contributors*

A central concern of his work has been with structures of theatrical persuasion, both within and beyond the professional theatre. His recent books include: *Theatre & Politics* (Palgrave Macmillan, 2009); *The Theatre of Societas Raffaello Sanzio* (with Nicholas Ridout and the core members of SRS, Chiara Guidi, Claudia Castellucci and director Romeo Castellucci, Routledge, 2007); *Contemporary Theatres in Europe: A Critical Companion* (co-edited with Nicholas Ridout, Routledge, 2006); and *Romeo Castellucci. To Carthage Then I Came. Exhibition* (with Claudia Castellucci and Nicholas Ridout, Actes Sud, 2002).

Sam Okoth Opondo is Assistant Professor of Political Science at Vassar College. His research is guided by an interest in colonialism, race and the mediation of estrangement. With an emphasis on violence, ethics and diplomacies of everyday life, he engages the problematics of humanitarianism, the politics of redemption and popular culture in urban Africa. His publications include *The New Violent Cartography: Geo-Analysis After the Aesthetic Turn* (Routledge, 2012).

Patrick Primavesi is Professor of Theatre Studies at the University of Leipzig and Director of the Dance Archive Leipzig, where he initiated a festival and conference on Movement in Urban Space. He also worked as a dramaturge and established a master's programme in dramaturgy (with Hans-Thies Lehmann) at the University of Frankfurt am Main. He wrote his PhD on Walter Benjamin's theories of translation and theatre and published widely on contemporary theatre, dance and performance art, and their inter-relations with film and new media. Present research projects focus on the politics of representation and performance in urban space and the changing conditions of the public sphere.

Michael J. Shapiro is a political philosopher and critical theorist and Professor at the University of Hawai'i, Mānoa, Honolulu, in the Political Science Department. His academic interests include political theory and philosophy as a tool to investigate international relations, media, culture, aesthetics and indigenous politics. His publications include: *Violent Cartographies* (1997); *Cinematic Political Thought* (1999); *Moral Spaces* (co-editor, 1999); *For Moral Ambiguity* (2001); *Reading 'Adam Smith'* (2002); *The Politics of Moralizing* (co-editor, 2002); *Methods and Nations* (2004); *Sovereign Lives* (co-editor, 2005); *Deforming American Political Thought* (2006); *Cinematic Geopolitics* (2008); and *The Time of the City* (2010).

Christine Sylvester is Professor of Political Science and of Women's Studies at the University of Connecticut, and is affiliated with the School of Global Studies, University of Gothenburg, Sweden. She has worked extensively outside the USA, including at the Australian National University (Canberra), The Institute of Social Studies (The Hague, Netherlands), Lancaster University (UK), and Lund University, Sweden. Her publications include: *War as Experience: Contributions from International Relations and Feminist*

Analysis (Routledge, 2013); *Experiencing War* (editor, Routledge, 2011); *Feminist International Relations: The Key Works* (editor of five volumes, Routledge, 2010); and *Art/Museums: International Relations Where We Least Expect It* (Paradigm, 2009).

Diana Taylor is University Professor and Professor of Performance Studies, Spanish and Portuguese at New York University, and founding Director of the Hemispheric Institute of Performance and Politics. Her publications include: *The Archive and the Repertoire: Performing Cultural Memory in the Americas* (Duke University Press, 2003); *Disappearing Acts: Spectacles of Gender and Nationalism in Argentina's Dirty War* (Duke University Press, 1997); and *Theatre of Crisis: Drama and Politics in Latin America* (University Press of Kentucky, 1991).

Maja Zehfuss is Professor of International Politics at the University of Manchester. She works on war and the politics of ethics. Her research examines how the problematic of ethics is produced, enacted and negotiated in war. This work focuses in particular on questions of targeting and training, the problematic of 'culturally sensitive war' and on instances in which soldiers have refused to fight. It aims to offer not least a critique of the just war tradition and thereby to open up space for more productive ways of thinking the ethical in relation to war. Her publications include: *Wounds of Memory: The Politics of War in Germany* (Cambridge University Press, 2007); and *Constructivism in International Relations: The Politics of Reality* (Cambridge University Press, 2002).

Introduction

Jenny Edkins and Adrian Kear

Preface: contingency, conversation and cross-talk
Jenny Edkins

It all began with a geographer. Or rather, with several geographers. And with an encounter at a dinner at the *Plas*—the Vice-Chancellor's official residence in wooded grounds next to the campus in Aberystwyth.

It was the first and only time I had been invited to such an event. I was there, as far as I know, not as Professor of International Politics, but because I'd recently been co-opted onto the editorial board of *Society and Space*. The new editor was an old friend of mine, Stuart Elden. Or rather, an old friend of someone who had been my doctoral student and was by now my co-author, Maja Zehfuss. He wanted to make the journal more interdisciplinary, or, to be precise, having made the move from political theory to geography himself on moving from Warwick to Durham, his vision was to bring more international politics into the journal. The geographers in Aberystwyth had noticed my elevation to the board of one of the most important journals in their field, and invited me along to meet Nigel Thrift, himself of course an Aber geography alumnus and co-founder of the journal. The dinner was held in his honour after one of his masterly expositions of the latest turn in critical thinking, the turn to affect, in a public lecture entitled 'Emotional Geographies: What and Why?'[1]

One of the other guests that night was Professor of Performance Studies Mike Pearson. I'm not sure why he was there—presumably because of his role in pioneering the development of site-specific theatre work, and the practice of auto-topographical performance.[2] In the archive entry for Nigel Thrift's talk on the Aber website, the preview does mention performance, so maybe that's why. Mike and I got talking, as one does on such occasions, and for some reason—Mike's presence and quiet intensity, I suspect—our conversation moved beyond the usual platitudes. Excited by the intellectual synergies that seemed to be emerging, we arranged to meet again, later, for a coffee in the Arts Centre.

It was an uncomfortable meeting, for me at least. I felt very much the novice, struggling to keep up, and at times we seemed to be talking past each other. However, my overriding impression was that we were talking about the same thing, and that in some profound sense we understood each other. We were using different words. Or rather, we were using the same words differently. A little like talking to someone who speaks North American English, perhaps. There was a common language to a certain extent. Many of the proper names that excited each of us were the same—Giorgio Agamben, Judith Butler, Jacques Rancière, Slavoj Žižek and Brian Massumi, for example—but the conventions of how we wove this language together were dissimilar. It seemed to me that we each had our own style of emphasis and nuance, and that our preferred modes, levels and genres of thought were distinct.

In the end it appeared—I think to us both—that there was something important here in terms of potential for productive intellectual engagement: some sort of a traumatic centre, an excess or lack around which our conversation orbited in a manner that conversations with colleagues in our own departments didn't always do. A shared emotional geography, perhaps. We decided to take things further, and explore the potential for a research group. We assembled interested and interesting colleagues around a table in the postgraduate seminar room in the Parry-Williams Building, the home of the Theatre, Film and Television Studies Department (TFTS), to see what would happen.

While a by now familiar self-consciousness and discomfort was present in the room, the feeling of excitement, exploration and potentiality grew as we talked. We went around the table outlining what we were working on. Those from a politics background disclaimed any knowledge of 'performance' and those from Performance Studies any expertise in 'politics'. It was a while before we discovered that no one in the room thought that 'politics' meant only what happens in parliaments, elections and political movements, or, on the other hand, that 'performance' was limited to a theatrical event or spectacle. We were not interested in looking at how all politicians inevitably 'perform' in front of the electorate, for example, or at how some theatrical productions take up current 'political' issues like Guantanamo or 9/11 directly.

By that time, February 2007, Adrian Kear had joined TFTS in Aberystwyth from Roehampton, as Head of Department. He brought with him, of course, an interest and expertise in a range of thinkers in contemporary continental philosophy congruent with that Mike and I had already discovered we shared. Alain Badiou and Jean-Luc Nancy were added to the list. Curiously, we discovered that both Adrian and I had already written on asylum seeker Abbas Amini's face-sewing protest.[3] Adrian is interested in appearance; I am interested in disappearance.[4] We have both written on mourning and memory.[5] These cross-overs confirmed our emerging sense of a strong research coherence. The gang of two rapidly became a gang of three, soon to be joined by others as new colleagues arrived and the group grew.[6]

Our decision to institute the Distinguished Speaker Series from which this volume springs was an attempt to develop an understanding of each other's languages, rather than a new interdisciplinary terminology. Its particular format was designed to allow time, space and a congenial atmosphere for gentle teasing out of diversity and accommodation of divergent and sometimes contradictory vocabularies. We would invite our speaker to give a talk, open to all comers, one evening. The talk would be followed by a dinner and there would be an extended seminar the following day with members of the research group. The seminar, sometimes lasting several hours, was where it all happened: where the warm-up of lecture and dinner bore fruit. I think what we were looking for, and what we found, was a way of continuing to speak our own languages but yet beginning to be mutually understood. Our invitations tapped into an already existing interest in the cross-over we were exploring. They were enthusiastically accepted and the series took off, with fifteen very distinguished speakers in the past five or six years.[7]

Twelve of these people have chapters in this volume, along with their 'hosts' in Adrian and me. What we have learned over the years is an acceptance and accommodation of each other's style and preferences. We don't ask that we develop a common language, but that we seek ways of understanding each other's idiom and appreciating the common questions that motivate us.

When we proposed this volume, we received reviews hugely supportive of the project on which we are engaged, but like all good reviewers of edited volumes, some wanted us to tighten up the argument and offer a firmer sense of direction for the new field that we were developing. That is the last thing we want to do. We are not developing a new field of study, nor are we doing interdisciplinary work. I would describe what is happening here as pre-disciplinary cross-talk. We are attentive to each other's different disciplinary constraints, but in our shared work, or in our sharing of work, we are, perhaps surprisingly, not bound by those constraints. Nor do we wish to modify our work to fit some supposed middle ground to be established between us. We are able instead to focus on the absent centre around which our work circulates. It's a bit like co-authorship. When I co-author a piece I always find it liberating. Instead of agonizing over the plausibility or intelligibility of what I am trying to say, I can share more or less unformed ideas with my co-author, who will immediately indicate whether there is anything there or not. In our pre-disciplinary cross-talk we can utter thoughts and receive affirmation or incomprehension, immediate support or puzzlement, and we can elaborate or enlarge accordingly. There is no need to be over-explicit, to pin things down, to categorize and classify. Instead, there are openings for what Rancière calls 'political being-together', which, as he reminds us, is 'a being-between: between identities, between worlds'.[8] Academic excitement, creative engagement, politics and critical humanities become possible.

Interlude: inhumanities
Adrian Kear[9]

Think pig

[*Standing with his back to a whiteboard, and face to face with his audience, the dark-suited young professor holds up his marker pen and begins speaking, in media res ...*]

Whilst Alain Badiou has argued that the subtractive aesthetics of Samuel Beckett attempted the 'formal reduction of "thinking humanity" to its indestructible functions, to its atemporal determinants',[10] it is possible to see how, in *Waiting for Godot*, he sought to condense the complex operation of the anthropological machine to a single exhortative imperative, directed by Pozzo towards the unfortunate Lucky: 'Think, pig!'[11] [*He writes* 'Think, pig!' *on the board as he says it.*]

The caesura introduced by Beckett's comma places Lucky's interpellation as 'human'—the thinking being—into suspension, producing a temporal and spatial barrier *within* the 'human animal' that marks, so to speak, its irremediably split condition. For if the anthropological machine functions, as Giorgio Agamben claims, 'by excluding as not (yet) human an already human being from itself, that is, by animalizing the human, by isolating the nonhuman within the human',[12] then the violence of Beckett's comma draws attention to this structure. Pozzo's line humanizes and animalizes simultaneously, or at least in a double movement; its performative effect is to produce the 'non-human' or 'less than human' within the *intellectual* capacity of the human being itself, whilst at the same time associating this figure with 'base' matter and *corporeal* insignificance. The punctuation mark, it might be said, inscribes precisely the 'zone of indifference' at the centre of the anthropological machine's operation, 'articulating' the otherwise invisible link between human and animal, thinking being and living being— the very stuff of *bare life*, as Agamben calls it, which Lucky appears to *represent*: a living, thinking being separated and excluded from the experience of itself by the *epistemic violence* and 'inhumanity' of the anthropological machine.[13]

What would happen, then, if Beckett's punctuation were to be removed? [*He erases the comma from* 'Think, pig!' *on the board, leaving the newly subtracted imperative,* 'Think pig!']. Not a lot, perhaps, other than a change of emphasis that instead of demanding that the animal *thinks* requires instead a *thinking of the animal*—which, as Martin Heidegger observes in *The Fundamental Concepts of Metaphysics*, is amongst the hardest things the thinking animal can do. This is because the animal must be recognized as absolutely other—'utterly unfamiliar'—if the 'error' of anthropomorphism is to be avoided; yet, as Heidegger makes explicit, this must also entail the suspension—and abstention—of the human as the 'anthropomorphous animal' whose very identity (or rather non-identity) relies on recognizing itself in what it is not (it must recognize itself as human in order to *be* human *as such*). This post-humanist 'human' is thereby rendered 'something ungraspable and absent' within the thinking of the animal's otherness, and yet, inexorably, it returns within the dialectic of the identity of identity and non-identity.[14] 'Think pig!' might therefore properly involve thinking openly about the pig's *metaphoricity*—its function as a literalized embodiment of the discourse of otherness—at least as much as any *putative* in-itself-ness. For if the pig itself has no sense of relation, it nonetheless has figured prominently in the historical 'staging' of human–inhuman relations (in which Heidegger, of course, is no less implicated).

So, let's try again to begin to 'Think pig!' [*He underlines this on the board*].

There's nothing particularly 'wild' about the story of my formative encounter with pigs: it took place on a farm and the animals concerned were already completely enclosed and thoroughly domesticated. Or, at least, that is what I *thought*. A child of about four years of age, I had been visiting this place for some time—the farmers were friends of my family—when the 'event' happened. I was standing on a gate at the entrance to the pigpen, watching the ravenous creatures feeding, when I decided, apparently, to jump in. No sooner had I hit the floor than I felt the enormous arms of my 'Uncle' Percy wrapped around me, hauling me back to safety. He scolded me in a gruff but caring tone: 'Did I want the pigs to eat me? They may look harmless enough but they will eat *anything*, little boys included! They just can't help it!' This 'lucky' escape left me somewhat bemused, I have to say: 'But *we* eat pigs,' I retorted, 'surely the pigs wouldn't dream of eating *me*!' Perhaps if Percy had read Heidegger he would have explained that the presence of 'food' acts as the pig's 'disinhibitor'—which, in a way, he did—for the implication of his lesson is that the pig has no way of *knowing* that I wasn't there to eat and, what's more, no way of stopping itself once set upon that course. The pig, if you like, eats indiscriminately and, I guess, *shamelessly*. My childish response was, of course, anthropomorphic in the extreme, in that I attributed to the animal the power of *thinking*. My capacity for thought—the *human* capacity for thinking the event that 'defines the very being of *thinking humanity*'[15]— was temporarily transferred onto it, and the result was a clouding of judgement. Yet, there is something more in this as well, as I remember thinking to myself, predictably, 'what would I taste like to a pig?' A further anthropomorphism, for sure, as if the judgement of 'taste' is not a culturally acquired *human* capacity, yet I remember all too clearly Percy's guttural response to my inquisitive pestering: 'Pork, probably!' This stopped me in my tracks, for if I were to taste like pork to a pig, and pig tastes as pork to me, then isn't there something *cannibalistic* in the relationship otherwise normalized between boy and beast?

I remember feeling a sense of shame at arriving at this recognition: *shame*, perhaps, as the operative condition of being 'human'. The shameless eating of the pig contrasts with the 'silent shame' feeding the *thought* of the human, even if the former is included in the latter's point of demarcation.[16] Perhaps this is why the pig's association—in the odious logic and bestializing epithets of the culture in which I was brought up—is with the very peoples who eschew swine-eating: Jews and Muslims. This is, for sure, absurdly and offensively literalizing, but then *literalization* is one of the key effects of the anthropological machine's *animalizing* metaphoricity. Agamben, of course, identifies the 'animalizing of the human'—the isolation of 'the nonhuman within the human'[17]—as one of the key historical determinants of anti-Semitism (and, one might add, current 'anti-terrorist' Islamo-hysteria). Following Primo Levi, he attributes the 'shame of being human'—a 'shame that in someway or another has tainted' *everybody*—to the 'shame of the camps', the shame of their 'exceptional' historicity.[18] Rather than consign the catastrophe of Auschwitz to the status of an cautionary anomaly, however, Agamben has argued consistently, and persuasively, that the camps' singularity reveals the foundational 'state of exception' at the heart of Western political machinery: that the 'state of emergency' in which Walter Benjamin and his contemporaries lived is not the exception but the rule, and the suspension of rights and citizenship that accompanies the designation of certain constituencies as operating 'outside' the rule of law (Jews in Nazi Germany; Islamic 'terrorist' suspects in post-9/11 USA and Britain) is inimical to the *continuing* literalizing attribution of categories of the 'less than human'.[19]

Perhaps the contrasting emotion to the feeling of 'shame' described above would not be the 'shamelessness' associated with the disinhibition of the animal but something like the recognition of 'dignity'. Dignity, classically—at least according to Immanuel Kant—is an end that is *unexchangeable*. It is the underlying principle of the ethical maxim: 'Act so that you treat humanity, whether in your own person or in that of another, always as an end and never as a means only.'[20] However, importantly, for Kant, dignity does not exist outside the field of instrumentality; rather, it organizes and legitimizes the constitution of its means *retroactively*. It functions, so to speak, *performatively*—creating the impression of an imperative behind an action that justifies the operation and deployment of certain 'means' tendentiously. It should not be surprising, then, to learn from Agamben that 'the humanist discovery of man is the discovery that he lacks himself, the discovery of his irremediable lack of *dignitas*'.[21] Kant re-orders this destabilizing recognition by directing it towards the establishment of objective exteriority: towards the imaginative construction of the *other* as the locus of an unexchangeable dignity. Whilst this is designed to ensure the just treatment of the other 'as an end and never as a means only',[22] the sentiment of 'respect' that it generates is as much—if not more—respect for the imperative of *law* governing means-ends relations as respect for the other in their inalienable alterity. In other words, Kant's framework is more than capable of accommodating a juridical attenuation of ends to means indefinitely: the *political* occupation and delimitation of the human being's *ethical* 'dwelling space' being decided by the sovereignty of *legal* principle and action.

'Respect for the other' thereby easily translates into respect for the law that designates which others are worthy of respect and which other others might be excluded from its remit (and one need only recall Kant's *Anthropology from a Pragmatic Point of View*[23] to see the violently *racist* implications of this). As Agamben suggests, any attempt to differentiate and decide between means and ends—human and inhuman—is, then, ultimately a matter of *politics*. 'If there is no animal politics, that is perhaps because animals are already in the open and do not try to take possession' of it; 'they simply live in it without caring about it'.[24] [*He writes* 'Think pig in shit!' *on the board.*] Human beings, however, transform the open into 'the battlefield of a political struggle', which 'goes by the name of *History*'.[25] [*He writes* 'Think, pig!' *on the board.*]

The anthropological machine is the apparatus whose operative mechanism structures this domain called *History*, alternating between the 'exclusion of an inside' (Jew, Islamic terrorist) and the 'inclusion of an outside' (Pig, respectable other), in deciding upon the strategic placement of the caesura between 'man' and 'animal', 'human' and 'inhuman':[26] hence, 'Think, pig!' [*He underlines* 'Think, pig!' *on the board.*]

If, however, this 'humanist' process functions *ex machina*, how might it be possible to conceive of an effective *anti*-humanist intervention into its mode of operation? How might it be possible to begin *thinking* again, with Lucky? How might it be possible to *think the event* without recourse to this anthropological machinery?[27]

Methods: thinking through performance and politics

In his recent book, *Studies in Trans-disciplinary Method* (2013), Michael Shapiro offers a timely reminder that the task of political critique is not merely to duplicate cultural 'common-sense' with 'empiricist, explanation-seeking social science', or simply to reproduce the explanatory apparatus of 'representational practices that already exist' as the taken-for-granted logic of a social formation, but to 'seek to displace institutionalized forms of recognition with *thinking*'. In privileging thinking over explanation and categorization as the fundamental *pre*-disciplinary methodology of creative and critical enquiry, Shapiro suggests that political critique constitutes a practice that seeks:

> to invent and apply conceptual frames and create juxtapositions that disrupt and/or render historically contingent accepted knowledge positions. It is to compose the discourse of investigation with critical juxtapositions that unbind what are ordinarily presumed to belong together ...[28]

Placing International Politics and Performance into critical conjunction is, then, less an inter-disciplinary move that seeks to bring the analytical insights, epistemological frameworks and disciplinary methods from each discipline and apply them to the other—thereby extending and enhancing their respective reach and explanatory power—but rather an attempt to open up the frames and practices of aesthetic and political enquiry emergent in the *post*-disciplinary landscape of critical humanities and creative arts research. It is, in this respect, not simply an opportunity to think through their points of correspondence and inter-relation, but to create the conditions for their inter-animation and mobilization of new ways of thinking. This approach is closely aligned to Jacques Rancière's exposition of the inter-determining relationship between art and politics, in which each constitutes a mode of practice of 'an aesthetic politics [which] always defines itself by a certain recasting of the distribution of the sensible, a reconfiguration of the given perceptual forms', and contributes to the disruption and re-orchestration of 'the relationship between the visible, the sayable, and the thinkable'.[29]

This way of thinking—emphasizing the need to think through politics and performance as modes and practices of *aesthetic thinking*, and to think them *together* as modes and practices of *aesthetic politics*—is in stark contrast to an alternative 'inter-disciplinary' approach, which remains primarily interested instead in elaborating the performance dynamics of politics (their ritual incarnations and modalities of practising citizenship) and the ways in which performance addresses politics and 'the political' through staging and interrogating its processes. In this empirically restricted view, we're still in the territory of examining 'performances *about*' political events, histories, experiences, etc. on the one hand, and explaining political events in terms of the logic of performance on the other. Whereas in this volume we see performance and politics as 'folded' in myriad and complex patterns, inter-animating one another as domains of political subjectivation and creative practices undertaken by aesthetic subjects,[30] a more conventional approach might be to see them as operating in 'dialogue'.[31] Our contention—explored throughout this book—is that politics and performance, *thought in relation* as practices of 'dissensus' and agentic creation,[32] reveal the fundamental interconnection yet ultimate separation of the aesthetics of politics and the politics of aesthetics in terms of form and effect, elaborating and demonstrating at every turn their inter-animation by aesthetic subjects in the practice of aesthetic politics. As Rancière puts it:

> If there is such a thing as an 'aesthetics of politics', it lies in the reconfiguration of the distribution of the common through political processes of subjectivation. Correspondingly, if there is a politics of aesthetics, it lies in the practices and modes of visibility of art that reconfigures the fabric of sensory experience.[33]

So how, then, are politics and performance enfolded as practices? How is this enfolding 'staged' or made manifest in specific instances and modes of aesthetic thought? What critical and creative methods are useful in drawing attention to the potentialities and limits of this thinking?

The present volume offers a series of specific micro-investigations of these meta-critical questions. The chapters each identify a specific aesthetic–political event or 'thought event'[34] and seek to develop a mode of articulating its 'staging' by analysing the operation of its set-up as an apparatus (*dispositif*)[35] producing aesthetic–political affects and subjectivating effects. Michael Shapiro outlines the workings of this aesthetic–political method in his contribution, demonstrating the deployment of a war crimes *dispositif* in the novel, *War & War* by László Krasznahorkai, and its effects in the construction of an 'aesthetic subject'.[36] Drawing on and elaborating Deleuze's 'Method of Dramatization', Shapiro utilizes dramatization as a framework for interrogating the relationship between history, memory and aesthesis in the representation and evocation of significant political events. Alexander García Düttmann also turns to a novel, John Cowper Powys's *A Glastonbury Romance*, and a short film by Jean-Marie Straub, *An Heir*, to provide the dramaturgical frame for his examination of the ways in which a distinctively aesthetic mode of thought enables the figuration of identity. Following Adorno,[37] he questions the boundaries of the relationship between art and politics and demonstrates how aesthetic practice resists instrumentalization and attenuation, offering an affirmative re-imagination of the limits of the thinkable. By contrast, Diana Taylor explores the ways in which the aesthetic passions of political subjects are animated by, and made manifest in, the forms of activism developed by contemporary protest movements. Examining the contested Mexican election of 2006 (in which 2 million protesters gathered in the Zócalo to challenge the official results by means of acts of civil disobedience) and the Occupy events in New York and London, Taylor contends that the forms of non-violent activism they deploy depend on the construction of politically subjectivating 'animatives' that contest the operation of hegemonic 'performatives'. The struggle between the two, she suggests, takes place in and through bodies and affects—in short, through the production of aesthetic–political subjects.

Likewise, Jenny Edkins explores the tension between the interpellative modes of subjectification deployed by the state apparatus and the creative invention of forms of riot and disorder. Examining the use of images of the face captured on CCTV in the English riots of 2011, during which the Assistant Chief Constable of Greater Manchester Police commented, '*we have your face … we are coming to get you*'—illustrating perfectly how, through recognition of *the face*, 'the abstract machine has you in its overall grip'[38]— Edkins investigates the ways in which the face is a politics, and how effacing the face, through wearing a hoodie or defacing property in a riot, may be understood as the performance of another kind of politics. Joe Kelleher's chapter also examines the politics of riot and the effects of the state apparatus, but in terms of their theatricalization in 'virtuoso' aesthetic performance. Taking as a prompt Italian theatre maker Romeo Castellucci's staging of a lamenter for protester Carlo Giuliani, killed by Italian police at the 2001 G8 summit, the chapter situates the 'operatic' lamenter in the theatre as virtuoso performer and at the same time political 'operator' and aesthetic figure of the representational apparatus deployed by the police. Kelleher then sets out to trace theatre's political rhetoric—and claim to politics—in terms of both its complicity with the state and its opening, through an aesthetic apparatus of illumination, of another way of reflecting and shaping the possibility of virtuosic 'acts' and political action.

Kelleher's concern with thinking the limits of the entwinement of performance and politics[39] is shared by Adrian Kear in his contribution to the volume. Focusing on the theatrical apparatus of Alfredo Jaar's exhibition, *It is Difficult*, Kear investigates the co-dependence of structures of presentation and strategies of representation in explicating the problematic of an aesthetic politics of spectatorship. The chapter seeks to interrogate the ways in which the relationship between the aesthetic and political apparatus is illuminated in the experience of the event, situating an understanding of the co-creative labour of spectatorship as central to explicating the aesthetic frame's indexing of the politics of co-appearance and deployment of the logic of representation in structuring the visual presentation of ontological presence. In so doing, it elaborates a specific instance of a politics of spectatorship which 'by appearing in the face of itself, faced with itself', enables a reflexive experience of 'co-appearing'.[40] The aesthetic practice of interrogating co-appearance similarly underlines Paul Dwyer's chapter setting out his ethnographic 'co-performance'[41] in the Bougainville Photoplay Project. This creative research project investigates the complexities of the geo- and chrono-political ties binding Australians and the people of Bougainville, Papua New Guinea, in the wake of the experience of a brutal civil war. Dwyer retraces three journeys made by his father Dr Allan Dwyer, an orthopaedic surgeon who visited Bougainville in the 1960s, treating dozens of wounded children. He entwines auto-ethnographic family stories with a theatrical staging of the co-appearance of others through these encounters, thereby situating the accounts he investigates within the larger narrative of Australia's colonial enterprise and attempts to develop a framework for restorative justice.

Sam Okoth Opondo's chapter similarly investigates the creative, political and ethical possibilities attendant on shifting the logic of cultural encounter away from the 'objectified bodies' presented through the ethnological representations and the inheritance of colonial regimes of recognition. Taking Chris Marker and Alain Resnais's essay film *Statues Also Die*, and the exhibitions and performances surrounding Saartjie Bartmann's body (and body image, and bodily remains), as his cues, Opondo examines the diplomatic and epistemological frames through which these performances operate, interrogating the disjunctive discrepancy between 'moving' images of the African body and the representational apparatuses that police and produce the possibilities of political 'mobility' itself. Naeem Inayatullah's investigation of the 'movement' of the teaching body similarly exposes the structures of performance—and *mis*performance—as revealing the political imbrications of performers and spectators as co-creative agents and interpreters. Using his own auto-ethnographic accounts of various teaching 'failures', Inayatullah draws our attention to the structures of co-appearance in the classroom 'set-up', examining how the participant bodies move around the im/possibilities of teaching, learning and grasping the moment.

The investigation of the political and aesthetic technologies governing the movement of an audience—how 'we' move and are moved intellectually, emotionally, experientially—is at the heart of the concerns of this book. It is also at the core of the practice-based performance research project *Coriolan/us*, directed by Mike Pearson and Mike Brookes and designed by Mike Brookes and Simon Banham[42] for National Theatre Wales at RAF St Athan, as part of the 2012 World Shakespeare Festival and Cultural Olympiad. The project examined how an audience might be assembled, divided, differentiated and reconstituted as a political entity; how the activity of listening, integrated into the spectacle of watching, might be constitutive of political subjectivation.[43] Patrick Primavesi's chapter offers a detailed exposition of the production, situating it within a history of dramaturgical investigations of the question of audience—Brecht's most especially—in order to account for the movement of the audience through the performance as an experience of relation and a way of indexing the politics of 'democratic' participation. By examining the organization of and deployment of space, speech and screen in the theatrical event, Primavesi explores the audience's movement through a landscape of political and theatrical division, elaborating how by occupying different positions in relation to the space and action, the spectators become aware of their co-implication in its aesthetic-political operation. The question of the politics of space and the movement of the body politic is somewhat differently taken up in Stuart Elden's reading of Shakespeare's *Coriolanus*. Drawing on Ralph Fiennes's film version of the play, which is very different in its approach to the question of representing political community than the Pearson/Brookes production, Elden addresses the representation of political banishment and the military conquest of territories. His literary-geographic analysis demonstrates how, in *Coriolanus*, territory as the body of the state is only one aspect of its corporeal nature. His interrogation of the discursive construction and deployment of the figures of territory and body reveals the play to be about the political body of the polity itself, its inside and outside; the aggressive wars fought to keep it safe externally and the politics of governmentality developed to secure its internal health and well-being.

Questions of security, territory and the imaginative politics of policing the borders of the nation-state and integrity of the body politic form the focus of the concluding chapters of this volume. Christine Sylvester's chapter examines how the looting of antiquities, evidenced in events such as the plundering of the Iraq Museum in Baghdad during the early days of the Iraq War, reveals the performative power and agency of nonhuman objects. She suggests that in conflict zones and other complex situations concerning the extension and retraction of the nation-state, objects such as antiquities might be considered actants that attract, engage and deterritorialize a host of subjective relations and political assemblages. Whilst Sylvester suggests that engagement with aesthetic research and creative cultural practice might expand the field of International Politics, Maja Zehfuss illustrates how a similar trajectory is already being followed by the US military in the development of Human Terrain Teams, albeit for very different political purposes. Zehfuss considers how 'cultural knowledge' has become central to military success, with both linguistic and performance skills being pressed into service alongside a social scientific understanding of the 'cultural specificity' of the population in areas of military contact and conflict. She argues that in the context of a political dispute or war, emphasizing conflicts as cultural downgrades their political significance and Human Terrain technology is ultimately deployed to deny a political voice to the populations of the territories being occupied. Performing cultural understanding can appear to replace the need for political discussion, disagreement and resistance, Zehfuss contends, enabling objections to be recast as merely a matter of misunderstanding or cultural misrecognition.

Investigating the politics and poetics of recognition and misrecognition central to the deployment of technological apparatuses of governmental power and concomitant strategies of resistance forms a key focus of this book. Whereas Jenny Edkins explores the importance of face recognition in the English riots of 2001, and Adrian Kear examines the disruptive capacity of the aesthetic image to look back at its spectator, Louise Amoore's chapter considers the specific mode of visualization at work in contemporary border security practices. Amoore sees security practices as operating within a visual economy of attention and attentiveness to 'cultural difference'. She suggests that a logic of cultural normativity is evident within the epistemological, imagistic and narrative frames[44] through which 'pixellated' data are integrated to produce a picture of a person and an anticipated set of performed behaviours. Whilst these restrictive and 'pre-emptive lines of sight' are utilized in contemporary security practice to envisage 'unknown futures', Amoore proposes that contemporary aesthetic practices produce creatively expansive modes of engagement and attention, thereby enhancing our political capacity to disrupt, question and re-imagine the subjectivating apparatus and visual machinery of security.

In all the contributions to the volume, the operation of the anthropological machine is illuminated and challenged, and how aesthetic practices and aesthetic subjects might evade the inventive arrangements of the machine is highlighted. If there had to be a condensing image for the volume it could be this: the aesthetic-political opening or holding open of a space of possibility in which, as in Foucault's famous phrase, 'if those arrangements were to disappear as they appeared, if some event ... were to cause them to crumble ... man would be erased, like a face drawn in sand at the edge of the sea'.[45] If man was the product of 'a change in the fundamental arrangements of knowledge', then what is taking place now is not interdisciplinarity, or some academic debate, but a shifting of the ground beneath our feet, and with

Introduction 13

it the ending of the discourse of the human sciences. Can we, perhaps, 'sense the possibility' of such an event, an event of 'the explosion of man's face in laughter'?[46]

Notes

1 Nigel Thrift graduated from Aber in 1971 with a degree in geography—something I hadn't appreciated. The lecture in question appears in the archive as the J.B. Willans Lecture, held on Tuesday 21 November 2006, just after he had become Vice-Chancellor at Warwick, in lecture theatre A12 in the Hugh Owen building at 7.00 pm. Nigel Thrift co-founded the journal *Environment and Planning D: Society and Space* in the early 1980s.
2 Mike Pearson and Michael Shanks, *Theatre/Archaeology*, London and New York: Routledge, 2001; Mike Pearson, *Site-Specific Performance*, Basingstoke: Palgrave, 2010; Mike Pearson, *In Comes I*, Exeter: Exeter University Press, 2006. Pearson also served on the steering group of the AHRC *Landscape and Environment* strategic theme, undertaking several projects with political and cultural geographers. See, for example, *Fieldworks, Performance Research* 15, no. 4, ed. Mike Pearson, Steve Daniels and Heike Roms, London and New York: Routledge.
3 Jenny Edkins and Véronique Pin-Fat, 'Through the Wire: Relations of Power and Relations of Violence', *Millennium: Journal of International Studies* 34, no. 1 (2005): 1–24; Adrian Kear, 'Intensities of Appearance', *Performance Research* 12, no. 4 (2008): 16–24.
4 Adrian Kear and Richard Gough, eds., On Appearance, *Performance Research* Vol. 13, no. 4, December 2008; Jenny Edkins, *Missing: Persons and Politics*, Ithaca, NY: Cornell University Press, 2011.
5 Adrian Kear and Deborah Lynn Steinberg, *Mourning Diana: Nation, Culture and the Performance of Grief*, London and New York: Routledge, 1999; Adrian Kear and Patrick Campbell, *Psychoanalysis and Performance*, London and New York: Routledge, 2001; Jenny Edkins, *Trauma and the Memory of Politics*, Cambridge: Cambridge University Press, 2003.
6 Central to the success of the group and the speaker series were Karoline Gritzner, Simona Rentea and Heike Roms; other members of the group have included Catherine Charrett, Megan Daigle, Carl Death, Andrew Filmer, Alison Forsyth, Richard Gough, Jill Greenhalgh, Carl Lavery, Aoileann Ní Mhurchú, Reiko Shindo, Sabine Sörgel, Erzsebet Strausz and Nick Vaughan-Williams.
7 We would like to acknowledge the financial support that the research group and its speaker series has received from the University Research Fund and both TFTS and the Department of International Politics at Aberystwyth.
8 Jacques Rancière, *Disagreement: Politics and Philosophy*, trans. Julie Rose, Minneapolis: University of Minnesota Press, 1999: 137.
9 This is a short version of a performance lecture written in response to dramaturgical prompts from theatre director and academic Simon Bayly. In memory of Jon Adams, teacher and theatre director, who died in the Qatar theatre suicide bombing, Saturday 19 March 2005. With thanks for introducing me to Godot, the theatre and the rigours of thinking.
10 Nina Power and Alberto Toscano, '"Think, pig!" An Introduction to Badiou's Beckett', in Alain Badiou, *On Beckett*, ed. and trans. Nina Power and Alberto Toscano, Manchester: Clinamen Press, 2003: xxii.
11 Samuel Beckett, *Waiting for Godot*, London: Faber and Faber, 1959.
12 Giorgio Agamben, *The Open*, trans. Kevin Attell, Stanford, CA: Stanford University Press, 2004: 37.

13 Agamben, *The Open*: 37.
14 Martin Heidegger, *The Fundamental Concepts of Metaphysics: World, Fortitude, Solitude*, trans. William McNeill and Nicholas Walker, Bloomington and Indianapolis: Indiana University Press, 1995.
15 Power and Toscano, '"Think, Pig"': xxix.
16 Giorgio Agamben, *Means Without Ends: Notes on Politics*, trans. Vicenzo Binetti and Cesare Casarino, Minnesota: University of Minnesota Press, 2000: 132.
17 Agamben, *The Open*: 37.
18 Agamben, *Means Without Ends*: 132.
19 Giorgio Agamben, *The State of Exception*, trans. Kevin Attell, Chicago, IL: Chicago University Press, 2005: 1–5.
20 Immanuel Kant, *Foundations of the Metaphysics of Morals* (1785), cited in Alphonso Lingis, *The Imperative*, Bloomington and Indianapolis: Indiana University Press, 1998: 186.
21 Agamben, *The Open*: 30.
22 Immanuel Kant, *Groundwork of the Metaphysics of Morals*, ed. and trans. Mary Gregor and Jens Timmermann, Cambridge: Cambridge University Press, 2012.
23 Immanuel Kant, *Anthropology from a Pragmatic Point of View*, ed. Robert B. Louden, Cambridge: Cambridge University Press, 2006.
24 Agamben, *Means Without Ends*: 93.
25 Agamben, *Means Without Ends*: 93.
26 Agamben, *The Open*: 37–38.
27 When I posted a notice about the death of Jon Adams on the SCUDD list-server for UK drama departments, a colleague who knew him replied that he found it 'ironic that Jon should have lost his life to a car-bomber who was so demonstrably intolerant of cultural difference'. However, there is as little solace to be found in 'anthropomorphically' attributing intentionality to an unknown other as there is productivity in recourse to a neo-Kantian discourse of respectful 'tolerance'; both positions need troubling if we are to begin to understand why it is that individual humans continue to be the principal victims of 'human' history.
28 Michael J. Shapiro, *Studies in Trans-disciplinary Method*, London and New York: Routledge, 2013: xv.
29 Jacques Rancière, *The Politics of Aesthetics*, trans. G. Rockhill, New York and London: Continuum, 2004: 63.
30 Shapiro, *Studies in Trans-disciplinary Method*: xiv.
31 For example, Jane de Gay and Lizbeth Goodman, eds, *Routledge Reader in Politics and Performance*, London: Routledge, 2000; see also Shirin Rai and Janelle Reinelt's forthcoming collection *The Grammar of Performance and Politics*, London: Routledge, 2014. For an alternative view stressing both the undecidability and the eventual incommensurability of performance and politics, see Joe Kelleher, *Theatre and Politics*, London: Palgrave, 2009.
32 Jacques Rancière, *Dissensus: On Politics and Aesthetics*, trans. Steve Corcoran, New York: Continuum, 2010: 140. See also Chapter 1 by Adrian Kear, in this volume.
33 Rancière, *Dissensus*: 140.
34 Gilles Deleuze and Felix Guattari, *What is Philosophy?* trans. H. Tomlinson and G. Burchell, New York: Columbia University Press, 1994: 66.
35 Michel Foucault, *Power/Knowledge: Selected Interviews and Other Writings, 1972–1977*, ed. and trans. Colin Gordon, Hemel Hempstead: Harvester Wheatsheaf, 1977: 194. See also Giorgio Agamben, *What is an Apparatus?* trans. David Kishik and Stefan Pedatella, Stanford, CA: Stanford University Press, 2009.
36 Shapiro, *Studies in Trans-discipinary Method*: xiv.
37 Theodor Adorno, *Aesthetic Theory*, trans. Robert Hullot-Kentor, New York and London: Continuum, 2004.

38 Gilles Deleuze and Felix Guattari, *A Thousand Plateaus: Capitalism and Schizophrenia*, trans. Brian Massumi, London: Athlone Press, 1987: 177.
39 See Kelleher, *Theatre and Politics*.
40 Jean-Luc Nancy, *Being Singular Plural*, trans. Robert D. Richardson and Anne E. O'Byrne, Stanford, CA: Stanford University Press, 2000: 59.
41 Dwight Conquergood, 'Rethinking Ethnography', *Communications Monographs* 58 (June 1991): 179–94, at 188.
42 Theatre makers Pearson, Brookes and Banham are also, respectively, Professor of Performance Studies, Creative Research Fellow, and Senior Lecturer in Scenography at Aberystwyth University's Department of Theatre, Film and Television Studies.
43 Adrian Kear, *Theatre and Event: Staging the European Century*, Basingstoke: Palgrave, 2013.
44 Judith Butler, *Frames of War*, London: Verso, 2009: 3.
45 Michel Foucault, *The Order of Things: An Archaeology of the Human Sciences*, London: Tavistock/Routledge, 1970: 387.
46 Foucault, *The Order of Things*: 385.

Part I
Logics of staging

1 Traces of presence

Adrian Kear

> The fundamental problem that now arises is that of the trace, or of the visibility of the visible ... Are there traces of the act? How can we isolate the act from its result without resorting to the ineluctably sacred form of the work?
>
> (Alain Badiou[1])

> This does not mean that there is no theatre ... But theatre, here, means the scene of representation: it means the extreme edge of this scene, the dividing line where singular beings are exposed to one another.
>
> (Jean-Luc Nancy[2])

Presence and representation

January 2009, and I'm walking through three feet of snow to get to what I hope is the entrance to Hangar Bicocca on the outskirts of Milan in order to see an exhibition of works by the Chilean artist Alfredo Jaar. *It is Difficult*, the title on the exhibition poster tells me—which is also what the taxi driver had said as he dropped me off some way from the venue. I think to myself 'it certainly is' as I try to find the way into the building, recalling as I move the remainder of the enigmatic quotation from William Carlos Williams: 'It is difficult to get the news from poems, yet men die miserably every day for lack of what is found there.'[3] Eventually a doorway presents itself and I stumble into the cavernous space of the gallery with Williams's curious inversion of the troubled relationship between art and politics reverberating in my head. I'm struck by two things on entering: it seems inhospitably empty, the emptiness echoing the space's post-industrial enormity, testament to the scale of the economic apparatus once housed here and now traced, associatively, by the art-producing machine; and it's cold—colder, if that's possible, than the snow-encrusted city outside. However, I'm here now, and the cold draws attention to my being there as an ontological experience. It runs through my body as an index of my own presence, a marker of my exposure, and of exposure as a locus of being opened up to the relational experience of others.

As I move round *It is Difficult*, I'm aware that my viewing of the exhibition is conditioned as much by my relation to the cold as by my relation to the works themselves; yet in spite of this, or perhaps because of it—because it draws attention to my being located geopolitically in a privileged Northern hemispheric context—I'm conscious that the images with which I'm being presented are less a set of artworks as objects than the effective traces of a number of inter-related artistic *acts* with representational outcomes that record the co-presence of the artist in a series of places, relations and situations that would otherwise not be made visible, would not otherwise be made available to be seen. The institutional frame and representational context of *exhibition* is thereby to be regarded as an essential co-determinant of the 'visibility of the visible' set into play by the artistic act, creating a space of encounter between the spectator and the visible trace of another's material presence as an essentially *theatrical* exposure of relational ontology. Without this gesture towards the spectator's co-appearance in the scene, to my relational co-presence with what is seen, the image itself would not be given to be seen. Put simply, the conditions of the appearance of the image provide the very ground for the recognition of the politics of the image, drawing attention to the theatrical politics of spectatorship as a relational exposure of—and to—*political ontology*. Watching scenes of others being exposed to excessive heat and extreme exploitation thereby seemed, in the context of the bitterly cold environment of the gallery, to act as a reminder that what was being rendered visible in these images could not be encountered with the dispassionate detachment of the expert observer but rather sought to invoke the relational co-presence and ethical implication of the critically and creatively engaged spectator.

The earliest piece in the retrospective seems to demonstrate the continuity of Jaar's commitment to examining the relational dynamics of exposure through interrogating the material interdependence of the form, content and context of the image's exhibition and staging. *Introduction to a Distant World* (1985) is a 9 minute 30 second digital video projection, installed in the Hangar in large-screen format and presented in a face-to-face audience relation. It depicts an extraordinary scene—or, more precisely, it presents an ordinary scene 'extraordinarily' by bringing it to visibility and allowing it to be seen. Jaar's video camera captures an open-cast goldmine in the northeastern Amazonian rainforest, populated by some of the 40,000 or more gold prospectors in the Serra Pelada. It starts with an extreme wide-angle shot of the physical landscape of the site itself, showing the precarious network of ladders, rock-hewn steps and rudimentary irrigation system that form the 'infrastructure' of the excavation. The miners are visible only in their multitude, navigating the treacherous slopes as they carry bags of slurry up and out of the site before descending to continue their Sisyphean labour. The spatial and temporal rhythm of *Introduction to a Distant World* becomes established by the camera angle narrowing to focus inward on the mine, revealing in mid-shot a seemingly chaotic and self-evidently dangerous mining 'machine' with human bodies as its essential element. The framing of the image becomes more and more concerned with the materiality of the environment, with the bodies of the miners, arms and legs exposed, as they carry sodden sacks of earth on their shoulders up the slippery pathway in intensely close proximity, with others passing them on the way back down. They walk together, always looking down, conjoined by their work and interdependent on each other's material presence, their inescapable *being there together*. Jaar's camera zooms in on the movement of the miners' feet and legs, mud-splattered and exposed to the immanent disaster of a slip, whilst the continuous pace of the editing resonates with the ineluctable rhythm of the machine. Thigh, knee, calf, ankle, foot—the artistic apparatus seems designed to present nothing short of the presence of the people in this place as the very ground of their aesthetic co-appearance; as the material substance which would otherwise not be brought to appearance. The project of the video would therefore seem to be the presentation of ontological co-presence, or at least the presentation of its trace in the work of representation. For in the editing and framing of the image, in the manual labour of constructing the work of art as such as well as in the material trace of its making, we see the coexistence of presence and representation, material relations and mediation. The artist's work is dependent on the miner's labour, mediation remains dependent on the stuff of matter, and the point is not lost on the engaged spectator.

In fact, and in order to make clear the political relations at stake in the work of art and their imbrications in the co-compositional processes of making and spectating, *Introduction to a Distant World* incorporates the implication of the spectator in the scene through an explicit moment of recognition. At the end of the piece, in a marked interruption of the camera's focus on the rhythm of feet and the materiality of bodies, a miner looks up and returns the artist's/spectator's gaze. The suddenness of the gesture, its startling instantaneity, is accentuated affectively by the introduction of a soft freeze and then fading of the image. The theatricality of the moment seems to insist on the appearance of the miner as subject, staged as a face-to-face confrontation, when in fact it serves more as an index of the presence of the artist and, by extension, the anticipated context of the spectatorial relation. In other words, the moment of interruption instantiates the appearance of subjectivity as produced by the anthropological machine of the artistic apparatus rather than the appearance of a singular subject as such. If anything, it is the spectator who comes into being at this point as witness to a highly orchestrated disruption of the 'visibility of the visible' as an event of—and in—representation. As Badiou writes:

> It is of the very essence of the event to be both what irrupts and what solely exists and organizes subjects in the form of traces which are immediately difficult to read. One could then say that performance takes place precisely between the active force of what emerges and its enigmatic dissemination.[4]

The 'performance' taking place here, then, in the artistic space of presenting co-presence and disseminating it through the economic and political relations of the gallery, tends to organize *the spectator* as subject or, rather, as the aesthetic subject of an ethical and political address. If *Introduction to a Distant World* makes apparent part of the contemporary world that would otherwise not be seen, it does so with a knowingness by which the making and viewing of the artwork is itself structured and implicated in that world and is built upon fundamental global inequality. What is at stake in looking at these images in this context? What is the nature of the difficult performance of relation unfolded through watching them? These are, of course, Jaar's questions, to which I would add: what difference does it make if the people presented in the work of representation are aware of themselves performing? What if the labour of making art is conceived as a shared act rather than one built on another kind of work, another kind of labour? What are the ethical, political and aesthetic implications of recognizing the co-presence of performer, maker and spectator as being in the world—*this* world—together?

It is Difficult seems resolutely determined to draw attention to the politics of these questions and to trace the co-dependency of presence and representation through a series of inter-related aesthetic inquiries and investigations. The exhibition includes one of several variations of the Serra Pelada materials which extend the video work's focus on the dynamics of the image's framing and the ontological relations at stake in its theatrical staging. *Out of Balance* (1989), is a series of six rectangular light-boxes (45 x 244 x 13cm) in which the dimensions of the frame greatly exceeds the singular image of a miner's face illuminated by it. Each colour transparency is located at the edge of the frame, drawing attention to the *excess* of the mechanism of double exposure utilized to capture and then reproduce it. As such, this display of light is simultaneously reflective of the ontology of photography, at least in its analogue state, as the product of the capture of light in the form of its negative imprint and the re-animation of its material trace, and of the political aesthetics of an ideology that designates the appearance of the visual 'as the realm of what manifests itself'.[5] At the same time, the radiance of the face contained within its aperture designates the materiality of the political ontology simultaneously in play in the image's locus of appearance and affective articulation of itself as a virtual trace of presence. For this is *someone*; someone whose sometime appearance in front of Jaar's camera is once again made manifest in the spectator's confrontation with the 'facingness' of the image illuminated and installed in the exhibition space. Here the details of environment and activity are excluded so that, as Rancière explains, the spectatorial encounter with 'the obtuse presence that interrupts ... becomes the luminous power of a face-to-face' through which 'presence opens out into presentation of presence' and 'the obtuse power of the image ... becomes the radiance of a face'.[6] However, as the title of the work, *Out of Balance*, suggests, the geopolitical conditions governing the relations of presence and representation are themselves inexorably over-determining of the nature of the co-appearance being made manifest. Jaar's concern is therefore not simply with facilitating the appearance of the image as such, but with making visible the political *apparatus of appearance* that produces luminosity (and opacity) as its effect. The aesthetic organization of his work draws attention to the structural tension between the economy of representation and 'that irregular net of event-symptoms that reaches the visible as so many gleams or radiances', described by Didi-Huberman as '*traces* of articulation'.[7] The aesthetic event might thereby be thought of as a double articulation, staging the relationship between the presentation of traces of presence and the representation of modalities of representation by demonstrating their affective inter-animation as loci of co-appearance, and creating in the process the theatrical conditions for what might be termed an aesthetic practice of spectatorship as the performance of co-appearance.

Of course, it is important to note that, in this visual art context, the subjects themselves remain mute; it is the apparatus of staging that produces the articulacy of the image and its spectatorial address. Here there is no face-to-face relation without mediation; there is only the theatrical mediation of *facingness*. This relation of non-relation is made explicit in Jaar's *Geography War* (1991). The installation comprises 100 oil barrels (91 cm high x 61 cm diameter) filled with water, above which are suspended five light-boxes (102 x 102 x 13 cm) with colour transparencies projected directly onto the surface of the liquid. The images themselves appear only in their reflection, broken and reframed by the circumference of the barrels. As pools of light on water, the weight and density of which seems to increase in opacity as a result, they produce the semblance of a darkly viscous material medium at the point of contact with the surface, framing the surface as substance as well as effect. The image animates the surface and the surface 'substantiates' the image, showing the face that appears upon it to be the product of the material context and the material relations that inscribe it. The faces are of Nigerian children, playing on a toxic dump in close proximity to an array of hazardous materials discarded by First World companies. Yet they are not presented directly: hands cover eyes, bodies turn away. Their presence in the immediate environment, captured by the image, is remediated across the space of a spectatorial relation that eschews the comfort of confrontation and identification. Its aesthetic codification as a relation of non-relation inscribes rather the distance—the material difference—between the contexts of appearing and looking, articulating the political framing of spectatorship as its problem as well as effect.

The theatrical dynamics of distance and proximity, critical engagement and ideational intimacy, seem to be at the heart of Jaar's conceptualization of the politics of spectatorship in *It is Difficult*. The centre-piece of the exhibition, *The Sound of Silence* (2006), stages the act of composition itself as a spectatorial relation of non-relation operating within a continuous ethical, aesthetic and political tension. The installation retells the story of the South African photographer, Kevin Carter, who in March 1993 published a photograph in *The New York Times* and *Johannesburg Mail & Guardian* of a famine victim in the southern Sudan. The analogue picture depicted a small starving child who had collapsed just outside a relief centre being watched over by a vulture stood a few feet away from her hopelessly exposed, emaciated body. The photograph, widely described as one of the 'photographs of the Century'[8] for its condensation of suffering into a tragic *image of* suffering, won Carter the 1994 Pulitzer Prize and a good degree of notoriety for the detachment and calculation of its staging.[9] Alternately derided for taking an exaggerated amount of time to compose the shot rather than indulging the immediate humanitarian impulse to intervene; or for having accentuated the scene's set-up by collapsing the distance between the vulture and the child by 'smashing' the foreground with a telephoto lens; the ethics of Carter's photographic act have remained the focus of discussions about the politics of the image's publication, circulation and impact. But rather than simply reproduce the content of the image and replicate the epistemic violence of its encoding and effect, *The Sound of Silence* offers a systematic explication of the relational exchange between the moment of its production and the context of its reception, situating the aesthetic experience of the spectator—and the affective politics of spectator ship—as intrinsic to the encounter with the relation of non-relation structuring the theatrical apparatus's tragic operation.

The installation consists of a zinc-enclosed wooden box—perhaps reminiscent of the process of *camera obscura* as the analogical *ür*-form and basic unit of photographic exposure—entry into which is controlled by red (horizontal) and green (vertical) strip-lights at the aperture of the doorway. The back of the box is constructed as a picture frame surrounding a vertical arrangement of open white fluorescent tubes that simultaneously functions as an image and as an image of the image-making process itself as the material framing, capture and containment of light. The box is therefore quintessentially a light-box: an illuminated space and a space of illumination. Yet once inside, the spectator is enveloped by silence and darkness—the conventional theatrical preface to the emergence of visibility and speech. The immersive environment is punctuated at first by the appearance of white printed words on a black screen, the typeface of which appears recognizably analogue. They mark the name of a figure called 'Kevin', silently calling out, and calling out to 'Kevin, Kevin, Kevin'. The sentences—all short statements—gradually accumulate to provide a skeletal biography of this figure: a young South African news photographer and a member of the 'bang-bang club' collectively responsible for documenting the brutal and brutalizing violence of the South African townships under the apartheid regime.[10] The narrative unveils the story of 'Kevin's' assignment to the Sudan and the immediate events leading to the photograph's capture, accounting for the processes of its 'staging' and their inter-relation: the aesthetic juxtaposition of 'bare life' against barren ground; the photographer's watchful waiting for the perfect moment of the vulture opening its wings (and its recalcitrant refusal so to do); his parental concern for children at home whilst observing, within touching distance, *this* child's fate unfold. Only then the image appears, with shutter-speed suddenness as an interruptive burst of light, exposed to sight only for the same duration it takes to capture the image as the trace of light through the exposure of a frame of film. The re-introduction of temporality into the image—its *theatricalization*, so to speak—enables the spectator to focus not on the photograph as such but on the questions of politics and ethics it frames in its trace: the degradation of the human (black, female, child) to 'bare life', victim of the violence of capital and the vicissitudes of indifference; the limits of artistic detachment, implicating the observer in the thing observed, context in content, relationality in singularity; the self-regarding nature of the discourse of humanitarian intervention, supported by a tacit politics of spectatorship dominated by 'tragic' ways of seeing and a tendency to reduplicate the mimetic logic governing the commodification of suffering through the circulation of images of suffering in the economy of signs. The interruptive burst of light in *The Sound of Silence* draws attention to the ontological appearance of the image within an ideologically 'determined regime of the perceptible',[11] exposing its conditions of visibility and destabilizing its status as spectacle. As the spectator learns of 'Kevin's' suicide within the space of a year of having taken the original photograph, and is informed that the destiny of the child remains unknown, the light-box reverberates with nothing but the sound of our own investments in the aesthetic-politics of the image and its framing of the reduction of human life to the very moment of its emptying.

Jaar's installation appears to demonstrate how the representation of the scene of suffering, so precisely and pitilessly undertaken by Kevin Carter's photography, continues to bear the traces of spectatorial co-presence within it. Its staging of the terrible exposure of the human being within the space and time of the exposure of the photograph not only exposes the (in)humanity on both sides of the camera but extends this thinking to the material relations of spectatorship inscribed in the installation. *The Sound of Silence* provides a theatrical context for thinking through the work of making and looking; for thinking the work of making and looking precisely *as* aesthetic practices of thinking. By staging the photograph within the *mise-en-scène* of a theatrical space designed for viewing, as illuminated by a burst of light lasting only the duration of the shutter speed with which the photograph was taken, Jaar identifies the political performativity of the image less with the narrative's illustration than its interruption. The image's moment of appearance becomes the point at which the activity of viewing is thrown into question, and the spectator is invited to occupy a different relation to the visible and its normative construction and distribution. As the perceptual apparatus is thrown open, however momentarily, an ethical and aesthetic thinking of the political logic of representation—and its disruption by the simultaneous co-appearance of presentation—is set in motion. In this sensate moment of fissure, this temporal burst of illumination, the political structure of spectatorship is opened up through a 'rupture in the relationship between sense and sense, between what is seen and what is thought, and between what is thought and what is felt'.[12]

Practices of dissensus

Jacques Rancière identifies the experience of such moments of disruption and dissociation as being essential to the recognition and recalibration of the political 'distribution of the sensible'.[13] He suggests that the aesthetic encounter's capacity to 'reconfigure the fabric of sensory experience' through altering the 'frames, scales and speeds' of perception, destabilizing the 'self-evidence of the visible' and making 'the invisible visible', exemplifies its operation as a practice of 'dissensus'.[14] For Rancière, the practice of 'dissensus' unites the domains of art and politics, albeit paradoxically, with the aesthetic re-opening of the sensate experience of the visible *qua* 'distribution of the sensible' acting as an index of the re-animation of *political* processes of subjectivation. Although there remains a necessary 'undecidability' in the specificity of its organization, Rancière argues that the aesthetic event operates as a key site for the *essentially political* 'manifestation of dissensus as the presence of two worlds in one'.[15] Artworks such as Jaar's would seem to operate 'dissensually' by placing co-appearance into political tension, re-opening the foundational gap between presence and representation at the heart of the 'fundamental grievance' articulated by politics as the locus of division and dispossession.[16] Experienced as 'a singular disruption', the aesthetic encounter takes place through the appearance of an image that '*interrupts* the smooth working' of representation and sets into play the recognition of the fact of presentation as 'a singular mechanism of subjectification'.[17] As a practice of dissensus, art—like politics—consists in revealing the distance, and the difference, between a social situation and its representation; the presentational appearance of the image functions not simply as an ontological fragment of the visible but as a political *staging* of the conditions of visibility making manifest 'the separation of the sensible from itself'.[18] Dissensual practices, according to Rancière, create 'a modification of the co-ordinates of the sensible'[19] and an opening for political subjectification precisely by re-opening the division, the foundational separation, between presence and representation.

Tellingly, Rancière argues that the essence of 'democratic' politics resides in the practice of dissensus rather than in the attempted 'annulment' of the differences it reveals in the social field.[20] With this reversal of the priority of dissensus over 'consensus', he effectively draws attention to the dialectical movement between them, thereby foregrounding the continuous re-opening of the political divisions and ontological gaps that 'the practice of ruling relentlessly plugs'.[21] In extending this critique from the domestic sphere to the domain of international politics, he notes that 'consensus' is the name given to the 'effective reconfiguration of the political field' conducted under the aegis of 'universal' human rights and citizenship, which in itself nominates 'an actual process of de-politicization'.[22] For Rancière, then, the practice of 'consensus' is an attempt to delimit the possibilities of democracy the productivity of which lies in the staging and enactment of 'specific scenes of dissensus'.[23]

The term 'dissensus' is used by Rancière to account for a division in 'the common experience of the sensible'[24] or 'common sense' that is no mere 'conflict of interests, opinions, or values', but rather a fundamentally *political* 'dispute about what is given, about the frame within which we see something as given'.[25] Consensus, as a representational practice, he argues, operates through a process of foreclosing spaces of dissensus in order to produce a social settlement, or ideological distribution, based on the economic coincidence of interests and identities. Accordingly, he suggests that consensus functions by attempting to excise the random element of participative politics—the presence of the 'surplus subject' whose affiliations, identifications and orientations are neither fixed nor co-extensive with a 'definite collective'—and thereby exclude the opening of a juridical/political 'dispute' about their continuing representation.[26] Substituted in their place are the 'representative' stand-ins of social groups attenuated to the state—'stakeholders', 'community leaders', constituencies of identities, and the like—whose role is to appear to legitimate the attribution of rights and demarcation of responsibilities within a stable cultural framework. For Rancière, then, 'consensus is the reduction of democracy to the way of life of a society, to its *ethos*',[27] achieved through the symbolic evacuation and exclusion of 'the *political* core constituting it, namely dissensus'.[28]

'Consensus' is also the term adopted by Alain Badiou, in the coruscating critique of the framework of international human rights he advances in *Ethics: An Essay on the Understanding of Evil* (2001), to describe the way in which the call of 'blind necessity' is staged in 'the spectacle of the economy' to produce passive acceptance of the 'logic of Capital'.[29] He sees the neutralization of the idea of need in global economics as being co-extensive with the valorization of suffering in human rights discourse, with both being directed, from the outset, towards the foreclosure of any form of dissensual politics. Badiou insists that 'the very idea of a consensual ethics ... is a powerful contributor to subjective resignation and acceptance of the status quo', the aim of which is to provide a bulwark against the realization of possible alternatives and to secure the de facto recognition of 'necessity as the objective basis for all judgements of value'. Genuine politics needs must be excluded from this tight-knit relation because what it offers, Badiou suggests, puts 'an end to consensus' through the irruption of the radically innovative and performatively re-subjectivating.[30]

Likewise, for Badiou the contemporary 'turn to ethics' represents an abandonment of the foundational principle of equality and the reintroduction of an essentially abstract, faux 'universalism' at the expense of a concrete, socially situated materialism. He regards the philosophical underpinnings of human rights discourse as essentially Kantian, and the contemporary 'turn to ethics' as being, as Simon Critchley has noted, essentially a 'return to Kant and to a Kantian conception of the subject of the moral law as universal and context-free and not situationally bound'.[31] In *Ethics*, Badiou rehearses a formalist reading of Kant's *Foundations of the Metaphysics of Morals* (1785), emphasizing 'how subjective action and its representable intentions relate to a universal Law' and the imperative of judgement.[32] He traces the extension of this position in the neo-Kantianism of human rights discourse to demonstrate how an 'ethics of judgement' correlates with an essentially negative conception of human beings and human actions.[33] The external imperatives privileged by this framework not only conceive of the subject as 'incapable of thinking the singularity of situations, that is, of being orientated to praxis';[34] they constitute a regulative matrix designed to guarantee obedience and—in cases of transgression—the justification of punishment and enforced compliance (which is especially important given their extension into the codes of international law). Badiou suggests that 'ethics is conceived here both as an *a priori* ability to discern Evil'—the acceptance of the negative as the fundamental consensual 'given'—'and as the ultimate principle of judgement, in particular political judgement: good is what intervenes visibly against an Evil which is identifiable *a priori*'.[35]

Whilst it is clear that according to this assessment, neo-Kantian 'ethical universalism' acts as an 'apologia for Western ideology'[36]—an ideology that determines in advance the criteria for what will 'count' as morally acceptable: Western criteria, devoid of contextual/situational considerations—this is by no means the end of the matter. Badiou extends his critique by insisting that the neo-Kantian discourse of ethics positions human beings primarily as *victims*. More particularly, by adopting a certain figure from tragic performance, he suggests that the so-called 'universal' 'subject of rights' is effectively split between a 'passive, pathetic, or reflexive subject'—a victim who suffers—on the one hand, and on the other, an 'active, determining subject of judgement' who occupies a classical spectator position in relation to suffering, exposed only to the vicarious experience of pity and fear. This latter position, he suggests, is by far the most important and powerful within this bifurcation, subordinating the politics of the situation to the 'sympathetic and indignant judgement of the spectator' and soliciting their concomitant desire for intervention.[37] This formulation resonates with Jaar's questioning of relations of representation in *The Sound of Silence*, for example, and opening up of the ethics of reproducing suffering through the image of suffering and its concomitant risk of reduplicating 'ethical' demands for intervention. Like Jaar, Badiou's provocation, in this context, acts to remind us that the 'judgement of suffering' from the spectator's perspective serves not only to confirm the victimization of those being 'represented', but concedes, at the same time, a self-reflexive conception of the human subject as 'the being who is capable of recognizing himself as a victim'.[38]

Badiou here is perhaps simply reiterating a certain Platonic anti-theatricality in associating spectatorship with the scopophilic enjoyment of victimization and subjective *in*capacity—or, at least, with the structural impossibility of the spectator's intervention into the domain of the act. In an essay concerned with challenging the notion of the spectator's 'passivity' and accrediting the role with intellectual and political agency, Rancière characterizes this conception as asserting that 'the theatre is the place where ignorant people are invited to see suffering people. What takes place on the stage is a pathos, the manifestation of a disease, the disease of desire and pain, which is nothing but the self-division of the subject'.[39] Whilst this is also potted Plato, for sure, Rancière is at pains to indicate its intransigence in structuring the theatrical relation as a mode of appearance that produces a split between activity and passivity, capacity and incapacity which remains evident even in forms of practice that celebrate their binary inversion. For Rancière, this structural bifurcation is integral to the theatre's role in maintaining a certain 'distribution of the sensible' that partitions capacity and incapacity, activity and passivity, knowledge and ignorance and attributes them to discrete social 'parties', with the gap between stage and audience serving as an 'allegory of inequality' imbricated in the play of 'domination and subjection'. So he proposes instead a theory of emancipated spectatorship that 'starts from the opposite principle, the principle of equality'. This entails rejecting the association of looking with passivity and the bifurcation of capacity and incapacity, and recognizing that spectatorship is a critical activity that confirms, contests and changes the 'distribution of the visible' with which it is presented.[40] In this way, the theatrical relation may be reconfigured as a mode of *dissensual* engagement and *democratic* political participation.

It should be clear, then, that for both Badiou and Rancière, the question of human rights as the rights of the victim is a question of the conceptualization of the subject and the process of subjectification. Badiou rejects the notion of an *a priori* universal subject and demonstrates how such a conception is both irremediably split and fundamentally nihilist, focusing on the negative construction of the victim and 'the underlying conviction that the only thing that can really happen to someone is death'.[41] The key site of application for the discourse of rights is therefore the deciding of death: 'who shall die and how?' becomes the central touchstone in decisions about judgements of responsibility and the ethics of 'humanitarian intervention'. Badiou's analysis points to a certain 'sordid self-satisfaction' permeating the construction of the spectator/victim relation—an essentially *tragic* configuration irremediably concerned with the dispensation of *eudaemonia* or happiness as the ultimate social good, which leads him to conclude that 'every definition of Man based on happiness is nihilist'.[42]

The reliance on an ethics derived from abstract universals is, then, both incapable of recognizing the fact that 'we are always dealing with a political situation, one that calls for political thought-practice, one that is peopled by its own authentic actors', and impervious to the recognition of its own reliance on representation.[43] Rancière similarly notes the vacuity and lack of utility of the rights derived from such abstractions. Tellingly, he suggests that Western society dispenses these as it does whatever else is deemed empty or of no further use, by giving them to the poor: 'Those rights that appear useless in their place are sent abroad, along with medicine and clothes, to people deprived of medicine, clothes, and rights. It is in this way, as a result of this process,' he says, 'that the rights of Man become the rights of those who have no rights, the rights of bare human beings subjected to inhuman repression and inhuman conditions.'[44] In other words, this process turns 'human rights' into 'humanitarian rights', and enables them to be re-manufactured and returned to their sender. For if those who suffer are regarded as incapable of exercising or enacting the rights afforded them, then it follows that these can be enacted for them on behalf of a certain gaze in the Other. This is what, for Rancière, forms the political and psychic fabric of 'humanitarian intervention'—a non-reciprocal relation (a quasi-theatrical relation of non-relation), which re-fashions 'disused rights' and gives them a concrete new dimension, which amounts to the 'justification' of invasion and occupation. He insists that this is in no way a matter of 'equality', as this new utility is instrumentalized on the world stage to achieve 'what consensus achieves on the national stage': 'the erasure of all legal distinctions and the closure of all political intervals of dissensus.'[45]

Rancière is clearly on the same page as Badiou when it comes to recognizing that the reign of ethics secures itself by precluding any political conception of the human subject and foreclosing any space of genuine politics. He further suggests that 'the "ethical" trend is in fact the "state of exception"'—the term taken up by Agamben to describe the attempted temporary suspension of the rule of law that reveals itself instead as the foundational exclusion sustaining the structure of law[46]—in that it seeks to ensure the erasure (not the completion) of the political and the forced identity of exclusion and law. In so doing, Rancière stresses that adherence to any sense of 'ontological destiny', in the Heideggerian stance adopted by Agamben, risks both privileging the inescapability of human animality and prioritizing 'faithfulness to the law of Otherness, which rules out any dream of "human emancipation"' or any possibility of a political process beyond the self-reflexive determinism of 'resistance'.[47] It would seem that, for Rancière, resistance attenuates ethics to legalesque 'responsibility' rather than to the possibilities of politics. It should come as no surprise, then, that Badiou is equally hostile (and, again, rather brusque) in his critique of Levinas's 'ethical radicalism', which prioritizes the role of responsibility for the other in the construction of human relations and subjectivity. Although anti-ontological in orientation, Levinasian ethics, according to Badiou, ends up reproducing some of the mimetic plays of self-identity that were supposed to be escaped from in the 'ethical opening to alterity'.[48] Specifically, Badiou suggests that Levinas's 'fleshy epiphany' of the face-to-face relation can only side step the narcissistic and aggressive logic of identification outlined by Lacan in the Mirror Stage, if it does, by recourse to 'an alterity or exteriority that transcends finite human alterity', namely the 'absolute alterity' and 'infinity' of God. This would appear to confirm Badiou's characterization of ethics as a moralizing and reactionary *ressentiment*—a practice of guilt and blame—which subordinates the stage of politics and aesthetics to the spectacle of tragedy and religion.

Badiou's conception of an *affirmative* ethic of practices, in contradistinction to the *negative* ethics he discerns in neo-Kantian and sub-Levinasian discourses of 'human rights', 'respect for the other and for difference', and even good old-fashioned 'tolerance', starts out from a fundamentally *secular* position which takes *equality* as its foundational category. This is an *ethic of singular truths*, borne of singular situations. For him 'there is no ethics in general. There are only—eventually—ethics of processes by which we treat the possibilities of a situation';[49] or, as Rancière suggests, the re-appearance of aesthetic-political practices of dissensus through which to counterpoint the emergence of consensual ethics as the 'ultimate form of the will to absolutize this dissensus'.[50]

Perhaps Jaar's aesthetic practice should be seen, in this context, as engaging an *international* mode of dissensus disputing the politics of global consensus. *Introduction to a Distant World* presents a compelling encounter with a part of the world normally foreclosed from representation, thereby presenting the differential 'presence of two worlds in one' rather than their homogenization.[51] It positions the spectator as co-present with the situation and the people to whose labour of appearance it draws attention, and yet facilitates only a gesture of ontological co-existence across the distance of the economic and environmental reality of living in fundamentally different worlds, composing the relational experience of the aesthetic event as exposing an essentially political relation of non-relation. *The Sound of Silence* examines the fallacious presumption that the discourse of human rights and ethics can somehow cross this structural divide, or that the work of art can somehow do the work of politics *sui generis* rather than simply attest to the opening-up of possible spaces of political subjectivation, recognizing its inexorable foreclosure by the 'aesthetic cut' as a process of formalization internal to the work of the artwork itself. Accordingly, the ontological difference in worlds separating the spectator and the image prevents any 'direct passage' to a space outside or beyond the world of the encounter with the image as a spectatorial event.[52] The installation's unpacking of the theatrical logic of the construction of the victim and attendant discourses of 'ethical responsibility' puts into question normative conceptions of relations of agency and action, making visible the traces of the acts, ethics and material relations of presence upon which representation builds its ineluctable political apparatus.

Illuminating the apparatus

The seemingly inescapable attenuation of the encounter with the image to the performative recuperations and political operation of the logic of representation is staged directly by Jaar in one of the key works sited in the Hangar Bicocca, *Lament of the Images (1)* (2002). This consists of a large light screen, onto which three illuminated texts describing the *absence* of an image from the space of visibility are projected. Written by photographic critic David Levi, they narrate the constitutive *excess* of representation through demonstrating the presentational gaps left open or deliberately vacated in the field of visible appearances, showing these absences themselves to be the product of 'excessive' political processes. The first of the sequential triptych notes that there are no photographs 'that show Nelson Mandela weeping on the day he was released from prison' as the 'blinding light from the lime' he was forced to mine 'had taken away his ability to cry'.[53] Here exposure is durational rather instantaneous, whilst reflection is utilized as a process of denigration rather than enlightenment. The second text records the exertion of considerable control over the collection, containment and circulation of some 65 million images by Corbis, a company owned by Bill Gates, the ownership and exertion of digital reproduction rights of which seems to threaten the very visibility of the photographic image by condemning the material traces of historical appearance to a cold storage facility in a disused limestone quarry. Here exposure is delimited and restricted, its impact kept in the dark rather than illuminated. The final text of the sequence is perhaps the most significant. It documents the decision by the US Defense Department to buy the rights to all available satellite images of Afghanistan on the eve of the 2001 invasion and occupation, despite the fact that its own satellite images were considerably more powerful and their coverage extensive. The move to purchase 'excess capacity' is therefore to be seen as a political move to determine what can be seen, producing 'an effective whiteout' of the event's visual presentation and its replacement by a highly mediated—and controlled—mode of representation.[54]

Each of the three texts in *Lament of the Images (1)* appears in place of an image, in the place of the image, as a marker of the image's failure to appear. The white light animating the words on the screens remains a constant, suggesting not only that 'words are image material too',[55] but that every image is a *staging* of something being made visible—the product of a political *apparatus* and regime of visibility—that concomitantly occludes something else from not being seen. The large screen presentation of *The Lament of the Images (1)* effectively asks the spectator to rethink the material ground of appearance as intrinsically political; to encounter the image as a representational staging in which absence as well as presence is brought into view. This staging of the visible as an apparatus of appearance is accentuated in *Lament of the Images (2)* (2002), in which two identical light tables are arranged face to face. Here neither text nor image appears, but rather the visible is made visible as an apparatus. The inverted light table, suspended by steel wires from the ceiling, descends on a pulley mechanism towards the other fixed on the floor beneath it. As it draws closer, the light generated by the tables intensifies through their mutual reflection and inter-animation, spreading outwards across the walls of the gallery. At the point at which their surfaces almost meet, two clearly defined lines of light are visible along with a dark void line marking their division, producing an image of image-making as an operation of intensification. The apparatus of visible appearance is thereby itself made visible as the continuous co-relation of absence and presence, and made sensible through the contiguous realization of their affective distribution in the material structure of representation.

Jaar has commented that 'there is always an element of light' in his work, suggesting that the calculation of 'how much light I should let through' is fundamental to the operation of its staging.[56] The exposure of, and to, light is not only essential to the image's ontological conditions of appearing but to the configuration of a specifically aesthetic space and orchestration of a precise temporal rhythm necessary to its performative exhibition. This quintessentially *theatrical* operation makes clear that 'the image is not in fact determined by the mere presentation of the visible',[57] but by the aesthetic and political apparatus governing processes of representation and intensification. As Badiou succinctly puts it, ontological consistency requires 'that all presentation is structured twice', with the structure of presentation being doubled by a 'metastructure' of representation ensuring 'that the structure be structured' as a political operation and performative moment of reduplication. Accordingly, Badiou observes that 'all situations are structured twice', and so in any given instance of ontological appearance 'there is always both presentation and representation'[58]—always the co-presence of both image and apparatus. Perhaps the political nature of the apparatus itself might be usefully characterized in Foucauldian terms as determined by, and determining of, the heterogeneous 'system of relations' between presence and representation operative in a particular conjunction, made evident through the 'interplay of shifts of position and modifications of function'[59] in its aesthetic manifestation. Certainly this seems to be the concern of Jaar's elaboration of the inter-relation of image and apparatus, and concomitant formalization of the interplay of presence and representation, in the various works comprising *It is Difficult*.

The second half of the exhibition, housed at Spazio Oberdan gallery on the other side of Milan, engages explicitly with the international politics of the representational apparatus and its mobilization of visible appearance. Of particular importance in this context are the series of works drawn from Jaar's *Rwanda Project, 1994–1998*, previously exhibited under the title *Let There Be Light*. The mechanism of staging underpinning their construction remains consistently demonstrated as the operation of a *double exposure*: a process of illuminating the relation between ontological presentation and aesthetic-political representation as the product of specific regimes and modes of visibility. In *Epilogue* (1998), for example, a large light screen frames the gradual emergence and subsequent fading of the dignified but pain-ridden face of an elderly, white-haired Rwandan woman. The digital image, projected as a continuous movement of appearance and disappearance over a fixed duration of three minutes, never comes fully into focus or close to capturing the intensity of her enigmatic countenance. The portrait seems to confront the spectator with a certain inter-subjective *aphanisis*—not so much the fading of the subject as such but rather the fading of the appearance of an inter-subjective relation across the mediating space of representation. In

Embrace (1996), the political positivity of the recognition of co-presence and the inter-animation of spectatorship and subjectivity is similarly put into question. The piece consists of a digital animation mounted on an LCD screen, a singular enclosure framing the movement between four still images of two Rwandan boys with their arms around each other, photographed from behind whilst they look upon an indeterminate scene. The transition between the stills, focusing closer and closer in on the boys, constructs a sense of intimacy and solidarity, offering a glimpse of the ontological *being there together* exposed by the apparent 'retreat of the political'.[60] The boys hold each other tightly as they watch attentively something happening outside the frame of the image, their co-presence reflecting and reflected in a crowd of other spectators gathered as an audience encircling the scene not seen. In the last frame, one of the boys turns away from the event he has been witnessing and rests his head touchingly against his neighbour's cheek. Whilst it may be tempting to see in this moment an index of the endurance of human community in the face of extreme adversity—seemingly situating the political ontology of being together as a form of resistance to the instrumental political organization of the social bond—and its capacity for effectuating a mode of inter-subjective spectatorial relation 'that can leave its own traumatic trace in the viewer',[61] it is important to recall that the context of its staging acts as a material counterpoint to any traffic in redemptive idealization. Around the lit but otherwise empty stage space of the black box 'theatre' in which the screen of *Embrace* is located are installed ten black matte light-boxes, each illuminating the name of a place in Rwanda designating and denoting the site of an internecine massacre: Kigali, Mibrizi, Butare, Amahoro, Cyahinda, Cyangugu, Gingongoro, Kibungo, Rukara, Shangi. The specificity of the place names themselves, juxtaposed to the temporal delineation of the two boys as intimate onlookers to an unspecified scene apparently *taking place*, serves to anchor the image of ontology in a concrete situation and ensemble of material relations. This is further accentuated by the aesthetic realization that the apparent image of inter-subjective tenderness displayed on the screen is situated within the historical and political reality of the activities of the 'Interahamwe'—the groups of boys bonded by 'fighting together' in the inter-subjective structure of the genocide's militias—who collectively carried out the regime's brutal murders.[62] Paradoxical as it may seem in this context, it is precisely the material *theatricality* of the image's exhibition that enables the exposition of its performative effect, creating a critical distance between the presentational ontology of the scene being witnessed and the aesthetic-political apparatus of representation organizing its spectatorial affect.

The aesthetic construction of the spectatorial encounter is perhaps most fully realized in the seminal work of Jaar's *Rwanda Project*, the exemplary theatrical *The Eyes of Gutete Emerita* (1996). Inscribed as a single jagged line of light scratched across, or rather into, the black matte surface of a scenographic gallery 'wall'—operating as a textual scar cut into the void space of the visual—the following words invite the spectator to undertake a close examination of the semiotic detail of the composition:

> Over a five month period in 1994, more than one million Rwandans, mostly members of the Tutsi minority, were systematically slaughtered whilst the international community closed it eyes to the genocide. The killings were largely carried out by Hutu militias who had been armed and trained by the Rwandan military. As a consequence of this genocide, millions of Tutsis and Hutus fled to Zaire, Burundi, Tanzania and Uganda. Many still remain in refugee camps, fearing renewed violence upon their return home. One Sunday morning at a church in Narama, 400 Tutsi men, women and children were slaughtered by a Hutu death squad. Gutete Emerita, 30 years old, was attending mass with her family when the massacre began. Killed with machetes in front of her eyes were her husband Tito Kahinamura, 40, and her two sons, Muhoza, 10, and Matigari, 7. Somehow, Gutete managed to escape with her daughter Marie-Louise Unumararunga, 12. They hid in a nearby swamp for three weeks, coming out only at night in search of food. Gutete has returned to the church in the woods because she has nowhere else to go. When she speaks about her lost family, she gestures to corpses on the ground, rotting in the African sun. I remember her eyes. The eyes of Gutete Emerita.[63]

The simple narrative delineation of the story is compelling, moving the spectator through the descriptive force of witnessing—or rather, of witnessing a witnessing. The event itself remains elsewhere, foreclosed from representation. It is gestured towards, remembered, but not given to be seen, for even in testimony it remains fundamentally *ob*scene. What is shown to the spectator is the witness's continuous *seeing*, not what she sees; as such, the invitation to see *The Eyes of Gutete Emerita* is not to see through them, but to encounter the historical fact of their *having seen*. Consequently, the line-run from the end of the text leads into the staging of a visual installation in the space behind the scenographic divide. A glow of light discernible from the other side opens out onto an extraordinarily powerful sight: a huge light table, over five metres square, serves as a platform for an enormous mound of 35mm photographic slides, seemingly sculpted as a mountainous landscape. The structure comprises over a million slides, each one containing the same image: an extreme close-up shot of a singular pair of eyes—the eyes of Gutete Emerita. Although the detail of the photographic image can be inspected by means of the dozen or so magnifiers placed around the edges of the light table, it seems clear that the installation is itself the image: the image of a landscape constructed out of looking—and not looking—at a million or more deaths; the visible remainder of both the fact and the failure of seeing. The aesthetic event, to this extent, operates as an indexical reframing of an historical and political event that remains unseen, the presentation of an absence made present only in the imprints and traces of its material effects. Yet at the same time, it makes visible and represents the constitutive dynamics of the apparatus of spectatorship as intrinsic to the political operation of both its *mise-en-scène* and its reduplicative *mise-en-abyme*.

The theatrical *dispositif* of *The Eyes of Gutete Emerita*, its setting up of a confrontation with the spectator on the very grounds of spectatorship, becomes directly apparent in an alternative iteration of the piece. In this version, two LCD computerized light-boxes, identical to the one used in *Embrace*, are placed side by side on a proscenium-enclosed scenographic wall. The text cited above appears in the two boxes in three stages for three specific durations, making evident its staging as a temporal as well as spatial mode of aesthetic encounter. The first block of text—10 lines in each screen, filling the black transparencies with heavily pixelated white words—appears for 45 seconds allowing the spectator to read to the point of Gutete's return to the site of the traumatic scene. A dissolve replaces the first lines of text with a further five in the lower half of each screen, taking the story to the point of her gesturing to 'the corpses on the ground, rotting in the African sun'. Thirty seconds elapse before the final dissolve reveals the last two lines of text, one placed in each box: 'I remember her eyes. The eyes of Gutete Emerita.' The words remain there for fifteen seconds, resonating slowly, but then they are suddenly replaced by an image bursting into temporary visibility with the split-second speed of photographic exposure, producing the interruptive shudder of the force of the shutter in the eye of the spectator. The moment is disorientating in that it forces an image drawn from another world—the extreme close-up shot of Gutete's eyes, split between the two screens—into the theatrical world of the gallery as the space of the seen/unseen. The illuminating burst of light appears almost to prevent the image from being visible, foreclosing the possibility of the spectator more than glimpsing the traumatic event of seeing, of capturing seeing as seen. Rather, the moment of illumination constructs 'a potent afterimage'[64] in the eyes of spectator which situates the aesthetic event itself in relation to another event—the historical and political event of the Rwandan genocide—which remains impossible to see in any form other than that traced by the political apparatus of spectatorship itself.

Interestingly, a photographic still of this version of *The Eyes of Gutete Emerita* appears on the front cover of the English translation of Jacques Rancière's book *The Emancipated Spectator* (2009).[65] The photograph captures the moment of the appearance of the image on the LCD screens, and yet precisely by rendering it as an *image* seems to evacuate it of its theatrical intensity. For it is the *staging* of the image as an event—an event indexing multiple other events—that generates its political affect. As an aesthetic event, the work constructs a relation between the experience of the spectator and the spectatorial experience of Gutete Emerita—an experience of the traumatic experience of looking—albeit one that can only really be described as a relation of non-relation, or a *theatrical* relation as such. For our world is not her world; our eyes do not see what her eyes have seen. Yet, that said, in this event we do experience ourselves *as* spectators, addressed by the distance in between. Her world *is* our world; her eyes *have seen* what ours failed, and fail, to see.

Traces of presence 37

Although apparently dissensual in its operation, the photograph renders this relation fixed, given, seemingly not subject to alteration. Perhaps this is the truth of the matter, running counter to the argument of Rancière's text. Perhaps even when encountered as an aesthetic event and regarded as a work of theatre, *The Eyes of Gutete Emerita*, like all the work exhibited by Jaar in *It is Difficult*, enables us to see only the apparatus of spectatorship in the moment of its illumination, staging the relation between art and politics as an enigmatic but nonetheless irremediable relation of non-relation.

Notes

1 Alain Badiou, *The Century*, trans. Alberto Toscano, Cambridge: Polity, 2007: 159.
2 Jean-Luc Nancy, *The Inoperative Community*, ed. and trans. Peter Connor, Minneapolis: University of Minnesota Press, 1991: 65.
3 William Carlos Williams, 'Asphodel, That Greeny Flower' (1955), in *The Collected Poems of William Carlos Williams, Volume II, 1939–1962*, ed. Christopher MacGowan, New York: New Directions, 1992: 310–38.
4 Alain Badiou, 'A Theater of Operations: A Discussion between Alain Badiou and Elie During', in *A Theater Without Theater*, ed. Manuel J. Borja-Villel *et al.*, Barcelona: Museu d'Art Contemporani de Barcelona, 2009: 26.
5 Georges Didi-Huberman, *Confronting Images: Questioning the Ends of a Certain History of Art*, trans. John Goodman, University Park: Pennsylvania State University Press, 2009: 31.
6 Jacques Rancière, *The Future of the Image*, trans. Gregory Elliott, London: Verso, 2007: 23.
7 Didi-Huberman, *Confronting Images*: 31.
8 See, for example, Jacques Rancière, 'Theater of Images' in *Alfredo Jaar: The Politics of Images*, Musée Cantonal des Beaux-Arts, Lausanne: JRP Ringier, 2007: 71–80, at 80.
9 See Griselda Pollock, 'Photographing Atrocity: Becoming Iconic?' in *Picturing Atrocity: Photography in Crisis*, ed. Geoffrey Batchen *et al.*, London: Reaktion Books, 2012: 65–78.
10 Pollock, 'Photographing Atrocity': 72.
11 Rancière, 'Theater of Images': 78.
12 Jacques Rancière, *Dissensus: On Politics and Aesthetics*, trans. Steve Corcoran, New York and London: Continuum, 2010: 143.
13 Jacques Rancière, *The Politics of Aesthetics*, trans. G. Rockhill, New York and London: Continuum, 2004: 12.
14 Rancière, *Dissensus*: 140–41.
15 Rancière, *Dissensus*: 37.
16 Jacques Rancière, *Disagreement*, trans. Julie Rose, Minneapolis: University of Minnesota Press, 1999: 96–97.
17 Rancière, *Disagreement*: 99, emphasis added.
18 Rancière, *Dissensus*: 42.
19 Jacques Rancière, 'Art of the Possible: Fluvia Carnevale and John Kelsey in Conversation with Jacques Rancière', in 'Regime Change: Jacques Rancière and Contemporary Art', *Artforum International*, March 2007: 252–85, at 259.
20 Rancière, *Dissensus*: 42.
21 Rancière, *Dissensus*: 54.
22 Jacques Rancière, 'Who is the Subject of the Rights of Man?' *South Atlantic Quarterly* 103 (2004): 297–310, at 306.

23 Rancière, 'Who is the Subject of the Rights of Man?': 304.
24 Rancière, *Dissensus*: 14.
25 Rancière, 'Who is the Subject of the Rights of Man?': 304.
26 Rancière, 'Who is the Subject of the Rights of Man?': 303.
27 Rancière, 'Who is the Subject of the Rights of Man?': 306.
28 Rancière, *Dissensus*: 188, emphasis added.
29 Alain Badiou, *Ethics: An Essay on the Understanding of Evil*, trans. Peter Hallward, London: Verso, 2001: 30–31.
30 Badiou, *Ethics*: 31–32.
31 Simon Critchley, 'On the Ethics of Alain Badiou', in *Alain Badiou: Philosophy and its Conditions*, ed. Gabriel Riera, New York: SUNY Press, 2005: 222.
32 Badiou, *Ethics*: 2.
33 Badiou, *Ethics*: 8.
34 Critchley, 'On the Ethics of Alain Badiou': 222.
35 Badiou, *Ethics*: 8.
36 Critchley, 'On the Ethics of Alain Badiou': 222.
37 Badiou, *Ethics*: 9.
38 Badiou, *Ethics*: 10.
39 Jacques Rancière, 'The Emancipated Spectator', in *Artforum International*, March 2007: 271–80, at 272.
40 Rancière, 'The Emancipated Spectator': 277.
41 Badiou, *Ethics*: 35.
42 Badiou, *Ethics*: 13, 37.
43 Badiou, *Ethics*: 13.
44 Rancière, 'Who is the Subject of the Rights of Man?': 307.
45 Rancière, 'Who is the Subject of the Rights of Man?': 309.
46 See Giorgio Agamben, *Means Without Ends: Notes on Politics*, trans. Vicenzo Binetti and Cesare Casarino, Minnesota: University of Minnesota Press, 2000.
47 Rancière, 'Who is the Subject of the Rights of Man?': 309.
48 Badiou, *Ethics*: 19.
49 Badiou, *Ethics*: 16.
50 Rancière, *Dissensus*: 201.
51 Rancière, *Dissensus*: 37.
52 Rancière, *Dissensus*: 151.
53 *Alfredo Jaar: The Politics of Images*, Musée Cantonal des Beaux-Arts, Lausanne: JRP Ringier, 2007: 144.
54 *Alfredo Jaar: The Politics of Images*: 144.
55 Rancière, 'Theater of Images': 78.
56 Alfredo Jaar, *Jaar SCL 2006*, Barcelona: Actar, 2006: 86.
57 Rancière, 'Theater of Images': 78.
58 Alain Badiou, *Being and Event*, trans. Oliver Feltham, New York and London: Continuum, 2005: 94.
59 Michel Foucault, *Power/Knowledge: Selected Interviews and Other Writings, 1972–1977*, ed. and trans. Colin Gordon, Hemel Hempstead: Harvester Wheatsheaf, 1977: 194.
60 Jean-Luc Nancy, *Being Singular Plural*, trans. Robert D. Richardson and Anne E. O'Byrne, Stanford, CA: Stanford University Press, 2000: 37.
61 Griselda Pollock, 'Not-Forgetting Africa: The Dialectics of Attention/Inattention, Seeing/Denying, and Knowing/Understanding in the Positioning of the Viewer by the Work of Alfredo Jaar', in *Alfredo Jaar: The Politics of Images*, Musée Cantonal des Beaux-Arts, Lausanne: JRP Ringier, 2007: 128.
62 David Levi Strauss, 'The Sea of Griefs is not a Proscenium', in Alfredo Jaar, *Let There Be Light: The Rwanda Project, 1994–1998*, Barcelona: Actar, 1998: unpaginated.

63 Alfredo Jaar, *Let There Be Light: The Rwanda Project, 1994–1998*, Barcelona: Actar, 1998: unpaginated.
64 Levi Strauss, 'The Sea of Griefs is not a Proscenium': unpaginated.
65 Jacques Rancière, *The Emancipated Spectator*, trans. Gregory Elliott, London: Verso, 2009.

2 Facing and defacing

Jenny Edkins

> At any rate, you've been recognized, the abstract machine has you inscribed in its overall grip.
>
> Gilles Deleuze and Felix Guattari[1]

Riots. In the UK a couple of names are evocative: Brixton 1981, Broadwater Farm 1985.[2] On 6 August 2011, it kicked off again, moving from Tottenham to multiple locations across London, then, rapidly, to other English cities including Manchester, Bristol, Birmingham.[3] Mark Duggan, whose death at the hands of police was the precursor to the 2011 riots, was born and brought up on Broadwater Farm Estate.[4] Of course there are other dates and places in between: Notting Hill 1958, St Pauls 1980, Handsworth 1981, Toxteth 1981 and 1985, Brixton again in 1985 and 1995. Before the summer of 2011, there had been civil unrest in the *banlieues* in France, turmoil in Greece, revolution in Egypt and Tunisia, and the Occupy movement in North America.[5] In August 2011, mayhem on the streets turned into looting: not looting in the imperial tradition or looting of art, but the theft of consumer goods from high street stores.[6] Were these food riots? Maybe: the start of the Arab Spring was linked with rising food prices.[7] At the beginning of Gillian Slovo's *The Riots*, a play about August 2011, the stage directions read like a reminder of Mike Pearson and Mike Brookes's *Coriolan/us*:[8]

> Large and prominent: Photographs and moving footage. The most dramatic that can be found of the riots in progress. Shops being looted, shopkeepers defending themselves. Anarchy on the streets of England. Loud surround sound coming at the audience from different directions. Noises of riot. Of sirens. Helicopters. Shouts.[9]

Substitute place and time and we are with Shakespeare on the streets of Rome in 'a company of mutinous Citizens, with staves, clubs, and other weapons' protesting their hunger with the claim that 'what authority surfeits on would relieve us'.[10]

Are the English riots 'criminality pure and simple', as Prime Minister David Cameron insisted?[11] Or were they part of 'the first stirrings of a global popular uprising' against what Alain Badiou calls 'this regression': the destruction of everything that 'the worker's movement, communism and genuine socialism had invented between 1860 and 1980, and imposed on a world scale, thereby putting liberal capitalism on the defensive'? Do we find ourselves in 'a *time of riots* wherein a rebirth of History ... is signalled and takes shape'?[12]

Certainly, as Badiou tells us, our masters 'are secretly trembling and building up their weaponry'.[13] This chapter examines one part of that armoury: the objectification of the person through the mythical technologies of CCTV imaging and face recognition that have replaced nineteenth-century photographic typologies of classes and races, and that continue to pin personhood down, demanding it be recognizable to the abstract machine of capital. To contest this instrumentalization is to contest an entire history and ideology of individualization, racialization and commodification.[14]

Following the riots in August 2011, politicians in the UK's governing coalition and the opposition alike moved swiftly to urge police to arrest those suspected of involvement and the courts to impose maximum custodial sentences, even for first offenders.[15] The shooting dead by police of a black suspect they were trying to arrest, Mark Duggan, and the way information about his death and details of what exactly had happened was kept from his family, led to peaceful demonstrations outside Tottenham Police Station two days later, on Saturday 6 August. The family received a dismissive response. Later that evening, anger spilled over into violence and disorder, which spread quickly to rioting in other areas of London and in other English cities, including Bristol, Nottingham, Manchester, Salford and Birmingham.[16] Shops were looted and businesses destroyed; buses, cars and buildings were set on fire; police and members of the public were injured; and three young men who were defending their area were killed in a hit and run incident.

The events of those few days and nights, and the responses to them, were hotly debated.[17] Views were polarized. Some wanted to search for deeper economic and social causes; others to blame individuals for their actions, which they saw as based on greed and consumerism.[18] The ready availability and widespread use of instant messaging and social media was blamed for enabling the co-ordination of the riots, and what was seen as the police's weak initial response for allowing the disorder to spread. Prime Minister David Cameron moved from first laying the blame on 'criminality pure and simple', to later identifying street gangs and a 'sick' society as to blame: a lack of respect for authority, fostered by the absence of father figures in the home, was the overriding cause and people needed to be taught to be responsible for their actions. In the debate in the House of Commons, the only one to draw attention to research showing that disorder and social unrest was more prevalent in societies with high levels of inequality was Green Party Member of Parliament for Brighton Pavilion Caroline Lucas.[19] However, amongst the wider public, deprivation and the austerity measures of the coalition government—and in particular cuts to youth services and funding for educational maintenance grants and the rise in university tuition fees—were pointed to as likely contributory factors. Whether or not what Deleuze calls the 'machine' of capitalism and the subsequent increase in inequality in the UK over the previous 30 years could be blamed for what had happened, against this background it is interesting to note the way in which the face was produced as part of the apparatus of power instrumental to the crackdown that ensued.

For Deleuze, 'if the face is a politics, dismantling the face is also a politics'.[20] The face is paradoxical. On the one hand it appears an obvious focus of interest. We pay attention to reading each other's faces—reading people's moods, personalities and origins in their facial appearance. We search for clues as to who the person opposite us may be and what they may be thinking. Present before us in its apparent materiality and corporality, the face demands to be read. There is a requirement that the face be available for scrutiny. Hiding one's face is taken as an indication of shame or embarrassment—or criminal intent; face-to-face encounters are seen as potentially more honest and open than those conducted by other means. In social interactions, we are aware of the importance of saving face, and loss of face by either party is something to be avoided. A literal loss of face, or a facial disfigurement, is shocking and calls for exceptional measures of surgical intervention. As well as judging—and indeed classifying—people by their faces, we identify those we know by their faces too. Most of us can recognize someone with whom we are familiar from the briefest of glimpses of their face. There appears to be an innate ability to recognize a face in the crowd with incredible speed. Faces seem special in this regard—wired into our brains. The face is embedded in everyday language and in philosophy: we are expected, for example, to face up to whatever problems life presents us with, and the face is seen as a source of ethics and ontology.[21] Its significance—whether literal or metaphorical—is taken for granted. We are surrounded by faces, and by images of the face.

I have a suspicion that a politics that makes the face is a politics that produces the person as object. Pinned down like a specimen insect, or, in Frantz Fanon's words, 'dissected under white eyes ... *fixed* ... laid bare', the person is immobilized and made present, available to the gaze of a bureaucracy, an administration.[22] The person is called on to give an account of themselves, to say who they are, to be unchanging, categorizable, knowable. As Agamben says, we have an identity without the person.[23] It does not allow for the person as such, a person never fully present, displaced, always arriving too late or too early, escaping categorization, unknowable—a person who is always missing, never fully grasped even by themselves.[24] The individual is tied down by biometrics and biopolitics, or at least that is what is attempted. However, the individual as such—complete, whole, either present or absent but not both—does not exist. The individual of the European Enlightenment is a chimera, an image of its time, a dream (or a nightmare) that is part of a politics that strives for presence, reassurance and certainty where there is none. Such striving produces only an uncanny form of absent presence.

The upshot of Kobo Abe's novel *Face of Another* is that the face itself is a mask—it is not *under* the mask, testimony to a person hidden beneath a veil.[25] There is no separation between face and mask. Agamben, in his essay 'Identity Without the Person', takes this further.[26] The identity we have today is an identity without the person. The person has *become* the mask—the social role—and is indistinguishable from it. There is no longer the person as such: the person is missing, objectified, instrumentalized, disappeared. His notion of identity without the person corresponds to my hunch that the contemporary face—the face of biopolitics and surveillance—forces the person into presence, but into presence as an object not as a person. The person as such, in all its mystery, its unknowability, is missing.[27]

'We have your face'

The Assistant Chief Constable of Greater Manchester, Garry Shewan, said at a press conference the morning after the riots in his city, addressing the 'hundreds and hundreds of people' involved, 'we have your image, *we have your face*, we have your acts of wanton criminality on film. We are coming for you, from today and no matter how long it takes'.[28] Manchester police published images of those it was seeking online, appealed for additional images of the looting from the public, and launched a 'Shop a Looter' campaign.[29] In Birmingham, the images were paraded through the streets on a 'digi-van' carrying a giant screen and asking, 'Do you recognise these people?'[30] The response from the public was said to be good. The police were 'inundated' with tip-offs about the identities of those shown in the published images.[31] It was not the first time that images had been paraded in Manchester; in March 2011 vans with mugshots, names and alleged offences of 'Manchester's most wanted' were driven around areas where the suspects were thought to be living.[32]

There had been some worries, apparently, that publishing the images would contravene the European Human Rights Act, but Prime Minister David Cameron urged police to disregard them. 'Picture by picture these criminals are being identified and arrested', Cameron said, 'and we will not let any phony concerns about human rights get in the way of the publication of these pictures and the arrest of these individuals.'[33] Pictures of individuals 'might well constitute private information, the release of which could breach confidence in their human rights', but the law allows for reasonable use of such information by the police. Apparently the legal position, set out in a decision that predates the Human Rights Act, is that police 'may make reasonable use of [a photograph] for the purpose of the prevention and detection of crime, the investigation of alleged offences and the apprehension of suspects or persons unlawfully at large'.[34] In his statement to the House of Commons the following day, Cameron noted that over 1,200 people had been arrested: 'We are making technology work for us, by capturing the images of the perpetrators on CCTV, so even if they have not yet been arrested *their faces are known* and they will not escape the law'.[35]

Police efforts were hampered by the way that so many of those taking part in the riots had worn hoods or scarves or otherwise attempted to conceal their faces. Among the measures Cameron set out in his Commons speech—the shutting down of social media and instant messaging sites and the eviction of those found guilty and their families from local authority and private housing—he announced the outlawing of face masks in response to a police request:

> I have also asked the police whether they need any other new powers. Specifically on facemasks, currently they can only ask for them to be removed in a specific geographical location and for a limited time. I can announce today that we are going to give the police the discretion to require the removal of face coverings under any circumstances where there is reasonable suspicion that they are related to criminal activity.

Sarah Wollaston, Conservative Member of Parliament for Totnes, tried to persuade him to go further and 'make it an offence for anybody involved in rioting and demonstrating to cover their faces'.[36]

As well as using images of the face to track down potential suspects, police mugshots of those later convicted were displayed online, together with dates of birth, addresses and details of conviction and sentence. This move was presented as part of a process of 'naming and shaming', aimed at deterring others, but one wonders whether the legal and ethical implications of disclosing such detailed personal information alongside clear images of people's faces were considered.

It is obvious from the widespread publication of images that police needed the public to identify their family, friends and neighbours among those pictured. Police are not able immediately to recognize faces from CCTV footage using automated facial recognition, although one of the reasons people who demonstrate go masked is a general fear of a surveillance society where the police keep records of political activists filmed at demonstrations and can readily identify them and track their movements.

Kelly Gates has argued that facial recognition technology is not as developed as people think it is, but that the belief that the technology does already work is instrumental in the spreading acceptance of its use. 'Computerized face perception is proving to be an incredibly difficult technology to engineer', she says, but 'the prevalent myth of inevitability surrounding this and other new forms of surveillance ... performs an important role in their institutionalization, and ... encourages public acquiescence ... Creating the illusion creates the reality'.[37] She argues also that these technologies serve a particular function; they should not be understood as mere technical developments, inevitable and incontestable. On the contrary, she argues, 'digital biometric identification technologies ... are being envisioned and designed to fulfil certain perceived social necessities and political-economic demands of large-scale, late capitalist societies—societies characterized by a predominance of mediated forms of social organization and vastly asymmetrical distributions of wealth'.[38] She links the development of facial recognition technology, where early research was shaped by military priorities, with the dependence of neoliberalism on 'mass individuation, social differentiation, and intensified security'. They provide 'a means of tying individuals into circuits of inclusion and exclusion, determining their status as legitimate, self-governing citizens or more problematic identities deemed to fall outside the realm of legal rights who can therefore be subjected to a range of repressive strategies'.[39] The face is more useful than other biometrics because it seems less obtrusive—it involves recognizing people the way other people do—and it allows for recognition at a distance, and without the knowledge or consent of the subject. It has 'the practical advantage of being able to build on the existing bureaucratic norms and practice of facial identification' and the 'billions of photographed faces already circulated on documents and resided in archives'.[40]

The experience in 2011 confirms Gates's conclusions that the technology is not as widely used or applicable as people think. Chief Constable Andrew Trotter of the British Transport Police said facial recognition technology was indeed being used in the aftermath of the London riots, but that it 'makes up only a fraction of the police force's efforts ... tips have mostly come from traditional sources, such as still images captured from closed circuit cameras, pictures gathered by officers, footage shot by police helicopters or images snapped by members of the public'.[41] As Trotter pointed out, people can be recognized by clothing, gait or tattoos as well as by their face. Though broadcasters defied calls for them to hand over footage without going through the normal procedure for unpublished footage, a court order obtained by police,[42] detectives were said to be scouring the internet for images and contacting photojournalist members of the public for copies of photographs they had posted and any additional material they had. A spokesperson at Scotland Yard confirmed that 'in most cases disseminating photographs to the general public remains a far cheaper and more effective way of finding suspects' than facial recognition technology.[43] The technology is only useful for identifying someone whose face is already 'on the record', and where the police have a good quality mugshot for comparison purposes.

In what could be seen perhaps as an attempt to counter the myth of the power of facial recognition technology that Gates identifies, and police claims that 'we have your face ... we're coming for you', a leaflet circulating in Tottenham during the riots urges people not to panic.[44] If they thought police might identify them they were urged to remember that the photos released were not evidence: 'just because the police have a blurry photo that might be of you doesn't mean they know who you are.' The pictures would be used to put psychological pressure on people to hand themselves in—and this should be resisted. People should get rid of the clothes they had worn, keep a low profile, not attend other demonstrations for a while, be careful what they say on the internet, and think about changing their appearance.

This picture may well illustrate the case at present, unless of course the police line is a question of the reverse of Gates's argument: an attempt to minimize the power of the technology. However, recent research by a group based at Carnegie Mellon University (CMU) has produced 'eye-opening' results that show the worrying potential of combining off-the-shelf facial recognition technology with the vast databases of faces available on social networking sites such as Facebook.[45] In a study entitled 'Faces of Facebook: Privacy in the Age of Augmented Reality', Alessandro Acquisti, Ralph Gross and Fred Stitzman carried out three experiments that demonstrated how strangers encountered either on the street or online could be identified from their faces alone, and how, once identified in this way, their social security numbers could be retrieved.[46] A number of developments have led to a situation where it is likely that in the near future, Acquisti and his colleagues argue, 'anyone may run face recognition on anyone else, online and offline'.[47] People are increasingly posting images of their faces and profiles on social networks, using their real names. Face recognition accuracy is improving, and cloud computing makes it possible to run millions of face comparisons quickly—and to do this from smartphones. This future would be one where it was as if everyone carried their name, address, date of birth and other sensitive data tattooed on their forehead wherever they went.

Following the English riots in August 2011, a group attempting to use facial recognition technology to identify rioters was set up on Google.[48] They planned to use the same techniques as those developed by the CMU researchers. These 'digilantes' abandoned their project after negative emails they received and when their attempt to identify rioters had anyway proved ineffectual, producing inaccurate results when they tried out their method using images of people they knew.[49] More recently, the Metropolitan Police have launched a smartphone crowd-sourcing app called Facewatch, which contains uploaded photos of CCTV images captured during the 2011 riots. The app has also been made available more widely.[50] People are asked to browse the images and inform on anyone they recognize: they can do this anonymously via the app.

Acquisti, Gross and Stitzman point out that notions of privacy will need to be reconsidered in a world where strangers will be able to guess the names and profiles of people on the street in real time. Our expectation that we are anonymous in a crowd will no longer hold. Our behaviour may have to change. While we are used to managing face-to-face encounters, they ask 'Will we rely on our instincts, or on our devices, when mobile devices make their own predictions about hidden traits of a person we are looking at?'[51]

Face and physiognomy

The use of images of the face to identify and track down criminals dates from the invention of photography in the nineteenth century. When it is applied to whole categories of people, such as suspected rioters, this idea is not too far removed from notions of the face as being a key to personality—ideas of phrenology and physiognomy closely linked with the science of eugenics. Face recognition measures the size and separation of facial features to identify individuals; eugenics does the same, this time in order to identify groupings of individuals according to their ethnic or racial origin.[52] Both phrenology and physiognomy were based on, or rather produced, the belief that internal characteristics of personality are expressed in external physical characteristics of the head and, in the case of physiognomy, the face in particular. While phrenology examined the topology of the skull, assigning mental faculties to particular areas of the brain measured in terms of their size and shape, physiognomy assigned significance to the various anatomical features of the head and face: eyes, forehead, nose, chin, ears.[53] The conviction was that the face, 'if it can be "read" correctly, may be seen to display the essential nature of the person within'.[54] In both cases, these were techniques that opened the way for sciences of personality and typologies of character, operating on a medicalized and quantified model. A third science, pathognomy, examined the expression of the emotions.[55]

Photography provided the ideal method of recording thousands of images of face and skull for phrenological or physiognomic examination and analysis. The photograph could isolate faces as objects for scientific scrutiny. One of the uses to which it was immediately put was that of producing sets of images of particular types of people: the poor, imbeciles, criminals, the deviant.[56] In his attempt to define particular types or races, statistician Francis Galton took this further, producing composite photographs generated by superimposing images of several specimens of particular types to create, for example, a generic criminal face or a generic Jewish boy.[57] His composite photographs were an attempt to discover 'the true physiognomy of a race' or type through a form of visual generalization that would eliminate distortions caused by exceptional cases.[58] Galton's statistical study of heredity was superseded by work in evolution and genetics, but his technique of image superimposition was copied by others and his eugenics movement flourished. The argument of eugenics was, of course, that society could be improved by selective breeding: encouraging only those with looked-for characteristics to reproduce. Galton's focus on a typology was paralleled in nineteenth-century uses of photography by the development of systems for identifying individual characteristics, as in the work of Paris police official Alphonse Bertillon, and in Duchene de Boulogne's use of photographic images of subjects whose expressions were manipulated by electric stimulation of facial muscles.[59] Bertillon was a precursor of the work of automatic face recognition.

Photography was the obvious tool to use in gathering data for phrenological and other forms of analysis when anthropology became established as a discipline in the late nineteenth century, or in attempts to prove or disprove theories of evolution, as Nancy Leys Stepan's examination of images of the tropics demonstrates.[60] In a broader sense it was a key component of practices of imperial domination as the British Empire and other European empires grew and colonial administration extended over vast territories such as the United States and Australia.[61] In particular it was used for photographing the natives, in the same way as it had been used in Britain for photographing the poor or the insane. As James Ryan notes, photography was 'one of the most powerful mediums ... for bringing the British public imaginatively face to face with people different from themselves, both abroad and at home'.[62] Commercial photographers were 'closely associated with discourses on ethnology and anthropology', but also took advantage of the thirst for 'portraits of exotic and little-known peoples from around the world'.[63] When the anthropological interest in types declined, there was still a commercial market for exoticism.[64] These forms of objectification survived in attempts to produce more documentary styles of representation. Once 'everyone had been safely conquered' such notions were embodied in the 'banal' *Family of Man* images of Edward Steichen and the photography of the US Farm Security Administration in the 1930s.[65] The impact was far from banal. Steichen's collection of images from around the world, exhibited from 1956 to 1962, can be seen as 'the deployment of a logic of control and domination that [constructs] the Family of Man exhibition as a worldwide visual spectacle and the medium of photography as a universal language'.[66] Though such images contested Cold War logics of enmity and anti-communism, they did so in a way that marginalized non-liberal views of the world and of community and imposed their own neo-colonial forms of exclusion.

Where previously living specimens of the exotic had been taken, measured and exhibited—Sara Baartman, the so-called Hottentot Venus, being the infamous example—by the mid-nineteenth century photographs were taken instead.[67] The photograph provided a substitute for the living specimen.[68] It became a trophy, like the scalp or the antler, and hunting could take place with the camera rather than the gun. The photograph's use in anthropological studies, like its use in criminology, depends in a large part on its materiality and its accepted evidentiary status.[69] Like the impression a finger makes in ink on card, the photograph records light reflected from the face falling on a photographic plate. Like the fingerprint, the photograph can be filed or archived and indexed for later retrieval. It can be shown in evidence.

As John Tagg has shown, these techniques were bound up with the emergence of new institutions of control and governance in both the metropolis and the colonies (and in particular with the biopolitical control of populations)—institutions that continue today, albeit in different forms. What this produced was discourses where:

> The working classes, colonised peoples, the criminal, poor, ill-housed, sick or insane were constituted as the passive—or, in this structure, 'feminised'—objects of knowledge. Subjected to a scrutinising gaze, forced to emit signs, yet cut off from command of meaning, such groups were represented as, and wishfully rendered, incapable of speaking, acting or organising for themselves.[70]

The camera was in this sense an instrument of objectification and de-politicization: a frame was produced within which certain people were rendered as bare life, without political voice.[71] Tagg again:

> A vast and repetitive archive of images is accumulated in which the smallest deviations may be noted, classified and filed. The format varies hardly at all. There are bodies and spaces. The bodies—workers, vagrants, criminals, patients, the insane, the poor, the colonised races— are taken one by one: isolated in a shallow, contained space; turned full face and subjected to an unreturnable gaze; illuminated, focused, measured, numbered and named; forced to yield to the minutest scrutiny of gestures and features.[72]

Tagg argues that the apparent contradiction between these 'technologies of surveillance and control' and the seeming 'democratisation' of image taking that the advent of photography made possible may be too strongly drawn.[73] The use of photography as a 'repressive' form was closely linked to its more 'democratised' role: photographers captured the faces of the 'beautiful' as well as the 'damned', and photography functioned 'honorifically' as well as 'repressively'.[74] The developing techniques of photography can be traced as it moved from the difficult, time-consuming and non-reproducible daguerreotype through the *carte de visite* to the mass-produced, cheap camera and flexible film that an amateur could operate. The process that led to the ready availability of the photographic portrait as a means through which the middle classes laid claim to the privilege of possessing images of themselves and their nearest and dearest simultaneously produced a new underclass: those subject to the burden of representation.[75]

This bifurcation was exploited, in the collection of photographs W.E.B. Du Bois produced for the American Negro Exhibit at the 1900 Paris Exposition, to challenge perceptions of race in America. The collection comprised a set of three albums containing nearly 400 images. Whilst the photographs at the start recall the scientific images of anthropologists, with small images of head and shoulders full face and in profile, 'as one progresses through [the] albums seemingly scientific photographs blend and fade into middle-class portraits ... Large feather hats, formal Victorian dresses, [and] ornate chairs ... come to fill the photographic frame. African-American "types" turn out to be middle class gentlemen and ladies'.[76]

The use of the photograph in technologies of control continues today. As Allan Sekula reminds us:

> Bertillon and Galton are still with us. 'Bertillon' survives in the operations of the national security state, in the condition of intensive and extensive surveillance that characterises both everyday life and the geopolitical sphere. 'Galton' lives in the renewed authority of biological

determinism [and] in the neoeugenicist implications of some of the new biotechnologies.[77]

It survives, too, in the manipulation and commodification of the image of the face in advertising and celebrity. In a more insidious yet more significant way, 'Galton' survives in our continuing propensity to read facial appearance as a signifier of character, feeling or experience. An exhibition that opened at the Los Angeles County Museum of Art in 1999, *Ghost in the Shell*, traces the history of photographic portraiture from its beginnings to the present day. Seemingly without irony, curator Robert Sobieszek writes in the book that accompanies the exhibition:

> Whatever it may be called—personality, individuality, self, soul, character ... what persists of being human continues to be found embedded within, lurking behind, projected upon, or subsiding beneath the human face, and the photographic representation of the face remains the principal tool of our time for delineating the ghost in the shell.[78]

Another exhibition held in 2002–03 in Copenhagen, *Geometry of the Face*, challenges the idea that the face is the mirror of the soul, but argues that the way we approach photographic images of the face today is still very much framed by the ideas that influenced physiognomy over a century ago: the idea that we can judge people on the basis of appearance.[79] The claim is that photography has played an important role in producing and maintaining these visual stereotypes, and continues to do so today: it 'confirms the assumed link between identity and appearance by which we all more or less take our bearings'.[80] In *The Beautiful and the Damned* at the National Portrait Gallery in London in 2001 a link is drawn between what it claims can be seen as two forms of surveillance: celebrity photography, where the image of the face is a route to fame, and the criminal mugshot or passport photograph, where the image is a form of control. All three exhibitions show a revival of interest in exploring the troubling history of the photographic portrait.

A later exhibition, organized at the Wellcome Collection in London in 2009, resonates in worrying ways with the parading of Sara Baartman in the early nineteenth century.[81] In a series of eight identical rooms purporting to explore questions of identity, eight figures are represented: April Ashley, famous as the first person in the UK to undergo a sex-change operation; Claude Cahun, noted for her adoption of an androgynous identity; Franz Joseph Gall, phrenologist; Francis Galton, founder of eugenics; Charlotte and Emily Hinch, identical twins from a family with three generations of twins; Alec Jeffreys, pioneer of DNA profiling; Samuel Pepys, diarist; and actor Fiona Shaw, who has undergone brain scans whilst reciting her lines. The room on Pepys includes 'the extraordinary diaries of Clive Wearing, an accomplished musician who experienced a rare form of encephalitis, leaving him with severe anterograde amnesia'.[82] The overall impression is of a freak show. We are allowed to gawp at a collection of identities constituted as in some ways exemplary of the extraordinary, the abnormal.[83] Our curiosity is authorized by the parallel scientific curiosity of phrenologist, eugenicist and DNA expert.

The function of all this is perhaps not so much, as Tagg implies, to turn these bodies into reformed and docile subjects of administration but to produce them as the exception that guarantees the necessity and continuance of biopolitical control. Through imaging 'them' as objects, it seems that 'we' are constituted as 'subjects' of the democratized photograph, apparently in control and able to choose whether and how we are pictured—though in the end, perhaps, we are the docile bodies too.[84]

Returning the gaze

However, the face in the photograph escapes any singularity of interpretation. Elizabeth Edwards cautions us when we look at anthropological practices of photography in colonial contexts to remember that 'the consideration of images cannot rest solely on homogenised models of colonial action visited on passive ... populations, nor can the consumption of images be formulated in simple causal terms'.[85] Jane Lydon's study of photography in Australia reveals 'a dynamic and performative relationship between photographer and Aboriginal subject', as does Deborah Poole's work in the Andes.[86] Histories of nineteenth-century photographic practice can elide complexity and ambiguity and forget that these practices were 'acutely inflected by matters of gender', for example.[87] Domination can be an ambiguous, fractured process, and the photograph itself has a certain 'rawness' or materiality, an 'infinite re-codability' that leaves it open to being seen differently in different contexts and by different people.[88] It escapes the constraints of its production or its exhibition in unpredictable ways.[89]

In London also the image was ambiguous. It functioned 'honorifically' as well as 'repressively'. Those who are generally invisible appeared in semi-heroic poses: the image of a magnificent figure clad in an Adidas tracksuit, gloved, hooded and masked, striding across the page silhouetted against the red flames of a burning vehicle that provided the front cover of one newspaper after the riots, or another showing rioters in their hoodies and masks facing police with their helmets and batons. The spectacle was seen on screens of different sizes by those who participated and those who were caught up in the events, as well as those who could be considered mere spectators.[90]

In the aftermath, the aim of digi-vans and police websites was for the rioter to be produced, exhibited and made to appear, their faces captured in the abstract machine. However, the face we scrutinize has the potential to scrutinize us: to return the gaze, as Adrian Kear describes in his chapter, and in carrying goods from stores, rioters turned the gaze of consumerism back on itself.[91] It was this return of the gaze that had to be refused through making the gaze appear as that of an underclass. Criminalization was to function to defuse any political effect: the production of rioters as criminals pure and simple as the end of the matter.[92] The fragile glass that separates you from us, your goods from our hands—legality with a vengeance—has been shattered, the law itself rendered defunct: we have a war.[93] As Zygmunt Bauman puts it:

> Steel gratings and blinds, CCTV cameras, security guards at the entry and hidden inside only add to the atmosphere of a battlefield and ongoing hostilities. Those armed and closely watched citadels of enemy-in-our-midst serve as a day in, day out reminder of the natives' misery, low worth, humiliation.[94]

The riots breached this crucial exclusion zone, challenged the separations it instantiates. The facelessness produced by the invisibility of personhood under capitalism is assumed in, or taken on by, the facelessness or bare life in the body politic of the riot, where both rioters and police are masked: rioters in their hoodies, police in their anti-riot visors. If, as Deleuze and Guattari claim, the face is a politics, dismantling or effacing the face, like defacing property in a riot, may constitute another politics. Is this the bare life that sovereign power cannot stand?

For Badiou the consensus demonstrated after the London riots is that 'the destruction or theft of a few goods in the frenzy of a riot is infinitely more culpable than the police assassination of a young man—the assassination that caused the riot'.[95] This view is in keeping with 'the principal alienation of capitalism: the primacy of things over existence, of commodities over life and machines over workers, which [Marx] encapsulated in the formula: "*Le mort saisit le vif.*"' Badiou continues: 'Of this lethal dimension of capitalism the Camerons and the Sarkozys are the zealous cops ... Here, by contrast, it will be asserted that the life of a young man is priceless.'[96] Badiou links the riots in London with those elsewhere—in China, Syria, Iran, Palestine, the United States: 'What they all have in common is that they stir up masses of people on the theme that things as they are must be regarded as unacceptable.'[97] However, for Badiou the London riots were an 'immediate riot': predominantly led by youths, localized (though imitated elsewhere), and importantly:

> indistinct when it comes to the subjective type it summons and creates ... In among the destruction of hated symbols, the profitable pillaging, the sheer pleasure in smashing what exists, the joyous whiff of gunpowder and guerrilla warfare against the cops, one cannot really see clearly.[98]

An immediate riot can be the precursor to an historical riot, but, according to Badiou, the subjects in such a riot are not political or even pre-political. The Arab uprisings of 2011 were obviously *historical* riots: riots 'that indicate the possibility of a new situation in the history of politics, without for now being in a position to realise that possibility'.[99] They are characterized by 'the construction of an enduring central site, where the rioters install themselves in an essentially peaceful fashion', a move from imitation to extension in terms of a mosaic of types of people involved and, finally, the invention of a single slogan that unifies all the disparate voices such that 'what is ... at stake ... has been decided'.[100]

Although Slavoj Žižek sees the rioters as a Hegelian rabble and not political subjects, his widely quoted characterization of the riots as a 'consumerist carnival of destruction' misses his elaboration of the point.[101] 'The riots,' he continues, 'contain a moment of genuine protest, a kind of ironic reply to the consumerist ideology ... "You call on us to consume while simultaneously depriving us of the possibility of doing so properly—so here we are doing it in the only way open to us!"' He concludes: 'the violence thus staged the truth of our "post-ideological society," displaying in a painfully palpable way the material force of ideology.'

Badiou's views are echoed by James Treadwell, Daniel Briggs, Simon Winlow and Steve Hall, who from their extensive interviews with rioters conclude:

> The rioters could not locate or articulate the objective structural and processual causes of their marginalization. Neither could they clearly recognize or ethically censure their structural antagonists. Thus, in the entire absence of truthful, comprehensible and unifying political symbolism, they had nowhere to go but the shops.[102]

The riots did indeed represent an ultra-consumerism, but in a somewhat different way. Winlow and Hall see August 2011 as the expression of a subconscious desire for political change that can find no other form of expression: 'the complexity of subjectivity and the emotional consequences of living a life in the shadow of ostentatious wealth and indulgent hedonism [meant that] those involved in the disturbances were unable to form an articulate political response to the pressures they face.'[103]

For me this is too narrow a reading of politics. The disturbances could not be described as not political—they constituted a challenge to the partition of the sensible, a claim to visibility by those rendered invisible.[104] That was why the immediate re-criminalization had to be so strong, the sentences so severe, the policing so firm and unrelenting. That was why a twenty-three-year-old university student with no previous convictions had to be sentenced to six months in prison for stealing bottles of water worth £3.50 (around $5.00). The London riots may only have been an immediate riot, not an historical riot in Badiou's terms, but the reaction they provoked was the visible sign of a not-so-secret trembling.

Notes

1 Gilles Deleuze and Felix Guattari, *A Thousand Plateaus: Capitalism and Schizophrenia*, trans. Brian Massumi, London: Athlone Press, 1987: 177.

2 'How Smouldering Tension Erupted to Set Brixton Aflame', *The Guardian*, 13 April 1981, www.guardian.co.uk/theguardian/1981/apr/13/fromthearchive; Gareth Parry, John Ezard and Andrew Rawnsley, 'Policeman Killed in Riot: Street Violence in Tottenham, North London', *The Guardian*, 7 October 1985, www.guardian.co.uk/uk/1985/oct/07/ukcrime.garethparry.
3 See, for example, *The Guardian* and LSE, 'Reading the Riots: Investigating England's Summer of Disorder', 2011, www.guardian.co.uk/uk/series/reading-the-riots; Daniel Briggs, ed., *The English Riots of 2011: A Summer of Discontent*, Hook, Hampshire: Waterside Press, 2012; Clive Bloom, *Riot City: Protest and Rebellion in the City*, London: Palgrave, 2012.
4 Bloom, *Riot City*: 76.
5 For a discussion of protests in Mexico in 2005 see Chapter 5 by Diana Taylor, this volume.
6 See Chapter 12 by Christine Sylvester, this volume, for the looting of antiquities.
7 Nafeez Mosaddeq Ahmed, 'Why Food Riots are Likely to become the New Normal', *The Guardian Environment Blog*, posted 6 March 2013, www.guardian.co.uk/environment/blog/2013/mar/06/food-riots-new-normal; for Zygmunt Bauman, 'these are not hunger or bread riots': Zygmunt Bauman, 'The London Riots—On Consumerism Coming Home to Roost', *Social Europe Journal*, 9 August 2011, archive.is/h8pp.
8 *Coriolan/us* from Shakespeare and Brecht, Vale of Glamorgan, National Theatre Wales, August 2012, directed by Mike Pearson and Mike Brookes in association with the Royal Shakespeare Company and commissioned for the World Shakespeare Festival, which was produced by the Royal Shakespeare Company for London 2012 Festival, www.nationaltheatrewales.org/coriolanus; see Chapter 10, by Patrick Primavesi, and Chapter 11, by Stuart Elden, this volume.
9 Gillian Slovo, *The Riots: From Spoken Evidence*, London: Oberon Books, 2011: 7.
10 William Shakespeare, *The Tragedy of Coriolanus*, Act I Scene I, shakespeare.mit.edu/coriolanus/full.html.
11 Alain Badiou, *The Rebirth of History: Times of Riots and Uprisings*, trans. Gregory Elliott, London: Verso, 2012: 17.
12 Badiou, *Rebirth of History*: 5.
13 Badiou, *Rebirth of History*: 5–6.
14 As I write this, the UK Cameron government is celebrating the life of Margaret Thatcher, in an effort to pre-empt any immediate reawakening of 'the "red years" (1960–80)' or the memory of the way that 'between 1950 at the earliest and 1980 at the latest, the ideas of revolution and communism were banally self-evident for masses of people throughout the world': Badiou, *Rebirth of History*: 14, 37.
15 'Public Disorder', Commons debates 11 August 2011, Hansard HC Deb, 11 August 2011, c1051, www.theyworkforyou.com/debates/?id=2011-08-11a.1051.0. For a discussion of the sentencing, see Julian V. Roberts and Mick Hough, 'Sentencing Riot-Related Offending: Where Do the Public Stand?' *British Journal of Criminology* 53 (2013): 234–56.
16 'From Peaceful Protest to Countrywide Riots: England Riots: Map and Timeline', BBC News, 11 August 2011, www.bbc.co.uk/news/uk-14436499.
17 See, for example, 'Street Riots: The Live Debate', presenter Krishnan Guru-Murthy, Channel Four, 12 August 2011, www.channel4.com/programmes/street-riots-the-live-debate.
18 David Harvey, 'Feral Capitalism Hits the Streets', *Reading Marx's Capital*, blog, posted 11 August 2011, climateandcapitalism.com/2011/08/11/david-harvey-on-english-riots-feral-capitalism-hits-the-streets/.
19 House of Commons Debates, Thursday 11 August 2011, Column 1051ff., www.publications.parliament.uk/pa/cm201011/cmhansrd/cm110811/debtext/110811-0001.htm#1108117000001; Caroline Lucas, Column 1083.

20 Deleuze and Guattari, *A Thousand Plateaus*: 188. I explore further what dismantling the face might entail in Jenny Edkins, 'Dismantling the Face: Landscape for Another Politics?' *Environment and Planning D: Society and Space* 31, no. 4 (2013) pp. 538–553.
21 I refer here to Emmanuel Levinas of course; see, for example, *Totality and Infinity: An Essay on Exteriority*, trans. Alphonso Lingis, Pittsburgh, PA: Duquesne University Press, 1969.
22 Frantz Fanon, *Black Skin, White Masks*, trans. Charles Lam Markmann, London: Pluto, 1986: 116.
23 Giorgio Agamben, *Nudities*, trans. David Kishik and Stefan Pedatella, Stanford, CA: Stanford University Press, 2011: 52.
24 Jenny Edkins, *Missing: Persons and Politics*, Ithaca, NY: Cornell University Press, 2011.
25 Kobo Abe, *The Face of Another*, New York: Vintage Books, 2003.
26 Agamben, *Nudities*: 46–54.
27 Edkins, *Missing: Persons and Politics*: 197.
28 'UK Riots: Trouble Erupts in English Cities', *BBC News*, 10 August 2011, www.bbc.co.uk/news/uk-england-london-14460554 (my emphasis).
29 GMP Wanted, www.flickr.com/photos/gmpwanted/page2/; Lisa O'Carroll, 'Police Beam Images of Wanted Riot Suspects onto Giant Screens', *The Guardian*, 12 August 2011, www.guardian.co.uk/uk/2011/aug/12/police-wanted-riot-suspects-looter.
30 'Looting Suspects Caught on CCTV Paraded on "Digi-van"', *The Guardian*, 12 August 2011, www.guardian.co.uk/uk/2011/aug/12/looting-suspects-cctv-digi-van?INTCMP=ILCNETTXT3487.
31 'Police Inundated with Calls to "Shop a Looter" Scheme', *BBC News Manchester*, 13 August 2011, www.bbc.co.uk/news/uk-england-manchester-14515631.
32 'Most Wanted on Wheels: Mug Shots of City's Top Suspects Plastered on Sides of Police Vans', *Daily Mail*, 28 March 2011, www.dailymail.co.uk/news/article-1370691/Mug-shots-Manchesters-suspects-plastered-sides-police-vans.html.
33 PM statement on violence in England, 10 August 2011, Number 10, Official Site of the British Prime Minister's Office, www.number10.gov.uk/news/pm-statement-on-violence-in-england/.
34 Matthew Flinn, 'Will Publishing Photos of Alleged Rioters Infringe their Human Rights?' UK Human Rights Blog, 11 August 2011, ukhumanrightsblog.com/2011/08/11/will-publishing-photos-of-rioters-infringe-their-human-rights/.
35 'Public Disorder', Commons debates 11 August 2011; Hansard HC Deb, 11 August 2011, c1051, www.theyworkforyou.com/debates/?id=2011-08-11a.1051.0 (my emphasis).
36 Public Disorder', Commons debates 11 August 2011; Hansard HC Deb, 11 August 2011, c1051, www.theyworkforyou.com/debates/?id=2011-08-11a.1051.0.
37 Kelly A. Gates, *Our Biometric Future: Facial Recognition Technology and the Culture of Surveillance*, New York: New York University Press, 2011: 5–6.
38 Gates, *Our Biometric Future*: 16.
39 Gates, *Our Biometric Future*: 33, 34.
40 Gates, *Our Biometric Future*: 47.
41 Paisley Dodds and Raphael G. Satter, 'London Riots 2011: Facial Recognition Technology Considered for Olympic Games used to Identify Rioters', *Huffington Post*, 8 August 2011, www.huffingtonpost.com/2011/08/11/london-riots-2011-facial-recognition-technology_n_924282.html.
42 Mark Sweney and James Robinson, 'Broadcasters Defy Cameron's Call to Hand Riot Footage to Police', *The Guardian*, 11 August 2011, www.guardian.co.uk/media/2011/aug/11/broadcasters-cameron-riots-footage-police?intcmp=239.
43 Dodds and Satter, 'London Riots 2011'.

56 *Jenny Edkins*

44 An image of the leaflet circulated during the London riots is available at: tctechcrunch2011.files.wordpress.com/2011/08/21cxauf.jpg?w=255&h=300.
45 Chenda Ngak, 'Facebook's Facial Recognition System, Why it's Scary', *CBS News, TechTalk*, 5 August 2011, www.cbsnews.com/8301-501465_162-20088678-501465.html.
46 Alessandro Acquisti, Ralph Gross and Fred Stitzman, 'Faces of Facebook: Privacy in the Age of Augmented Reality', paper presented at BlackHat, Las Vegas, 4 August 2011, draft slides, www.heinz.cmu.edu/~acquisti/face … /acquisti-faces-BLACKHAT-draft.pdf; Face recognition study: FAQ: www.heinz.cmu.edu/~acquisti/face-recognition-study-FAQ/.
47 Acquisti, Gross and Stitzman, 'Faces of Facebook', draft slides.
48 Kashmir Hill, 'Will London Riots be Turning Point for Facial Recognition as a Crime-fighting Tool?' *Forbes*, 9 August 2011, www.forbes.com/sites/kashmirhill/2011/08/09/will-london-riots-be-the-turning-point-for-facial-recognition-as-crime-fighting-tool/.
49 Kashmir Hill, '"London Riots Facial Recognition" Vigilantes Abandon their Project', *Forbes*, 11 August 2011, www.forbes.com/sites/kashmirhill/2011/08/11/london-riots-facial-recognition-vigilantes-abandon-their-project/.
50 David Wilcox, 'Police "Facewatch" App Targets London Riot Suspects', *Independent*, 26 June 2012, www.independent.co.uk/news/uk/crime/police-facewatch-app-targets-london-riot-suspects-7887778.html.
51 Acquisti, Gross and Stitzman, 'Faces of Facebook', draft slides. See also Willie D. Jones, 'The Future of Riots: Video Surveillance of London's Rioters Points to Future of Facial Recognition', *IEEE Spectrum*, November 2011, spectrum.ieee.org/computing/software/the-future-of-riots. This article reports research by James Orwell at Kingston University on recognition and tracking systems that make viewing of CCTV more efficient.
52 Face recognition software demands extensive databases of similar, racially classified faces.
53 Allan Sekula, 'The Body and the Archive', in *The Contest of Meaning: Critical Histories of Photography*, ed. Richard Boulton, Cambridge, MA: MIT Press, 1989: 342–88, at 347.
54 Peter Hamilton and Roger Hargreaves, *The Beautiful and the Damned: The Creation of Identity in Nineteenth Century Photography*, Aldershot: Lund Humphries, in association with the National Portrait Gallery, London, 2001: 63.
55 Robert A. Sobieszek, *Ghost in the Shell: Photography and the Human Soul 1850–2000*, Los Angeles: Los Angeles County Museum of Art; and Cambridge, MA: MIT Press, 1999: 17.
56 Sekula, 'The Body and the Archive'; Hamilton and Hargreaves, *The Beautiful and the Damned*.
57 Susanne Regener, 'Reading Faces: Photography and the Search for Expression', in *Geometry of the Face: Photographic Portraits*, ed. Ingrid Fischer Jonge, Copenhagen: National Museum of Photography, 2003.
58 Francis Galton, quoted in Sekula, 'The Body and the Archive': 367.
59 Sekula, 'The Body and the Archive': 353–65; Hamilton and Hargreaves, *The Beautiful and the Damned*: 64–75; Sobieszek, *Ghost in the Shell*: 32–79.
60 Nancy Leys Stepan, *Picturing Tropical Nature*, London: Reaktion Books, 2001.
61 James R. Ryan, *Picturing Empire: Photography and the Visualization of the British Empire*, Chicago, IL: University of Chicago Press, 1997; James C. Faris, *Navajo and Photography: A Critical History of the Representation of an American People*, Albuquerque: University of New Mexico Press, 1996; Jane Lydon, *Eye Contact: Photographing Indigenous Australians*, Durham, NC: Duke University Press, 2005; Christopher Pinney, *Camera Indica: The Social Life of Indian Photographs*, Chicago, IL: University of Chicago Press, 1997.

62 Ryan, *Picturing Empire*: 140. For discussions of the later use of film in anthropology, see Anna Grimshaw, *The Ethnographer's Eye: Ways of Seeing in Modern Anthropology*, Cambridge: Cambridge University Press, 2001; David MacDougall, *Transcultural Cinema*, Princeton, PJ: Princeton University Press, 1998; and Peter Ian Crawford and David Turton, *Film as Ethnography*, Manchester: Manchester University in association with the Granada Centre for Visual Anthropology, 1992.
63 Ryan, *Picturing Empire*: 140.
64 Ryan, *Picturing Empire*: 181.
65 Faris, *Navajo and Photography*: 15; see Edward Steichen, *The Family of Man*, New York: Museum of Modern Art, 1955; and Cara A. Finnegan, *Picturing Poverty: Print Culture and FSA Photographs*, Washington, DC: Smithsonian Books, 2003.
66 Louis Kaplan, *American Exposures: Photography and Community in the Twentieth Century*, Minneapolis: University of Minnesota Press, 2005: 57.
67 Ryan, *Picturing Empire*: 144–45. Her remains were returned to South Africa from France in 2002: 'Hottentot Venus Goes Home', *BBC News*, 29 April, 2002, news.bbc.co.uk/1/hi/world/europe/1957240.stm; Clifton Crais and Pamela Scully, *Sara Baartman and the Hottentot Venus: A Ghost Story and a Biography*, Princeton: Princeton University Press, 2011. See the discussion of Baartman in Chapter 8, by Sam Okoth Opondo, in this volume.
68 A substitute for so-called 'anthropological displays': Anne Maxwell, *Colonial Photography and Exhibitions: Representations of the 'Native' and the Making of European Identities*, London: Leicester University Press, 1999.
69 The 'materiality' of the photograph came to attention a while ago; see, for example, Elizabeth Edwards and Janice Hart, eds, *Photographs Objects Histories: On the Materiality of Images*, London: Routledge, 2004; and for the general context in anthropology, Daniel Miller, ed., *Materiality*, Durham, NC: Duke University Press, 2005. For an important early critique of this 'material turn' that suggests we see 'images and objects as densely compressed performances unfolding in unpredictable ways', see Christopher Pinney, 'Things Happen: Or, from Which Moment Does that Object Come?' in *Materiality*, ed. Daniel Miller, Durham, NC: Duke University Press, 2005: 256–72, at 269.
70 John Tagg, *The Burden of Representation: Essays on Photographies and Histories*, Basingstoke: Palgrave Macmillan, 1988: 11.
71 'Bare life' is Giorgio Agamben's term: Giorgio Agamben, *Homo Sacer: Sovereign Power and Bare Life*, trans. Daniel Heller-Roazen, Stanford, CA: Stanford University Press, 1998.
72 Tagg, *The Burden of Representation*: 64.
73 Tagg, *The Burden of Representation*: 16.
74 Sekula, 'The Body and the Archive'; Hamilton and Hargreaves, *The Beautiful and the Damned*.
75 Tagg, *The Burden of Representation*: 59.
76 Shawn Michelle Smith, *Photography on the Colour Line: W.E.B. Du Bois, Race, and Visual Culture*, Durham, NC: Duke University Press, 2004: 63–65.
77 Sekula, 'The Body and the Archive': 376.
78 Sobieszek, *Ghost in the Shell*: 15.
79 Ingrid Fischer Jonge, ed., *Geometry of the Face: Photographic Portraits*, Copenhagen: National Museum of Photography, 2003.
80 Mette Mortensen, 'Photography in the Public Arena', in *Geometry of the Face: Photographic Portraits*, ed. Ingrid Fischer Jonge, Copenhagen: National Museum of Photography, 2003: 10–39, at 11.
81 Wellcome Collection, 'Identity: Eight Rooms, Nine Lives', London, 26 November 2009–6 April 2010, www.wellcomecollection.org/whats-on/exhibitions/identity.aspx.
82 Wellcome Collection, 'Video: Man without Memory', www.wellcomecollection.org/whats-on/exhibitions/identity/video-man-without-memory.aspx.

83 Traces of such an approach can be found in the responses to Suzanne Opton's photographs of soldiers, as I have discussed elsewhere: Jenny Edkins, 'Still Face, Moving Face', *Journal for Cultural Research* 13, no. 4 (2013). D01: 10. 1080/ 14797585. 201792657

84 Visual securitization works in an analogous way: it relies on these stereotypes and reproduces them: it produces the subject it securitizes: Matt McDonald, 'Securitization and the Construction of Security', *European Journal of International Relations* 14, no. 4 (2008): 563–87.

85 Elizabeth Edwards, *Raw Histories: Photographs, Anthropology and Museums*, Oxford: Berg, 2001: 152. Paul Dwyer's study of photographs taken by his father, orthopaedic surgeon Allan Dwyer, in Bougainville explores many of these issues (Chapter 7, by Paul Dwyer, this volume).

86 Jane Lydon, *Eye Contact: Photographing Indigenous Australians*, Durham: Duke University Press, 2005: xiii; Deborah Poole, *Vision, Race and Modernity: A Visual Economy of the Andean Image World*, Princeton, NJ: Princeton University Press, 1997.

87 Lindsay Smith, *Women, Children and Nineteenth-Century Photography*, Manchester: Manchester University Press, 1998: 16; see also Susan Bernardin, Melody Graulich, Lisa MacFarlane and Nicole Tonkovich, *Trading Gazes: Euro-American Women Photographers and Native North Americans*, New Brunswick: Rutgers University Press, 2003.

88 Edwards, *Raw Histories*: 235.

89 I examine the politics of the portrait photograph from a Lacanian perspective in Jenny Edkins, 'Politics and Personhood: Reflections on the Portrait Photograph', *Alternatives: Local, Global, Political* 32, no. 2 (2013) pp. 139–154; Roland Barthes's writing on the *punctum* is useful here; see Chapter 7, this volume.

90 For a fascinating exploration of the iconization of an image of Carlo Giuliani, a young man shot dead at the G8 protests in Genoa in 2001, see Chapter 6, by Joe Kelleher, this volume; and for a discussion of the predominance of screened modes of attention, see Chapter 14, by Louise Amoore, this volume.

91 See Chapter 1, by Adrian Kear, this volume.

92 Michel Foucault, *Discipline and Punish: The Birth of the Prison*, trans. Alan Sheridan, London: Allen Lane, 1991; see also Stuart Hall, Chas Critcher, Tony Jefferson, John Clarke and Brian Roberts, *Policing the Crisis: Mugging, the State, and Law and Order*, London: Macmillan, 1978, a text that remains both prescient and perennially apposite.

93 Jenny Edkins, 'Legality with a Vengeance: Famines and Humanitarian Relief in "Complex Emergencies"', in *Poverty in World Politics: Whose Global Era?* ed. Sarah Owen Vandersluis and Paris Yeros, Basingstoke: Macmillan, 1999: 59–90.

94 Bauman, 'The London Riots'.

95 Badiou, *Rebirth of History*: 19–20.

96 Badiou, *Rebirth of History*: 20.

97 Badiou, *Rebirth of History*: 21.

98 Badiou, *Rebirth of History*: 25. Slavoj Žižek argues similarly that the rioters represent a Hegelian 'rabble', not an emerging revolutionary subject: Slavoj Žižek, *The Year of Dreaming Dangerously*, London: Verso, 2012: 53.

99 Badiou, *Rebirth of History*: 27.

100 Badiou, *Rebirth of History*: 33, 35.

101 Žižek, *The Year of Dreaming Dangerously*: 12 and 60.

102 James Treadwell, Daniel Briggs, Simon Winlow and Steve Hall, 'Shopocalypse Now: Consumer Culture and the English Riots of 2011', *British Journal of Criminology* 53 (2013): 1–17.

103 Simon Winlow and Steve Hall, 'Gone Shopping: Inarticulate Politics in the English Riots of 2011', in *The English Riots of 2011: A Summer of Discontent*, ed. Daniel Briggs, Hook, Hampshire: Waterside Press, 2012: 149–67.
104 Jacques Rancière, *The Politics of Aesthetics: The Distribution of the Sensible*, trans. Gabriel Rockhill, London: Continuum, 2004. For a discussion of Rancière, see Chapter 1, by Adrian Kear, this volume.

Part II
Aesthetic thought and the politics of practice

3 Justice and the archives
'The method of dramatization'
Michael J. Shapiro

Introduction: a war crimes *dispositif*

In a recent exploration entitled 'Zones of Justice', my analysis was inspired by a passage in a novel by Mathias Énard.[1] His protagonist/narrator is Francis Servain Mirković, a former soldier who participated in atrocities while a fighter in a Croatian militia during the Balkans War. Having been reformed, he is on a train from Milan to Rome with an archive of atrocities that have occurred in the 'zone' (the Mediterranean region), which he intends to deliver to the Vatican. The passage is his recollection of seeing his former Croatian commander, Blaškić, on trial at The Hague's War Crimes Tribunal. Blaškić is:

> in his box at The Hague among the lawyers, the interpreters, the prosecutors, the witnesses, the journalists, the onlookers, the soldiers of the UNPROFOR who analyzed the maps for the judges commented on the possible provenance of bombs according to the size of the crater determined the range of the weaponry based on the caliber which gave rise to so many counter-arguments all of it translated into three languages recorded automatically transcribed ... everything had to be explained from the beginning, historians testified to the past of Bosnia, Croatia, and Serbia since the Neolithic era by showing how Yugoslavia was formed, then geographers commented on demographic statistics, censuses, land surveys, political scientists explained the differential political forces present in the 1990s ... Blaškić in his box is one single man and has to answer for all our crimes, according to the principle of individual criminal responsibility which links him to history, he's a body in a chair wearing a headset, he is on trial in place of all those who held a weapon ... [2]

As I have noted, the passage articulates a justice *dispositif*, where a *dispositif*, as Michel Foucault has famously elaborated it, is 'a thoroughly heterogeneous ensemble consisting of discourses, institutions, architectural forms, regulatory decisions, laws, administrative measures, scientific statements, philosophical, moral and philanthropic propositions ... the said as much as the unsaid ... the elements of the apparatus'.[3] As my analysis proceeded, I briefly addressed the Vatican as an archive, while at the same time pondering the stability of the entries in archives in general:

> [To submit materials to the] Vatican, implies that once they are situated in the archives of political or religious authorities, the records are sealed, locked up, immune from modification, because those authorities (archons) administer 'the law of what can be said'.[4] However, as the novel's construction of its plastic aesthetic subject, Mirković (as he goes 'backwards toward his destination'[5]) shows, and its testimony to the fragility of historical recollections and allegiances to which his journey indicates, the archive is never finally secured. However institutions, agencies, and bureaucracies may try to hold onto words and meanings (for example reifying them in the architectural sites and icons in the Vatican) they will ultimately be modified or supplanted.[6]

In this chapter, I turn again to the instability of archives and approach that issue by exploring another invented archivist, while framing that archivist's adventures within what Gilles Deleuze calls 'The Method of Dramatization'.[7]

Authorial invention

In a brief parable, 'The Truth about Sancho Panza', Franz Kafka offers an ironic twist to Miguel de Cervantes's epic novel, *Don Quixote*:

> Without making any boast of it Sancho Panza succeeded in the course of years, by feeding him a great number of romances of chivalry and adventure in the evening and night hours, in so diverting from himself his demon, whom he later called Don Quixote, that this demon thereupon set out, uninhibited, on the maddest exploits, which, however, for the lack of a preordained object, should have been Sancho Panza himself, harmed nobody. A free man, Sancho Panza philosophically followed Don Quixote on his crusades, perhaps out of a sense of responsibility, and had of them a great and edifying entertainment to the end of his days.[8]

Although the focus of the parable seems to be on Sancho Panza, doubtless what is more important is how the parable thinks about concept of 'truth', which arguably is applied to Sancho Panza's invention to provide a critique of the traditional concept of a timeless truth, i.e. to show that so-called truth is a function of signifying practices, in short that it is an effect of language. Kafka's parable challenges the usual way of raising truth questions; it suggests that rather than interrogating what truth is, the important questions are: whose truth is being dramatized, from what perspective, and to what purpose.

Kafka's Sancho Panza is very likely an inspiration for another fictional character, György Korin, the protagonist in László Krasznahorkai's novel

War & War. Briefly, Korin, a clerk/archivist in an office in the outskirts of Budapest, travels to New York with a manuscript of unclear authorship he has 'discovered'. His intention is to interpret/translate it and load it onto the internet where, he has speculated, it will be part of history's permanent archive. Apart from his geographic migration—from Hungary to New York—Korin undergoes symbolic/identity migrations, from minor archivist working in a records office in what he regards as a peripheral location, to the place he regards as the centre of the earth, the contemporary equivalent to Rome ('why, he asked himself, why spend his time in an archive some two hundred kilometers southwest of Budapest when he could be sitting in the center of the world'[9]). He thus also migrates from being a marginal Hungarian to being a New Yorker, and at the same time from a monolingual Hungarian speaker to one using a hybrid language (his Hungarian is increasingly peppered with English words as the narrative progresses). Like Kafka, Krasznahorkai regards intelligibility as an enigma rather than as an unambiguously positive achievement. Every mode of intelligibility operates within a discursive economy. To alight on a meaning is to jump to an arbitrary place that excludes alternatives. Thus as Korin reads and rereads the manuscript (which he seems to be embellishing, but many clues point to the entire narrative as his invention), he finds that there is no clear way to do justice to what it contains. At several points in his rereading, he concedes that he cannot understand the manuscript: for example, 'He had read it through countless times ... but the manuscript's mystery was by no means diminished ... '[10] He nevertheless dedicates himself to 'recover the dignity and meaning whose loss he had been mourning', even as he wonders why 'it did not respond to the pressure of expectation', was not 'a work of literature' (or any familiar genre), and has an ambiguous 'form of address'. 'At a minimum,' he surmises, 'it's perfectly clear that it was not addressed to anyone in particular.'[11]

Throughout the novel, Krasznahorkai's narrative structure—long sentences that frequently comprise entire chapters—articulates the manuscript's unusual narrative structure, which follows a journey of four travellers on an Odyssey through both time and space to return home. The journey begins in ancient Minoan Crete, passes through Cologne, Germany in 1812, continues through Venice and then proceeds on to Spain in the fifteenth century. Bracketing for the moment the sentence structure, Korin's rendering of the manuscript constructs it with what M.M. Bakhtin calls 'chronotopes', which render 'the intrinsic connectedness of temporal and spatial relationships that is artistically expressed in literature'.[12] In the case of *War & War* the narrative of the manuscript Korin is describing/inventing fits Bakhtin's examples of chronotopes of emergence and encounter. In the former, the 'emergence' is dual; it connects the 'hero's' individual becoming with a historical becoming, as the person and the world emerge in new forms. With respect to the latter, Bakhtin refers to chronotopes of the road 'which is a good place for random encounters ... On the road the spatial and temporal series defining human fates and lives combine with one another in distinctive ways, even as they become more complex and more concrete by the collapse of *social distances*'.[13]

As for the novel's grammatical style, the protagonist helps us appreciate why it has such long sentences. Well into the novel, Krasznahorkai has Korin speculate on the manuscript's formal structure, which turns out to be homologous with the formal structure of Krasznahorkai's novel as a whole. Here is what Korin says about the manuscript at one point:

> There is an order in the sentences: words, punctuation, periods, commas all in place ... and yet the events that follow in the last chapter may be characterized as a series of collapses ... for the sentences have lost their reason, not just growing ever longer and longer but galloping desperately onward in a harum scarum scramble—*crazy rush* ... [14]

Krasznahorkai's long sentences gallop along as well; they make the reader *present* to Korin's musings as Krasznahorkai 'draws us toward the consciousness of his archivist character'. The vertigo-inducing sentence structure buttresses Korin's testimony making it evident that the archivist may well be delusional, while at the same time demonstrating the vagaries of archival construction (the ways in which particular forms of memory-as-invention can constitute what ends up as history). The novel's grammatical rhythms, delivered in a third-person narrative, therefore unite the reader with the protagonist, 'offering a stance that is distanced yet remarkably intimate'.[15] Crucially, the flow of the sentences, without interruption, gives the reader an appreciation of all the aspects of Korin's experience—the ways in which he is sensing the manuscript, the relevance of how he is dwelling in the New York life-world, where he is inventing it, and how his interactions with his interlocutors (a Hungarian landlord/interpreter and the landlord's abused Puerto Rican lover/housekeeper) contribute to his interpretations. The way the novel-as-form develops makes it evident that rather than *representing* things, the protagonist is *expressing* them. As a result, 'truth' is not a matter of discovery but of expression.[16] In what follows, I offer a close reading of Krasznahorkai's novel in order to derive its implications for what I am calling the justice of the archives. However, to situate that reading, I turn first to the 'method of dramatization', which inspires my approach to that reading.

The method of dramatization

> Given any concept, we can always discover its drama ... [17]

> Gilles Deleuze

Deleuze's discussion of the method of dramatization is inaugurated by one of his interlocutors, who identifies Deleuze's major concern: how to ask questions. 'It is not certain that the question *what is this*? is a good question for discovering the essence or the Idea.'[18] Beginning his response to that provocation, Deleuze states, 'The Idea responds only to the call of certain questions', and goes on examine the question forms of Platonism: 'The question *What is this?* reveals itself to be confused and doubtful, even in Plato and the Platonic tradition.' He continues by insisting that, 'The question *What is this?* prematurely judges the Idea as simplicity of the essence ... '[19] Resisting such a representational mode of questioning, Deleuze seeks to recover what he calls the dynamisms at work in concepts such as truth and justice. He evokes 'a strange theatre' in which 'a drama ... corresponds to this or that concept',[20] and adds that 'pure spatio-temporal dynamisms have the power to dramatize *concepts*, because in the first place they actualize or incarnate *Ideas*'.[21] What then is the appropriate grammar for such dramatization? Inspired by Nietzsche's suggestion that rather than asking what something is, we should ask who is interpreting it and from what perspective, Deleuze puts it this way:

> ... when Nietzsche asks *who,* or *from what perspective*, instead of *what*, he is not trying to complete the question *what is this?* he is criticizing the form of this question and all its possible responses. When I ask *what is this?* I assume there is an essence behind appearances, or at least something ultimate behind the masks. The other kind of question, however, always discovers other masks behind the mask, displacements behind every place, other 'cases' stacked up in a case.[22]

How then can a grammatical shift away from 'what' questions apply to the problem of justice? Edward Mussawir provides some assistance. Edified by the Deleuzian/Nietzschean mode of questioning, he applies the 'method' to a jurisprudence which 'does not just reflect the stable social reality of the time but one which "dramatizes" it'.[23] Approaching the problem of justice, he resists the typical 'what is justice?' and 'who is just?' questions in order to develop a theatrical account of justice, one that substitutes personae for stable subjects: 'The person is not a "subject" but a device or contrivance ... [which makes possible] a profoundly aesthetic account of the masks that define civil and juridical existence.'[24] While Mussawir adapts his personae to what he regards a practical, personal jurisprudence, I turn to Krasznahorkai's conceptual persona, Korin, to develop a politics of archival justice.

Korin

Krasznahorkai's Korin is by his own admission losing his identity coherence as his work on the manuscript proceeds, increasingly disintegrating as a persona: '*something in me is breaking up and I'm getting tired*'.[25] Rather than turning inward, he aggressively externalizes his fractured self. In Jacques Lacan's words, he 'throw[s] back on the world the disorder of which his being is composed'.[26] Nevertheless, Korin is not a static self. Early in the novel, after he gets to New York, he refers to himself as a 'head-archivist-in-waiting'[27] with a lot to do to prepare himself for the task, not the least of which is acquiring and becoming competent with a computer. Lacking facility in English, Korin has his landlord/interpreter Mr Sarvary accompany him to one of New York's most venerable (if not immortal) institutions, 47th Street Photo, to buy a computer because he has concluded that the internet is the best place to enter a text that you want archived permanently: 'For the first time in history,' Korin thinks, 'the so-called internet offered a practical possibility of immortality, for there were so many computers in the world by then that computers were for all practical purposes indestructible [and] ... that which is indestructible must perforce be immortal.'[28]

Korin's musings on the internet resonate with his perspective on New York as the new Rome, the implication being that the internet is a better place than the Vatican archive to secure the immortality of the text. Doubtless that is the case in part because the open access of the internet implicates countless witnesses to the documents, whereas the Vatican archive has opened itself very slowly and with various hindrances to access. For example, after Pope Leo XIII opened the archives for scholars in 1881, a time in which the 'opening was intertwined with Italian politics', access was afflicted thereafter by ecclesiastical conflicts associated with the papacy. The apparatuses of archival management hindered access then and has frequently done so since; for example, there has been a reluctance of Vatican archive managers (the archons) to grant access to researchers who have wanted to investigate Pope Pius XII's attitude toward the Holocaust.[29] While the internet, the ultimate venue for Korin's 'discovered'/invented manuscript, has implications for a discernment of the politics of archiving and access, the venues of the spaces of its preparation are arguably even more telling with respect to the contingencies of archiving.

The relevance of the spatial Odysseys of an archivist becomes evident as the novel progresses. In the process of working on the manuscript, Korin is also in the process of inventing himself as an American and as a New Yorker. He is a becoming subject, one who is 'axiologically yet-to-be'.[30] To do justice to the manuscript and its archiving, he has to invent a just self as well. With respect to his American location, the novel describes it succinctly: 'He had become quite a different person in America',[31] and that difference is engendered by the narrative of being (a being toward death) that Korin has decided to embrace. At one point he enquires as to whether 'the entire notion of America had ultimately come about as a result of his decision to put an end to his life' (once the archiving is completed).[32] With respect to his more specific location, his first New York experiences made him delirious: 'The traffic made him dizzy ... he was in constant fear of assault at every road and traffic sign.'[33] At this stage, Korin is prey to the dizzying effect that Georg Simmel famously describes in his analysis of the way the 'metropolis' affects 'mental life', a vertigo engendered by 'the rapid crowding of changing images, the sharp discontinuity in the grasp of a single glance, and the unexpectedness of onrushing impression. These are the psychological conditions which the metropolis creates. With each crossing of the street, with the tempo and multiplicity of economic, occupational and social life, the city sets up a deep contrast with small town and rural life with reference to the sensory foundations of modern life'.[34]

However, as Korin continues exploring the city on foot, urban impressions became increasingly a stimulus to critical reflection, as for example at one point when he 'journeyed further and further into the heart of town ... [and] odd small details, the apparently insignificant parts of the whole ... struck him ... he felt most intensely that he should be seeing something that he wasn't seeing, that he should be comprehending something he was not comprehending ... '[35] He thus increasingly becomes the urban persona that Walter Benjamin famously described, a 'flaneur' who is busy 'botanizing on the asphalt' rather than the delirious one suggested by Simmel. As Korin continues to read the city, it inflects the way he reads the manuscript; the city turns him into a lexical flaneur.[36] Rather than a disruption to mental life, the city, 'as a kind of force field of passions that associate and pulse bodies in particular ways',[37] helps to create the conditions of possibility for a critical mental life. It stimulates Korin's interpretive work as he reads and rereads (or most likely invents) the manuscript he has decided to submit to the permanent archive of the internet.

The novel also implicates yet another spatial determinant of Korin's creativity. The architecture of the apartment in which he dwells affects his reading/inventing process. On the one hand, there is the privacy of his room where Korin enters the manuscript into his computer file; on the other there is the apartment's kitchen—effectively the apartment's public sphere—where he attempts to communicate his insights about the manuscript to 'the woman', the lover/housekeeper of the 'interpreter'. Moreover, the various doors and walls aid his work process; they allow him to avoid the censorious presence of the interpreter, who inhibits his attempt at 'publicity', occasionally attempting to bar his access to the woman/interlocutor with whom he needs to communicate what he is thinking in order to validate his reading/interpretation of the manuscript. For example:

> He had read it through countless times, thought Korin as he sat in the kitchen next day—when, after a long period of silence behind the door, he judged that the interpreter must be out of the way—for really, he had been through it at least five, maybe as much as ten times, but the manuscript's mystery was by no means diminished ... even as he continued devouring the pages ... the mystery obscured by the unknowable and inexplicable was more important than anything else ... by now impossible to shake he felt no great need to try to explain his own actions to himself, to ask why he should have dedicated the last few weeks of his life to this extraordinary labor, since what after all did it consist of he asked the woman rhetorically ... [38]

In effect, the apartment where Korin dwells is one of the novel's protagonists. More than merely an inert physical structure, it shapes the way Korin creates the manuscript as the novel has him in a spatial Odyssey from room to room. It becomes evident that his becoming as an archivist is a drama that is dynamically shaped within the apartment—as well as in the city. Thus the spatial framing of Korin's archiving helps to specify what Deleuzian method identifies as the drama in the concept of archives that the novel develops. There is the protagonist, Korin, whose antics elaborate the 'who' of the archive creation (where who is interpreting must trump the 'what' of the archiving). However, there is also the theatre, i.e. the spaces of interpretation. Although Korin is arguably crazy, he is best construed as an 'aesthetic subject' rather than a psychological subject. The concept of the aesthetic subject to which I am referring is developed in Leo Bersani and Ulysses Dutoit's analysis of Jean-Luc Godard's film *Contempt* (1963). At a psychological level, the film narrative involves a process in which a couple becomes estranged. Although much of the dynamic is about how the wife, Camille (Bridget Bardot), has her feelings for her husband Paul (Michel Piccoli) turn from love to contempt, Bersani and Dutoit focus on the way the camera explores space and note that Godard's focus is not on 'the psychic origins of contempt' but on 'its effects on the world', which the context of cinema is articulated through 'what contempt does to cinematic space … how it affect[s] the visual field within which Godard works, and especially the range and kinds of movement allowed for in that space'.[39] Their characters' movements and dispositions are less significant in terms of what they reveal about their inner lives than what they tell us about the world in which they are inserted.

Similarly, although Korin's mental condition is monitored throughout the novel (among other things his plan to end his life once his task is completed), the narrative is intensely involved in both the spaces of the manuscript interpretation and the spatial Odyssey of the manuscript's characters. The novel turns the world into an interpretation-inspiring stage that shapes the way the archiving drama unfolds as a work of the venue-inspired 'creative imagination' of Korin.[40] Certainly the political subjectivity that Korin is acquiring throughout the novel is as much a part of his performance as is the manuscript he is creating to submit to the archive. However, two aspects of the novel's voice must be appreciated to heed the archive drama unfolding. First, in addition to apprehending Korin as a lexical flaneur, we must recognize his 'audiography', a concept that emerges from a tracing of the spaces in which Michel Foucault responded orally to queries about his historico-philosophical works. The 'audiography is … associated with a number of physical locations. Some are institutional and expected—the university auditorium or radio studio—others are more incongruous—for example the exchange on intellectuals and power which took place in a conversation with Gilles Deleuze and others in the kitchen of Gilles and Fanny Deleuze in Paris'. As the summary of the tracing puts it, 'this geography has left its imprint in the archives'.[41] As is the case with discerning the significance of Foucault's remarks in various interviews and recorded conversations, to grasp the significance of the 'where' of the way Korin creates an entry to the archive, we need to heed the geography of the language events that add up to its content—Korin in the kitchen of the New York apartment verbalizing to a non-comprehending interlocutor what he understands (or fails to understand) about the manuscript.

Second, the rhythms of Krasznahorkai's novel articulate a phenomenology of perception, for example in this long passage on the beauty of a flight attendant who helps Korin get his visa papers so he can board his plane to New York. Although the passage may seem to be an irrelevant aside, it is exemplary:

> The nipples delicately pressed through the warm texture of the snow-white starched blouse while deep *decollage* boldly accentuated the graceful curvature and fragility of the neck, the gentle valleys of the shoulders and the light swaying to and fro of the sweetly compact masses of her breasts, although it was hard to tell whether it was these that drew the eyes inexorably to her, that refused to let the eyes escape, or it was the short dark-blue skirt that clung to her hips ... that arrested them; in other words men and women caught in the moment ... —they stared quite openly, the men with crude, long-suppressed hunger and naked desire, the women with a fine attention to the accumulation of detail ... dizzy with sensation but, driven by a malignant jealousy at the heart of their fierce inspection ... [42]

This seeming aside on how beauty achieves its effects—beauty as a drama of encounter—is illustrative. It serves as a preview of the phenomenological density of the parallel simultaneous texts—Krasznahorkai's and Korin's—which treat the ways in which the creation of the history of war archives is a function of events of encounter, of the dramas through which the archives have been assembled as archiving subjects encounter others whose presence disrupts the tendency toward a proprioceptive (non-reciprocal) relationship to the world. Thus in *War & War* there is a dual dramatic narrative: one involving the encounters that shape the archivist's (Korin's) work of reading and inscription, and the other, the contrived encounters of the characters in the manuscript, which shapes their tale as they serve as aesthetic subjects in a chronotope of historical encounter. In that narrative, the protagonists report on the history of war's atrocities, as they come to recognize (as a result of an encounter with an interlocutor Masterman) that 'the spirit of humanity is the spirit of war'. The comment, for example, on 'the triumph of Koniggratz, or rather the hell of Koniggratz as anyone would say had they witnessed the Prussian victory on that notorious July 3 three years ago, a victory bought at the price of forty-three thousand dead, and that was just the Austrian casualties';[43] and they ponder (through Korin's interpretation) the means of security or defence in the vast scheme of life's desires and motives:

> ... *the primary level of human*, said Korin—lay in the longing for security, an unquenchable thirst for pleasure, a crying need for property and power

and the desire to establish freedoms beyond nature [and] ... to offer security in the face of defenselessness, to provide shelter against aggression ... the creation of peace instead of war ... [44]

The genres and temporality of the archives

In his analysis of Bergsonism, Gilles Deleuze writes, '[O]f the present we must say at every instant that it "was", and of the past, that it "is"'.[45] The manuscript that Korin is submitting to the internet archive is a patchwork of historical shards. Instead of a linear history of the events of war and post-war experiences, the protagonists bring the past into evolving presents in a way that encourages reflection on the implications of reliving the past in light of subsequent events. One way of conceiving the approach to war that the novel's temporal tropes express is afforded by Walter Benjamin's notion of 'temporal plasticity'. Reflecting on the poetry of Friedrich Hölderlin, Benjamin refers to what he calls a 'plastic structure of thought'.[46] It is a 'temporal plasticity',[47] a time 'wholly without direction'.[48] Benjamin's notion of temporal plasticity articulates with the ethos of historical sensibility that he promotes, a history that permits new beginnings instead of being seen as 'a sequence of events like the beads of a rosary'.[49]

What kind of new beginning can emerge from the way the novel *War & War* treats history and archiving? In the process of doing justice to the manuscript he has discovered/invented, Korin is in effect seeking an archival justice. Inasmuch as the drama of Korin's work is literary rather than juridical, we should address the contrast for which Shoshana Felman provides the relevant gloss. After posing the question, 'What indeed is literary justice, as opposed to legal justice', she answers, 'Literature is a dimension of concrete embodiment and a language of infinitude that in contrast with the language of the law, encapsulates not closure but precisely what in a given legal case refuses to be closed and cannot be closed. It is to this refusal of the trauma to be closed that literature does justice'.[50] Moreover, as she adds—indicating the ways in which justice responds to the theatricality of the trial—' ... the body of the witness is the ultimate site of memory of individual and collective trauma [as a result] ... trials have become not only memorable discursive scenes, but dramatically physical theaters of justice'.[51]

We are thus positioned to recall Deleuze's methodological injunction, 'Given any concept, we can always discover its drama ... '[52] and are encouraged, more specifically, to reflect on the drama of the archives. While the courtroom constitutes a drama that is ultimately closural, literature, as Felman insists, resists closure. The contrast is enacted effectively in Énard's novel *Zone* with which my analysis began. In a playful passage, describing the war crimes trial noted earlier, he writes:

> ... in the Great Trial organized by international lawyers immersed in precedents and the jurisprudence of horror, charged with putting some

order into the law of murder, with knowing at one instant a bullet in the head was a legitimate *de jure* and at what instant it constituted a grave breach of the law and customs of war ... peppering their verdicts with flowery Latin expressions, devoted, yes, all these people to distinguishing the different modes of crimes against humanity before saying *gentlemen I think we'll all adjourn for lunch ... the Chamber requests the parties to postpone the hearings planned for this afternoon until a later date, let's say in two months*, the time of the law is like that of the church, you work for eternity ... [53]

However, Énard himself is not, like the lawyers, 'immersed in precedents and the jurisprudence of horror'. Like Krasznahorkai, he creates the drama of a becoming archivist in order to create a counter-effectuation of the official archives of atrocity. His novel thus encourages a more open archive. At the same time that his protagonist is becoming an archivist, as he heads toward Rome to deliver the catalogue of atrocities in his briefcase, the novel offers a series of glosses on the role of writers who evince a 'literary justice' bringing the past into various presents. In the process of exploring the history of atrocity in the 'zone', Énard creates a literary archive that contains the writers whose fiction explores issues of atrocity and justice: Apollinaire, Butor, Homer, Joyce and Pynchon, and the canonical fictional responses to war and atrocities by Joseph Conrad, Ernest Hemmingway and Ezra Pound, among others. Many of these latter writers were personally affected by a history of violence in the 'zone'.

I want to call particular attention to Conrad because the route he took, which inspired his anti-colonialism, has inspired a powerful recovery of the injustices visited on Africa by colonial powers. Conrad's route was retraced by the Swedish writer/activist Sven Lindqvist, who follows Conrad's footsteps in order to tell the story of the extermination of much of Africa's native population by Europeans in the nineteenth century. Fashioning himself as an aesthetic subject, Lindqvist articulates a literary justice as he visits the extermination sites to reflect on the violent nineteenth-century European–African encounters, while at the same time including the archival testimony that rehearses the rationales used to justify the slaughters.[54] Lindqvist's work is one genre among many within which the past has been drawn into the present in order to seek justice for victims whose experiences have not had extensive coverage in official archives and/or in juridical venues.

In effect, Lindqvist fashions himself as one of justice's conceptual personae. He enters the historical drama by reliving an era of atrocity and blending his own creative imagination with shards from the historical record. He fashions his journey as a narrative of a man (Lindqvist) travelling by bus through the Sahara desert while simultaneously travelling by computer through the history of the concept of extermination. Krasznahorkai's Korin—simultaneously doing justice to the manuscript he is entering into the internet and to moments in the history of war through his four personae who see 'only war

74 *Michael J. Shapiro*

and war everywhere'[55]—also exercises a creative imagination that he commits to his computer: ' ... the manuscript that preoccupied him was a work of art of the highest caliber, so he was very much in a position to understand the problems of the creative imagination ... '[56]

What would a just archive be with respect to histories of atrocity, and what aspects of what kinds of genre can recover the dramas that open the archives of justice that official institutions have tended to fetishize (where a fetishized archive is one that is inanimate rather than historically mobile)? Part of the issue is addressed in Adam Gopnik's reflections on academic responsibility. Referring to what 'we' as academics owe to such histories in response to suggestions that the histories contain 'a sense of proportion', he writes:

> Whatever academic scholarship may insist, surely a sense of proportion is the last thing we want from history—perspective certainly, not proportion. Anything, after all, can be seen in proportion, shown to be no worse a crime than some other thing. Time and distance can't help but give us a sense of proportion: it was long ago and far away and so what? What great historians give us instead, is a renewed sense of sorrow and anger and pity for history's victims.[57]

While I endorse Gopnik's suggestion (although I am more partial to the contributions of artists and writers than to 'great historians'), I want to conclude by heeding two significant aspects of Krasznahorkai's *War & War*: its turn to the internet as the space of archives and its 'plastic temporality'. With respect to the former, of late reality is imitating Krasznahorkai's fiction. On 8 March 2013, *The Jerusalem Post* reported that France has released and placed on the internet the documents from one of history's most dramatic trials, the trial of Alfred Dreyfus, the French Jewish soldier wrongfully accused of spying for Germany in 1894.[58] Without going into the sordid details of the case (after years in prison, Dreyfus was exonerated and reinstated in the army as a lieutenant-colonel in 1906), I want again to evoke the difference between legal and literary justice. Whereas the French courtroom had closed the Dreyfus case with a verdict, French writers kept the case open. In addition to Emile Zola's well-known *J'accuse*, an open letter in 1898 in a French newspaper, accusing the government of anti-Semitism while pointing to flaws in the court's procedures and evidence collection (ultimately forcing the writer into temporary exile), I want to call attention to Anatole France's satiric novel *Penguin Island* which ridiculed the evidentiary process used by the military against Dreyfus. Using a pseudonym for Dreyfus and the accusing army officers, France has a 'General Panther' state 'with patriotic satisfaction ... proofs against Pyrot [Dreyfus]? ... We had not got them when we convicted him, but we have plenty of them now'.[59] 'Six months later the proofs against Pyrot filled two stories of the Ministry of War [and were so heavy that] the ceiling fell in beneath of weight of the bundles, and the avalanche of falling documents crushed two head clerks ... '[60]

Turning to the second aspect of *War & War*, its 'plastic temporality', I want to call attention to the way treatments of ongoing war atrocities in artistic texts have the effect of rethinking those in the past. For example, in her *Hiroshima after Iraq*, Rosalyn Deutsche provides specific cases that speak to the implications of Benjamin's concept of plastic temporality. She explores how to rethink the bombing of Hiroshima now that the Iraq wars are part of the historical archive of war. Highlighting the critical temporality that derives from the grammatical tense that locates the past in the future—the future anterior (the will have been)—she dwells on the significance of several returns to Hiroshima. In one example, she analyses Silvia Kolbowski's video *After Hiroshima Mon Amour*, which 'returns to Hiroshima to confront the legacy of the atomic bombing, linking it to the present invasion and occupation of Iraq'.[61] Recasting the Duras/Renais film, *Hiroshima Mon Amour* (1959) by using a different temporal pacing and different mode of oral address, while including images from Iraq, Kolbowski's heterogeneous temporal association of the two wars gives both the past and the present different interpretive weight and significance. It is one artistic event among many in which the arts participate in challenging the official archive of war. Summing up the significance of Kolbowski temporal inter-articulation of the Hiroshima bombing and the Iraq invasion and occupation, Deutsche writes, 'The word *after* in Kolbowski's title raises the question of time and therefore of history, which is to say of the meaning of past events'.[62]

The drama of the archives of war that Deutsche rehearses in her survey of the arts is what is accomplished in Krasznahorkai's *War & War*. The novel is a critical response to the temporally oriented questions and suggestions about archives that Jacques Derrida has famously explored. After focusing on the 'when' rather than the 'what' of archives, Derrida states, 'I asked myself what is the moment *proper* to the archive'.[63] Like Deutsche, Derrida evokes the future anterior: 'The archive: if we want to know what that will have meant, we will only know in times to come.'[64] Like Krasznahorkai's Korin, he heeds the new technologies that give the archive its current 'moment' as well as its *where*: 'The technical structure of the *archiving* archive determines the structure of the *archivable* content ... email is privileged ... because electronic mail today, even more than fax, is on the way to transforming the entire public and private space of humanity' (i.e. the theatre of the archiving drama is increasingly the internet).[65] Like Korin, Derrida's evocation of the internet responds to the question about doing justice to the archives. As he puts it, the archive must partake of 'a responsibility for tomorrow'.[66] It is in this sense that he, like Krasznahorkai, renders the justice of the archive as an historical drama.

Notes

1 See Michael J. Shapiro, *Studies in Trans-Disciplinary Method: After the Aesthetic Turn*, New York: Routledge, 2012: 71–85.
2 Mathias Énard, *Zone*, trans. Charlotte Mandell, Rochester, NY: Open Letter, 2010: 72–73.

3 Michel Foucault, 'The Confession of the Flesh', A Conversation, in *Power/Knowledge: Selected Interviews and Other Writings 1972–1977*, ed. and trans. Colin Gordon *et al.*, New York: Pantheon, 1980: 194.
4 Michel Foucault, *The Archaeology of Knowledge*, trans. Alan Sheridan, New York: Pantheon, 1972: 129.
5 Énard, *Zone*: 127.
6 Shapiro, *Studies in Trans-Disciplinary Method*: 80.
7 See Gilles Deleuze, 'The Method of Dramatization', in *Desert Islands and Other Texts, 1953–1974*, ed. David Lapoujade, trans. Michael Taormina, New York: Semiotext(e), 2004: 94–116.
8 Franz Kafka, 'The Truth about Sancho Panza', in *The Complete Stories*, trans. Willa and Edwin Muir, New York: Schocken, 1971: 430.
9 László Krasznahorkai, *War & War*, trans. George Szirtes, New York: New Directions, 2006: 19.
10 Krasznahorkai, *War & War*: 103.
11 Krasznahorkai, *War & War*: 201.
12 M.M. Bakhtin, 'Forms of Time and Chronotope in the Novel', in *The Dialogic Imagination*, trans. Caryl Emerson and Michael Holquist, Austin: University of Texas Press, 1981: 84.
13 M. M. Bakhtin, *The Dialogic Imagination*, trans. Caryl Emerson and Michael Holquist, Austin: University of Texas Press, 1981: 243.
14 Krasznahorkai, *War & War*: 196.
15 The quotations in this paragraph are from an interview with Krasznahorkai, online at: timesflowstemmed.com/2012/01/29/war-and-war-by-laszlo-krasznahorkai/.
16 For a treatment of that difference, see Gilles Deleuze's treatment of Spinoza's philosophy in *Expressionism in Philosophy: Spinoza*, trans. Martin Joughin, New York: Zone Books, 1990.
17 Deleuze, 'The Method of Dramatization': 98.
18 Deleuze, 'The Method of Dramatization': 94.
19 Deleuze, 'The Method of Dramatization': 95.
20 Deleuze, 'The Method of Dramatization': 98.
21 Deleuze, 'The Method of Dramatization': 99.
22 Deleuze, 'The Method of Dramatization': 113–14.
23 Edward Mussawir, *Jurisdiction in Deleuze: The Expression and Representation of the Law*, New York: Routledge, 2011: 22.
24 Mussawir, *Jurisdiction in Deleuze*: 22–23.
25 Krasznahorkai, *War & War*: 130.
26 The quotation is from Jacques Lacan, 'Agressivity in Psychoanalysis', in *Écrits*, trans. Alan Sheridan, New York: Norton & Co., 1977: 20.
27 Krasznahorkai, *War & War*: 23.
28 Krasznahorkai, *War & War*: 84.
29 See Nicholas J. Tussing, 'The Politics of Leo XIII's Opening of the Vatican Archives: The Ownership of the Past', *The American Archivist* 70 (Fall/Winter 2007): 364–86.
30 The quotation is from M.M. Bakhtin, 'Author and Hero in Aesthetic Activity', in *Art and Answerability*, trans. V. Liapunov, Austin: University of Texas Press, 1990: 13.
31 Krasznahorkai, *War & War*: 91.
32 Krasznahorkai, *War & War*: 92.
33 Krasznahorkai, *War & War*: 63.
34 The quotation is from Georg Simmel, 'The Metropolis and Mental Life', in *The Sociology of Georg Simmel*, ed. Kurt Wolff, New York: The Free Press, 1950: 409–24. I am quoting it from a contemporary analysis of modernity's hyperstimuli: Ben Singer, 'Modernity, Hyperstimulus, and the Rise of Popular Sensationalism',

Justice and the archives 77

     in *Cinema and the Invention of Modern Life*, ed. Leo Charney and Vanessa R. Schwartz, Berkeley, CA: University of California Press, 1995: 73, which acknowledges its debt to Simmel's original formulation of the phenomenon.
35 Singer, 'Modernity, Hyperstimulus, and the Rise of Popular Sensationalism': 64.
36 On the flaneur, see Walter Benjamin, *Charles Baudelaire: A Lyric Poet in the Era of High Capitalism*, London: Verso Books, 1983.
37 The quotation is from Ash Amin and Nigel Thrift, *Reimagining the Urban*, Malden, MA: Polity, 2002: 84.
38 Krasznahorkai, *War & War*: 103–4.
39 See Leo Bersani and Ulysse Dutoit, *Forms of Being*, London: BFI, 2004: 21–22.
40 Krasznahorkai, *War & War*: 143.
41 See Michel Foucault, *Speech Begins After Death*, trans. Roberto Bonnono, Minneapolis: University of Minnesota Press, 2013: 6.
42 Krasznahorkai, *War & War*: 37.
43 Krasznahorkai, *War & War*: 133.
44 Krasznahorkai, *War & War*: 175.
45 Gilles Deleuze, *Bergsonism*, trans. Hugh Tomlinson and Barbara Habberjam, New York: Zone Books, 1991: 55.
46 Walter Benjamin, 'Two Poems by Friedrich Holderin', trans. Stanley Corngold, in *Walter Benjamin: Selected Writing 1913–1926*, Cambridge, MA: Harvard University Press, 1996: 31.
47 Benjamin, 'Two Poems by Friedrich Holderin': 34.
48 The quotation is from Peter Fenves, *The Messianic Reduction: Walter Benjamin and the Shape of Time*, Stanford, CA: Stanford University Press, 2011: 3.
49 Walter Benjamin, 'On the Concept of History', trans. E. Jephcott, in *Walter Benjamin: Selected Writings 1938–1940*, Cambridge, MA: Harvard University Press, 2003: 397.
50 Shoshana Felman, *The Juridical Unconscious: Trials and Traumas of the Twentieth Century*, Cambridge, MA: Harvard University Press, 2002: 8.
51 Felman, *The Juridical Unconscious*: 9.
52 Deleuze, 'The Method of Dramatization': 98.
53 Énard, *Zone*: 75.
54 See Sven Lindqvist, *Exterminate All the Brutes*, trans. Joan Tate, New York: The New Press, 1992.
55 Krasznahorkai, *War & War*: 203.
56 Krasznahorkai, *War & War*: 143.
57 Adam Gopnik, 'Headless Horseman: The Reign of Terror Revisited', *The New Yorker*, June 5, 2006: 84.
58 See: JTA, 'France Releases Documents from Dreyfus Trial Online', *Jerusalem Post*, 3 July 2013, www.jpost.com/Breaking-News/France-releases-documents-from-Dreyfus-trial-online.
59 Anatole France, *Penguin Island*, New York: Modern Library, 1984: 171.
60 France, *Penguin Island*: 192.
61 Rosalyn Deutsche, *Hiroshima After Iraq: Three Studies in Art and War*, New York: Columbia University Press, 2010: 10.
62 Deutsche, *Hiroshima After Iraq*: 21.
63 Jacques Derrida, *Archive Fever: A Freudian Impression*, trans. Eric Prenowitz, Chicago, IL: University of Chicago Press, 1995: 25.
64 Derrida, *Archive Fever*: 36.
65 Derrida, *Archive Fever*: 17.
66 Derrida, *Archive Fever*: 36.

4 The 'little cold breasts' of an English girl, or art and identity

Alexander García Düttmann

Aesthetic thought, a sensuous affection that touches upon spirit, is a thought that conceives of the image. Doubtless, such a definition is not exhaustive, yet it seems sufficient. What is an image? An image is something that has detached itself from the object, a doubling of the world in the domain of semblance, or a doubling of the world that brings about the domain of semblance as a domain drifting between being and non-being, matter and spirit. The image need not be understood as a copy or a reproduction. The copy, like the image, is ambiguous, but its ambiguity differs from that of the image. The image's semblance is a shimmering that hovers ambiguously between being and non-being. A copy is ambiguous because its semblance has the effect of denying the fact that a copy, too, is an image. This is why the copy can posit itself as an object: as the object copied and as an object with a consistence of its own, with a consistence that resembles the consistence of beings, of the image carrier, of the extension of the canvas and the density of the frame, if one looks at the case of paintings. Inasmuch as one must distinguish between image and copy, or between two forms of ambiguity, or between two effects of semblance, an image is something that proves to be fleeting, something that appears, flares, shines forth and vanishes, something that turns toward the beholder and away from him, not something that perseveres in its being or that belongs essentially to being. Images exist only as a flight of images. It is as if the image did not present the world but exhibited the relation to the world and thereby distanced the world, loosening its coherence and consistence. The image is a trace of the world. It is as much a form of participation as a sign of solitude. It is both a bond and a rupture that splits the world. Whatever enters or becomes an image, whatever comes into being as an image, raises the question of whether one can say that it was there, to allude to *The Death of Empedocles*.[1] The absence of images is thus not the contrary of the image, and it is never simply imposed from the outside, as it were. It is for this reason that one can turn to Adorno and speak of 'aesthetic comportment'[2] as a 'gaze' under which 'the given is transformed into an image', or of 'imageness' as constitutive of art, detecting even in music an image-like element that characterizes art itself and not merely programme music. If art is the objectification of 'aesthetic comportment', then 'aesthetic thought' stands for such comportment since the transformation into an image must be

Art and identity 79

considered a sensuous affection touching upon spirit. At the same time, 'aesthetic thought' also designates the labour of the concept that refers to 'aesthetic comportment' and that feeds off the sensuous and spiritual affection at work in art.

The fact that images are produced does not entail that images are nothing but a product and that, as a consequence, they can be arbitrarily replaced and put together. For it is always possible that in its very fleetingness, an image comes to bear upon something that is not another image without therefore being an object. Upon what might an image come to bear? It might come to bear upon something new. Not upon something new that distinguishes itself from something old and then eventually turns into something old from which something else will distinguish itself as new, but upon the new under the aspect of the inexhaustible, of that which keeps recurring in a different manner. The new upon which the image, the flight of images or aesthetic thought come to bear, is the newness of the idea that communicates itself to the image or to the thought and that indeed is mere communicability. Such communicability is located in the communication of a thought as an image, in the artistic instantiation of aesthetic thought. It cannot be separated from this communication or instantiation. The idea is the unthought of aesthetic thought that allows this thought to exist in the first place. Hence communicability means that there is not just one single image, but that there is always a flight of images or that there are always flights of images, and that aesthetic thought must always begin anew, both in the creation and in the discovery of a new flight of images.

If, at this point, one asks whether aesthetic thought in the present has also a political relevance, the question could be answered in the affirmative, for aesthetic thought can shatter a prevailing prejudice, namely the prejudice that an identity—the identity of a person, a group, a people, or a nation—must be regarded as a construct, a construct founded in a social history but ultimately arbitrary and replaceable by a different construct. Recently, Jean-Luc Nancy has pointed out the dilemma one faces when conceiving of identity, be it the identity of a person, a group, a people, or a nation. On the one hand, Nancy claims that identity is linked to a lineage, and to a history, at least to the extent that it refers to itself and that its assertion is also an opening and an exposure. Identity in this sense is a point one encounters by chance, a point from which a path departs, a point at which a trajectory begins. On the other hand, Nancy also claims that identity always indicates what is one and remains one because no doubt can ever touch it. Identity in this sense is a remainder that only a meaningless proper name can designate. External descriptions, listings of qualities and attributes will miss it, as will self-examination and introspection. The 'absolute unity' of this oneness, of this remainder of identity disappears, fizzles out, expires within 'the infinitesimal point of its origin and destination'.[3]

According to Nancy's argument, identity and identified identity must be told apart. Identified identity is an attempt to make available and accessible that which must be unavailable and inaccessible, that which imposes itself and emerges as a point of reference, all the more so the less it allows for an identification and the more difficult it proves to locate.

Yet the point one encounters by chance and the point that sticks out from the sphere of doubt, from the domain of chance, are not two different points, as if one had to conceive of identity from two contradictory perspectives and thereby entangle oneself in an inconsistency. Rather it is the unavailability and inaccessibility of the infinitesimal, of an infinitesimal that challenges all calculation, that draws the Janus-faced image of identity, the image of a face with accidental and variable traits and the image of a face with necessary and invariable traits. Both faces cannot but appear vague and blurred, as in a portrait by Gerhard Richter; one face because its mutability turns every single trait into a trait that is out of focus, the other face because its immutability makes every single trait protrude with such exactness that it becomes unrecognizable and ceases to be a trait, or because in relation to the face's immutability every single one of its traits is already fuzzy.

It follows from this characterization of identity that two types of prejudice might arise, the prejudice of a rigid identity that comes with an attempt to identify identity itself and the prejudice of a fictitious identity that amounts to its denial, or that reduces it to chance and arbitrariness. How can aesthetic thought as a thought of the image confront these prejudices, especially the prejudice prevailing today, the prejudice of identity as something entirely fictitious, and in this way claim political relevance, that is, represent a challenge to politics? It can do so, for example, by producing images of a landscape that hold fast and at the same time let go whatever it is that turns this landscape into a distinctive and unique landscape, into a landscape that despite its transformation, its industrial devastation, its preservation as an artificial sanctuary, or the defacement brought about by the installation of huge wind turbines, is so tightly connected with the historical processes that have informed and shaped it, with the people who have grown old in it, who have lived or still live there, that it cannot be seen as a replaceable cultural product. How a landscape might fashion and stamp the identity of a person in an image can be gauged from a novel by John Cowper Powys set in Norfolk's harsh and watery landscape and in Somerset's mystic landscape. John Crow, who has returned to Norfolk because of an inheritance, decides to go for a walk with his cousin as winter gives way to spring. He has fallen in love with her:

> And John thought, 'I'm English and she's English and this is England. It's more lovely to feel her little cold breasts under these stiff clothes, on this chilly grass, than all the Paris devices.' And without formulating the thought in words he got the impression of the old anonymous ballads writ in northern dialect and full of cold winds and cold sword-points and cold spades and cold rivers; an impression wherein the chilly green grass and the peewits' cries made a woman's love into a wild, stoical, romantic thing.[4]

On the one hand, the identity of the English which here is bound to an experience of landscape and love and tinged by a vivid literary reminiscence, appears under the spell of a cliché as if it were an identified identity, at least to the extent that it is described in contrast to something fundamentally French. On the other hand, however, it hangs in the balance of an image and has something suspended and ungraspable about it because of the attributes Cowper Powys chooses when describing 'a woman's love'. The reader feels how the stoical is linked to the wild and the romantic, as a kind of unyieldingness that fosters rather than lessens the exuberant abandonment, yet he also knows that these predicates exclude one another.

In a later passage from the same novel, it is said about the 'fancies' of a woman who lives in Glastonbury:

> [They] were simply her sudden recollection of certain moments of intense realisation of life as they had occurred several years ago. They were nothing more than the look of a particular wall, of a particular tract of hedge, of a particular piece of road, of a certain hay-wagon on a certain hillside, of a particular pond with ducks swimming on it and a red cow stepping very slowly through the mud, of a load of seaweed being pulled up from the beach by struggling horses, of the stone bridge crossing the Yeo at Ilchester, of a little toll-pike at Lodmore that seemed to be made up, as she had seen it from the top of a bus beyond Weymouth once, of nothing but white-washed stones and tarred planks and tall brackish grasses and clouds of white dust. Nancy could never tell which of her fancies would rise up next like a fish, making a circle of delicious ripples round it, from the depths of her mind, nor did she know whether these mental pictures stored up in her brain were limited in number, and whether, at a certain point, they would begin recurring all over again, or whether they were inexhaustible and need never repeat themselves.[5]

As difficult as it might prove to call the identity of the female figure by another name than her proper name, the identity that crystallizes itself in a feeling of life pervading intensely the images of the landscape, as difficult as it might prove to say of exactly what this identity consists, the reader of the passage quoted will still sense how the feeling of life lets the figure grow beyond herself and at the same time become who she is, and how her identity lies neither in the person nor in the landscape but in an unfathomable in-between, in the landscape as the person's being and non-being, in the person as the landscape's being and non-being. This in-between is nothing but the in-between of the image.

When, in his essay on *Der Freischütz*, Adorno writes that one must seek the 'specifically German quality of the Romantic opera'[6] in the fact that musically a 'breeze comes wafting in through windows and openings' and brings 'air that is normally kept out by the dense landscape of culture', when he situates the 'specifically German quality' of an opera and of Romanticism, of a whole period in music, in an experience of natural beauty, in a sigh of relief 'out in the open', he actually relates what is German to an experience of the non-identical. The non-identical discloses the work of art inasmuch as 'identity'[7] is not to be its 'last word', as Adorno puts it in his *Aesthetic Theory*, and inasmuch as each artwork must meet the double demand of integration and disintegration, of making every detail its own and interrupting this process, at least if it is to be an 'authentic' work of art. Once again identity is given only in an image since both the experience of natural beauty and the 'experience of art'[8] are said to be an experience of 'images', of nature as a landscape.

Who will want to claim, following the automated reflex of enlightened foolishness, that the section in Adorno's monograph on Mahler in which the 'Jewish element' is attached to an experience of natural beauty, is a deeply 'problematic' one? '*Das Lied von der Erde*', Adorno states,

> has colonised a white area of the intellectual atlas, where a porcelain China and the artificially red cliffs of the Dolomites border on each other under a mineral sky. This Orient is pseudomorphous also as a cover for Mahler's Jewish element. One can no more put one's finger on this element than in any other work of art: it shrinks from identification yet to the whole remains indispensable. The attempt to deny it in order to reclaim Mahler for a German music infected by National Socialism is as aberrant as his appropriation as a Jewish nationalist composer.[9]

That the 'Jewish element' withdraws from attempts to identify it, or to remove the image that 'covers' it; that it does not present itself as a 'folk element'; that, in Mahler's late style, it does not express itself in the 'manner of composition' but 'without extenuation', in 'the shrill, sometimes nasal, gesticulating, uproarious aspect' of the material itself; that it pertains either to unmediated matter or to the totality, to a totality that, were this element to go missing, could not constitute itself as a totality; all of this indicates for Adorno that the interpretation of the 'directly musical qualities and their technical organisation' depends on philosophy. Philosophy alone can discern the 'spirit of music' and the relevance of unmediated matter, or of the material, beyond the specific shape, or form, it is given in the composition. Adorno suggests a proximity of aesthetic to philosophical thought. Perhaps spirit is merely the image as it appears in the element of the concept. In the wake of such a suggestion, an entirely different access might be gained to Joachim Ritter's idea that theory is the contemplation of God and of nature as a whole, and that in modern times it has been replaced by the aesthetic sense of landscape.[10] Totality, spirit, could be understood in terms of non-identity, so that the aesthetic would cease to be a compensatory supplement designed to institute an overreaching unity.

The aesthetic thought contained in the short film *Un héritier* (An Heir), shot by Jean-Marie Straub in 2011, can be considered a challenge directed at politics and even at art itself to the extent that art seeks an awareness of its own political implications. The camera follows two figures through the Alsatian forest and accompanies them until they arrive at an inn where the young and the old man pursue their conversation. In the last series of shots, the camera shows the young man in the middle of a green landscape, standing in front of the remains of a wall. The voices of the two figures recite dialogues and read out passages from a novel on the German annexation of Alsace-Lorraine, a novel by the writer Maurice Barrès, who is commonly regarded as an anti-Semitic representative of the blood-and-soil ideology in France. Repeatedly, imageless, black sequences interrupt the flow of images on the screen. What can one say about identity in this context? Can aesthetic thought appropriate polemically the legacy of ideological motives and instigate their conversion? In Straub's view, Barrès was the only intellectual in Paris who dared to speak out against surrendering Alsace-Lorraine to Germany, the war winner in 1871, because 'the French state bank happened to be insolvent'.[11]

Notes

1 Friedrich Hölderlin, *The Death of Empedocles: A Mourning Play*, trans. David Farrell Krell, New York: SUNY Press, 2008.
2 Theodor W. Adorno, *Aesthetic Theory*, London: Continuum, 1997: 330.
3 Jean-Luc Nancy, *Identité*, Paris: Galilée, 2010: 38.
4 John Cowper Powys, *A Glastonbury Romance*, New York: The Overlook Press, 1996: 38.
5 Cowper Powys, *A Glastonbury Romance*: 754 ff.
6 Theodor W. Adorno, 'The Pictorial World of *Der Freischütz*', in *Night Music. Essays on Music 1928–1962*, London: Seagull Books, 2009: 52 ff., translation modified, AGD.
7 Theodor W. Adorno, *Aesthetic Theory*: 63; see also Alexander García Düttmann, 'Life and Beauty: In the Middle, in the Extreme', *The New Centennial Review* 10, no. 3 (Winter 2010): 17 f.
8 Adorno, *Aesthetic Theory*: 65.
9 Theodor W. Adorno, *Mahler: A Musical Physiognomy*, Chicago, IL.: Chicago University Press, 1996: 149.
10 Joachim Ritter, 'Landschaft. Zur Funktion des Ästhetischen in der modernen Gesellschaft', in *Subjektivität*, Frankfurt am Main: Suhrkamp, 1974: 161 f.
11 sites.google.com/site/straubethuillet/3-nos-notes-critiques/2010-un-heritier/un-heritier-entretien.

5 Animating politics

Diana Taylor

This chapter explores the ways in which individual bodies and affects define today's political struggles taking place at the margins or outside traditional political parties and hierarchies. We have only to think of movements driven by outrage against political and economic injustices such as the so-called Arab Spring, European summer, Occupy Wall Street last fall, and Chilean winter as a few notable examples of affects that transcend individual feelings to form transnational conditions (perhaps unspoken coalitions) of resistance or even revolt. Words like contagion and entrainment suggest the ways that suddenly, unpredictably, people can become seemingly not only of one mind but of one body. Groups share and further transmit and elaborate what Teresa Brennan called 'energetic affects'.[1] The Indignados, or as Manuel Castells refers to them, the Indignadas of Spain, the over two million people who manifested in over 800 cities around the world between May and October 2011 fuelled by indignation, we might say, enact pure affect.[2] However, unruly acts and passions cannot be limited to the 'outside'—they cross ideological and structural bounds, showing the fears, anxieties, prejudices and hopes that animate the attitudes and actions of the state itself. While usually commentators assign affect to the opposition, characterizing those outside established political systems as irrational or angry, what Freud observed just after World War I remains true today: ' ... it would seem that nations still obey their passions far more readily than their interests.'[3] Hitler's Germany offers an extreme illustration of the ways in which the mobilization of poisonous affects can lead to passionate identifications and dis-identifications that overwhelm all systems designed to contain them. The politics of passion can be as murderous as they can be liberating: context is all.

Once again, it seems, political decisions during the past decade have been increasingly forged through affective and embodied struggle. Mexican theorist Rossana Reguillo has noted the move towards the de-politicization of politics through a politics of passion that exceed (and reject) traditional institutions.[4] Convinced that the electoral process has been violated or corrupted, that the media are sequestered in the hands of the power brokers, and that official institutions cannot adjudicate in a way that is seen as transparent and legitimate, people across political persuasions throughout the world have been gathering, demonstrating, demanding and pressuring for change through enacted, rather than discursive or representational, practice. The activism I look at here, committed to non-violent resistance, relies on bodies, digital networks and performance—marches, rallies, amusing and disruptive acts, media coverage, solidarity networks, cultural events such as teach-ins and discussions, and other embodied and virtual practices. The streets make manifest some of the connections among these various elements. WE ARE HERE. Visibly. Hormonally. Experientially. Politically. Not an abstraction like the 'American' or in this case 'Mexican' people. Not a poll number, not an easily divisible subgroup or constituency. Clearly, to think of political performance more broadly, we would need to look beyond the streets and digital networks. Ricardo Domínguez reminds us that the 'indigenous avant-garde' demands that we consider lands without streets and communities without networks.[5] However, for now, I will think about bodies acting in public space—bodies that due to specific historical, phenomenological and political reasons give at least the illusion of ontological stability and coherence.

Here, I focus on Mexico's contested election of 2006 in which 2 million protesters gathered in the Zócalo (Mexico's central square) to challenge the election results through acts of civil disobedience. This example, I hope, will shed light on the importance of bodies in politics that we can extend to the more recent Occupy Wall Street movement and other youth-driven protests.

I will not go into all the ins and outs of the election and Mexican politics as such or in relation to the elections of July 2012. Instead I focus on the efficacy and limitations of performance as politics—using the 2006 election as a stunning case study of several performances taking place simultaneously in the public sphere:

1 Andrés Manuel López Obrador (AMLO), the mayor of Mexico City and the popular presidential candidate for the PRD (the ever so slightly left-of-centre party) gathered millions in the Zócalo when he heard the elections had gone to his opponent, Felipe Calderon, candidate of the PAN, on the political right. AMLO knew he would no longer have access to TV or other media. It was now all about bodies. YouTube and Twitter had not yet become part of the distributive network that politics take for granted today. Millions of Mexicans, concerned that the PAN might have stolen the elections after seven decades of make-believe democracy, demanded a recount.

2 Protesters, organized by the performance and cabaret artist Jesusa Rodríguez, took to the streets and organized a massive sit-in and tent city (or *plantón*) that lasted for fifty days and clogged the Zócalo of Mexico City and the main boulevard Reforma (see Figure 5.1). Protesters enacted non-violent resistance during which 3,400 performances took place.

3 AMLO was sworn in as the 'legitimate president' in a 'pretend' inauguration—'pretend', that is, in relationship to the 'real' one that was out-performed as illegitimate (see Figure 5.2). The official swearing-in could not be celebrated

Figure 5.1 Plantón
Source: Photo credit, Diana Taylor

in a public place for fear of popular outrage; rather, it took place at midnight, during a three-minute ceremony in the midst of a congressional brawl.

These competing utterances, displays and ceremonial acts illustrate the degree to which performance and/as politics comprise multiple, overlapping and often contested cultural repertoires and legitimating practices. I will look at the staging, the power of political performatives and what I will call animatives, and the role of spectatorship which characterized the scenario of democratic participation that has yet to come into being.

Performatives, in the J.L. Austin understanding of the term, refers to language that acts, that brings about the very reality that it announces (i.e. the preacher's declaration 'I now pronounce you man and wife' has the force of law;[6] legally, in some religions, they are now 'one'). These utterances are verbal performances that take place within highly codified conventions; their power stems from the legitimacy invested in authorized social actors rather than individuals (the priest, the judge, or the Electoral Commission). Animatives, as I define them—are grounded in bodies—the becoming of 'one body' exceeds discursive formulation.

Animatives are part movement as in animation, part identity, being, or soul as in anima or life. The term captures the fundamental movement that is life

Animating politics 87

Figure 5.2 AMLO
Source: Photo credit, Cristina Rodriguez, courtesy of La Jornada

(breathe life into) or that animates embodied practice. Its affective dimensions include being lively, engaged and 'moved'. 'Animo' in Spanish, emphasizes another dimension of the Latin 'animatus': courage, resolve, perseverance. Animatives, thus, are key to political life. As Castells reminds us, 'emotions are the drivers of collective action'.[7] Animatives refer to actions taking place 'on the ground', as it were, in the messy and often less structured interactions among individuals. Performative, in my example here, might index the Electoral Commission's declaration of the winner in the 2006 election with its binding legal force, while animative signals the ruckus that broke out in the Zócalo and in the country. Clearly, as I argue, this apparent binary is far more complicated than my distinctions suggest here. Performatives and animatives only ever work together—nothing pronounced means much without the re-action of those addressed or invoked. The terms call attention to different political acts, uptakes and positionalities encompassed by the broader word, performance.

The efficacy of performatives depends on the acknowledgment/agreement of those in attendance. The addressee also always enacts a position—it might be one of agreement or consensus, it might be one of dis-identification, dissensus, or radical rejection. The two million people in the Zócolo overtly denounced the results announced from above. They supported their own candidate as *presidente legítimo* whether or not that act produced a widely recognized 'real'. I use these terms, then, not to illustrate clear-cut distinctions between some high/low, elitist/populist, 'real'/'pretend' understanding of politics. The space between those terms, the space of friction, contradiction and interface seems far more productive to me in understanding how traditional political hierarchies and structures have been upended by contemporary participatory politics.

The multiple Mexican political 'performances' (like all performances) of course need to be understood in situ, within the context of the political acts that gave rise to them—the decades of electoral fraud and corruption, endemic poverty (half of all Mexicans live in poverty and 20% live in extreme poverty), the brutal battle of images waged through the media during this specific election, the traditionally marginalized poor bursting in on the electoral process, the show of force by the Mexican military following the election, and the escalating waves of violence and human rights abuses evidenced in parts of Mexico since 2006 that have left some 100,000 people dead or disappeared.

The Sunday following the announcement of the election results, a million people converged in Zócalo to show their support for AMLO. From that moment onwards, the various protest acts broke new ground, social actors improvised as they went along. The contest of power was clear—on one hand, the PAN was the party in government controlling the resources, the armed forces and legitimating institutions. It made alliances with the PRI (the party that ruled Mexico for over 70 years and which is now again in power), with media conglomerates, wealthy industrialists in the north of Mexico and the US right. On the other side were millions of people—progressives, intellectuals, young people and a huge number of indigenous and mestizo people who had finally found a role in a political party. Mexico became a massive training ground for staging scenarios of democracy through civil disobedience.

AMLO started the march at the Auditorio Nacional, walking down Reforma to the Zócalo, the seat of executive power for the past 700 years when the Aztecs built their *cue* (or main temple) on the same ground. There he met his followers, who had come from throughout the country to join him. His proposal was that every single ballot be recounted: *voto por voto, casilla por casilla*.

From a conceptual point of view, this performance had political and symbolic force, but the staging posed a real problem. Jesusa Rodríguez (Mexico's most famous cabaret performer and activist) went to the Zócalo that first Sunday only to find a huge platform structure—an empty stage. During the three hours it took for AMLO to walk from the Auditorio to the Zócalo, the million people waiting there had nothing to do. When AMLO finally did arrive, all his political advisers and followers crowded around him. No one could see him. Jesusa remembers thinking 'a stage is a stage. It has its rules and norms. Someone has to organize it—people have to be able to see and hear things'. As Rodríguez pointed out, many politicians don't understand 'live' *teatro politico*.

For the second massive rally in the Zócalo, Jesusa had orchestrated the event (see Figure 5.3). The platform now had risers so that AMLO could stand centre stage; party members would line up behind him. While AMLO walked from Reforma to the Zócalo, well-known actors and writers read, sang and entertained the public. As mayor of Mexico City, AMLO was able to have huge TV monitors installed along the route so that those walking could see what was going on in the Zócalo, and those waiting in the Zócalo could see their leader coming closer. The walk itself took on a sense of dramatic crescendo, symbolically building on and amplifying the effect of AMLO's approach to occupy the centre of power. When he arrived, he was greeted with open arms by the admiring PATRIA—the actress Regina Orozco as Motherland (see Figure 5.4).

More importantly, the participants could see themselves magnified as a collective body both on and off screen; they were now visibly a part of an historic movement they could visualize and identify with. The staging did not in fact change what happened. Its efficacy, rather, lay in changing everyone's sense of participation in the event. Performance, the poor person's media in this case, made it possible for people to represent themselves (in the democratic rather than mimetic sense of the word, as in political *representation*) and to see themselves *in* and *as* a political force. By fuelling passionate identification, the force of the event created the very 'body' it claimed only to 'represent', but instead of language that acts, here bodies act—bodies that feel themselves robbed of their language in the form of their vote. They were voting with their feet, as the saying goes. Political participation begins to take other, more affective forms.

The *plantón* was a different kind of performance—the animative challenged the official performative. This was both an embodied claim to inclusion and the performance of belonging, of establishing a different 'city' that people

Figure 5.3 AMLO and Jesusa Rodriguez
Source: Courtesy of Jesusa Rodriguez

would occupy and control for over 50 days. The tent city enacted an alternative vision of what communal social life might look like. A disruptive animative—in the face of powerful performatives—enacted a more open and equitable society. Representatives from all around Mexico lived in the makeshift tents installed along several miles of the protest route. Gender roles underwent change as men cooked and cleaned and new forms of collaboration came into being. The *plantón* inverted the private/public we've become used to—the use of 'public' space as if it were private. Cell phone conversations and iPods have

Animating politics 91

Figure 5.4 Regina Orozco
Source: Courtesy of Jesusa Rodriguez

created a new etiquette—we take our private world with us wherever we go. These daily acts reaffirm the private publics of capitalism with its privatization of public space. My bubble world allows me to lock out all and everyone else. Here, however, the private became public as people literally rubbed shoulders and lived together peacefully in one of the world's largest cities. A different notion of politics was not only envisioned but enacted. 'The radical utopian character' of the *plantón*, to recall Herbert Marcuse's words about the 1968 uprisings, were 'expressions of concrete political practice'.[8]

Living *as if* culminated in the strangest performance of all—AMLO's swearing in as the *presidente legítimo*, head of a parallel government that boasts about 1 million constituents. The performative declaration failed on one basic level—he did not have the recognized authority to enact the claim—but it worked to question the authority of the 'official' decision. Rather than participate in the 'simulated democracy' of the Right, his performance accentuated not only the theatricality and make believe quality of the 'real', but the very real potential of the what if. The scenario offered another framework for envisioning a way forward by calling attention to the sham and imagining alternative, plausible futures. The *as ifs* and *what ifs*, as Aristotle noted, are very 'serious business ... [and] the poet's job is not to report what has happened but what is likely to happen: that is, what is capable of happening according to the rule of probability or necessity'.[9] Political *as ifs* create a desire and demand for change; they leave traces that reanimate future scenarios. In Mexico, this means imagining the political as a space of convergence and potentiality rather than (as we know it to be) a pact brokered behind closed doors by those in control.

I asked Jesusa what, from her experience as a cabaret artist, had prepared her for this task of choreographing an entire political movement. Judging from her response, cabaret might indeed be essential training for politics. While she had to keep the general structure of the scenario in mind—the 'creative' non-violent struggle against fraud and oppression—she had to act without a script. Her body became central to the performance (with advantages and drawbacks that we will see later). The improvisational nature of her work in cabaret, where she constantly pulled topical issues and figures into a loosely structured art piece, had trained her to stay on her feet and respond creatively to what was going on around her. Improvisation, as a methodology, is practice-based—'you can only learn to improvise by improvising', she reminds me. She also stressed the quality of bodily presence—developing a deep focus and connection to the people and place around her, allowing herself to become a body of transmission for the energy that circulates in and through her to the crowd. Affect, as Teresa Brennan reminds us, circulates among and between us; we as individuals are not self-contained.[10] Presence of mind is equally important as she weighed various options. A good imagination and a sense of humour are key, not only to performance and cabaret, but to envisioning a better world. Moreover, running El Habito, an alternative performance space for fifteen years with her wife Liliana Felipe, Jesusa had learned to plan, programme activities and look ahead six months. While performance is always in the now, it also has an eye to the future.

The politics of passion and the scenarios of a more equitable society to which these sometimes give rise, can prove politically efficacious. Since 2000, popular marches by ordinary citizens have peacefully toppled five undemocratic governments in Latin America—Ecuador, Bolivia, Venezuela, Argentina and Peru. However, there are dangers and risks to relying so heavily on performance as politics—some of them having to do with the highly unstable nature of performance itself. A couple of months after the contested elections, many of those who voted for AMLO said that if the elections were held again, they would not vote for him. They were put off by all the acting out. Still, AMLO has continued to be a public presence since 2006, and he and his party—the PRD—were a close second in the 2012 presidential elections. The 2012 elections, animated with a cry, 'Out with the idiots, in with the thieves', as one anti PAN slogan puts it, backfired. Now, with the PRI's Peña Nieto in power, protesters scream at the horror of a president whom some consider both an idiot and a thief.

So the rejection of AMLO following the 2006 election seemed to be a rejection of the performance of a more equitable society. The *plantón* was depicted as a strategic disaster—turning off supporters and giving spectators and critics occasion to paint AMLO as a radical. It's fine for the middle class and even progressives to embrace 'equality' on an abstract level, yet become afraid when they actually see the power of a dynamic and motivated working class. Animatives terrify governments whose main goal is to control bodies through the use of performative edicts, decrees and official utterances with the force of law. They also challenge onlookers who can be moved by acts of empowerment, but it's important to remember that even these acts (or especially these) are framed by many mediated forces. An important ambiguity, thus, attends to animatives—one key to understanding performance and/as politics. In *Ugly Feelings*, Sianne Ngai explores 'animatedness' or the 'non-stop technology' of cartoons and animations which, she writes, are 'unusually receptive to outside control'.[11] Control, she states, comes from the outside, the inanimate body usurps the 'human speaker's voice' and agency.[12] The bodies on the streets and in the squares were framed by the media as racialized rabble. So who controls whom? Who is watching? Who witnesses the battle of presentation and representation to decide whether to join to protest or to turn off the TV?

Political spectatorship, then, is a force or even *the* force to be reckoned with. Spectators are neither the stupefied mass Brecht maligns nor the emancipated actor Rancière envisions.[13] Revolutions and transformations succeed, Kant noted, when bystanders join in. The people in the tents, many of them of indigenous and mestizo racial origins, triggered a deep-seated fear and racism. For some participants, the tent city offered a utopian possibility of trust and collaboration, but for too many onlookers the tents, especially as they were pictured through the hostile media, foretold the 'fall' of the middle class that the ads had announced. AMLO (another Castro or Chávez), the Right had warned, will take all your property and belongings away, and here they were: his followers sleeping on the streets! A dreadful performative. For others, still supportive of the movement, the daily grind of navigating a complex city further complicated by the *plantón* proved too much—they would not forgive AMLO for what came to feel like, so very literally, the enactment of 'obstructionist politics'. Performance, a highly powerful yet unstable form, is always a two-edged sword—it can cut officials down to size but it's hard to know when resistance, civil disobedience and protest might trigger a violent backlash.

The politics of passion, I believe, explains the resurgence and even centrality of the body in politics. As political parties fail to represent their constituencies, people are re-learning to represent themselves. The Protester was *Time Magazine*'s Person of the Year for 2011. In each case, I submit here, we need to understand the work of performatives and animatives. Take Occupy Wall Street. Critics called on the protesters to name their demands! Slavoj Žižek, who was against the protests until he was for them, accused protesters in the UK of being 'thugs' whose 'zero-degree protest' was 'a violent action demanding nothing'. Where were the performatives? As political scientist Benjamin Arditi writes, Žižek stated that participants had no message to deliver and resembled more what Hegel called the rabble than an emerging revolutionary subject. The problem for him is not street violence as such, but its lack of self-assertiveness: 'impotent rage and despair masked as a display of force; it is envy masked as triumphant carnival.'[14] Later, of course, Žižek called for 'occupy first, demand later'—animatives before performatives. What caught on in Mexico, in Spain, in Occupy Wall Street, however, were the animatives. The occupation of public space with tents, libraries, meeting spaces, food centres, digital communication centres and much more caught on around the world. These movements, all *gestus*, involved repetition, citationality and improvisation. Everyone came up with all sorts of acts to instruct and amuse. Figures such an Anonymous refused the lure of clearly individuated leadership—they all form part of the 99%. These animated gestures enact a politics of massive unified presence. Occupy's unwillingness to make a demand, to narrow their force to one or more specific claims, speaks for itself, but here again, this only works if others join in. I would argue that our role (and by this I mean mine, and Žižek's, and Arditi's, and all of those who write about Occupy) is not to try to lead, or prescribe, but to assist, especially in the Spanish *asistir* which means also to be present. It means to legitimate the act of occupation by being there, physically or virtually, as consenting addressees. Again, as in the case of Mexico, the very 'REAL' is under debate and construction. Who gets to decide? Asistir means to defend, to augment, to assure that the injustices they name are not just theirs, a disenfranchised group as the media often calls them, but ours as well. We are, after all, invoked in the 99%. However, the beauty of the 99% is that it calls for solidarity and for identification, not for the individual protagonism of the famous, recognizable figures. Here, too, we're talking about distributive networks. The Žižeks, and even the Jesusas, cannot lead this kind of movement that requires an individual, everyday practice that exceeds them. As Mexican protesters said, democracy is not about voting once every six years, it's about defending the vote. One protester in Occupy Wall Street put it slightly differently (though I still edited it): You don't have intercourse every four years and call it a sex life. Politics is a process, a daily engagement, a way of envisioning a future, a doing and a thing done—which, incidentally, is also the definition of performance.

Notes

1 Teresa Brennan, *The Transmission of Affect*, Ithaca: Cornell University Press, 2004: 51.
2 Manuel Castells, *Networks of Outrage and Hope: Social Movements in the Internet Age*, Cambridge: Polity, 2012: 113.
3 Sigmund Freud, 'Thoughts for the Times on War and Death', in *The Standard Edition of the Complete Psychological Works of Sigmund Freud, Volume XIV (1914–1916): On the History of the Psycho-Analytic Movement, Papers on Metapsychology and Other Works*, trans. and ed. James Strachey, London: Hogarth Press, 1957 [1915]: 288.
4 Rossana Reguillo, 'Sujetividad sitiada. Hacia una antropología de las pasiones contemporáneas', *E-misférica* 4, no. 1 (June 2007), issue entitled 'Passions, Performance, and Public Affects', hemisphericinstitute.org/hemi/en/e-misferica-41/reguillo.
5 Ricardo Domínguez, teach-in, 'Convergence' Conference, Duke University, October 2012.
6 J.L. Austin, *How To Do Things With Words*, 2nd edn, Cambridge, MA: Harvard University Press, 1975: 6–8.
7 Manuel Castells, *Networks of Outrage and Hope: Social Movements in the Internet Age*, Cambridge: Polity, 2012: 134.
8 Herbert Marcuse, *An Essay on Liberation*, Boston, MA: Beacon Press, 1969: ix.
9 Aristotle, *Poetics*, trans. Gerald F. Else, Ann Arbor: University of Michigan Press, 1973: 32.
10 Brennan, *The Transmission of Affect*: 14.
11 Sianne Ngai, *Ugly Feelings*, Cambridge, MA: Harvard University Press, 2005: 91.
12 Ngai, *Ugly Feelings*: 123.
13 Jacques Rancière, *The Emancipated Spectator*, London: Verso, 2009.
14 Slavoj Žižek, 'Shoplifters of the World Unite', *London Review of Books*, 19 August 2011, cited in Benjamin Arditi, 'Insurgencies don't have a plan—they are the plan. Vanishing mediators and viral politics', delivered at 'Política y performance en los bordes del neoliberalismo: tramas contemporáneas' roundtable, King Juan Carlos of Spain Center, New York University, 20 September 2011.

6 A golden surface
On virtuosity and cosmopolitics
Joe Kelleher

On virtuosity and rhetoric

Virtuosity is a quality upon which much performance still depends. It involves, as Susan Melrose has argued, the sorts of operations and capabilities that enable the expert practitioner—the ballet dancer Darcey Bussell, for example—to 'genuinely be able to do more, in terms of the spectator or listener's own engagement, than she does'.[1] Virtuosity is also, though, something that can get in the way of affective engagement, or indeed any other sort of engagement, with what the performer may be doing, or trying to do. Theatre maker and performer Matthew Goulish put it well when he said in a lecture some years ago 'that it is a condition of performance that virtuosity, once recognised, becomes the subject of the performance, and displaces other ostensible subjects'.[2] Put another way, virtuosity generates a very particular distribution of the sensible: if it draws attention to itself, then it tends to do so at the expense of other topics of attention. This understanding, of course, has itself long been shared by all sorts of virtuoso performers—actors, orators, teachers, politicians—for whom the value of a performance that is 'impressive' in one sense may need, if it is also to be 'effective', to be tempered with other considerations, to do with credibility, believability and such, or the focus that is drawn towards particular ideas and values. To the extent that virtuosity is at times a useful part of persuasion, one part amongst others of the contemporary performer's rhetorical armoury, choreographer Jonathan Burrows, for instance, would appear to agree. As Burrows points out in his *A Choreographer's Handbook*, a volume that in its title and format might be thought of as imitating the classical and early modern handbooks on rhetorical technique, virtuosity is a useful hook for an audience's attention. It is, he remarks, 'just another way to help the audience to care what happens next'. It achieves this, as often as not, by raising the stakes 'to a place where the audience knows something may go wrong', which, for Burrows, 'is as much of a pleasure for the performer as for the audience'.[3] This, we might add, brings a particular *temporality* of attention to bear; or perhaps better, a certain temporal suspension. So it is that we 'hold our breath', or we perch 'on the edge of our seats', as we project towards what might be about to happen, for the performer and for ourselves. Just as, when the performance is done, we are suspended in another way in relation to something remarkable in which we participated, and to which report can hardly do justice (although report will try). Even so, for Burrows too, virtuosity can get in the way. As he says, 'if everything is virtuosic then there's nothing against which to read the virtuosity: it has to be in balance with other modes of engagement'.[4] Virtuosity functions—or needs to function, we might even say—ecologically: in relation to other aspects of performance practice, or other sorts of practice than performance, or perhaps other sorts of values generated from practice.

If considerations of virtuosity from the point of view of the expert practitioner have a tendency to focus on the temporal quality of the audience's attention, in and around the event, to what the performer is doing (and how well they are doing it), then a different sort of perspective is opened by more spectator-based, or scholarly or writerly approaches. For dance scholar Judith Hamera, for instance, virtuosity is—after Hayden White—one of the 'typical "plots" which histories of bodies are destined to inhabit'.[5] The plot of the virtuoso performing body, Hamera proposes, is put together by artists and spectators in their mutual creation of a 'social, interpretive occasion'. Virtuosity, then, for Hamera, is less 'a state or quality of individual bodies' than it is 'a communal organizing fiction'.[6] Hamera's approach to the topic of virtuosity, framed as it is within a wide-ranging study of the intersections of diverse urban cultural practices (professional and amateur) in Los Angeles, in relation to global political frameworks, is itself both political and historical. This sort of approach, not only to virtuosity itself but also the genres of fiction and the climates of attention that it generates, is very much the way of an important essay that was published by Gabriele Brandstetter in 2007. As we shall see, however, there are areas where the insights of practitioners and scholar-observers overlap, not least regarding what virtuosity lends to persuasion—and its disturbance.

Brandstetter, without overlooking the view of virtuosity as a capability, at least, of certain individual bodies, locates virtuosic practices in relation to a history of rhetoric. She draws attention, for instance, to one of the earlier forms of the virtuoso *topos*, arising amongst the so-called 'virtuosi' scholars of sixteenth- and seventeenth-century England, figures such as Richard Burton, the author of *Anatomy of Melancholy*, or Francis Bacon, gentleman amateur mediators of the marvels to be found in nature, in art, in antiquity. If, though, these virtuosi of early modern science were like oratorical midwives, dedicated to bringing nature's body to light, there was already no lack of concern amongst them around the extent to which a virtuoso eloquence might, as we've been saying, get in the way. As Bacon himself writes, 'But yet notwithstanding it is a thing not hastily to be condemned, to clothe and adorn the obscurity even of philosophy itself with sensible and plausible elocution … surely to the severe inquisition of truth and the deep progress into philosophy, it is some hindrance, because it is too early satisfactory to the mind of man and quencheth the desire of further search before we come to a just period'.[7] To return to Brandstetter, departing from the scholar virtuosi the larger history of virtuosity is one in which these mediators of the amazements of 'nature' morph, by virtue of the rhetorical-theatrical *topos*, into the performers of amazing 'acts' themselves.

The rhetorical question, meanwhile, remains. So it is that Brandstetter's account refers to ways and moments in which concepts of the 'natural' in eighteenth-century theories of performance are given to replace the rhetorical, but only so far as they displace the rhetorical stakes, as she says, to 'another stage'.[8] What remains in particular—on any of the stages where virtuosity is encountered—are the typical lineaments of the virtuosic *topos* (the term to indicate a commonplace theme or site of argument in classical rhetoric). These include the capacity of virtuosity to draw an audience's attention, 'even their awe and amazement';[9] its association with an unlikelihood of accomplishment that verges on 'sheer human impossibility';[10] the relation of virtuosity with the evidential, both the self-evidential aspect of an event that has to be experienced to be believed, and the likelihood then that testament to such experience should circulate as story, as anecdote, as legend; and, above all, ways in which this same evidentiary aspect lends itself to ambivalence and controversy. As Brandstetter puts it, 'the virtuoso is controversial because he constitutes a figure of evidence for the utterly improbable, which is necessarily and self-evidently tied to the event of his performance'.[11] Paradoxically, however, as she then goes on to argue, this same ambivalence, falling as it does between an event that one can speak of but which at the same time can only attest to itself, lends itself to a further site of controversy or *querelle*: that between text and performance, 'which—in its various permutations and in its inability to decide whether it is "for" or "against" the virtuoso— forms the basis of his charismatic performance'.[12] How, to put it banally, are we to know if the virtuoso 'means' it? How, indeed, to know *what* the virtuoso means, or what their performance is worth? Or, to take the questions more in the sort of direction that Brandstetter would lead us, how is it that the virtuoso is so often the one we find ourselves talking about, at those moments when we might be realigning in a more general or historical way our sense of what a performance—any performance—is 'worth', and the sort of meanings we might want to take from it?

Brandstetter herself discusses the virtuoso's 'seismographic function' in nineteenth-century debates around the relation of the performer to the 'work' that they represent, whether as stand-in *for* the work or, later, subsumed rather as an element in an author's, or composer's 'composition'. The terms of such debates, she points out, extend, in the nineteenth century, to the understanding of political models, so that for some contemporary commentators 'the end of the "virtuoso jamboree" (the great age of Paganini, Liszt and Thalberg) appears to parallel the change in the political situation and the 1848 revolution'.[13] Brandstetter then takes this into considerations of the geometrical and *mechanical* codification of the dancer in nineteenth-century ballet and, tellingly, the displacement of the human virtuoso in our own age by the virtuosic machines of the new media.

Brandstetter's question, at the end of her essay, is to ask what remains of virtuosity, today, as a 'transgressive scene'? Might those of us concerned with such a question, she suggests, look for an answer not 'in the milieu of the stars in sports, Hollywood, arena of politics or even in economy and management' but rather in those spaces of the contemporary performing arts where we find an 'undermining of the virtuoso, as a (nevertheless virtuoso) play with the risk and as well with the failure as performance'.[14] As it is, the sort of research project proposed here has indeed been taken up in recent performance studies by scholars such as Sara Jane Bailes, Sarah Gorman and Simon Bayly, each of whom, in their very different ways and in the course of substantial projects, offers invaluable insight into ways that thinking alongside the sorts of '"small transgressions" in passing' of which Brandstetter speaks, can enhance our understanding of theatre and performance's purchase on, and contribution to, the progressive political imagination.[15] I share with these and other authors an interest in how and why a certain virtuosity, typically conceived along the lines of the remarkable, the unfamiliar (if not unimaginable), can 'get in the way' of the theatre's aspiration to imagine the political. What I also wish to propose, however, is that this obstruction may itself prove productive, not least for thinking about relations between the local 'reciprocal capture'[16] of attention that takes place in any theatre around the virtuosic event, and the theatre's ambition to speak for itself—let alone speak on behalf of others—rhetorically as it were, which may be to say also politically, in and amongst other practices, other *forms* of practice, on the international (or cosmopolitical) stage.

On confusion and complicity

My first example derives from the scene of a contested international politics. Carlo Giuliani was a young man who, at the age of 23, was shot dead by Italian police during a demonstration at the Group of Eight (G8) summit in Genoa of leaders of some of the world's wealthiest nations, on 20 July 2001. Images of Giuliani after he was killed quickly circulated around the world, through newspapers and other media. The images, we would say, are iconic, or quickly became so. Giuliani wears black trousers, a white vest and a black ski mask or 'balaclava'. In most of the images the red fire extinguisher that Giuliani had raised before he was shot, as if to throw it at the police, lies a short distance from his outstretched body. Some months later, in January 2002, at the Teatro Comandini in the city of Cesena in northern Italy, the home town of theatre company Sòcietas Raffaello Sanzio (SRS), Giuliani—or that same iconic rendering—appeared again in a scene of SRS's *C.#01*, the first 'Italian' episode of their three-year, trans-European project *Tragedia Endogonidia*.[17] There is a scenographic virtuosity already to this rendering. 'Giuliani' is played not by a young man, but by an adolescent boy. The boy is smaller than a grown man, and by virtue of the conventions of visual perspective, the Giuliani figure appears, when the lights come up on the scene, as further away than it is. It is, indeed, as if we are looking not at a young man lying on the ground, but at an image of that, with all the operations of visuality, which would include our own relations to the image of appropriation and disavowal, built into the image substance.[18] All the familiar attributes of the image are also there: the 'clothes',[19] the posture, the fire extinguisher, and the ski mask that identifies Giuliani both as himself and also, as it were, marks the figure's iconic significance, as an icon of anonymity, as one of us. As if to emphasize the point, the 'stage' where all of the action of the episode is shown is a five-sided gold cube, so that the theatrically rendered photograph of Giuliani appears as if against the gold background or *iconostasis* that we associate with the Orthodox Catholic Church. We are, however, not done with virtuosity yet. A young man enters the space. Like 'Giuliani' he will only appear for this one scene. He wears black trousers and boots and is bare chested. He stands in the space, side-on, some distance in front of the Giuliani figure, and sings what we can only take as a lament for the dead figure. The song is beautiful, strange and archaic, a song of mourning. The performance is also—the words are appropriate—virtuosic, even awe-inspiring. The singer, Radu Marian, is a natural male soprano singer. He sings, that is to say, in the register of the *castrati*, a register which, as Brandstetter remarks, was '*the* virtuoso voice' in the eighteenth century, and also a primary locus for the sort of ambivalence we were discussing earlier, around 'the ethos of the interpreter and the artificiality of the "performance"'.[20]

As it is, somewhat different uncertainties arise for spectators in the early twenty-first century, for whom the castrato singer is no longer a part of the usual cultural provision, and where a rare appearance such as this is embedded anyway in the illusionistic machinery of the theatre. I was no less amazed, or impressed, than any of my fellow spectators, but given that testimony of the virtuoso experience is in a sense all about the circulation of report, I hand over to another to comment:

> it is ... the extraordinary and genuine male soprano voice that demands attention. And his breathing. His ribcage seems huge compared to his stomach. In the movement of his flesh we see the voice itself making its way out of the body; we see the breath move the flesh; and we don't know what it is that this breath articulates. Is his a song of praise for the deeds of the fallen, or a lament over the wasted youth of the too-soon-dead?[21]

There is, though, even more to the ambivalence than that. 'We don't even know,' commentator Nicholas Ridout continues, 'if we are witnessing a killer at the scene of a murder, or a mourner at a funeral, or both.' That further ambivalence is due to a dramaturgical virtuosity that reveals itself about half way through the lament. At a certain moment, in a break between strophes, Marian turns through 180 degrees, allowing us to see stitched along the length of his other trouser leg the red stripe of the *carabinieri* police uniform.

What to make of this? Up to that point, the singer had occupied a classical position on stage appropriate to the *epideictic* rhetoric of the lament or funeral oration. By extension, the theatre in which this scene is given has been making its own claim of honour and sympathy in relation to the fallen protester, the hero of civil disobedience, the anonymised exemplum of (us) all. Now, in a literal twist, the mourner to whose song the theatre has given space is discovered to be the police, perhaps Giuliani's murderer. Whatever ambivalence we may feel in relation to the physiognomy of Radu Marian's virtuoso performance—I remember for my own part feeling unable to decide whether *that* sound was being produced by *that* body, not quite sure that the song wasn't after all the playback of a recording—this ambivalence is compounded by reflections on the role being played by the theatre itself. As a place of illusion and duplicity for sure (not that we did not know that already), but also, more interestingly perhaps, as a place where the gesture of revealing—of the illusion, so to speak, that constitutes the truth of the situation—will reveal also, or at the very least allude to, a complicity on the theatre's part with the rhetorics and instruments of political power, of church and state, from which it might have been supposed to set itself apart. Arguably, though, the complications go further than this. As touched on already, the golden box stage serves to remove the figure of Giuliani—literally—from the context of his death, replacing the familiar setting of street and crowd and daylight and tear gas and riot police and spilled blood and armoured police vehicles, as well as replacing the 'chatter' of newspapers and other media commentary, with the reflective—and archaic—background of the iconostasis.[22] The golden cube—to echo Jonathan Burrows's comment cited earlier—functions as a setting 'against which to read' the *artisanal* virtuosity of the theatre image, as something set against its generic background, illuminated in a manner akin to the venerated icon.[23] However, the cube is also—as a set of surfaces turned in on each other, rather than a screen—reflective of everything that is there in the theatre, not least its own representational operations. Those operations include, of course, the engagement of our attention as spectators, there and, as it were, in the heat of the passing moment, the temperature of which the shimmering, yellow metallic environment seems only to intensify. As we give our attention to the images before us, as we ourselves *reflect* upon the scene, suspended in that reflection, projecting forward and back as best as we are able, what are we to make of what the theatre is already reflecting back on us—not only of ambivalence and complicity, but simply of confusion? What to make of a theatre that addresses, as this one happens to do, the international political scene with such operational precision, such rhetorical deliberation, only to churn it all up again, itself included, ourselves included too? Or, to come at the question another way, and to pick up another part of Burrows's comment: What if '*everything* is virtuosic'?

On other sorts of virtuosity

There are anyway, other sorts of virtuosity than human virtuosity. We noted briefly, but without going into it, how Brandstetter's essay involves an extended discussion of mechanical and instrumental principles in the codification, and training, of the virtuoso performing body in early nineteenth-century ballet. More recent studies have also begun to investigate the virtuosity of non-human performing bodies in contemporary and historical theatre. A recent issue of *Theatre Journal* on 'Theatre and Material Culture' includes, for example, an essay by Aoife Monks that explores the 'potential "virtuosity"' of stage props, to the extent that these function on stage like relics, not least when the objects' signifying and affective force is heated up by the ready circulation of testimony, in the form of theatrical anecdote. In Monks's argument, the virtuosity of objects, at least for actors devoted to Stanislavskian naturalism, is both something that 'gets in the way', in the sense I was discussing earlier, but also potentially what enables the virtuoso performance to emerge from the actor's communion with the object—a donated skull, an old coat, or in a post-Stanislavskian example, the cremated ashes of a precursor performer—'which takes over the actor' and, for the Stanislavskian anyway, 'releases the secret and repressed aspects of the actor's unconscious self'.[24] Also in the same issue of *Theatre Journal* is Nicholas Ridout's essay on Heiner Goebbels's machine-based theatre work *Stifters Dinge*. The self-playing pianos and weather-generating systems and other mechanical marvels we encounter in that piece, Ridout suggests, are experienced as having a touch more vitality to them—not just liveliness but, as it were, thinking, feeling life—than they need in order to function as mere things, as mere commodities for example. For Ridout, these performing objects represent, through what they embody of the theatre-making labour required to put them into motion, something of the virtuosity of what Marx referred to as the 'general intellect', the capacity for communication and collaboration held in common by all people. In the extra, unforeseen animation that the objects bring to the stage in Goebbels's production—and here perhaps there is a chiming with Monks's argument—they promise to do more than is required of them as objects in a play (to engage us by doing more than they *do*, as Melrose might remark): even to 'connect up' with other actors in the building—ourselves the spectators, for example—and 'produce some social relations together'.[25]

It is worth adding that the performance *C.#01* discussed earlier, like much of director Romeo Castellucci's work, includes its own version of a virtuoso mechanical performer, in this instance a self-loading, repeating mechanical cross-bow situated at the side of the theatre that launches several arrows—just as the image of Giuliani is revealed—across the faces of the audience into the side wall of the stage. Perhaps the only thing to remark here is that the social relations in which the theatre machinery may invite us to engage are not necessarily *friendly* ones. They may even be deadly. The same goes, it may be, for whatever apparently self-animating objects we encounter outside, or to borrow Brandstetter's phrase on 'another stage', in the theatre of the immediate political situation. This, for example, would appear to be the focus of a recent work, *The Pixelated Revolution*, by visual artist Rabih Mroué, exhibited at the 2012 dOCUMENTA exhibition in Kassel, Germany. Mroué's piece is a performance lecture and exhibition of documents that looks at deaths in public during the Syrian revolution through video documentation made by the victims themselves filming the act of shooting with their mobile phones.[26] At once, though, with these understandably brief and shaky video strips that Mroué renders as highly magnified stills or flip-books as if to get a better, closer or frozen look at what the video never quite makes clear (the identity of the military or police snipers), there would appear also to be a different sort of virtuosity at work.

Ridout's essay is one that would remind us that there is, as far as recent debate is concerned, more than one sort of—or more than one way of reflecting upon—human virtuosity. As noted, Brandstetter's account of virtuosity as a theatrical topos—i.e. virtuosity as we tend to imagine it when we think of exceptionally skilled, or awe-inspiring performances—itself includes discussion of the economic division of labour and the historical deployment of the figure of the virtuoso as an emblem for certain forms of political praxis. Even so, the theoretical tradition that tends to be drawn upon when such matters are considered is one that goes back not to seventeenth-century gentleman scholars, eighteenth-century castrati singers or even nineteenth-century ballet dancers, but rather develops this same Marxian concept of general intellect alongside a theorization of the forms of 'immaterial labour'. The latter, for Marx, were essentially forms of servile or non-productive labour, but which have proven very conducive to the generation of value within those modes of production that are dependent upon affective, social relations. What emerges from this intellectual tradition, for example in the work of Paolo Virno, is indeed a much less spectacular conception of virtuosity.

To rehearse the argument briefly, Virno takes the virtuoso performance artist as a model to examine, as he puts it, contemporary forms of life; in particular, contemporary forms of working life.[27] Virno defines virtuosity, simply enough, as the special capabilities of the person who performs for a living, the performance artist whose work depends upon their cognitive and linguistic capabilities, be they a dancer, orator, teacher, or a priest. There are, though, two main aspects to what we might think of as the virtuosic situation. First, virtuosity finds its fulfilment as an activity—its 'purpose in life'—only in itself. It has no other end product; it creates its own value. Virno's chosen example of a modern virtuoso, the pianist Glenn Gould, comes in here as someone who withdraws from live concert performance to the recording studio so as to challenge this condition and be productive, as it were, in something other than a strictly virtuoso way. Second, because virtuosity lacks a product external to itself, it requires the presence of others, it relies on witnesses. We might, to stretch a point, given the discussion so far, think here of Florensky's characterization of the iconostasis screen with its rows of saints and angels as itself 'a manifest appearance of heavenly witnesses ... who proclaim that which is from the other side of mortal flesh'.[28] Virno then goes on to remark that virtuosity, thus conceived, is rather similar to what Aristotle imagined political action or *praxis* to be like, as distinct from labour which produces an object from which the act of production can ultimately be separated. Political action—just like performance—requires the presence of others. That is, it requires—or as Hannah Arendt argues, it brings into appearance[29]—a publicly organized space. Performance and political action, then, also share with each other a sense of contingency, to do with the immediate and unavoidable presence of other people: the contingency, we might say, of what 'happens' to us, when we are amongst each other.

Taken so far, there is much in what Virno says to encourage someone who recognizes their work in such terms, and who aspires to have their work contribute to a political—or better, a progressively political—life. Virno's next move, however, is to point out that the special characteristics of virtuosity are those very qualities most readily appropriated by post-industrial or post-Fordist forms of capitalism. These are, of course, the same skills that we inculcate in our students in the universities, both when we seek to inspire engaged, capable and free citizens, and when we argue for the 'employability' value of our degrees in the educational marketplace. Virno itemises some of the sorts of skills involved: communication skills, or as we might say rhetorical abilities, the ability, for instance, to strike a balance between convincingness and responsibility; or, where responsibility is concerned, a responsible relation to risk, 'knowing how to put one's own soul in danger', as Virno puts it, and being able to respond effectively to the contingencies of a situation. These are the sorts of skills that make us dependable, trustworthy, in all sorts of situations. These start to sound less like 'specialist' capabilities, and more like the *special* capabilities—or species-specific capabilities—that might be cultivated in any human being, and which are equally important to political activity, social relations and various forms of waged labour, sometimes to the point where it is hard to tell the difference.

If, though, there is more than one sort of human virtuosity, there would also potentially be some scope for confusion, to return to our earlier topic, at least where certain sorts of values are being decided upon and contested. The sorts of confusions that might arise, not least for those with a professional, scholarly and we might say activist interest in performance and performance-related arts, are taken up in a recent essay by Shannon Jackson, which deals in some detail with what crosses in various arts-world discourses between the type of virtuosity that Virno is talking about with respect to the politics of immaterial labour, and the type of 'lay' virtuosity, as Jackson calls it, that we would associate with what prima ballerinas do, or the singing of Radu Marian. Summarizing Virno, Jackson writes of 'a dispersed virtuosity that uses the linguistic and cognitive "talents and qualifications" that used to be associated with "political action," but that are now incorporated into the everyday post-Fordist workforce'.[30] What follows, she says, for some—and here again we glimpse Brandstetter's intimation of an 'undermining' of the virtuoso in the pursuit of a renewed potential for 'transgression' within contemporary arts—is the image of a 'democratized and awkward' virtuosity, one that 'all of us have the capacity to access', but which also means 'you can deliver a mediocre performance and still be a virtuoso'.[31] As Jackson remarks, this sort of reversal of an old *topos* throws up some new puzzles. For example, while certain forms of recent performance—for example in contemporary choreography—might subscribe to the sort of virtuosity Virno outlines, invested practitioners of these forms may well at the same time—in the wake, say, of Yvonne Rainer's famous *No Manifesto* ('No to Spectacle. No to virtuosity', it begins)[32]—hold out against the other sort of virtuosity, as a mode of service to or complicity with the capitalist spectacle. Are, though, Jackson asks, the two sorts of virtuosity mutually exclusive? What does appear to be the case, however, is that some modes of virtuosity—or just some modes of performance—will be championed as being intrinsically more politically progressive or regressive than others. It is also the case that 'theatrical terms' in particular 'continually appear in discourses that cannot decide whether theatre is an agent *of* disruption or a vehicle of social constraint that needs *to be* disrupted'.[33]

That last remark chimes with Brandstetter's argument—and, we might add, Societas Raffaello Sanzio's practice, as far as our earlier example indicates—which points to the theatrical *topos* of virtuosity as a particularly likely site of difficult decision, or *aporia*, with regard to such concerns. Jackson, too—as she says, whatever her own sympathies for the arts of social practice out of which the anti-virtuosic or anti-theatrical prejudice is more likely to be articulated—also faces in the direction not of championing one sort of virtuosity or another, but rather focusing on the sorts of decisions that get made around virtuosity, and how those decisions get made, and what sorts of values (including 'political' values) those decisions produce. As she says, 'it seems important to notice that perceptions of immateriality and virtuosity are context-specific and relationally-produced'. These notions emerge, she notes, 'when local habits for defining materiality or for defining skill have been challenged'. She adds: 'Meanwhile, those local habits also produce the sense that such challenges have radical potential.'[34] Ultimately, Jackson's argument around virtuosity and immateriality[35] comes round to a pondering on complicity, for instance with regard to high-profile arts-world operators who mobilize 'an anti-theatre or anti-dance stance' but whose activities may be 'more in league with what Guy Debord called "the Spectacle" than most theatre or dance productions could ever hope to be'.[36] It is, I have been arguing, something of the order of the undecidable—or at least a suspended *decision* that neither absolves nor suspends the work of feeling or thought—that characterizes SRS's engagement with the aesthetics of complicity, through their deployment of the icon and the virtuoso, as it were, in the field of political reflection. It would appear in this case that the theatre—no more than the scholars whose arguments we have been following—will offer no easy way to resolve this thought. We remain, if not in confusion, then in a certain aporetic relation to the image, the occasion, the situation of virtuosic practice.

On practice and cosmopoetics

If not to resolve the discussions here, but perhaps to set more reflections in play, I turn for this last section to a performance much less spectacular than

Castellucci's theatre and with significantly fewer production resources behind it (or so we will assume), but in its way, no less engaged in putting onto the theatrical stage—as it were a problem offered for attention, for engagement—the practice of the virtuoso performer. Artist Sarah Vanhee's work *Turning Turning (a choreography of thoughts)* has been shown in various iterations, as a solo performance and as a stage piece for several performers. I encountered the work at the Frascati theatre in Amsterdam, during October 2011, as a show involving three performers, including Vanhee herself. I set out here the basic lineaments of the piece.[37] This is a live event, which is to say it presents itself as taking place at one and the same time for all the participants to the theatrical situation: the makers, the performers, the spectators. The show itself involves little more than the direct presentation of a practice, a mode of doing and producing that takes place according to particular constraints. Those constraints are the following: there are three performers who will speak as quickly or as immediately as they can, whatever speech comes to mind for each of them (dealing with the full demands of speech, i.e. syntax and deliberate, continuous sense, not just random words or vocables). They do this in turn, one at a time, for a pre-determined period, measured by a small stop-clock that is visible and audible to the spectators, but small enough so that we cannot see how much time is being measured. We might say the performers are speaking before thinking, or speaking as they think, although that begs a question perhaps of what we might mean by thinking. There is anyway a manifest virtuosity at work, which is to say special capabilities are on display.

To pick up on our earlier discussion, virtuosity can be taken here in two—I would say now, related—senses. One sense refers to the specialist capabilities of the artists, Vanhee and her collaborators, who have conceived and developed the work, rehearsed it, devised its form, structured its presentation, and who have the skills—the expert practitioner *nous*, to recall Melrose's emphasis cited at the start of this essay—to deliver it competently in a professionally run theatre to a paying public. The second sense—related, as we have been saying, to Virno's concerns with the exploitability of human intellectual, affective and social capabilities under the conditions of contemporary 'post-Fordist' capitalism—has to do with the 'special' capabilities that all of us in that theatre share, as creatures able to think and move and speak. In Vanhee's work these two senses of virtuosity, the special and the specialist, the held in common and the held apart, the ordinary (we all of us at times speak before we think) and the rather hard to do, are combined in a very particular intensity of attention. This attention is at the same time shared and divided between the concentration of the performers on their task, and the attention drawn from the spectators as the task is performed; as we attempt to listen at speed, to follow and anticipate the various tracks of thought; as we marvel at the difficulty; as we enjoy the differences and judge the relative accomplishment of the three performers; and as we wonder if at any point any of them might fail in what they are doing, whether before the alarm sounds, to echo Burrows, something might go wrong.

I have referred throughout to virtuosity as a site where value—or specific 'values'—might be generated and contested. The same is the case here, and indeed is explicitly accounted for. At the back of the stage, above the performers, there is a row of video screens, and at various times an 'expert' from another practice—a linguist, a neurologist, a psychoanalyst, a performance theorist—will appear on one of the screens, recorded on a previous occasion, speaking in an analogous situation to the performers themselves, i.e. responding 'live' to a video of the thinking-talking practice. In turn, each of these experts will say something about what—for them—Vanhee and her collaborators are doing or have done, about what sorts of discoveries their experiments bear witness to, what sort of thing—if any—the work makes apprehensible: giving that thing, whatever it may be (and for a linguist and a neurologist it may not be the *same* thing), a respectable name, giving it a value, so that something noticed, something shown, invented, conjured into being, may be acknowledged as having been 'there'—*in potentia*, as it were—before this began. The observations of the one group, the experts, depend upon the activity of the others, the expert performers, the virtuosi, constrained into a practice and acknowledged as such.

What, then, is a practice? Philosopher Peter Sloterdijk has written a large book on the topic (*You Must Change Your Life! On Anthropotechnology*), but offers a concise account in a published lecture series (*The Art of Philosophy*) focused upon practices of thought and scholarly theory, where practice is defined in general as a 'mixed domain' of human action made up of contemplative and active elements. More specifically for Sloterdijk practice involves a form of 'self-reflexive training' that is not so much to do with the producing of objects or the influencing of circumstances as it is with developing 'the practicing person's state of capability. Depending on the context, this is defined as constitution, virtue, virtuosity, competence, excellence, or fitness'.[38] As that stands, this is a concept with which we are all presumably familiar, although Sloterdijk's concern is also with how practices become unfamiliar, or mis-recognize each other, or are transformed or become difficult to sustain as times and circumstances impose themselves.

However, it was not Sloterdijk I was reading when I saw the performance of Vanhee and her colleagues in late 2011, but the recently translated first volume of philosopher and science historian Isabelle Stengers's *Cosmopolitics*. A way in to saying a little about Stengers's conception of practice, with regard to the brief outline above of Vanhee's work, may be to remark that the performers—or practitioners—on this stage or any other are not the only ones sharing the air. The cosmopolitics that Stengers proposes, in which there is no sort of universalism to be taken for granted and where any claims on the part of science—or politics—to speak for 'nature' once and for all must remain in question, involves what she calls an 'ecology of practices'.[39] For Stengers, to ask what a practice is, is to ask what sorts of constraints and responsibilities it has to negotiate in order to sustain itself; it is to consider also what kinds of values it produces (right here, right now and for whom); and it is to register how any particular practice 'presents itself' to others in a world where all sorts of different practices (theoretical physics, laboratory-based chemistry, verbal choreography, the maintenance and use of underground transport systems, witchcraft, you name it) exist, or are performed, in an 'ecological' interdependence with each other. Constraints, according to Stengers, are a matter of requirements and obligations: requirements having to do with experimental procedure, the satisfying of measurements and the behaviour of phenomena, whereas obligations have to do with, say, the history in which a practice is produced, or with our own behaviour when we enter situations of controversy, or when we present our work to colleagues who may recognize or dispute its value.

What follows from this is that there is no practice that does not involve at some level an element of rhetorical persuasion, and there is no rhetorical persuasion without an element of unpredictability, some possible disagreement, some instability or interference or misunderstanding to disturb how any practice moves in the world, or is taken to move. In these lights Stengers reminds us of the Greek word *pharmakon*, something that can be a cure but in the wrong dose or the wrong circumstance can also be a poison. She points us towards various pharmacological practices, or as we might say now various professions of affective labour, pre- and post-industrial—charlatan, populist, astrologer, ideologue, magician, hypnotist, charismatic teacher—while insisting on the rhetorical-pharmacological element even in those practices or professions we might consider the most materially, technically, 'scientifically' grounded: particle physicists, too, have to persuade that their neutrinos and Higgs bosons have satisfied the requirements of experimental proof, so that the particle—newly identified, newly fabricated we might say—can be acknowledged in its autonomous existence, an existence dating back, for any 'factish'[40] such as these, not only to the event of its discovery but to the origin of the universe, as if its existence had a time frame independent of human knowledge, existing both 'in itself' and 'for us'.

The ecology of practices, then—or so I take the argument—is a function of the multiplicity of constraints and causalities and unintended meanings and effects that go to make up the situations in which particular forms of value or usefulness are produced. These are situations of co-dependence—or events, as Stengers puts it, of 'reciprocal capture'—such as the relation between a parasite and its host, a predator and its prey, the underground transport system and the heterogeneity of its users, or—we might say—the virtuoso performer and her public, where what matters here and now is a certain 'holding together with others', although not in consensus so much as symbiosis. Here what counts, for some if not for all, is in the event that something 'works', as need and desire and circumstance determine. I think, for instance, of a performer—some performer or other, any performer it may be—on the high wire of their virtuosity, the wire working for them as well as it must, while the rest of us 'hold our breath'. Or else a performance in which words and images—a countless number of both—swirl randomly, in a sort of *cosmopoetics*, like a splash of oil thrown onto the reflective surface of thought. Vanhee's choreography of thoughts, like much virtuoso performance, has the strange effect of seeming to promise us everything and anything, while leaving us with something else that is at once more than that everything and at the same time less than itself: the singularity, the fragility of the capable being, the bare actor as it were, attempting to think, attempting to speak.

Notes

1 Susan Melrose, 'Who Knows—and Who Cares (about performance mastery)?' Melrose's lecture was one of the contributions to the symposium Virtuosity and Performance Mastery, Middlesex University, 31 May–1 June 2003. The full collection of papers are archived in e-PAI 2003–04: www.sfmelrose.org.uk/e-pai-2003-04/.
2 Matthew Goulish, lecture given by Goulish and Lin Hixson for the Centre for Performance and Creative Exchange at University of Roehampton, January 2011.
3 Jonathan Burrows, *A Choreographer's Handbook*, London: Routledge, 2010: 76.
4 Burrows, *A Choreographer's Handbook*.
5 Judith Hamera, *Dancing Communities: Performance, Difference and Connection in the Global City*, Houndmills: Palgrave Macmillan, 2011: 40; see Hayden White, 'Bodies and Their Plots', in *Choreographing History*, ed. Susan Leigh Foster, Bloomington: Indiana University Press, 1995: 230–34.
6 Hamera, *Dancing Communities*: 41.
7 Francis Bacon, 'From *The Advancement of Learning*', in *Renaissance Debates on Rhetoric*, ed. Wayne A. Rebhorn, Ithaca, NY: Cornell University Press, 2000: 267–70.
8 Gabriele Brandstetter, 'The Virtuoso's Stage: A Theatrical Topos', *Theatre Research International* 32, no. 2 (2007): 178–95, at 181.
9 Brandstetter, 'The Virtuoso's Stage': 178.
10 Brandstetter, 'The Virtuoso's Stage': 178.
11 Brandstetter, 'The Virtuoso's Stage': 183.
12 Brandstetter, 'The Virtuoso's Stage': 183–84.
13 Brandstetter, 'The Virtuoso's Stage': 185.
14 Brandstetter, 'The Virtuoso's Stage': 192.
15 See Sara Jane Bailes, *Performance, Theatre and the Poetics of Failure*, London and New York: Routledge, 2010; Sarah Gorman, *The Theatre of Richard Maxwell and the New York City Players*, London and New York: Routledge, 2011; Simon Bayly, *A Pathognomy of Performance*, Houndmills: Palgrave Macmillan, 2011.
16 The phrase is from Isabelle Stengers, of whom more later. Isabelle Stengers, *Cosmopolitics I: I. The Science Wars. II. The Invention of Mechanics. III. Thermodynamics*, trans. R. Bononno, Minneapolis: University of Minnesota Press, 2010: 35.
17 The work is documented extensively in Claudia Castellucci, Romeo Castellucci, Chiara Guidi, Joe Kelleher and Nicholas Ridout, *The Theatre of Societas Raffaello Sanzio*, London: Routledge, 2007.
18 For a rigorous setting out of the operations of visuality in the theatre see Maaike Bleeker, *Visuality in the Theatre: The Locus of Looking*, Houndmills: Palgrave Macmillan, 2008.
19 As Pavel Florensky remarks, in a discussion on theology and traditional icon painting, '"flesh and blood do not inherit the Kingdom of God," but clothes do'. Pavel Florensky, *Iconostasis*, trans. Donald Sheehan and Oolga Andrejev, New York: St Vladimir's Seminary Press, 2000 [1922]: 118.
20 Brandstetter, 'The Virtuoso's Stage': 182.

21 Nicholas Ridout in *The Theatre of Societas Raffaello Sanzio*: 34–35.
22 As director Romeo Castellucci remarks, 'Carlo Giuliani is not nobody. He is one of us. He is the name of the case. And, in this case, we worked on the photograph, extracted from the newspaper, removed from all the chatter. The background of the image was rubbed out and substituted with the gold of the icon'. *The Theatre of Societas Raffaello Sanzio*: 221.
23 For Florensky the iconostasis, as an element of Orthodox church architecture, is 'the wall that separates two worlds'. It may be thought of as 'the boards or the bricks or the stones' but 'in actuality, the iconostasis is a boundary between the visible and invisible worlds'. Florensky, *Iconostasis*: 62.
24 Aoife Monks, 'Human Remains: Acting, Objects, and Belief in Performance', *Theatre Journal* 64 (2012): 355–71, at 367.
25 Nicholas Ridout, 'On the Work of Things: Musical Production, Theatrical Labor, and the "General Intellect"', *Theatre Journal* 64 (2012) 389–408, at 408.
26 dOCUMENTA (13), *Das Begleitbuch/The Guidebook*, Ostfildern: Hatje Cantz Verlag, 2012: 354.
27 Paolo Virno, *A Grammar of the Multitude: For an Analysis of Contemporary Forms of Life*, trans. Isabella Bertoletti, James Cascaito and Andrea Casson, Los Angeles: Semiotext(e), 2004.
28 Florensky, *Iconostasis*: 62.
29 Hannah Arendt, *The Human Condition*, Chicago: University of Chicago Press, 1998 [1958]: 199.
30 Shannon Jackson, 'Just-in-Time: Performance and the Aesthetics of Precarity', *TDR: The Drama Review* 56, no. 4 (T216) (Winter 2012): 10–31, at 16–17.
31 Jackson, 'Just-in-Time': 17.
32 Yvonne Rainer, 'Some Retrospective Notes on a Dance for 10 People and 12 Mattresses Called "Parts of Some Sextets"', *Tulane Drama Review* 10, no. 2 (T30) (1965): 168–78.
33 Jackson, 'Just-in-Time': 18.
34 Jackson, 'Just-in-Time': 19.
35 Jackson also raises some questions as to just how 'immaterial' the bodily-based practices of performance can really be considered to be, especially for gendered workers whose performance skills have typically 'anchored' the cognitive creativity of others. Jackson, 'Just-in-Time': 24.
36 Jackson, 'Just-in-Time': 20.
37 The comments that follow are rehearsed at greater length in a 2013 article on Sarah Vanhee's work commissioned by Myriam van Imschoot for Sarma.be, and which appears at www.sarahvanhee.com/turning and http://sarma.be/docs/2928.
38 Peter Sloterdijk, *The Art of Philosophy: Wisdom as Practice*, trans. Karen Margolis, New York: Columbia University Press, 2012: 6.
39 Stengers, *Cosmopolitics I*: 1–86.
40 The term is borrowed from Bruno Latour, but see Stengers, *Cosmopolitics I:* 19.

Part III
Ontological and ethnographic co-performance

7 Theatre as post-operative follow-up
The Bougainville Photoplay Project[1]

Paul Dwyer

In February 2003, I sent an email to Brother Pat Howley, a Marist missionary and co-founder of the nongovernmental organization (NGO) Peace Foundation Melanesia, one of many groups involved in the work of reconciliation and rebuilding civil society in Bougainville, Papua New Guinea (PNG), following a decade of violent conflict:

Dear Brother Pat,

> I wonder if you could offer some advice. I'm an academic working in the Department of Performance Studies at Sydney University. It's a department where we study theatre but also dance, sport, festivals, rituals and so on—something like a cross between a Theatre Studies, a Sociology and an Anthropology department.
>
> I'm looking to develop a post-doctoral research project into 'restorative justice', ideally by comparing and contrasting the way it works in an urban, Western setting (like the New South Wales juvenile justice system) to the way it looks in a rapidly changing Melanesian society. (There's a significant sentimental reason for focusing on Bougainville which I'll come back to in a minute.)
>
> Obviously restorative justice is not what we normally think of as performance. The participants are not actors in a play engaging with an audience sitting in neat rows in a theatre auditorium. There is so much more at stake for all the participants in a restorative justice ceremony. Nevertheless, it does seem to me that the way in which the participants conduct themselves in this event—the way they dress, the way they speak, the kind of gestures of reconciliation they make, the place where they agree to meet—all of these 'performance' factors are closely related to the social healing process that the event is meant to foster. There's no way restorative justice will work if the participants simply go through the motions: their performance is going to be carefully assessed by all those present. It seems to me that there is a lot to learn about these different

societies—urban Sydney and the villages of Bougainville—by studying the different ways they enact such ceremonies of reconciliation.

Five years later, the academic research so speculatively envisaged in that email has taken shape as a cross-cultural ethnographic project. With colleagues from the Department of Linguistics at Sydney University, I have been documenting and analysing the discourse, across all modes of communication, of participants involved in 'youth justice conferences', a diversionary programme in the New South Wales (NSW) juvenile justice system whereby young offenders, victims, their families, friends and selected community participants come together to discuss the consequences of a crime, to negotiate reparation for the victim and, it is hoped, reintegration of the offender into family and community networks.[2] I have also been able to make two brief field trips to Bougainville, establishing relationships at the grassroots level with village mediators involved in work that melds customary approaches to dispute resolution with Western concepts of 'restorative justice' such as those that inform youth justice conferencing.[3] The initial gambit of analysing these legal processes through the conceptual lens of performance is proving productive but there is still a long way to go.[4]

Developed over the same period, *The Bougainville Photoplay Project* began partly as an attempt at coming to terms with that 'significant sentimental reason' which, at the time of emailing Brother Pat, I had understood as mainly coincidental to the more 'proper', scholarly questions I wanted to ask about reconciliation and restorative justice. In what follows, I will try to explain why this process of devising a performance has become so closely imbricated with the larger ethnographic research project and, in particular, how a small collection of photographs have served as a key point of intersection between the performance and the ethnography. My explanation will involve, in roughly equal parts, a theoretical exegesis and something like a 'show and tell' demonstration of method; in other words, the text accompanying the images below is designed to make explicit some of the critical theory informing the *Photoplay Project* but also to evoke a feel for how some of the images are actually presented in performance, a sense of the show's own internal logic.

Looking at photographs: standing before history

The *Photoplay Project*, as I often advise spectators in the opening remarks I make at the start of each performance, is a 'mixed bag' in terms of genre and the balance tends to shift depending upon the audience and the context. To date, these contexts have included: a 'performed paper' at an academic conference; the opening of an exhibition by Bougainvillean artists at a Sydney art gallery; a gathering, in the open air, under a galip nut tree, of about 350 parishioners from Monoitu Catholic Mission (south-west Bougainville); a fundraiser at Buka District Hospital (with the president of Bougainville sitting in the front row, helping to light the show with his torch after a power failure); and a season at the National Multicultural Festival in Canberra.[5] Thematically and in its narrative structure, the performance interweaves three main strands: i) accounts of the recent history of Bougainville, in particular events leading up to, and during, the decade of violent conflict from the late 1980s to the late 1990s; ii) an attempt to recover early childhood memories and oral history (both of my own family and families in Bougainville); iii) a commentary on my ethnographic fieldwork in progress. While the opening of the show may have the feel of a more or less formal lecture, it soon slides into other territory, including a Berlitz-style crash course in *tok pisin* ('*raskol i kam stilim ol samting bilong mi*'; '*dispela dog i kaikai pinis olgeta kaikai bilong dispela kakaruk*'),[6] performative renditions of ethnographic field notes (the tale of a night-time trek from Sovele to Moratona, through mud and swollen creeks, talking with Peter Kebono about reconciliation rituals and the National Rugby League salary cap), the recreation of a complex surgical procedure, readings from old diaries and letters, archival film footage and so on.

From my very earliest attempts to conceptualize the performance, however, and absolutely central to the mix of genres and registers hinted at above, there has always been this small collection of Kodachrome slides (hence, when pushed to define the genre of my performance, I have taken to saying: 'slide show with fireside chat'). I discovered these slides in a box, tucked away in the attic of my mother's house, shortly before embarking on my first field trip to Bougainville in 2004. The photographs are mostly amateur holiday snaps, not obviously 'dramatic' images. Their theatrical potential seems to reside, first, in the action of pointing or showing which they so readily invite. As Roland Barthes suggests, unless you have the trained eye of a professional photographer, it is often almost impossible to disentangle a photograph as *signifier* from whatever its real-world *referent* may be. As with the fundamentally deictic qualities of theatrical discourse, the photograph 'is never anything but an antiphon of "Look", "See", "Here it is"; it points a finger'.[7]

Against the commonplace notion that photography's development as an art form is related to the emergence of a realist aesthetic in nineteenth-century painting, Barthes goes on to argue for a different, more fundamental connection between photography and theatre:

> We know the original relation of the theatre and the cult of the Dead: the first actors separated themselves from the community by playing the role of the Dead: to make oneself up was to designate oneself as a body simultaneously living and dead: the whitened bust of the totemic theatre, the man with the painted face in Chinese theatre, the rice-paste makeup of the Indian Kathakali, the Japanese No mask ... Now it is this same relation which I find in the Photograph; however 'lifelike' we strive to make it ... , Photography is a kind of primitive theatre, a kind of *Tableau Vivant*, a figuration of the motionless and made-up face beneath which we see the dead.[8]

Contemplating this 'return of the repressed', for Barthes, becomes a bodily encounter. It is the luminous rays emanating directly from the photographed subject which have been captured on film and they will reach us sooner or later 'like the delayed rays of a star. A sort of umbilical cord links the body of the photographed thing to my gaze'.[9] Arresting the flow of history, the photograph arrives in our present, asserting simply that 'this has been' yet thereby it opens up the most fundamental ethical questions. What came before this moment? What came after? What relation do I have (did I have) to this history (future)? 'Why is it that I am alive *here and now*'?[10]

In Figure 7.1, that's my father, Dr Allan Dwyer, the tall man on the right, standing behind the Marist nun with the crucifix on her chest—Sr Therese-Anne, also a skilled anaesthetist. The other nun is Sr Mary Leo, by all accounts an outstanding general surgeon. The four boys standing between them are my eldest siblings (from left to right, Damien, Garrett, Denis and Terry). It's 1962. Dad is on the cusp of a radical breakthrough in the treatment of scoliosis (severe and, if untreated, fatal twisting of the spine), a discovery that will earn him a worldwide reputation as one of the outstanding orthopaedic surgeons of his generation.

The photo shows his arrival at Tearouki, on the north-east coast of the main island of Bougainville, having accepted an invitation from the Marists to work *pro bono* during a two-month tour of the many small mission hospitals. The boys are travelling with him at the suggestion of my mother, who is looking after four younger children back in Sydney. These other children will accompany my father on subsequent trips to Bougainville in 1966 (my sister

Figure 7.1 Tearouki, Bougainville, 1962
Source: Photographer unknown

Mary and brother Patrick) and 1969 (Martin and Genevieve). For all of my siblings, their recollections are of a proverbial tropical island paradise, an ostensibly calm and peaceful Bougainville governed, along with the rest of Papua New Guinea, by an Australian colonial administration operating under a mandate from the United Nations. Like many Australians of my generation (I was born in 1963), and certainly those younger than me, I had largely forgotten this history of Australia as a colonial power. I had even forgotten that my father ever visited Bougainville until the first few essays I read about the conflict there brought this slender family connection back to consciousness.[11]

Jump-cut to 5 August 1969: The Rorovana 'incident', Central Bougainville. Australian colonial authorities deal with an act of civil disobedience by sending police in to clear the area with a series of baton charges and tear gas grenades. It's barely six months after my father's third and final visit but, as I now realize, events had been moving swiftly towards this point of crisis throughout all the years he had been travelling there. In 1964, Australian authorities gave CRA, the Australian subsidiary of Rio Tinto, permission to prospect in the mountains around Panguna, Central Bougainville. In 1966, we pushed legislation through the PNG House of Assembly making land on Bougainville private property which the colonial administration could forcibly resume and lease to the mining company for a pepper-corn rent. A small number of male leaders—so-called 'big men'—were identified by the authorities as the best conduit through which to provide monetary compensation (risible amounts if compared to what Australian citizens would have demanded) to the communities that were going to be displaced by the mine. However, nearly all Bougainvillean societies are matrilineal: the protests at Rorovana were led by senior women unwilling to give up their ground for the construction of port facilities and a port-mine access road.

When it opened in 1972, Panguna was one of the largest open cut mining operations in the world. Over the next 17 years, it produced half of PNG's exports. While vast profits flowed to the central PNG government, and to shareholders in Britain and Australia, Bougainvillean people watched as tailings from the mine were simply flushed down the Jaba River, destroying wildlife and making once fertile valleys uninhabitable. These environmental concerns helped rekindle a longstanding secessionist movement and, in 1989, the Bougainville Revolutionary Army was formed: they closed the mine and declared independence for Bougainville. The PNG government responded by sending in riot police and, soon after, the PNG Defence Force (PNGDF). Before the end of hostilities in 1997, this dirty, brutal post-colonial war had cost the lives of somewhere between 15,000 and 20,000 people, either as a direct result of the fighting or through treatable conditions for which there was no medical help available. This is a figure roughly equivalent to one in every ten inhabitants of Bougainville.[12]

Throughout the conflict, in an effort to protect PNG and Australian interests in the mine, the Australian government supplied the PNGDF with almost everything they needed. We posted military advisers to Bougainville; we organized combat training in Australia for 2,000 PNGDF personnel; we supplied guns, ammunition, mortars, bombs, patrol boats, search planes and—most notoriously—four Iroquois helicopters: we paid $1 million a year so that these helicopters could be serviced and flown by Australian pilots. While the Australian government strenuously maintained that the helicopters were used for nothing more than troop transportation, even PNGDF officers admitted on Australian national television that they were being used as offensive 'gunships'.[13]

I have before me on my desk a dossier with information regarding thousands of human rights abuses and atrocities committed during the decade-long Bougainville 'crisis'.[14] Scanning this database, reading reports of indiscriminate torture, rape and extra-judicial executions, again and again I come across the same names of villages as my father, in his slightly cramped handwriting, has written across the bottom of his Kodachrome slide frames. Partly by chance, partly by design, these are also the villages where I have made the strongest contacts with mediators involved in the work of reconciliation and restorative justice. So we share quite a long and difficult history before we have even spoken a word.

Between ethnography and performance

How to begin a dialogue, in circumstances such as these, with (as anthropologists used to say) 'native informants'? It seemed to me that my father's photos, in their very naivety, say a great deal about the culture of the time in which they were taken, a late colonial moment of apparent stability, order and coherence, just before the opening of the Panguna mine. The new readings of these images that the passage of time has allowed are, as I have learned, readings that can be fruitfully undertaken in collaboration with Bougainvillean people. While I would not want to claim that the *Photoplay* is, in and of itself, a work of ethnography, the relationships I have made in fieldwork would not be what they are if I had not introduced the ancillary task of researching and devising a piece of theatre. Nor would the *Photoplay* be what it is as a performance without some attempt to engage explicitly with key debates in anthropology regarding ethnographic research methods.

In some respects, *The Bougainville Photoplay Project* can also be seen as part of the recent resurgence of 'verbatim' or 'documentary theatre'.[15] However, rather than simply asserting—through the use of authentic archival documents—the truthfulness of the performer's account of historical events, the *Photoplay Project* invites its audience to consider the 'slipperiness' of documentary truth and the ways in which interpretation of archival material is always shaped by ideology, memory and imagination.[16] While it is no doubt clear to the audiences for whom I have performed (both in Australia and in Bougainville) that my father's photographs have a deeply personal meaning for me, the performance is also asking: how do these photographs make sense to a Bougainvillean audience for whom they were not originally intended? What is their way of seeing my father's (and my own) way of seeing their history? Where do Australian citizens today stand in relation to the shared elements of this history?

Throughout the project, my goal has been not so much, or not simply, to 'collect' the stories of Bougainvillean people and then to speak *for* them; rather, by digging up stories from my own family history and exploring just a few points of contact with the stories of Bougainvillean families, I have aimed to *'speak nearby'* in an act of intimacy and solidarity.[17] As I describe below, the challenge has been to move the experience of Bougainvillean people back into the centre of frame, so to speak, without pretending that I do not still retain a strong authorial voice as the teller of the *Photoplay*. The mode of 'performance ethnography' towards which I have gravitated in developing the project seems to lend itself extremely well to staging these tensions over authority/authorship in an unresolved form. However much the narrative focus may shift towards reporting the attitudes and actions of various Bougainvillean acquaintances I have made, the audience always knows that their access to this information is being filtered through the white guy in front of them—a *Verfremdungseffekt* that's pretty hard to miss, particularly for audiences in Bougainville.

Live performance is also, as Dwight Conquergood and others have stressed, an especially appropriate medium if one wants to foreground—in a way that many written ethnographies do not—the fact that fieldwork is an embodied practice and an 'intensely sensuous way of knowing'.[18] Indeed, much has changed since Douglas Oliver, in his 1955 account of fieldwork in south-west Bougainville, calmly described his goal as being 'to put the Siuai [people] on paper' and to summarize 'the total Siuai culture'.[19] As Johannes Fabian has argued, the detached, contemplative stance affected by many ethnographers is perhaps better understood as a visualist bias, translating all too easily into a voyeuristic, even dehumanizing account of people with whom the researcher is in fact interacting in a shared time and place.[20] Drawing a link between the poetics and the politics of ethnography, James Clifford makes a similar point:

> Anthropology no longer speaks with automatic authority for others defined as unable to speak for themselves ('primitive', 'pre-literate', 'without history'). Other groups can less easily be ... represented as if they were not involved in the present world systems that implicate ethnographers along with the peoples they study. 'Cultures' do not hold still for their portraits.[21]

What kind of unspoken 'contract', what *rapport de forces* between photographer and 'subjects' made possible an image such as Figure 7.2, which my father took in the village of Pateaveave, in the mountains above Tearouki? Dad's trips required, of course, approval from the colonial administration and considerable support from the Catholic Church. On the one hand, while the Church is often credited with having done much to stop inter-tribal warfare, as well as providing healthcare and education, it is sobering to recall

Figure 7.2 Villagers of Pateaveave, Bougainville, 1962
Source: Photograph: Allan Dwyer

that the very first Marists were deposited on Bougainville courtesy of a German gun boat which, when the local people became hostile, started firing cannon shells into the jungle. Presumably the German administration of the time saw the missionaries as front-line troops in a campaign to produce the 'docile bodies' that would later be needed for work on coconut plantations.[22]

On the other hand, as an ideological and political project, colonialism was never underpinned by a completely stable, homogenous set of beliefs: there were always areas of indigenous cultures where the colonial influence was relatively weak and there were often inconsistencies between the projects of particular colonial institutions which, as Nicholas Thomas has argued, allowed indigenous people, in some respects, to adjust the culture of colonialism to their own ends.[23] Thus, resistance to the Panguna mine was actively encouraged by some (not all) Catholic missionaries and many of the most outspoken Bougainvillean independence leaders have been the best and brightest graduates of Marist schools and seminaries.[24] This is not to deny, of course, the often brutal exploitation of indigenous people under colonial rule. It is simply to affirm that indigenous people have always been 'actors in world history', and that there is much to learn once we 'recognize the value of their analyses of the political and economic forces that connect our lives'.[25]

My father's caption for Figure 7.3 reads simply: 'Fr McConville and Denis at Pateaveave', so I am presuming it was taken on the same day as the preceding image. In his caption, Dad has forgotten to mention Damien, the other small white boy, just to the right of centre. Having picked up this detail,

Theatre as post-operative follow-up 121

Figure 7.3 Pateaveave, Bougainville, 1962
Source: Photograph: Allan Dwyer

I then had to look four or five times more at this photo before I realized what else Dad (and I) had missed: the black man in the foreground, his head turned, his gaze directed straight down the lens of the camera. What exactly did this man see? How might my father's presence in his village have made sense for him? Turning back to all the other photos in my father's collection, I began to realize what should have been self-evident: their main purpose being to document my siblings' holidays in Bougainville, it is my brothers and sisters who appear in the centre of almost every frame, with Bougainvilleans left occupying the margins. Alternatively, on the few occasions when Bougainvillean people are centrally framed, they appear in large groups, assembled before a colonial gaze that is mostly implicit but occasionally made more explicit.

In Figure 7.4, the Tarlena Girls' High School Choir is on the right, rehearsing for the 1966 Hanahan Choral Festival in front of teachers and missionaries. (A curious fact: I have met many Bougainvillean people who can name over half the people in the picture on the left; the retired missionaries to whom I have spoken have trouble recalling more than one or two of their former colleagues.)

When, in 2004, I first began to show these photographs to the people I was meeting in Bougainville, I hoped that, among other things, they might be able to help me locate the places where my father must have stood with his camera. Whenever this turned out to be possible, I would try to take a photograph myself and would spend time talking with my Bougainvillean hosts about their knowledge of events that had occurred in these places

Figure 7.4 Tarlena, Bougainville, 1966
Source: Photograph: Allan Dwyer

during the forty years since Dad was there. Some of these new images (not too many—I wouldn't even rate myself an amateur photographer) and many of the stories people have told me have now found their way into the *Bougainville Photoplay Project*. (Another curious fact: despite my protestations that it was only by good luck, not good management, that I found all these photos in my mother's attic, many people in Bougainville have responded to the *Photoplay* by saying how much they appreciate its demonstration of the benefits of literacy, of careful archival documentation and so on. While, for me, the photos have been valuable as a stimulus to Bougainvillean people's memories, opening up a rich vein of storytelling in what is a very strongly residual culture of orality, I have also heard Bougainvillean people bemoan the fact of having lost, during the 'crisis', all the photos and written documentation they ever possessed.)

Figure 7.5 is a photograph, taken by my father in 1966, of my sister Mary and a group of Marist nuns at Chabai mission, on the north-west coast of Bougainville's main island. In 2004, I also stopped at Chabai and, standing in almost the same spot, took a photo of the nuns who are there now. That's Sr Catherine Mona, head of the congregation of the Sisters of Nazareth, on the right of Figure 7.6. Next to her is Sr Lorraine Garasu, renowned for her involvement in peace making and reconciliation work.[26] The older nuns— Sr Margaret (in the middle, with a bandaged leg) and Sr Elizabeth (far left)— are also important figures in this process. I spent an evening sitting with these nuns, telling stories and looking at photographs. To my delight, they were able to identify at least five of the girls in the Tarlena High School Choir whom my father had photographed in 1966. To my amazement (and to their delight), one of those choir girls (third row, second from the right) was none other than the young Catherine Mona, now sitting with us in the lounge room of the convent.

As our conversation progressed, it soon became clear that by the time my father returned to Bougainville, three years after the Tarlena Girls Choir photo was taken, Sisters Catherine, Margaret and Elizabeth had all finished school and were working as nurses in the little hospital at Tearouki mission.

Theatre as post-operative follow-up 123

Figure 7.5 Mary and the Sisters at Chabai, 1966
Source: Photograph: Allan Dwyer

Figure 7.6 Nuns at Chabai, 2004
Source: Photograph: Paul Dwyer

These women assisted my father in the operating theatre. They were thus able to describe in detail the kind of surgery he did, including numerous operations to fuse the ankle joints of young people who'd been crippled by polio. Indeed, they introduced me to a man of my age who'd been operated on by my father in 1969: I noticed a scar above the ankle that my father had repaired and Jack told me it was a wound made by an Australian-supplied bullet, fired by a PNGDF soldier. Jack and I agreed it was a good thing the ankle operation had given him the ability to run fast.

Shortly after returning home from my 2004 trip to Bougainville, subsequent research (to be honest, another fortuitous find in the attic of my mother's house) produced a faded manila folder containing correspondence that my father had maintained with Fr Jim Harding, one of the missionaries at the time and also a fine general surgeon. One thing that becomes abundantly clear upon reading these letters is that my father was still seeking follow-up X-rays and was still offering advice on patient management for months, in some cases even years, after each of his three trips to Bougainville (this at a time when the recognition for his work on scoliosis meant that he was in high demand to present lectures/demonstrations of his technique at major conferences and teaching hospitals around the world). In one of Fr Harding's letters, he has attached, as requested by my father, a list of 19 patients from villages near the Monoitu and Sovele missions on whom my father operated in 1966.

Tenai, whose name appears in the detail of this list, was three years old at the time: my age. The surgical procedure undergone by Tenai—'bilateral medial release and triple arthrodesis'—suggests he was quite badly crippled in both feet. Looking closely at the other letters and clippings in the folder of Dad's Bougainville correspondence, I then came across a brief note, written in *tok pisin*, by Samuel Liobo (his name also appears in the list, though it is misspelt as 'Liombo'). Samuel writes:

Dear Doctor Dwyer,

> Mi say thank-you long you bikosi you bin stretim lek bilong mipala [thank you for fixing up our legs]. Nau mipala ken amamas taim mipala wokabaut gut [Now we feel happy about being able to walk properly]. Na mi happy tumas long yutupela wantaim Fr. Doctor [And I'm very happy with both you and Fr. Doctor (a reference to Jim Harding)]. Because em i gutpela job [Because you did a good job]. Mipela i happy tumas taim mipela looking lek bilong mipela em i stret i pinis [We're all very happy when we look at how our legs have turned out straight]. Na mipela i pein liklik [We have a little bit of pain still]. Na Tenai emi no wokabaut [And Tenai is not walking yet].

God bless you,
Yours faithfully,
Samuel Liobo

Last year I made my second field trip to Bougainville with the intention not only of advancing the research into restorative justice and the reconciliation process but also—however quixotic it may have seemed—with a determination to find out what might have become of Samuel Liobo and all the other Monoitu and Sovele patients listed in Jim Harding's correspondence. Was Tenai walking, I wondered? What life was he or any of the other patients able to walk into?

I took a low-tech (in fact, 'no tech') travelling version of the *Photoplay* with me, performing it at every opportunity and stopping to ask after patients on whom my father had operated. Five weeks later, I had knowledge of all 19 of the Monoitu and Sovele patients as well as others: as far as I am aware, all of them managed to live through the 'crisis' and only five have died since. A number of these former patients were able to watch performances of the *Photoplay* with their families and afterwards we spent considerable time discussing its content and method of presentation. As for Lawrence Tenai, we have not as yet been able to meet but there is every chance he could become a collaborator on my research into restorative justice: the day after I attended a major reconciliation ceremony at Moratona, I learned that Lawrence had been one of the key organizers of the event (so I know at least that he is walking well, as it's more than a three-hour trek from his village to Moratona).

Unfinished business

Such moments of serendipity, when the 'proper' ethnographic research project I first envisaged in the email to Pat Howley and the 'sideline' performance-making project appear to dovetail, have served as a forceful reminder that no researcher ever enters 'the field' without becoming personally entangled in the history of a place and the lives of those who dwell there. In my own case, recognizing the extent of these entanglements, I have slowly come to abandon the idea that there will ever be a definitive version of the *Bougainville Photoplay:* it will be an ongoing project, always an effort towards placing myself, as a researcher and an artist who is also a citizen of a former colonial power, in a new ethical relationship with Bougainvillean people. What kind of dialogue is possible between us? Why, and for whom, does any of this matter?

John Berger and Jean Mohr—towards the end of their photo-essay *A Fortunate Life: The Story of a Country Doctor*—face a somewhat similar problem in trying to assess the value of a doctor's work:

> Supposing he is an intelligent but careless doctor—how much must he forfeit from his record for treating one case, ten cases, a hundred cases carelessly? Supposing that he is an intelligent and unusually dedicated doctor, how much must be added to his record? What would his bonus be? Such accounting seems absurd. Then, let us ask: What is the social value of a pain eased? What is the value of a life saved? How does the cure of a serious illness compare in value to one of the better poems of a minor poet? How does making a correct but extremely difficult diagnosis compare with painting a great canvas? Obviously the comparative method is equally absurd ... [W]e in our society do not know how to acknowledge, [... or how] to take the measure of a man doing no more and no less than easing—and occasionally saving—the lives of a few thousand of our contemporaries. Naturally, we count it, in principle, a good thing. But fully to take the measure of it, we have to come to some conclusion about the value of these lives to us now.[27]

Figure 7.7 Torokina, Bougainville, 1962(?)
Source: Photographer unknown

On the frame of the slide of Figure 7.7, my father has written simply: 'Me and Short Foot Leper.' The photograph must have been taken during a clinic at Torokina, on the west coast of Bougainville's main island, where a hospice for lepers had been established. I can't see that Dad is doing anything more complex than changing the dressing on this patient's foot (from which the toes are missing). While I understand that the relationship depicted here between my father and this Torokina man was obviously heavily mediated by the particular institutional histories and ideological investments of the Catholic Church and the Australian colonial administration, the suggestion of closeness and intimacy—the placement of the patient's foot, the shared focus of the two men, the sense of their touching one another—attracts my attention like the sort of *punctum* or stimulus that Barthes is always seeking in the photographs he describes.

These are the details, according to Barthes, that strike, prick or wound the spectator, without which the photograph exists only as *studium*—something we might like or be interested in but not the kind of thing to provoke desire or pain. Of course, no sooner does Barthes set up this binary opposition than he deliberately sets about muddying the waters. 'What I can name does not really prick me'[28]—our desires fluctuate; we lose a photograph, find it again and discover the *punctum* is not where we first thought it to be; indeed, the passage of time is itself a *punctum*: 'In front of the photograph of my mother as a child, I tell myself: she is going to die: I shudder ... *over a catastrophe which has already occurred*. Whether or not the subject is already dead, every photograph is this catastrophe.'[29] Perhaps, in the end, what counts most is

Barthes's notion of the *punctum* as something the spectator wishes to add to a photograph while sensing that *it is already there in some way*.

Of all the photographs I have found that document my father's visits to Bougainville, the one above is the one to which I most often return. I suppose I have always seen it as making an implicit demand along the lines of John Berger and Jean Mohr's final question: What value do the lives of any of my father's former patients have today? What kind of relationship is possible between Australians and Bougainvilleans today? I have often shown this photograph and asked such questions in performances of the *Photoplay*, but the clearest answers, I have to say, have tended to come from the spectators in Bougainville. For them, there is nothing rhetorical about these questions and nothing particularly 'artful', it seems, in my way of posing them. Their responses make virtually no reference to aesthetic concerns or, rather, none that are not immediately anchored with reference to their lived experience of the historical relationship between Australia and Bougainville and to their hopes for the future of this relationship.

Often the reply will run into another very practical, pragmatic issue, expressed more or less as follows: 'It's nice that you have come with this *Photoplay*, Paul. It's a good thing for you to know about the good work your father did and we are happy to be reminded of it again. You are very welcome ... *But* if you want to talk to us about reconciliation between Australia and Bougainville, then we need to take this matter very seriously: next time, you should try to come with your leaders—where are your leaders?' While this is obviously not something I can deal with on my own, I hope that *The Bougainville Photoplay Project* creates for future audiences in Australia a context inwhich the question can at least be heard. Clearly, there is much that Australians can learn from the current process of post-violence reconciliation in Bougainville but the most important lessons will only be learned if we see ourselves as protagonists in, and not merely spectators of, the process.

Notes

1. This piece first appeared in *About Performance* 8 (2008): 141–60, and we are grateful for the kind permission of the editors to reprint it here.
2. Lily Trimboli, *An Evaluation of the NSW Youth Justice Conferencing Scheme*, Sydney: NSW Bureau of Crime Statistics, 2000; Janet Chan, ed., *Reshaping Juvenile Justice: The NSW Young Offenders Act 1997*, Sydney: Institute of Criminology, 2005.
3. Sinclair Dinnen, ed., *A Kind of Mending: Restorative Justice in the Pacific Islands*, Canberra: Pandanus Books, 2002; Pat Howley, *Breaking Spears and Mending Hearts: Peacemakers and Restorative Justice in Bougainville*, Sydney: Federation Press, 2002; see also Chris Cuneen, 'Restorative Justice and the Politics of Decolonization', in *Restorative Justice: Theoretical Foundations*, ed. Elamir Weitekamp and Hans-Jürgen Kerner, Cullompton, Devon: Willan Publishing, 2002: 32–49; and Kathleen Daly, 'Conferencing in Australia and New Zealand: Variations, Research Findings, and Prospects', in *Restorative Justice for Juveniles: Conferencing, Mediation and Circles*, ed. Allison Morris and Gabrielle Maxwell,

128 *Paul Dwyer*

      Oxford: Hart Publishing, 2001: 59–83 for dissenting views regarding the parallels between Western and indigenous justice forms.
4 See Michele Zappavigna, Paul Dwyer and James Martin, 'Just Like, Sort Of, Guilty, Kind Of: The Rhetoric of Tempered Admission in Youth Justice Conferencing', paper delivered at the Australian Systemic Functional Linguistics Congress, Woollongong, 2007, for early work in progress.
5 Creative development of *The Bougainville Photoplay Project* has been supported by the Department of Performance Studies at the University of Sydney, for which I sincerely thank my colleagues. Along with staff from Peace Foundation Melanesia, I must also acknowledge Marilyn Taleo Havini, Moses Havini, Taloi Havini and Sr Lorraine Garasu for their generous support. The work has been produced by *version 1.0* and was most recently presented at the 2008 National Multicultural Festival in Canberra (writer/performer: Paul Dwyer; director: David Williams; video installation: Sean Bacon; technical production: Russell Emerson). For full credits, acknowledgments and more information, see the company website: www.versiononepointzero.com.
6 'The raskol stole all of my belongings'; 'this dog has eaten all of this chicken's food': from the early 1980s textbook that is still used as a staff-training tool for Australian diplomats!
7 Roland Barthes, *Camera Lucida: Reflections on Photography*, trans. Richard Howard, London: Vintage, 1993: 5.
8 Barthes, *Camera Lucida*: 31–32.
9 Barthes, *Camera Lucida*: 81.
10 Barthes, *Camera Lucida*: 84.
11 John Connell, 'Compensation and Conflict: The Bougainville Copper Mine, Papua New Guinea', in *Mining and Indigenous Peoples in Australasia*, ed. John Connell and Richard Howitt, Sydney: Sydney University Press, 1991: 55–75; James Griffin, 'Bougainville: Secession or Just Sentiment?' *Current Affairs Bulletin* 48, no. 9 (1972): 258–80; Paul Quodling, *Bougainville: The Mine and the People*, Sydney: Centre for Independent Studies, 1991.
12 There is not the space here for anything like a full overview of geographic and cultural factors that fuelled Bougainvillean secessionist tendencies even before the mine, nor for a detailed account of the Bougainville 'crisis' (a euphemism but also common usage in Bougainville where participants in the post-violence reconciliation process are generally trying to move beyond blaming and retribution—without losing sight of the need for justice). Needless to say, the history of the conflict is often hotly contested. Useful introductions may be found in Geoff Harris, Naihuwo Ahai and Rebecca Spence, eds, *Building Peace in Bougainville* (National Research Institute Special Publication No. 27), Waigani: NRI, 1999; Anthony Regan and Helga Griffin, eds, *Bougainville Before the Conflict*, Canberra: Pandanus Books, 2005; Josephine Tankunani Sirivi and Marilyn Taleo Havini, eds, *As Mothers of the Land: The Birth of the Bougainville Women for Peace and Freedom*, Canberra: Pandanus Books, 2004.
13 Sean Dorney, *The Sandline Affair: Politics and Mercenaries and the Bougainville Crisis*, Sydney: ABC Books, 1998: 44–45; Mary-Louise O'Callaghan, *Enemies Within: Papua New Guinea, Australia, and the Sandline Crisis*, Sydney: Doubleday, 1999; Naomi Sharp, 'Bougainville: Blood on Our Hands', Sydney: Aid/Watch Report, 1997.
14 Marilyn Taleo Havini, ed., 'A Compilation of Human Rights Abuses Against the People of Bougainville, 1989–95', Sydney: Bougainville Freedom Movement, 1995.
15 Stephen Bottoms, 'Putting the Document into Documentary: An Unwelcome Corrective?' *TDR: The Journal of Performance Studies* 50, no. 3 (2006): 56–68; Derek Paget, *True Stories? Documentary Drama on Radio, Screen and Stage*, Manchester: Manchester University Press, 1990.

16 Paul Dwyer, 'The Inner Lining of Political Discourse', *Australasian Drama Studies* 48 (April 2006): 130–35.
17 Trinh Minh-ha, in Anna Grimshaw, *The Ethnographer's Eye: Ways of Seeing in Modern Anthropology*, Cambridge: Cambridge University Press, 2001: 6; see also James Thompson, *Digging Up Stories*, Manchester: Manchester University Press, 2005.
18 Dwight Conquergood, 'Rethinking Ethnography: Towards a Critical Cultural Politics', *Communication Monographs* 58, no. 2 (1991): 179–94, at 180; see also Dwight Conquergood, 'Performing as a Moral Act: Ethical Dimensions of the Ethnography of Performance', *Literature in Performance* 5, no. 2 (1985): 1–13; Norman Denzin, *Performance Ethnography: Critical Pedagogy and the Politics of Culture*, Thousand Oaks, CA: Sage Publications, 2003; Della Pollock, 'Marking New Directions in Performance Ethnography', *Text and Performance Quarterly* 26, no. 4 (2006): 325–29.
19 Douglas Oliver, *A Solomon Island Society: Kinship and Leadership among the Siuai of Bougainville*, Boston, MA: Beacon Press, 1955: x, xiii.
20 Johannes, Fabian, *Time and the Other: How Anthropology Makes Its Object*, New York: Columbia University Press, 1983; see also Grimshaw, *The Ethnographer's Eye*: 64–68, for a refinement of Fabian's critique.
21 James Clifford, 'Introduction: Partial Truths', in *Writing Culture: The Poetics and Politics of Ethnography*, ed. James Clifford and George Marcus, Berkeley: University of California Press, 1986: 1–26, at 10.
22 Hugh Laracy, *Marists and Melanesians: A History of Catholic Missions in the Solomon Islands*, Canberra: Australian National University Press, 1976.
23 Nicholas Thomas, *Colonialism's Culture: Anthropology, Travel and Government*, London: Polity Press, 1994.
24 Wally Fingleton, 'Bougainville: A Chronicle of Just Grievances', *New Guinea and Australia, the Pacific and South-East Asia* 5, no. 2 (1970): 13–20; Griffin, 'Bougainville: Secession or Just Sentiment?'
25 Stuart Kirsch, *Reverse Anthropology: Indigenous Analysis of Social and Environmental Relations in New Guinea*, Stanford, CA: Stanford University Press, 2006: 5.
26 Carl, Andy and Sr Lorraine Garasu, eds, *Accord #12: Weaving Consensus: The Papua New Guinea-Bougainville Peace Process*, London: Conciliation Resources, 2002.
27 John Berger and Jean Mohr, *A Fortunate Man: The Story of a Country Doctor*, Harmondsworth: Penguin, 1967: 164–65.
28 Barthes, *Camera Lucida*: 51.
29 Barthes, *Camera Lucida*: 96.

8 Stagecraft/statecraft/mancraft

Embodied envoys, 'objects' and the spectres of estrangement in Africa

Sam Okoth Opondo

> Not Marshall McLuhan's 'the medium is the message', but a new formula; 'The medium is the maker'. Poesis means 'making'. The poet is a maker. Usually, people once thought, the poet is the maker of beautiful lies. But 'maker' also implies a performative force. The medium itself makes something happen.
>
> (J.H. Miller, 'The Medium is the Maker')

> ... you do not know beforehand what good or bad you are capable of; you do not know beforehand what a body or a mind can do, in a given encounter, a given arrangement, a given combination.
>
> (Gilles Deleuze, *Spinoza, Practical Philosophy*)[1]

Poetics and histrionics of death and estrangement

'When men die, they enter history. When statues die, they enter art. This botany of death is what we call culture.' These are the opening lines to *Les Statues Meurent Aussi* (Statues Also Die, 1953), an essay film about African statues (and bodies) by Alain Resnais, Chris Marker and Ghislain Cloquet. Commissioned by Présence Africaine, *Les Statues* is concerned with the politics surrounding the expropriation, classification and exhibition/storage of African statues in European museums. As Alain Resnais puts it, the initial provocation for the documentary was the differential treatment accorded to statues from different parts of the world. As such, the documentary seeks to respond to a basic question: '*why is the black African art located in the Musée de l'Homme* (an ethnographic museum), *whereas the Greek or Egyptian is in the Louvre* (an art museum)?'

Filmed in European museums and supplemented with archival footage about colonial Africa, the film depicts the way statues lose meaning and use when taken out of their context or when they are cut off from their active environment.[2] Just like the statues put in European museums as objects for European edification and cultivation of aesthetic selves, the black bodies that the film treats have also been transformed into machines: sites for the extraction of cheap labour and more recently entertainment. Through an effective use of montage and compelling voice-overs, the film provides a map of estrangement that shows how colonial aesthetics robs the African statues of their symbolic and spiritual value thus transforming them into curio art. By juxtaposing the displaced statues with shots of the black body in action, *Les Statues* offers a compelling critique of the 'uses' to which Europeans and Americans have put the black body: from the choreographed work of colonial labourers ('Tarzan meets Ford'), to the pugilism of Sugar Ray Robinson and the theatrical/spectacular athleticism of the Harlem Globetrotters.

The rhythmic shift from static 'worked objects' in the European museum to mobile 'objectified bodies' (the colonial *homo faber* and *homo ludens*) draws our attention to different ways of seeing/looking and their relationship to the politically framed regimes of recognition. Through a series of editorial cutaways, the film makes us aware of problematic positions and dispositions which range from the complicit viewers peering into glass cabinets (where the African statues are exhibited) to voyeuristic voyages into the African hinterland where African bodies are exploited for their labour and entertainment value. However, a different way of seeing and counting emerges as the documentary progresses. Unlike the complicit ways of seeing that take the staging of statues and bodies in the museum or the colony for granted, the later part of the film transforms 'us' into more attentive and empathic 'witnesses' of the multiple possibilities and capacities of the black body—from pleasure and ritual performance to the black body in pain as evinced by the violent police crackdown on striking workers. In staging the entanglement of lives, objects and practices, the film points towards a more ethical and politically inclined reading of the conditions under which Africans and other colonized peoples mediate estrangement (where estrangement includes not only alienation from other people and other cultures but also from one's labour, the environment and gods).[3]

Perhaps one should read Resnais and Marker's *Les Statues* not just as a cinematic critique of colonialism and ethnological reason but also as an elaborate map of African/black estrangement derived from a politically saturated relationship between beings and apparatuses. Read this way, the genres of expression, peoples and mediation practices that the film summons offer insights into how the ethnological frame affects both the colonizer and the colonized (in the colonial context) and remains a dominant mode of assigning meanings, counting bodies and effacing what can be known, used and felt in the encounter with another being. Most significantly, *Les Statues* reveals the multiple sites of the colonial and diplomatic 'production of man'. Not only does it engage *heterology*—a discourse/science of the other—but the film also provides an opportunity for us to revisit and interrogate *homology*, thus disturbing ethnological and colonial ways of sensing and making sense of the world.[4]

As *Les Statues* illustrates, the ways of organizing and consuming the world that were thought to be specific to the museum have become pervasive as a result of the religiosity of capitalism and colonialism. In this sense, the film has resonances with Giorgio Agamben's observation that modernity/capitalism's operation and architectonics are predicated on 'the impossibility of using' and are in effect some form of 'museum'.[5] Agamben goes on to state that capitalism, as the religion of modernity, makes it difficult for us to return things to their common use (profanation) given that it is predicated on radical forms of separation (sacrifice).[6] As a site of estrangement where 'what cannot be used is given over to exhibition and spectacular exhibition', the museum, or world as museum, often privileges separation and/or 'secularization' which is 'a form of repression' that leaves 'intact the forces it deals with by simply moving from one place to another'.[7]

The diplomatic and colonial *mancraft* derived from the web of estrangement and the forms of 'museification' exemplified by the scenes in *Les Statues* is well captured by the film's voice-over:

> The subject is the black man cut off from his own culture and not in contact with ours. His work no longer has either spiritual or social consequences. It has no prospects; it leads to nothing but a derisory wage. In those countries of gift and barter, we introduced money. And so the black's work is bought and his art degraded. Religious dance becomes a spectacle. We pay the Negro to give us the amusing spectacle of his joy and enthusiasm. And in this way there appears alongside the Negro as slave, a second figure—Negro punch.[8]

Not only does *Les Statues* raise questions about the politics and poetics of museum exhibitions (the difference between ethnographic and art museums and the nature of objects on display), but it also exposes the racial and cultural partialities that inform the process of collection and display of worked objects. In posing these questions, Resnais and Marker provoke us to interrogate the mediatory capacities of collected objects and the forms of knowledge that make it possible or even desirable to collect and mark objects or bodies from another place/culture as ethnological or aesthetic objects.[9] The film also points to the forces and operations at play in the 'museification' of the world which, according to Agamben, is an 'accomplished fact':

> ... art, religion, philosophy, the idea of nature, even politics—have docilely withdrawn into the museum. 'Museum' here is not a given physical space or place but the separate dimension to which what was once—but is no longer—felt as true and decisive has moved. In this sense, the museum can coincide with an entire city ... , a region ... and even a group of individuals ... but more generally, everything today can become a Museum, because this term simply designates the exhibition of an impossibility of using, of dwelling, of experiencing. Thus in the museum, the analogy between capitalism and religion becomes clear.[10]

That is, the cinematic juxtaposition/inter-articulation of worked objects and working or worked on bodies in *Les Statues*, rather than offer a mere critique of the ethnology/aesthetics divide in museums, forces us to think about the 'museification' of the world, 'cultural modes of regulating affective and ethical dispositions' and the positions, frames or apparatus that make them possible.[11] As the film illustrates, ethnological frames impact not only on how we apprehend worked objects from Africa but also how we apprehend lives or beings in general. Such frames, Judith Butler tells us, are at 'once epistemological and ontological'. They work to 'differentiate the lives that we can apprehend and those that we cannot' and in the process 'organize visual experience and generate specific ontologies of the subject'.[12]

It is precisely these acts of 'museification' and framing in general and ethnological framing in particular with which this essay is concerned. Through an exploration of the differential staging and valuation of African objects, images, bodies and 'objectified bodies', I illustrate how colonial and postcolonial *statecraft*, *handicraft* and *mancraft* are entangled with the 'ethnological frame' and the regimes of diplomatic recognition and 'museification' it produces or authorizes. From the exhibitions and performances surrounding Saartjie (or Sarah) Bartmann's dissected body at the *Musée de l'Homme* in Paris to the diplomatic negotiations to retrieve her remains for dignified burial in South Africa, ethnological spectres and spectacles persist and are identifiable in multiple forms of comparison of human groups and the apparatuses that produce those subjects. Zeroing in on the ontology–apparatus relationship that makes the figure of man imaginable and manageable in the postcolony, I conclude with some reflections on the humanitarian production of man and the diplomacies, sympathies or moral imaginaries it mobilizes. The objective here is to interrogate humanitarian common-sense in order to speculate on the possibilities of more ethical and aesthetically creative encounters with precarious lives or people with incommensurate practices of identity.

On the whole, I engage multiple sites of estrangement and 'museification' to illustrate that diplomacy is as much a dialogue between states as it is an encounter between states of mind, states of being and modes of becoming. That diplomacy is an encounter between human beings and beings in general that can be usefully enhanced through an appreciation of profanations and encounters predicated on dramatization and ethology (rather than mere ethnology).[13] At work here is what Costas Constantinou calls *homo-diplomacy*— a human non-professional, experimental and experiential diplomacy of everyday life—which makes sense of a life-world outside the space of nation-state discourses.[14]

However, attentiveness to the dominant forms of *mancraft* in Africa means that our interest in homo-diplomacy has to go beyond 'the human' and explore not only how '*the Other but the Self become[s] strange, a site to be known or known anew*'.[15] Ultimately, concern with the question of the human, *thingification* and diplomacy beyond the state means that one has to take seriously the multiple forms of *mancraft* which exceed, complement and sometimes disturb the poetic vision of the world derived from modern *statecraft* and humanitarian *mancraft*.[16] At stake here is a pluralization, profanation and dramatization of various diplomatic imaginaries in order to reveal the ontologies and apparatuses that set beings apart or aggregate them while seeking different ways of being with the other and other ways of being.

Beautiful/ugly: ethnological reason and the embodiment of the diplomatic body

True to the trope of anachronistic space, civilizational absence and/or cultural degeneracy, African spaces, bodies, objects and mediation practices often act as an alternative site for European self-knowledge and reassurance. As illustrated by *Les Statues*, African people and things are often viewed and politicized through a *negative interpretation* that enables Africa to be inscribed in the 'dominant Western aesthetic discourse as the figure of the ugly' or as the 'sign of a lack'.[17] In the introduction to the edited volume *Beautiful/Ugly*, an anthology that explores the 'unpredictability, mutability and volatility of beauty and its relationship to ugliness in Africa and its intersections with the world', Sarah Nuttall notes that 'beauty in Africa, as it has been dealt with by the world at large, has an ugly history'.[18] Citing Immanuel Kant's 1764 essay 'On National Characteristics So Far as they Depend upon the Distinct Feeling of the Beautiful and the Sublime', Nuttall illustrates how aesthetic discourses on African beauty (or lack thereof) authorize moral discourses that limit the possibility of ethical encounters with Africans.[19] Turning to the disciplines of anthropology and art history, Nuttall notes that the ethnological discourses that animate them seek to account for the beauty of the savage that does not exist for itself unless it is 'conferred by the white slave trader, colonial soldier or merchant'. Within such a configuration, reflection on African beauty/ugliness and representation of other cultures becomes a pathway to a 'Western vision of human possibilities'.[20] This way of thinking about Africa is replicated in the realm of history, philosophy, religion, and can be summarized thus: there is a standard and recognizable way of being human or diplomatic that is linked to a standard of beauty, official histories, writing practices and recognized philosophical orientations. Africans, in the all too familiar Hegelian formulation, have no history, no philosophy and no civilization; therefore, they cannot be diplomatic or engaged in a 'diplomatic' manner unless they are translated into more familiar historical forms through processes that erase, subordinate or appropriate their Africanness as ahistoricity/otherness.

Nuttall is not alone in the interrogation of ethnological framing of beauty/ugliness in Africa and the moral or aesthetic worlds and selves it makes possible. In an interesting 'critique of ethnological reason', V.Y. Mudimbe engages the political significance of an ethnological mode of thought that creates not only a community of sense, but also provides a way of making sense of that community. According to Mudimbe, the ethnologicist perspective 'always extracts elements from their context, aestheticizes them, and then uses their supposed differences for classifying types of political, economic, or religious ensembles'.[21] That is, ethnology as a mode of comparing and contrasting cultures 'establishes a relation between the technical development of material arts and mentalities' which is used to confirm the inferiority of the primitive. It operates by 'isolating a datum from its "real" context', in order to make it 'analyzable', classifiable and ultimately assigning it a label that locates it in time and space, thus fixing its function.[22]

The aforementioned formulations and the desire to know and transform a people and the spaces they occupy contributed to the desire to pool 'existing knowledge about Africa and opening routes along which civilization could penetrate the interior of the African continent'.[23] For instance, the epistemological cartography concerned with the division of disciplines and the 'subjects' of their investigation established by the German Society for the Exploration of Equatorial Africa (formed by the German ethnologist Adolf Bastian) and Leopold II's convention of the 1876 Geographical Conference of Brussels, set the stage for the establishment of 'hospitable, scientific, and pacifying stations' for Africa. As the conditions of research changed, *the subjects of ethnological study became colonial Subjects*. Similarly, these national and transnational research and exploration institutes and their representatives were transformed into agencies responsible for imperial governance over large parts of Africa. The logic of partition, aggregation and management was soon transformed into multilateral diplomatic initiatives like the November 1884 Berlin conference where the spatial partition and cultural translation of Africa into European colonies and spheres of influence was formalized so as to minimize intra-European warfare while justifying the application of brute force against Africans who had since ceased to be considered viable diplomatic subjects.[24] In short, the desire to know and secure the figure of the human contributed to a quest for authoritative knowledge about the other which was conventionalized and then fixed as a factual basis for classification, theorization, organization and, most important, managing the non-European other.[25]

Like the ethnological knowledge and classification of worked objects that *Les Statues* treats, the diplomatic and philosophical discourses that developed alongside the idea that Africa was the marker of 'absolute otherness'—an Other that could be annihilated, converted or abused with impunity—contributed to regimes of recognition where Africans were accorded a lesser value based on strict notions of the relationship between the European 'original' (England, France, Portugal) and the colonial 'copy' (anglophone, francophone and lusophone Africa).[26] While a lot of these discourses contributed to African thingification, there were also instances where the discourse on African otherness was erased in favour of a discourse on universal sameness, care or progress.[27] Here, African subjects and objects were valued and evaluated based on their cultural and physiological deviation from the dominant European standard of which they were seen to be part, albeit in a degenerate or incomplete form.[28]

Whereas the macropolitical renditions of the mediation of estrangement in colonial Africa contributed to colonial state governance and institutionalized forms of diplomatic recognition, there were a number of non-geopolitical mediation practices in which individuals and collectivities encountered each other through affective exchanges that either disturbed or enforced colonial frames and the idea of diplomacy and humanity that they privileged. By invoking the embodied rather than abstract self, the (institutional/professional) 'diplomatic body' becomes animated and the sites where diplomatic encounters take place are pluralized, thus making it possible for us to put diplomacy to 'common use' as a way of interrogating the racial and gendered aspects of modern diplomatic relations.[29] For instance, attentiveness to the homo-diplomatic significance of the female body enables us to stage a diplomatic encounter with embattled lives and the racialized, sexualized and colonized bodies like that of Saartjie Bartmann (the so-called Hottentot Venus), which are often abjected from dominant readings of diplomacy.

Dramatis personae: Saartjie Bartmann's dramatizing and racing of the diplomatic/colonial body

Between freak-show performance, scientific knowledge and museum exhibition, Saartjie Bartmann's body/figure (more so her buttocks, hips and genitalia) served as a site for popular entertainment, 'diplomatic' ceremonial, confirmation of royal and imperial power, and scientific inquiry into the hierarchies of man based on physiological and aesthetic differences. In line with the multiple mediatory roles she played, Bartmann reveals the relationship between colonial and diplomatic forms of *mancraft* through the 'unofficial' and 'experimental' diplomacy that she embodies. Similarly, her circulation as body, thing and sign reveals the numerous ethnological frames of recognition that underline consensual senses of community and the various acts of *dissensus* that seek to disturb them.[30]

At a minimum, Bartmann's body's circulation within multiple spaces reveals how colonial homo-diplomatic ventures pursued the 'knowledge and control of the Other' as a means of 'knowledge of the Self'.[31] It also highlights the extent to which postcolonial diplomacy contests or reproduces colonial logics, scripts and technologies (of the self) and 'credo of power' while creating new sites of estrangement or forms of mediation.[32] The internal mediation and forms of sameness and otherness that accrue from parading Bartmann's body are worth mentioning. At one level, Bartmann's body was incorporated into an already elaborate idea of the diplomatic self predicated on European aesthetico-anthropological discourses and popular conceptions of beauty, common sense and humanity.[33] On a different level, the parading of Bartmann's body and the various discourses around it sheds light on the notions of absolute otherness and the diplomacies that made it possible for multiple African 'Venus' figures to appear as entertainment items in Duchess du Barry 1829 Parisian ball and at a fair in Hyde Park on the Coronation Day of Queen Victoria in 1838.[34] Attentiveness to Bartmann's potentialities and the relations, rhythms, desires and intensities around her enables us to ask questions that go beyond the ethnological obsessions of her 'time'—*What* is Saartjie Bartmann? Is she human? *What type* of (human) being is she?—which serve to disallow ethical encounters by outlining tasks and 'operations' to be done.

However, we can shift our focus to questions of *how* Bartmann's body and figure is given or deprived of force, quality and vitality.[35] We can engage Bartmann in a manner that points to the numerous, though less visible and ultimately forgotten bodies that acted as sites of popular entertainment, sovereign performance and racialized reassurance of the self or as evidence of 'hierarchies of man'. We can ask questions that force us to see and think that which was rendered unthinkable, mute or erased by colonial desires and regimes of recognition that set Bartmann apart as a way of arriving at the truth of 'man *par excellence*'.

Writing about the banality of figures like Bartmann within the colonial imaginary, Sadia Qureshi calls for the 'contextualization and recapturing' of Bartmann's agency in order for us to have a more 'legitimate basis for her cultural status as a representative of colonized peoples' experiences'.[36] As Qureshi puts it:

> In many ways, Sara Bartmann is not an unusual woman, despite all the attention she has inspired. Throughout her life, processes can be identified that contributed to her objectification, allowed her trade as a human commodity, underlay her exhibition as a curiosity, aroused scientific interest, and reified her as a museum artefact. None of these events is in itself exceptional in the sense that they occur only in her tale. Rather, a historicization of her collection and display embeds her within a range of related contexts.[37]

For Qureshi, locating Bartmann in a given spatio-temporal plane in order to think the conditions of possibility for her exploitation is a significant practice. At a minimum, it enables Bartmann to dramatize this plane such that it comes to 'constitute a special theatre' where the 'forces' and ideas at play within the colonial and postcolonial worlds in which she circulates (or fails to circulate) become apparent. Such a dramatization makes it possible for us to determine 'something more important concerning the idea' by paying attention to how the 'idea incarnates or actualizes itself, differentiates itself'.[38]

For example, Bartmann's exhibition in 'Piccadilly relates her to the human curiosities upon display in the vicinity, from obese giants to emaciated dwarves', thus offering a glimpse into the conventions and discourses on the body of the Victorian era.[39] Similarly, the historical period in which the exhibition took place was characterized by the presence of abolitionists in London thus complicating the discourses surrounding the popular reception of the exhibition of her body.[40] Finally, Qureshi provides a perspective on 'the museological context' of Bartmann's display by highlighting the 'artefactual' significance of her body and its implications for diplomatic thought given that the display takes place 'within an ethnographic museum' in which 'ethnographic objects serve as tangible metonymic fragments of foreign cultures'.[41]

In death, Bartmann's body became the subject of General George Cuvier's racialized scientific inquiry into her human status, thus investing it with further diplomatic and colonial significance. That is, Bartmann's body was considered a specimen/model upon which scientific generalizations could be based, thus providing a site where the knowledge of the non-European other reinforced prevailing notions of the European self and by extension humanity. As recently as the early 1980s, Bartmann's dissected genitalia, along with her skeleton and brain, were still exhibited at the *Musée de l'Homme* in Paris. The presence of this diplomatic/colonial body in the museum transforms this space into both a temporal embassy and colonial relic—a constant reminder and perpetuator of the violent homo-diplomatic venture that made it possible to stage, cage and exhibit non-European others.[42]

In 1995, following the African National Congress's (ANC) victory and the formal end of apartheid in South Africa, Bartmann's diplomatic plane of operation shifts again when the Griqua National Conference began raising with President Nelson Mandela the issue of the repatriation of her remains.[43] The quest for the return of Bartmann's remains to South Africa for a humane burial was also used to highlight the present position of indigenous peoples like the Griqua and Khoe-San, the material and spiritual violations that they suffered in the past, and 'their need for recognition, constitutional accommodation and land restitution' in the post-apartheid era.[44] As a result of the GNC's political claims, the repatriation of Bartmann's remains became part of a diplomatic 'dialogue between states' characterized by the 'charged political row between the French and South African governments' and a summit diplomatic agenda involving a personal request from President Mandela to successive French presidents: first François Mitterrand, and subsequently to Jacques Chirac.

Following Mandela's request, the return of Bartmann's remains became part of a multi-track diplomatic agenda characterized by petitions from the National Council of the Khoisan Consultative Conference (NKOK) and the unsuccessful negotiations between Professor Philip Tobias from the University of the Witwatersrand and Dr Henry de Lumley, the director of the Musée del' Homme and the National Museum of Natural History in Paris. Citing the museum's lack of legal powers to de-accession the remains, Bartmann's case was turned over to the French parliament where case-specific provisions for the de-accession were to be enacted. Interestingly enough, the French Senator Nicolas About included a French translation of Diana Ferrus's poetic tribute to Sarah Bartmann in his 22 January 2002 submission to the French parliament to apply the bio-ethics law to the Bartmann case.[45]

It is claimed that Ferrus's poetic intervention/mediation played a key role in the French government's decision to change its position on the repatriation of Bartmann's remains. Most significantly, the poem puts Bartmann to common use and evokes a complexity/multiplicity of senses that her 'public exhibition' and concealed storage in Europe denied her. Unlike the historical reality of a woman caged/closeted and turned into a spectacle—an object of the 'knowing look' and the 'knowledgeable' gaze and dissection—Ferrus's poem 'offers to take Sara Bartmann home' where she is free to roam the *veld* and partake of that which her position in Europe has denied her. As such, the poem's persona has a relationship with Bartmann that is not based on objectification and public inscription but a quest for friendship. In contrast to popular treatments of Bartmann as a sight and site of desire, ethnological knowledge or 'positivist' scientific investigation, Ferrus's Bartmann is an affective being. One who, in an act of reciprocity, brings peace to her poetic interlocutor as she derives the same from her:[46]

> I have come to take you home
> Home! Remember the veld
> and the lush green grass beneath the big oak trees?
> The air is cool there and the sun does not burn.
> I have made your bed at the foot of the hill …
> I have come to wrench you away
> away from the poking eyes of the man-made monster
> who lives in the dark with his clutches of imperialism
> who dissects your body bit by bit,
> who likens your soul to that of satan
> and declares himself the ultimate God!
> I have come to soothe your heavy heart …
> I have made your bed at the foot of the hill.
> Your blankets are covered in buchu and mint.
> The proteas stand in yellow and white—
> I have come to take you home
> where I will sing for you,
> for you have brought me peace,
> for you have brought us peace.[47]

It is important to note that the negotiation agenda and parties to the negotiation on Bartmann's repatriation were already mediated by histories, institutions and dispositions that made the politics of return a site of overlapping and sometimes conflicting meanings and practices. This contestation is apparent when one pays attention to the fact that some of the scientific and aesthetic entities involved in negotiations to retrieve Bartmann's remains had enabled and perpetuated ways of knowing of which the Bartmann story is symptomatic. Writing about the South African memory complex, Ciraj Rassool notes that some of the symbolism, institutions and personalities surrounding the repatriation of Bartmann 'obscured wider legacies of gendered racial science in South Africa'.[48] Zeroing in on the mediatory role of Professor Philip Tobias, Rassool goes on to point out that:

> It is indeed ironic that Phillip Tobias featured prominently in these processes, as the appointed negotiator, part of the Sara Bartmann reception committee

as well as member of the Reference Group. The reference group itself was composed of a mix of academics, human rights and gender commission representatives, members of government and Khoesan representatives. Tobias had been a protégé of physical anthropologist and racial scientist Raymond Dart ... building on Dart's legacy, Tobias was positioned as the director, mentor and facilitator of the South African field of palaeoanthropology, which continued to feed South Africa's need for a scientized modernity after apartheid ... For Tobias—and for the discourse—palaeoanthropology and anatomical study were now the disciplines of the long-dead ancestors of South Africans, Africans and indeed, of all people, and were no longer framed by typology and the classification and comparison of the fossil record with the 'living fossils' of primitive races.[49]

Interestingly enough, the 'successful' return of Bartmann's remains opened a space for further management of her body/image/sign through a series of political and diplomatic credentials that accorded her remains a time(liness) attuned to the new spaces they occupied. Through a recourse to Afro-centric historicism, nation-statist and human rights discourses, Bartmann was inscribed into the 'public rituals of the constitution of the post-apartheid nation', not only as the 'great Foremother', who had experienced 'the great and enduring disgraces of Western civilization' but also as a 'human rights icon' adequate to the new political dispensation in South Africa.[50] In a speech given at Bartmann's funeral on 9 August 2002, Thabo Mbeki, the then South African president, offered some useful homo-diplomatic reflections that raise questions about the forms of gendered and racial estrangement characteristic of colonial encounters and their reproduction in the post-apartheid nation.[51]

According to Mbeki, the occasion of Bartmann's funeral 'can never be a solemn ceremony in which we bury her remains and bury the truth'. Not only does Bartmann's 'diplomatic funeral' act as a testament to 'the particular place attributed to African women' by colonizers who saw themselves as 'man *par excellence*', but the funeral also acts as an occasion to 'summon the courage to speak the naked but healing truth' that speaks to the past and the present 'with the knowledge that women have borne the brunt of the oppressive and exploitative system of colonial and apartheid domination' in the past and continue to carry 'the burden of poverty' while being exposed to 'unacceptable violence and abuse' today.[52]

Noting the significance of Bartmann's story for the post-apartheid reconciliation agenda, Mbeki went on to designate Sarah Bartmann's 'final resting place' at Hankey, Kouga Municipality in the Eastern Cape Province as a National Heritage Site, where one can reflect on South Africa and Africa's encounter with the West. According to Mbeki:

> The story of Sarah Bartmann is the story of the African people of our country in all their echelons. It is a story of the loss of our ancient

freedom. It is a story of our dispossession of the land and the means that gave us an independent livelihood. It is a story of our reduction to the status of objects that could be owned, used and disposed of by others, who claimed for themselves a manifest destiny 'to run the empire of the globe' ... It is an account of how it came about that we ended up being defined as a people without a past, except a past of barbarism, who had no capacity to think, who had no culture, no value system to speak of, and nothing to contribute to human civilization—people with no names and no identity, who had to be defined by he who was 'man *par excellence*'.[53]

Accorded such an iconic status by the state, Bartmann's body 'does not rest'. It continues to circulate as part of a public diplomatic discourse and ritual where the figure of Bartmann is mobilized for national and homo-diplomatic edification. The multiple uses of this 'diplomatic body' are well captured by the Republic of South Africa's Government Gazette No. 30987, of 25 April 2008. In this notice, the South African Heritage Resources Agency (SAHRA) declares that Bartmann's burial 'site has spiritual, cultural, social, and historical significance'.[54] The SAHRA notice, much like Mbeki's burial speech, summons the 'treatment of Sarah Bartmann during her life and after her death' to engage the question of 'dispossession, sadness and loss of dignity, culture, community, language and life', and claims that these are the symptoms of the inhumanity of people. In both cases the return and burial of Bartmann was seen as an opportunity to look to the atrocities of the past in order to imagine a different future for the South African nation and humanity as a whole.

Thus, Bartmann's travelling body, in all its excessiveness becomes a 'symbol to all South Africans and the world to strive towards recognizing past injustices to Khoi-San people, to women and vulnerable communities and to work towards building a nation that shows respect to human life, human rights and human dignity'.[55] More specifically, and in line with his fidelities to an African Renaissance and his Truth and Reconciliation prerogatives, Mbeki sees the story of Bartmann as a provocation to 'eradicate the legacy of apartheid and colonialism in all its manifestations' so as to 'build a truly non-racial society in which black and white shall be brother and sister'; a society where people 'join in a determined and sustained effort to ensure respect for the dignity of the women of our country, gender equality and women's emancipation'.[56]

Necromancies and profanations: calling up and 'recalling' postcolonial ontologies and apparatuses

The diplomacy of life/death, objectification and public inscription articulated by the exhibition and return of Saartjie Bartmann's 'body' and the attention to the 'death of statues' and objectification of men/women in *Les Statues Meurent Aussi*, raises many interesting questions about the ontology–apparatus (*dispositif*) relationship in colonial and postcolonial societies.[57] Especially relevant here is the relationship that Giorgio Agamben maps out between 'living beings (or substances)' and 'apparatuses in which living beings are incessantly captured'; a relationship between 'the ontology of creatures' and the 'apparatuses that seek to govern and guide them toward the good'.[58]

In the colonial/ethnological context, the ontology–apparatus relationship is characterized by the knowledge and management of human beings and worked objects from 'overseas spaces' by inserting them into 'ethnographic spaces' (like museums, libraries and universities) while the overseas spaces are converted into colonies and the people that inhabit them are converted into colonial subjects attuned 'to the self and imagination of the West'.[59] The 'science of man' and vision of the world and humanity derived from the set of relationships, dispositions and institutions that propped entities like the Berlin Ethnological Museum (also founded by Adolf Bastian in 1873) created the conditions of possibility for modes of recognition through which Africans (and African objects) were presented as strange, yet knowable and ultimately manageable parts of a shared humanity.

Today, *we* see the emergence of other sites of traffic in otherness where a vision of humanity and cultural encounters are imaged/imagined and relationships and managerial institutions invented to deal with the forms of life and objects that are aggregated under the category of the human. While such sites can act as a form of meta-diplomatic 'forum'—a 'place for confrontation, experimentation and debate' on the meaning of diplomacy, Africanness, the state, humanity, art and life[60]—they sometimes fail to offer sufficiently critical questions thus enabling a consensus to emerge about humanity and with it genres of expression and discourses that moralize the figure of man and the practical dispositions used to secure humanity, by managing vulnerable human 'life'.

As we engage the humanitarian *apparatus* that has become one of the dominant sites for the aggregation, evaluation and management of life in Africa through recourse to the category of the human or human rights, it is important that we also engage its ethnological *apparition* and the partialities it creates. Commenting on the *aporia* of humanitarian governmentality, Didier Fassin notes that the tension between the 'politics of life and an evaluation of humanity' and 'the practice of difference and an ideal of universality' lies at the core of humanitarianism. Thus, humanitarianism determines how 'we' value lives and evaluate human beings making it an operation predicated on the 'inequality of lives and hierarchies of humanity'.[61]

Given that we are witnessing the deepening rather than questioning of existing political categories, habits and partialities in the name of humanity (much like colonial ethnology), it becomes increasingly important for 'us' to reconfigure, disturb or present alternatives to the life-managing and other-managing moral discourses and aesthetic practices that have become part of the dominant humanitarian apparatus and the idea of 'man', space, time and life that it privileges. The objective here is to politicize and dramatize the concern for other/injured lives. The objective is not to try to destroy the humanitarian ethos of concern for the pain of distant others, or use it in the 'right' way, but to profane it—to 'restore its use to common men' rather than the experts and Western philanthropic subjects whose province it seems to be.[62] By paying attention to the ontology-apparatus relationship that conditions not only humanitarianism's declarations but also its interventions, abstentions and ultimately its subjections, we can ask how and why the logic and moral of humanitarianism seems to be one of sacrifice;[63] a logic that always 'sanctions the passage of something from the profane to the sacred, from the "human" sphere to the divine' or, we might add, to the sphere where the human is divine.[64]

Conclusion

The death of African statues and the dissection and storage of Bartmann in European museums was part of the ethnologically mediated 'ritual separation' of objects and women from the spaces of everyday operation in order to shore up a given idea of the human that was accorded a quasi-divine status. The museum, the colony and the colonial library/archive form part of an elaborate apparatus that makes possible and legitimizes these acts of separation in the name of man *par excellence*. In the face of such a colonial 'museification' of the world, the act of 'profanation is the counter-apparatus that restores to common use' the people, objects and lives that the colonial/capitalist 'sacrifice had separated and divided' in order to enable other ways of being and relating to emerge.[65]

Today, the humanitarian 'museification' of the world finds its full force through discourses on the 'well-being' of humanity or man as any-subject-whatever. Here humanity is accorded a quasi-divine status thus contributing to the proliferation of techniques and technologies that allow the West to mount 'a revisionary practice of cultural introspection and self-reinvention' through recourse to a 'cultural politics of affect' and the various technologies of 'humanization'.[66] For instance, the extensive *redemptive dispositif* enacted in the recent Invisible Children film '*Kony 2012*' calls for both US military intervention in northern Uganda and popular awareness and advocacy on the part of American citizens in an attempt to stop the Joseph Kony-led Lord Resistance Army. Well-meaning as they may be, such campaigns mobilize and legitimize a Humanitarianism-Military-Industrial-Media-Entertainment network (H-MIME-NET) and serve as a symptom, spectre and schema of the *salvific* and sacrificial forces characteristic of the recent, and not too recent, history of diplomacies of redemption in Africa.[67] Here the saving of 'African' lives becomes a means of producing and managing humanity.

While contemporary humanitarianism offers a different imperative, ethic of relation and engages different apparatuses than those privileged by colonial ethnology, the manner in which it poses the question of the human and the data and categories it organizes in the service of a bio-politics of humanity contributes to the privileging of categories that uphold its assumptions rather than open new ways of relating with others. As Liisa Malkki illustrates in her engagement with 'Speechless Emissaries'—Hutu refugees from Burundi living in Tanzania—a concern with authenticity and manageability has led to the privileging of categories like the 'refugee' which becomes 'an object of concern and knowledge for the international community and for a particular variety of humanism'.[68]

According to Malkki, 'refugee issues are one privileged site for the study of humanitarian interventions through which "the international community" constitutes itself'. The International Community then goes on to use social processes and modes of administration and representation that make it possible for refugees to stop 'being specific persons and become pure victims in general: universal man, universal woman, universal child, and, taken together, universal family'.[69] Such acts of knowing, managing and then universalizing particular displaced people through marking them as refugees in this case 'dehistoricizes' them and 'abstracts their predicaments from specific political, historical, cultural contexts'. In so doing, 'humanitarian practices tend to silence refugees' while reproducing them or images of them.[70] For Malkki:

> Pictures of refugees are now a key vehicle in the elaboration of a transnational social imagination of *refugeeness* ... This global visual field of often quite standardized representational practices is surprisingly important in its effects, for it is connected at many points to the *de facto* inability of particular refugees to represent themselves authoritatively in the inter- and transnational institutional domains where funds and resources circulate. The first thing to be noted about the mutual relationship between image and narrative, spectacle and self-representation, is that photographs and other visual representations of refugees are far more common than is the reproduction in print of what particular refugees have said. There are more established institutional contexts, uses, and conventions for pictures of refugees than for displaced persons' own narrative accounts of exile. Indeed, some of these visual conventions seem to speed up the evaporation of history and narrativity.[71]

'Moving' images like those in *Kony 2012* and the representations of which Malkki is critical tend to essentialize and fix the conditions under which one can have concern for other lives. The privileging of the wounded body or categories like refugeeness sometimes fail to raise critical questions about the conditions and perspectives under which political life arises and thereby elude the political negotiations required for the condition to change. While the proliferation of images and the vulgarization of diplomatic thought and subjects in the age of humanitarianism are useful, these images, as Jacques Rancière puts it, are sometimes the 'effigies' of those who produce them.[72] They are part of an elaborate 'theatre of images' that at once make us aware of the suffering of others while actively incorporating other practices, bodies and actors into existing modes of recognition, thus establishing a new consensus that attempts to restore the tranquillity required for the realization of a 'desirable' homo-diplomatic habitus and the habits of thought that comport with it.

In their different ways, the above explorations illustrate that the mediation of estrangement is always already mediated. Rather than reproduce the well-worn ethnological and humanitarian questions and moralities that privilege the knowledge and management of men, cultures and lives, we can explore ethology, which, Deleuze tells us, poses a different question for life by asking:

> How do individuals enter into composition with one another in order to form a higher individual, ad infinitum? How can a being take another being into its world, but while preserving or respecting the other's own relations and world? And in this regard, what are the different types of sociabilities, for example? What is the difference between the society of human beings and the community of rational beings?[73]

Unlike *ethnology* and, by extension, humanitarian morality, which is concerned with what the human IS and what it *must* do by virtue of its essence—its responsibility to catalogue, conserve, protect or civilize—the *ethological* quest allows us to raise questions about *what a body can do* such that the death of statues becomes apprehendable and their loss grievable. It raises not only the question of difference, but that of power and relationality and provokes 'us' to pursue a more patient reading of postcolonial homo-diplomacies (in Africa) by carrying out a critique of the habits of mediation and maps of estrangement made possible by calling up the familiar categories—essential Africanness or Europeanness, the human, the refugee, the genocidaire, peace or the state—as the determinants of diplomatic possibilities and responsibilities.

Attentiveness to ethology reveals the ontology-apparatus relationships at play in a modern-day humanitarianism that values/evaluates life and manages humans, thus foreclosing the possibilities for relating otherwise by stating how 'we' ought to relate with bodies in pain or moving images of the body in pain depending on our 'proximity' and disposition rather than raise questions about position and potentiality. In asking what a body can do, and acknowledging that we 'do not know beforehand what a body or a mind can do, in a given encounter, a given arrangement, a given combination', it becomes possible for us to think about the possibilities of violence and tyrannies, of hope, horror and various in-between states; to think about the possibilities of an ethics of encounter and experimental and experiential diplomacies that engage 'a people who are missing', or 'a people who are yet to come';[74] and thereby to conceive of diplomacies that mis-identify with humanitarian clichés and regimes of recognition for the sake of enhanced ethico-political and aesthetic possibilities.

Notes

1 J.H. Miller, 'The Medium is the Maker: Browning, Freud, Derrida, and the New Telepathic Ecotechnologies', *Oxford Literary Review* 30, no. 2 (December 2008):

161–79, at 161; Deleuze cited in G. Agamben, *Profanations*, trans. Jeff Fort, New York: Zone Books, 2007: 84.
2 Manthia Diawara, *African Cinema: Politics and Culture*, Bloomington and Indianapolis: Indiana University Press, 1992: 22.
3 The concept mediation as used in the essay refers to a 'method that makes social meanings possible'. As an instrument of meaning, mediation can take place across various social contexts, genres of expressing, bodies and cultural practices. For various treatments of diplomacy as the mediation of estrangement, see James Der Derian, *On Diplomacy: A Genealogy of Western Estrangement*, New York: Basil Blackwell, 1987; Costas M. Constantinou, *On the Way to Diplomacy*, Minneapolis: University of Minnesota Press, 1996; Costas M. Constantinou, 'On Homo-diplomacy', *Space and Culture* 9, no. 4 (2006): 351–64; and Francois Debrix, 'Rituals of Mediation', in *Rituals of Mediation: International Politics and Social Meaning*, ed. Francois Debrix and Cynthia Weber, Minneapolis: University of Minnesota Press, 2003.
4 Michel de Certeau, *Heterologies: Discourse on the Other*, trans. Brian Massumi, Minneapolis: University of Minnesota Press, 1986; Constantinou, 'On Homo-diplomacy'.
5 Giorgio Agamben, *Profanations*, trans. Jeff Fort, New York: Zone Books, 2007: 83.
6 Agamben, *Profanations*: 80–81.
7 Agamben, *Profanations*: 77.
8 Jean Negron voice-over, quoted in Nwachukwu Frank Ukadike, *Black African Cinema*, Berkeley: University of California Press, 1994: 49.
9 Matthias de Groof, 'Statues Also Die—But their Death is not the Final Word', *Image & Narrative* 11, no. 1 (2010): 29–46.
10 Agamben, *Profanations*: 84.
11 Judith Butler, *Frames of War: When is Life Grievable*, London: Verso, 2009: 1.
12 Butler, *Frames of War*: 3.
13 Gilles Deleuze, 'The Method of Dramatization', in *Desert Islands and Other Texts: 1953–1974*, trans. Michael Taormina, ed. David Lapoujade, New York: Semiotext(e), 2004: 94–116; Gilles Deleuze, *Spinoza, Practical Philosophy*, trans. Robert Hurley, San Francisco, CA: City Lights Books, 1988.
14 See Constantinou, 'On Homo-diplomacy': 352; Der Derian, *On Diplomacy*.
15 Constantinou, 'On Homo-diplomacy': 352.
16 Richard Ashley notes that 'modern statecraft is modern mancraft. It is an art of domesticating the meaning of man by constructing his problems, his dangers, his fears'. Given that I am interested in the forms of diplomacies that exceed statecraft, the forms of mancraft that I treat exceed those prescribed, sanctioned or invented in response to statecraft. For more on the relationship between statecraft and mancraft, see Richard K. Ashley, 'Living on Border Lines: Man, Poststructuralism and War', in *International/Intertextual Relations: Postmodern Readings of World Politics*, ed. James Der Derian and Michael J. Shapiro, Massachusetts: Lexington Books, 1989. Drawing upon Heidegger's reflection on the 'craft of the hand', Costas Constantinou suggests that the 'theme of diplomacy could be illustrated not only in statecraft but also in handicraft, that is, in the inscription, arrangement and authentication of diplomas ... in the etymological thematics of diploma, therefore, the theme of diplomacy gets rewritten, reread and redefined'. See Constantinou, *On the Way to Diplomacy*: 74–88.
17 Sarah Nutall, ed., *Beautiful/Ugly: African and Diaspora Aesthetics*, Durham: Duke University Press, 2006: 9; Achille Mbembe, *On the Postcolony*, Berkeley: University of California Press, 2001: 1.
18 Nutall, *Beautiful/Ugly*: 8.
19 Nutall, *Beautiful/Ugly*: 9.
20 Nutall, *Beautiful/Ugly*: 10.

21 V.Y. Mudimbe, *The Invention of Africa: Gnosis, Philosophy, and the Order of Knowledge*, Bloomington & Indianapolis: Indiana University Press, 1988: 52.
22 Mudimbe, *The Invention of Africa*: 59.
23 Johannes Fabian, *Out of Our Minds: Reason and Madness in the Exploration of Central Africa*, Berkley: University of California Press, 2000.
24 Sam Okoth Opondo, 'Decolonizing Diplomacy: Reflections on African Estrangement and Exclusion', in Costas Constantinou and James Der Derian, eds, *Sustainable Diplomacies*, Basingstoke: Palgrave Macmillan, 2010: 109–27.
25 Arjun Appadurai, *Modernity at Large: Cultural Dimensions of Globalization*, Minneapolis: University of Minnesota Press, 1996: 115; David Ludden, 'Orientalism Empiricism: Transformations of Colonial Knowledge', in *Orientalism and the Postcolonial Predicament: Perspectives on South Asia*, ed. Carol A. Breckenridge and Peter van der Veer, Philadelphia: University of Pennsylvania Press, 1993: 250.
26 Susan Bassnett and Harish Trivedi, *Post-Colonial Translation: Theory and Practice*, London: Routledge, 1998: 4.
27 According to Aimé Césaire, the colonial encounter requires the reinvention of the colonized, the deliberate destruction of his/her past through discourses and practices that rob him/her of his/her subjectivity. For Césaire, colonization = thingification. The colonial process involves practices that dehumanized the colonized such that he/she is reduced to 'an instrument of production' to serve the purpose of the colonizer. For more on thingification of colonized peoples, see Aimé Césaire, *Discourse on Colonialism*, trans. Joan Pinkham, New York: Monthly Review Press, 1972.
28 See Deleuze and Guattari's elaborate treatment of faciality in the section 'Year Zero: Faciality', in Gilles Deleuze and Felix Guattari, *A Thousand Plateaus: Capitalism and Schizophrenia*, Vol. II, trans. Brian Massumi, Minneapolis: University of Minnesota Press, 1987: 167–91.
29 Within the convention of diplomacy as a state practice, the diplomatic corps is that corporate body of diplomats from all states resident at one post and serves the purpose of fostering diplomatic standards, lobbies for the defence of diplomatic privileges and immunities among other collective/professional interests. See G.R. Berridge, *Notes on the Origins of the Diplomatic Corps: Constantinople in the 1620s*, Discussion Paper No. 92, Clingendale Netherlands Institute for International Relations, 2004.
30 Jacques Rancière, *The Politics of Aesthetics*, trans. Gabriel Rockhill, New York: Continuum, 2004.
31 Constantinou, 'On Homo-diplomacy'.
32 Mbembe, *On the Postcolony*.
33 See Harold Nicolson, *Diplomacy*, Oxford: Oxford University Press, 1950.
34 Sander L. Gilman, 'Black Bodies, White Bodies: Toward an Iconography of Female Sexuality in Late Nineteenth-Century Art, Medicine, and Literature', *Critical Inquiry* 12, no. 1 (Autumn 1985): 204–42, at 213.
35 Deleuze, 'The Method of Dramatization'.
36 Sadia Qureshi, 'Displaying Sara Bartmann, the "Hottentot Venus"', *History of Science* 42 (2004): 233–57.
37 Qureshi, 'Displaying Sara Bartmann': 249.
38 Deleuze, 'The Method of Dramatization': 94.
39 Qureshi, 'Displaying Sara Bartmann': 249.
40 Gilman, 'Black Bodies, White Bodies': 213.
41 Qureshi, 'Displaying Sara Bartmann': 249.
42 See Stephan Jay Gould, 'The Hottentot Venus', in *The Flamingo's Smile: Reflections in Natural History*, ed. Stephan Jay Gould, New York: Norton, 1985: 291–305; Janell Hobson, 'The "Batty" Politic: Toward an Aesthetic of the Black Female Body', *Hypatia* 18, no. 4 (2003): 87–105; Partha Mitter, 'The Hottentot

Venus and Western Man: Reflections on the Construction of Beauty in the West', in *Cultural Encounters: Representing Otherness*, ed. Elizabeth Hallam and Brian Street, London: Routledge, 2000: 35–50.
43 Jatti Bredekamp, 'The Politics of Human Remains: The Case of Sarah Bartmann', in *Human Remains & Museum Practice*, ed. Jack Lohman and Katherine Goodnow, London: UNESCO and the Museum of London, 2006: 28.
44 Michael Paul Besten, 'Transformation and the Reconstitution of Khoe-San Identities: AAS le Fleur I, Griqua Identities and Post-apartheid Khoe-San Revivalism (1894–2004)', unpublished PhD dissertation, Leiden University, 2006, www.griquas.com/griquaphd.pdf: 275.
45 Diana Ferrus, 'I've Come to Take You Home' (Tribute to Sarah Bartmann Written in Holland, June 1998), in Deborah Willis, *Black Venus 2010: They Called Her 'Hottentot'*, Philadelphia: Temple University Press, 2012: 213–14; Bredekamp, 'The Politics of Human Remains': 28.
46 See Pumla Dineo Gqola, '"Crafting Epicentres of Agency": Sarah Bartmann and African Feminist Literary Imaginings', *QUEST: An African Journal of Philosophy/ Revue Africaine de Philosophie* XX (2008): 45–76.
47 Extract from Ferrus, 'I've Come to Take You Home'.
48 Ciraj Rassool, 'Human Remains, the Disciplines of the Dead and the South African Memorial Complex', paper presented at The Politics of Heritage, Museum Africa, Newtown, Johannesburg, 8–9 July 2011, sitemaker.umich.edu/ politics.of.heritage/—schedule_and_papers: 3–4.
49 Rassool, 'Human Remains': 3–4.
50 Rassool, 'Human Remains': 6.
51 Qureshi, 'Displaying Sara Bartmann'; T. Mbeki, *Presidential Speech at the Funeral of Sarah Bartmann*, 9 August 2002, www.dfa.gov.za/docs/speeches/2002/mbek0809.htm.
52 Thabo Mbeki, *Presidential Speech at the Funeral of Sarah Bartmann, 9 August 2002*. For an elaborate treatment of the diplomatic funeral see G.R. Berridge, 'Diplomacy After Death: The Rise of the Working Funeral', *Diplomacy & Statecraft* 4, no. 2 (2007): 217–34.
53 Mbeki, *Presidential Speech*.
54 Department of Arts and Culture, South African Heritage Resources Agency (SAHRA), Declaration of the Burial Site of Sarah Bartmann as a National Heritage Site, Government Gazette, No. 30987, 25 April 2008: www.info.gov.za/ view/DownloadFileAction?id=80983.
55 SAHRA, Declaration.
56 Mbeki, *Presidential Speech*.
57 I thank Michael J. Shapiro for calling my attention to the ontology–apparatus relationship as explored by Giorgio Agamben's, Michel Foucault's and Gilles Deleuze's writings on the *dispositif*.
58 Giorgio Agamben, *What is an Apparatus?* trans. David Kishik and Stefan Pedatella, Stanford, CA: Stanford University Press, 2009: 13.
59 V.Y. Mudimbe, *The Idea of Africa*, Bloomington: Indiana University Press, 1994: 61.
60 Steven D. Lavine and Ivan Karp, 'Introduction: Museums and Multiculturalism', in *Exhibiting Cultures*, ed. Steven D Lavine and Ivan Karp, Washington, DC: Smithsonian Institution Press, 1991: 1–9, at 3.
61 Didier Fassin, 'Inequality of Lives, Hierarchies of Humanity: Moral Commitments and Ethical Dilemmas of Humanitarianism', in *In the Name of Humanity: The Government of Threat and Care*, ed. Ilana Feldman and Miriam Iris Ticktin, Durham, NC: Duke University Press, 2010: 238–55, at 238.
62 Agamben, *What is an Apparatus?*; Agamben, *Profanations*.
63 Fassin, 'Inequality of Lives, Hierarchies of Humanity': 255; Agamben, *What is an Apparatus?* 19.
64 Agamben, *What is an Apparatus?* 19.

65 Agamben, *What is an Apparatus?* 19.
66 H. Härting H., 'Global Humanitarianism, Race, and the Spectacle of the African Corpse in Current Western Representations of the Rwandan Genocide', *Comparative Studies of South Asia, Africa and the Middle East* 28, no. 1 (2008): 61–77, at 61.
67 By illustrating MIME-NET'S intersection with various forms of philanthropic practices or redemptive discourses, I illustrate how this differs from the military prosthetics and virtualization of weapons that is the focus of James Der Derian's *Virtuous War* essay.
68 Liisa H. Malkki, 'Speechless Emissaries: Refugees, Humanitarianism, and Dehistoricization', *Cultural Anthropology* 11, no. 3 (1996): 377–404, at 378; Kate Manzo, 'Imaging Humanitarianism: NGO Identity and the Iconography of Childhood', Antipode 40, no. 4 (2008): 632–57.
69 Malkki, 'Speechless Emissaries': 378.
70 Malkki, 'Speechless Emissaries': 378.
71 Malkki, 'Speechless Emissaries': 386.
72 Jacques Rancière, 'Theater of Images', in *Alfredo Jaar—La Politique des Images*, exhibition catalogue, Musée Cantonal des Beaux-Arts, Lausanne. Zurich: JRP Ringier, 2002: 71–80.
73 Deleuze, *Spinoza*: 125.
74 Deleuze, *Spinoza:* 125; Gilles Deleuze, *Cinema 2: The Time Image*, trans. Hugh Tomlison and Robert Galeta, Minneapolis: University of Minnesota Press, 1989: 130.

9 Impossibilities

Generative misperformance and the movements of the teaching body

Naeem Inayatullah

Introduction: after the end of the world

Allow me to start, dear reader, with the *tragic sensibility*: the idea that creativity emerges when we accept and face impossibility.

In graduate school, I was struggling with how Hegel and Marx employ dialectics. With the guidance of one my teachers, I came upon the work of the British philosopher R.G. Collingwood. I read everything I could find of Collingwood's. Then I selected three of his books, and re-read them for many months.[1] Somewhere in those works is a phrase Collingwood attributes to Hegel: 'the present is perfect'.

Collingwood does not mean we live in the best of worlds, that things cannot get better, or that we have no option but to celebrate the status quo. The aphorism suggests that given a riven past, the present condition is already the result of our best effort. The proposition 'the present is perfect' moves me to appreciate the intricacy of past troubles. It asks me to accept the sincerity and determination of those whose attempts to solve past problems have resulted in our current predicaments. It shifts my attention from our misperformed solutions to grasping the deeper intractability of problems.

From intractability it is a short step to impossibility. Impossibility might be expressed this way: problems are impossible because their origins are contested, their very constitution as 'problems' are read from competing values, and the execution of their 'solutions' moves us towards divergent ends. It follows that if the problems are impossible then the solutions are unlikely.

Most react with despondency, depression, or denial when faced with such impossibility. I find this utterly understandable, but this posture also denies available resources. A direct engagement with the impossible can provide energy, courage, stamina and creativity for a lifetime. How? Let me answer by quoting Henry Kariel in his 'Becoming Political'. Kariel writes, 'When exits close and options are cancelled our vision is suddenly sharpened and we can catch ourselves in the act of seeing. An auspicious moment for educators'.[2] When 'exits close' and 'options are cancelled', our urgency increases and we begin to recognize that all performance fails. Paradoxically, but also intuitively, such failure can be more fruitful than the righteous but anxious imperialism of teaching projects.

Following from the above, the starting premise of teaching—whether in a classroom, or on a more global stage—might be this: 'no one wants to learn.' This premise generates an infinitely fertile question: how does one teach when no one wants to learn? Or, what performance does one bring to the classroom, to conversations, to demonstrations, to presentations, when one accepts that no one wants to learn? My autobiographical vignettes below react to this question.

Before I get to those stories, I respond to a prior question: why is it that no one wants to learn? Because learning is dangerous. Learning reveals ruptures within the self, alienates us from our loved ones and threatens the national identity. Indeed, like tectonic shifts, it shakes the social order. Usually we cannot risk such convulsions of the body.

However, the principle 'no one wants to learn' does not face the impossible. Rather it only freezes the status quo into permanence. Thus, its opposite must be present: we are driven by a desire to satiate our curiosity, to make life meaningful, to come to an accurate understanding of the actual world, and to relate to each other in some deeper way. This hidden, subordinated but equally powerful desire presents possibilities within the impossible. In sum: no one wants to learn but everyone has an irrepressible curiosity. Either without the other presents an easy exit. The principle that 'no one wants us to learn' tempts us into defeatist inaction, whereas a belief in the straightforwardness of learning takes us easily to imperial teaching projects. Only grasping them together opens us up to the impossible.

Misperformance

Backpack and blue jeans

It is Spring 1986. I am a graduate student teaching my first class at the University of Denver. Condoleezza Rice has already come and gone. I remember only that her dissertation defence was not memorable.

My classroom is a small, flat room that easily holds the ten of us. I sit cross-legged on the table with my blue backpack next to me. The talking, the conversing and the interaction seem easy and natural. It goes well.

Nevertheless, I obsess, putting in 30 hours a week to the neglect of my dissertation. I give up the one pleasure of my graduate student life: lunch hour pick-up basketball games. At the end of the course, I am pleased, but three of the nine evaluations find the course mediocre; another three detail my failure. For days and weeks I cannot be consoled. My partner wonders what she has got herself into; the word 'dissertation' is already banned from the house and now *this*.

I take my disbelief and despondency to three mentors. Two of them offer advice: effective performance requires markers that produce distance. Replace the blue jeans and back pack with ties and a briefcase. Don't sit on the table.

Game theory

It's fall 1986. I am teaching three courses at the University of Colorado in Boulder. Despite three buses and a ninety-minute commute, my energy abounds.

I have spent the summer reading utterly lifeless textbooks after having lied to my adviser that I can deliver courses on International Relations. I am teaching five days a week and coming home only to prepare more lecture notes. I feel fortunate.

On the first day of classes, I arrive forty minutes early. Ready in tweed jacket and beige tie. I look west at the rock-faced mountains framed by the impeccably blue Colorado sky. I recall how many times I have hiked there. Heights and public speaking are my two great fears. Will a voice emerge from my throat in a few minutes? I am not sure. Then again, the mountains are no less daunting.

I enter the class now: 120 students fan out above and around me. They are eager. At the top are large windows where the ivy plays with the light. My lower torso is hidden by black tables with built in sinks. I am exposed from the waist up.

I summon my voice but there is nothing. Panic. I have no back-up plan. Then I hear a voice as it climbs up towards them. I recognize it as mine. I wonder who is speaking.

Weeks have gone by and, one by one, I am covering the various schools of International Relations theory. I have reams of lecture notes on yellow note pads. I relax; humour and stories emerge. They respond to the material and to my bodily presence. Then I arrive at the section on game theory.

I had problems with game theory. Still do. It reduces all human motivations to acultural and ahistorical rationalities. I think of it as a kind of epistemological Death Star threatening suffocation to the rebels. I take a deep breath, thinking that despite my Third World body, I owe this to them and to the profession. Game theory must be covered says the man in the tweed jacket.

Twenty minutes in, I look up and they are gone. Vacant eyes. Their spirits search for better engagement. Or is it that they sense that I myself am not really there? I stop. Seconds of silence feel like minutes. I am making a calculation. I say: 'You know, I hate game theory. I really think it's bullshit and I am not at all sure why I am presenting it.' They glance. I'm at a pivotal moment of my teaching career. 'To hell with it,' I say, 'no more game theory.' They re-embrace me. Afterwards, though, I cannot shake the question: was I responsible?

Body to body

It's the end of my advanced course on International Relations. The room has a stage three feet higher than the main room. Their eyes are level with my shoes and socks as I pace from wall to wall. After class, the semester done, a few of the 120 students come to the front of the class happy to convey their impressions. A thin young man with blue eyes and blonde hair cannot seem to express enough how much he enjoyed the course. Bereft of small talk, I ask: 'what did you like?'

I know what I want him to say: it was my visionary syllabus that combined International Relations theory with issues of global political economy; my meticulous and insightful lectures; my perfect balance between script and improvisation; and, most important, how the sequence of topics all developed up into a holistic and exact overview of International Relations. Overcoming my desire to answer my own question, I keep pressing him to articulate. Exasperated, he says finally: 'It was you. I liked you, okay?' Disappointed, I let him go. I am befuddled and angry. What about my precision, my effort, my skill?

For years I have turned over his comment. I think I understand what he tried to convey. If teaching is possible at all, it occurs from body to body. It is not the books, nor the ideas. We teach with our moving bodies and with little else.

Faint praise

I work myself into an emotional pitch, building a sax solo as Coleman Hawkins or Dexter Gordon might do. As my voice reaches a crescendo it breaks—as Archie Shepp or Pharoah Sanders might do. At the apex of my solo, I deliver a witty and disdainful jab at an abstract villain. It is not my meaning but my sound they absorb. As I dislodge the scream caught in my throat the room bursts into applause. Random occurrence, I think, like a hail storm. I ignore it.

It happens again. Different stage and different audience but the same performance and result. Easy, unearned, dangerous. 'This can never happen again', I mutter as I glare at my feet.

Love the one you're with

The following spring I have a lighter load: 120 students but only one class. My anger carries over. I translate the success of the previous semester to mean that I am too easy, too populist, not serious. Time for a new performance: the jaded professor who accuses students of wasting planetary resources. I prick them with condescending jibes.

Five weeks into the course I receive a letter from a student who sits in the front left, near the fifteen-foot windows facing north. She is short, wearing glasses and gravitas. She writes: 'there are five of us in the front who do the readings, never miss class, take good notes, and want to learn. Could you stop your bitching and teach us?' I read that letter twenty times. It saves me.

Learning silence

I am at Syracuse University, having unwillingly traded 320 days of sunshine for eternal clouds, cold and wind. I am teaching two sections of a graduate course on International Relations theory—thirty students per section. The morning goes well, always. However, the afternoon section replies to my thirty-minute presentations with a Dada-esque silence. My frustration moves me into crisis mode. I have just read Henry Kariel's brilliant essay on teaching, titled 'Becoming Political'. I try his methods. I become comfortable with silence; I welcome silence; I hone my ears to its textures.

Discussion ensues because they cannot bear the silence and I outlast them with my new techniques, but my posture lacks anything productive. We are miserable. I hate this class forever.

The coup

The Kariel piece has me thinking radical pedagogy. My student Mary Markowicz worries for me. She senses my negative self-assessment in our Third World politics seminar. She shores up my flagging confidence by lending me two books by Paulo Freire. I read. She and he set me on the path to theorizing the teaching body.

Most of the thirty students and I sit on the floor in a circle. We remove all the chairs. I enjoy the pleasures of silence. Some weeks into the course, three of the students stage a coup, because, as I learned later, a teacher-less space readily generates teachers. They announce they will be running things—democratically, of course, indeed far more democratically, they are sure, than I had run them. I cannot contemplate a fascist counter-coup. Also, I am intrigued by the danger, novelty and anxiety their intervention invokes. This will be a great adventure, I think.

Some two-thirds of the students privately express their displeasure with the new regime. We arrange a second three-hour meeting every week in students' apartments. These are cramped and heterogeneous spaces. I re-accept my authority and we follow the syllabus.

News travels fast across some segments of the campus. A supportive anthropology professor allows me not so much to explain as to express myself. My chair also calls me in: 'I am tired,' he says, 'of the fallout from your experiments.' As I absorb the admonishment I note his body seems more pleased than tired.

War! What is it good for!

It is spring of 1991 and I am teaching 'Politics of South Asia'. The room is square with no stage. The walls are sodden with thousands of lectures. There are windows but no view. I have no qualifications for the course but my Pakistani origins seem sufficient. At some cost, I have said 'no' to those who would reduce me to a native informant. How then have I said 'yes' to this course?

The Gulf War is battering my unexamined assumptions about scholarship. Do I incorporate the war into my class? Do I declare my partisanship? What is my responsibility?

I cannot locate my duty. I lose my temper and yell at the fifty or so students. Perhaps it's something about their complicity in Iraq's destruction. Afterwards, in my basement office, I think: I've lost them, I've been irresponsible, and I am a terrible teacher. We make it to the end of the course, somehow. I dread the evaluations. Many of the students mention my eruption as the turning point of the course. I am surprised. They did not experience my flare up and melt down as wholly negative. I call a few of students into my office and ask them to explain. They say: 'that's when we knew you had something at stake.' When bodies speak, more is heard then what is said.

This class comes with a second story. A paper makes the following argument: if the British had improved their communication skills and paid more attention to India's culture they would have been able to sustain their empire. Had the British taken the author's suggestions, they might still be there today. Not the irony of Monty Python but the bad faith of an aid concert.

I slap down an 'F'.

I get up. I walk around the stone pillars of Maxwell Hall a few times. What shall I say in my comments? I sit on the paper for a few days and cross out the grade. How can I fail an effort that portends sincerity? Also, though, how can I let this pass? What can I do? It finally comes to me: make my chasm visible. I will ask her to read the paper to the class, hoping they will provide the well thought-out critique that my censored scream cannot.

She reads the paper. All but five of the students agree with her. The dissenting five, I can see, burn with fury but are unable to express their anger. My rage doubles. I leave that scene stumped, utterly confounded. I consider resigning.

Years later, that defeat prepared me when Michael Walzer—a leading figure in our field and counsel to the prince—made a similar argument about the US occupation of Iraq. I knew what to say. I asked him if he thought we were living the 'colonial present'.[3]

The Blues come from Mali

I plead with Assistant Provost Dr Tanya Saunders to include me in the planning committee to stage a series of concerts and lectures on the music of the African diaspora. At each meeting, Dr Saunders hints we need a course on the music of the African diaspora. My ears do not hear because I have every reason to believe she is calling to our committee's four music faculty.

I finally surmise the obvious: the only response to her call will be mine. However, now I face a problem: I don't play an instrument, I can't read music and I have no musical training. All I have is my pilgrimage to jazz giants and a devotion to the music.

To decrease my teaching anxiety, I sit in on my friend Steve Pond's 'Survey of Jazz', course at Cornell. Bad mistake. Steve spent most of his life singing in a choir, most of his life dancing, most of his life as a jazz drummer. Academia is a mid-life fling. As I witnessed Steve dance, sing and lecture—all at the same time—I thought: I can't do that; not in this lifetime.

Despite my fears, I offer the course. The balance is perfect. I facilitate but they can see that I am learning from them. A coup, but bloodless. My singular worry concerns whether I have a right to claim myself as a teacher in the first place. I do not realize I am suffocating my students as I drone on about my unease.

At mid-semester, Kara Pangburn storms into my office. Kara has taken a few courses with me, she plays the French horn but gave it up upon arriving at Ithaca College, and she is weeks away from graduation. She screams at me: 'This course is too important for me to have you fuck it up. You need to get out of our way and let us do the work.' Her face is so red, her investment so palpable, that I cannot but sit and smile. I am released.

Slacker's paradise

It's fall 1996 and I am teaching my first four courses at Ithaca College, including three sections of Ideas and Ideologies. The requirements are a mid-term and final paper, or perhaps it was three essays. I barely recall that sleep-deprived semester because my wife and I were submerged by waves of fevers and infections brought home by our four-year-old and transmitted to our six-month-old.

It's the last week, and somehow we have survived the semester. One of the students walks in to applaud the course. I don't recognize him. Always suspicious, I ask him what he enjoyed. He liked that he could turn in two (or was it three) papers and never attend class. Alarm bells ring for me. He informs me of his many calls to friends who search for just such courses. Oh yeah, I think, *that's* the list I want my name on.

I start redesigning the course even as he speaks. I plead with him to tell his friends *not* to enrol in my courses. He is perplexed and asks why I would mess with such a good thing.

Surprise

In confessing my misperformances, I want to suggest that risking mistakes turns the classroom into a living, breathing, experimental, experience-filled place. Not a smooth utopia, nor a *terra nullius* absent of rifts, but a place where the already riven can be recognized, addressed and performed upon.

Allow me to zoom out and return to the larger frame. Thucydides, like the rest of the ancient Greeks, believed in a cyclic theory of history. I read his famous Melian dialogue as a confession about the impossibility of learning from history. He seems to accept that while we can uncover history's patterns, we cannot change them. Yet Thucydides performs his confession for us. Adam Smith believes that the public good appears if we each act in our self-interest. Individuals and the state need not engage in learning or in teaching because a providential invisible hand bridges the gulf between the narrow interests of citizens and the public good. Hegel, who is a student of Smith and the Scottish Enlightenment, believes not in the invisible hand but in the human capacity to learn—even if such learning comes too late. The limits of market activity, he says, teach citizens their need for the state. Self-interest begets public ethics—not automatically, but through a process of struggle and social strife. I gesture towards these giants of Western political theory because we can read their work as a commentary on the possibilities of learning and teaching: a commentary, that is, on how learning comes into being—if it comes into being.

If so, then my discussion of classroom performance is hardly tangential. We perform and misperform on the stage of social theory and political philosophy. More important, when we discuss teaching and learning we are never far from the impossibilities of life itself. In a way we know this, and this is why we have placed a taboo on the question of learning's impossibility. Exposing this taboo, like exposing any taboo, does little more than strengthen it. Enter art. Tragic performance and earnest misperformance encircle the real. They create just enough slight-of-hand distance to bypass our repressive triggers while creating just enough space to lure us into impossibilities.

Every performance is a misperformance, I can say with confidence. Yet the body moves; it re-performs, searching. Perhaps this small miracle can sustain us.

Notes

1. R.G. Collingwood, *Essay on Philosophical Method*, Oxford: Oxford University Press, 2008; *The Idea of Nature*, Oxford: Oxford University Press, 1960; and *The Idea of History*, Oxford: Oxford University Press, 1994.
2. Henry Kariel, 'Becoming Political', in *Teaching Political Science: The Professor and the Polity*, ed. Vernon van Dyke, Atlantic Highlands, NJ: Humanities Press, 1977: 129.
3. The phrase is Derek Gregory's from *The Colonial Present: Afghanistan, Palestine, Iraq*, Malden, MA: Wiley-Blackwell, 2004.

Part IV
Bodies politic and performative

10 Performing audience

The politics of relation and participation in *Coriolan/us*

Patrick Primavesi

This chapter investigates the role of the audience in *Coriolan/us*, directed by Mike Pearson and Mike Brookes for National Theatre Wales as part of the World Shakespeare Festival and 2012 Cultural Olympiad. Beginning with an examination of how Shakespeare's play reflects the public and the political in relation to performance and theatre, the particular approach of the production project is outlined: to explore the political impact of *Coriolanus* today, almost 60 years after Bertolt Brecht's attempt to redefine the role of the people and the audience in an epic reading of this play. Integrating some interview and other material from Pearson and Brookes, the essay analyses the performance as a practice-based research investigation into the relational process that enables the spectators to experience their 'being singular/plural' (Jean-Luc Nancy)—co-constituted in relation to others. By examining the organization and deployment of space, speech and screen technologies in *Coriolan/us*, the essay seeks to interrogate the performance as a theatrical experiment which challenges the idea of the public sphere (as a place of discourse and political subjectivation) between crowd, audience and individual positions.

Coriolanus, a play in public

Compared to Shakespeare's more famous and more frequently staged dramas, *The Tragedy of Coriolanus* remains somehow problematic. Although it shares the realm of mythical greatness, heroic rigour and tragic conflict with plays such as *Julius Caesar* and *King Lear*, *Antony and Cleopatra*, *Hamlet* and *Macbeth*, this piece was often criticized or even scandalized for its lack of moral coherence and the absence of any didactic perspective that could help the audience to judge about the central figure, its character and its fate.[1] Spectators or readers may still feel lost in a conflict that seems not only to be unsolvable but also incompatible with the tragic model of cathartic reaction and assimilation. The way in which Shakespeare transformed his source material is quite unconventional, placing the Roman people and their tribunes in a central position. Based mainly on Thomas North's translation of Vitruv's report on a legendary king of the early Roman republic,[2] this first dramatic version of Coriolanus's triumph and fall clearly exceeds the conventions of

(Greek) tragedy in highlighting the class struggle between plebeians and patricians with theatrical craftsmanship and sometimes even with elements of comedy and travesty.[3] Some new aspects are added to the story, and the dramaturgical framework is focused on the conflict between warlord Caius Martius and the people of Rome. An outline of the plot, paying attention to the stage action as implied by Shakespeare's text,[4] will indicate the particular potential of the play text that Pearson and Brookes identified and sought to reinforce by experimenting with the space of the public and the movement of the audience itself.

In the opening scene, the nature of the political conflict dividing the world of the play is exposed quickly and directly. On a street in Rome 'a company of mutinous citizens, with staves, clubs, and other weapons' enters, as the unusually precise stage directions of the play describe it.[5] They express their anger about the exploitative policy of the Roman senate and its wealthy members, arguing that it would raise the price of bread and exacerbate the plebeians' poverty and hardship (for economical and political reasons). Then Caius Martius's friend Menenius Agrippa enters and tells his famous parable of the belly that supplies the other parts of the body, as a symbol for the charitable function of the senate. While seemingly convincing and pacifying the citizens, this speech has an ironic undertone and ignores the real suffering of the people. In fact, the logic of Menenius's story does not apply to the actual situation, because the unfair speculation on prices and the delayed distribution of food are the concrete reasons for the protest. Moreover, he finishes his tale by bluntly accusing the first citizen of being a rebellious rascal who would only provoke a foolish battle between 'Rome and her rats' (I/1).

Now Martius appears and introduces himself by insulting the citizens as 'dissentious rogues', demonstrating his contempt for the people. He behaves exactly like the angry voices portrayed him beforehand, as 'chief enemy to the people' and 'a very dog to the commonalty'. The assumption that all his virtuous military actions for the city were driven only by the proud ambitions of himself and his mother Volumnia, together with the brutal verdict, 'Let us kill him, and we'll have corn at our own price', anticipate the agonistic development of the play. The *scenario* is already there, and Martius acts according to the projections and purposes of his environment. Paradoxically, this man of action and unshakable will is performing not only the intentions of his mother, but also those of his direct opponents. Throughout the play he is presented, as it were, from the outside: hardly ever through self-reflection and soliloquies, but mostly in controversies and as an object of reports and projections. A main element of his character, besides his pride, military prowess and aggression, is his repeated refusal 'to play a part, to act politically'.[6] In fact, the drama reflects its own theatricality by constantly producing scenes of external judgement, report and test, where the figure of Coriolanus is staged, directed and shaped as phantasm and fetish of others' political positions.

The extraordinary dramatic dynamic of the play is based in the movement of the people, rushing forward again and again, mostly in one direction: 'to the Capitol!', as the repeated slogan of the coming uprising goes. As indicated

Performing audience 163

by the very first line of the play, many scenes take place only as a temporary halt of this move: 'Before we proceed any further, hear me speak.' After the First Citizen's intervention, Menenius Agrippa and then Caius Martius create further scenes of attention to something spectacular rather than situations of dialogue and mutual exchange. Messengers prolong this series of speeches in front of the public. At first a message arrives from the senate that has granted to the people their right to elect tribunes who are able to intercede against any decision of the municipal council. The situation is changed by the messenger who reports the actual threat of the Volscian army approaching the city of Rome. Towards the end of the first scene, the movement of the people to the Capitol is taken over by a military mobilization led by Martius and other nobles, with the rebels suddenly retreating, as the stage direction explicitly notes: 'Citizens steal away.'[7]

The following scenes underscore the importance of *opinion* as medium of the people's interest, both for the tribunes who are suspicious about Martius's position in the present action (end of I/1), and for the noble women who are urging each other to appear in public, to perform their roles as proud patricians (I/3). Meanwhile the battle of Corioli takes place in which Martius himself appears as conqueror of the Volscian city, asking his soldiers to fear less their person 'than an ill report' (I/6). After his triumphant victory he seems too modest to stand any acclamations, but in fact he behaves as arrogantly and proudly as the tribunes had foreseen, counting on his 'soaring insolence' (II/1) to undermine his political intent. At the Capitol, in front of senators and tribunes, the highly praised 'Coriolanus', by now almost

Figure 10.1 Richard Lynch, John Rowley and Gerald Tyler
Source: Mark Douet, National Theatre Wales

approved as Consul, tries to avoid the ceremonial exposition of his wounds to the people. This necessary ritual performance at the forum, although understood on both sides as spectacle and role play, fails to deliver its performative function and thereby marks the turning point of his career. Because he cannot hide his contempt for the citizens and even mocks them in begging for their voices, he acts exactly in the way that helps the tribunes to accuse him of 'manifest treason' (III/1). The following trial enacts a repetition of this spectacle. Although his mother Volumnia and his former general Cominius have tried to make him play his part better and even try to 'prompt' him like a bad comedian, he only acts according to the needs of the tribunes that manage to provoke him, to 'put him to choler straight' and to present him in front of the public *audience* as 'enemy to the people and his country' (III/3).

Having finally lost his chance of accommodation and having been banished from the city, he changes sides and promises Aufidius, the leader of the Volscians, to help him to destroy Rome. Immediately he is accepted and praised by Aufidius and the Volscian people whom he will lead against Rome: 'He is their god: he leads them like a thing/Made by some other deity than nature' (IV/6). The only force that can stop him from his disastrous revenge is another spectacle: his mother, wife and son kneeling in front of him to beg for his mercy.[8] Once again his performance is ruined: 'Like a dull actor now, I have forgot my part and I am out' (V/3). Confronting him with the vision of her and her family dying in the burning Rome, Volumnia lets him fall into *silence* and change his mind, both knowing that this new treason against the Volscians would cost his life. Once again in a public place, he is accused by

Figure 10.2 Matthew Thomas, Richard Lynch and Jonny Glynn
Source: Mark Douet, National Theatre Wales

Aufidius and killed by conspirators before he is able to defend himself and to justify his behaviour. Yet, immediately after his death Coriolanus is mourned and (like Hamlet) raised high upon the stage. At least to the corpse the honours shall be paid for which the living Caius Martius has so desperately fought. This sudden change may come as something of a surprise, but it continues a process of depersonalization that Martius has experienced already: being treated as a thing, as a weapon, as an object. Therefore, the same Aufidius who has just stood on the corpse of the assassinated traitor, in the very next moment commands his soldiers to expose the dead hero for a mourning ceremony that would give him 'a noble memory' (V/6). The body of Caius Martius has become an object, an 'empty' sign that can be staged, directed and interpreted by his opponents according to their actual purposes. The irreducible ambivalence in the figure of the (untragic) hero in *Coriolanus*[9] is an important issue in particular when the relation between performance and politics is at stake. Shakespeare's drama raises the question of the political in a complex way that is not confined to the representation of state politics, conflicts of power and influence. As the outline of the plot has shown, *Coriolanus* is a play about politics *as* performance, about the public itself as a scene and a theatre, moving through the city of Rome. This movement includes the experience of performing and of becoming a spectacle, but also of becoming a spectator, a witness and a possible participant.

Political impact: ' ... then all power to the audience!'

Learned spectators in Shakespeare's audience may have sensed the irony in the abrupt ending, knowing from Plutarch and Livy about the development of the historical situation: the Volscians were finally defeated and subjugated to the state of Rome that was just rising in its power which would last for the following centuries.[10] Probably for everyone in the audience of the first performances the political topicality of the play would have been obvious: the experience of the Midland uprising (1607–08) and other political turmoil may even have inspired this dramatization of the legendary figure of Coriolanus.[11] By linking the experience of political conflicts in his own times with the early history of the Roman republic, Shakespeare chose a referential framework that was quite common in the Renaissance. However, the political impact and importance of the play derives not only from its theme, but rather from the way in which it treats the representation of the people's interest by the tribunes, and in particular the *conflict* between individual and community. The fact that the hero is killed in the end as a traitor to both sides marks the final result of this political parable about the strong individual as a necessary element of a democratic state which, at the same time, is also its worst enemy from within. Coriolanus, as the figure can be interpreted today, is not just an isolated traitor and therefore an individual case, but a stand-in for the individual in relation to the theatre of politics, and in this sense a political figure. Coriolan is *us*, and at the same time, as the title of the performance by Pearson and Brookes precisely indicates, remains divided from *us*. On the other hand remains the question about the identity, unity or diversity of the people: who are they? *Us?* The very *us* divided from Coriolanus? Is a crowd an anonymous mass, an assembly of individuals, or a *political* subject as such?

As Mike Pearson has underscored, politics is the 'overarching theme' of the play, which appears today as 'a fascinating counterpoint to current political events—with their unreliable leaderships, ad-hoc factions and coalitions, fleeting allegiances and shifting loyalties, civic uncertainties and disturbances, military adventurism and fledgling democracies'.[12] The challenge of the play and its contemporaneousness is based in the uncomfortable and unsettling way it confronts us with the problems of democratic representation, but these complex relations should not be reduced to obvious thematic parallels with this or that particular political situation. Sceptical about earlier attempts to strengthen the topicality (for instance, the film adaptation by Ralph Fiennes that is located in the internecine Balkan wars of the 1990s), Pearson and Brookes refrain from all too obvious linkage of the play with the 2012 uprisings in Egypt and Syria. For them, it is the very ambivalence in Shakespeare's play with regards to the people's movement that enables contemporary spectators to draw some parallels to our times, to the so-called Arab Spring revolutions or to the Occupy movement. However, the performance leaves these associations to the audience, avoiding direct allusion to a specific current conflict.

Pearson and Brookes's *Coriolan/us* let the spectators experience for themselves that the relevance of the play is based on the analysis of communal movement in times of protest and rebellion and, at the same time, on the theatrical structures and functions in all public action. In this sense, the political impact of this project is closely related to the politics of staging and performance inherent to Shakespeare's play already. It is important to note that the play text for this performance[13] partially includes the version of Bertolt Brecht (in Ralph Manheim's English translation).[14] Brecht's approach to *Coriolanus* is as complicated as it is revealing: He could not finish his version before his death in 1956. However, as he was fascinated by the play as early as 1917, and quite fond of Erich Engel's production in Berlin in 1926 (with Fritz Kortner), it is not an exaggeration to see *Coriolanus* as an important source for Brecht's understanding of an *epic* theatre. He commented that the changes made in his own adaptation of the play in the early 1950s tended to reinforce the people's resistance. Shortly before his death he thought it would also be possible to stage the play almost untouched, thereby acknowledging the epic quality of Shakespeare's text. It seems that he regarded his adaptation partially as a test case for the ability of the German Democratic Republic (GDR) (after the workers' uprising in 1953) to allow for a critical reflection on the relationship between leading politicians and the masses in a socialist system (a key issue for Günther Grass's anti-Brechtian piece 'Die Plebejer proben den Aufstand' from 1966). The version performed in 1962 (Frankfurt/Main), 1964 (Berlin) and 1971 (London) by Brecht's students Manfred Wekwerth and

Joachim Tenschert became somehow canonical, but has reduced the complexity of his approach (also by filling the gaps of his version with the romantic translation of Dorothea Tieck).[15] In fact, Brecht's approach should be taken not so much as another version of Shakespeare's text, but as a fragmentary way of reading it for the theatre, rather challenging than maintaining dramaturgical and political positions.

An awareness of this most interesting case (which finally manifests the modernity of Shakespeare's text) brought Pearson and Brookes in their own production to a new modus of re-framing the text.[16] They focused on the first scene, which Brecht had also identified as pivotal in a dramaturgical consideration of the crucial points of his interpretation, examining whether there is a reliable unity among the citizens due to their misery, or whether, for the same reason, they are divided by individual interests. In 1951 Brecht realized that the *unity of contradictions* ('Einheit der Gegensätze') would have to be studied as a precondition for any staging of the first scene (as the basis for the whole play).[17] What he reflected in his approach towards a *Dialectics at the theatre* ('Dialektik auf dem Theater'), had been partly demonstrated by the way in which he lets the citizens in the first scene talk explicitly about their common interest, and also in the discussion with Menenius Agrippa. However, as he stated later on, he felt he had overdone it. Therefore, in taking only a few parts of Brecht's 'clarifying' changes, Pearson and Brookes acted in accordance with Brecht's later insight into the dialectical potential of Shakespeare's text. The instructive discussion 'Study of the First Scene of Shakespeare's "Coriolanus"' (1953–55) indicates that he became more and more confident about the chances of the staging process ('Inszenierung') to expose the open problems and ambiguities of the original text. This made it possible to develop, contrary to all stereotypes about an over-didactic authority of epic theatre, a different attitude towards the audience as well:

B: But there must be no playing down of the contribution which the Volscian's attack makes to the establishment of the Tribunate; it's the main reason. Now you must start building and take everything into account.
W: The plebeians ought to share Agrippa's astonishment at this concession.
B: I don't want to decide. I also don't know if that can be acted without text, by pure miming. Moreover, if our group of plebeians includes a particular person, it might no longer be seen as representing half of the plebeian Rome, as a part representing the whole. But I note your astonishment and inquisitiveness as you move around within this play and within these complex events on a particular morning in Rome, where there is much that a sharp eye can pick out. And certainly if you can find clues to these events, then all power to the audience![18]

In the discussion (the initials indicate at least the names of the participants: B for Brecht, W for Manfred Wekwerth, R for Käthe Rülicke and P for Peter Palitzsch),[19] Brecht insists on the point that theatrical solutions can only be based on the insight that *all* the questions about the attitude of the plebeians are still unanswered, which means that they have to be raised in the performance. Transforming the political slogan 'All power to the people!' into 'All power to the audience!', Brecht suggests the decisive step towards an open dramaturgy that would enable and provoke the spectators really to think and decide for themselves.

However, as Jacques Rancière has argued, this very act of empowerment and enabling implies already a certain kind of paternalism and manipulation. The old political problem of a revolution 'from above', imposed on the masses by intellectuals or functionaries, seems to lurk behind the well-minded attempt of theatre makers to *activate* their spectators. This very gesture of activation remains problematic because it implies and requires passivity, although spectatorship may include a whole range of active behaviour. Therefore, Rancière introduces the notion of a truly *emancipated spectator* in a sense that goes beyond the Brechtian approach of activation:

> We have not to turn spectators into actors. We have to acknowledge that any spectator already is an actor of his own story and that the actor also is the spectator of the same kind of story. We have not to turn the ignorant into learned persons, or, according to a mere scheme of overturn, make the student or the ignorant the master of his masters ... The crossing of the borders and the confusion of the roles should not lead to some sort of 'hypertheatre' turning spectatorship into activity by turning representation to presence. On the contrary, it should question the theatrical privilege of living presence and bring the stage back to a level of equality with the telling of a story or the writing and the reading of a book. It should be the institution of a new stage of equality, where the different kinds of performances would be translated into one another. In all those performances in fact, it is a matter of linking what one knows with what one does not know, of being at the same time performers who display their competences and visitors or spectators who are looking for what those competences may produce in a new context, among unknown people.[20]

Before examining more in detail the extent to which Pearson and Brookes's *Coriolan/us* succeeded in creating such a 'new stage of equality', the issue of the audience itself should be considered further. Rancière's formula of being 'among unknown people' comes close to what Jean-Luc Nancy has described as the genuine situation of theatre spectators: that they are assembled together, becoming plural, as singular beings.[21] The particular community of an audience in the theatre can therefore be described as having the status of a being among others that are unknown and still at a certain distance; the spectacle and the actors remain at a remove, however close they approach physically to the body of the spectator. What may appear as a theoretical and meta-theatrical question becomes quite concrete in the context of Shakespeare's *Coriolanus* and its reanimation by Brecht. He sensed already that the question of the people's identity in the first scene is directly related to the question of the audience—in this particular play much more than in other theatrical works (not only by Shakespeare).

The way in which the citizens are presented is almost as complicated as the mode of appearance of Caius Martius himself. In a similar, almost reciprocal way, 'the people' of the crowd are attributed and thereby created by others: whereas they introduce themselves just as 'poor', they are characterized first as 'mutinous', mocked as 'honest neighbours', then insulted as 'dissentious rogues' and 'rabble', 'ridiculous subjects' and 'beastly plebeians'. However, there is also the important moment in the Forum, when the citizens ask themselves about their appearance as a 'many-headed multitude' (II/3), just before giving their individual voices to Coriolanus: 'He's to make his requests by particulars, wherein every one of us has a single honour, in giving him our own voices with our own tongues; therefore follow me, and I'll direct you how you shall go by him' (II/3). Like Coriolanus himself, the people perform as they are directed and 'staged', either by leading citizens or by the tribunes that manipulate them. Thus their real interest, identity and probable behaviour remains volatile and unpredictable, their appearance as chaotic mass seemingly confirming the picture constantly highlighted by Coriolanus: 'the mutable, rank-scented many' and the 'Hydra' that can never be seized (III/1).

At the end of the dramaturgical discussion, when Brecht and his collaborators focus again on the heterogeneity both of the oppressed and the oppressor's classes as the main result of an advanced staging, they finally reflect their overall aims in relation to the identity and the potential of the audience:

R: Is it for the sake of these perceptions that we are going to do the play?
B: Not only. We want to have and to communicate the fun of dealing with a slice of illuminated history. And to have first-hand experience of dialectics.
P: Isn't the second point a considerable refinement, reserved for a handful of connoisseurs?
B: No. Even with popular ballads or the showbooth panoramas at fairs the simple people (who are so far from simple) love stories of the rise and fall of great men, of eternal change, of the ingenuity of the oppressed, of the potentialities of mankind. And they search for the truth that is 'behind it all'.[22]

The 'people' in the audience appear as a phantasm as much as the citizens of Rome do. Whether the spectators would be united in the process of the performance into a kind of community, or rather divided by controversial opinions, remains an open question. Of necessity, one might add, because it is exactly the question of the public that links the discourse on the Roman people in the opening scene of the play to the question of what kind of theatre would be needed to install the equality wherein the various stories and performances in the common space can be translated into each other. As historically informed interpretations of the play have shown, we can imagine the earliest performances of *Coriolanus* in Shakespeare's times on different stage levels (probably at the Blackfriars Theatre), which must have allowed the actors, in particular Caius Martius, Menenius Aggripa and the tribunes Brutus and Sicinius Velutus, to speak closer to the spectators, on their level and 'among them'.[23] However, there is still a split between the theatre audience and the people of Rome, because all scenes of the masses, the political turmoil such as the fighting scenes, are indicated by the stage directions (and reported by messengers) to come 'from inside', meaning the off-scene behind the stage entrance doors. For a contemporary staging, these conventions seem hard to cope with, perhaps even unnecessary. Thus the question of the public sphere remains as a crucial point and perhaps the main challenge for any approach to staging *Coriolanus* after (and with) Brecht.

Coriolan/us: experimental set-up

Reflecting on the possible ways in which theatre may still, or again, be connected to a public sphere, leads inevitably to the fact that the public today is influenced, controlled and maintained to a high extent by technical media. Pearson mentions this context as another impulse for the production: 'A conjoined world of celebrity and surveillance: of constant media attention and intrusion, of embedded transmission, of improvised recording and uploading, of covert monitoring ... '[24] The dramaturgical structure of the play, in which Coriolanus is hardly alone but constantly acting in public, with most of the scenes take place outside in the presence of the people, may be difficult for small indoor theatres and rather calls for big spaces and the employment of media technology. The co-appearance of Caius Martius and the Roman people, configured as a mutual process of projected images and constructed phantasms, also suggests the need for a contemporary production to work on mediated images, to deploy live camera and screens. Last but not least, the situation of the people, moving and being moved in a crowd, and the battle scenes outside of Rome, produce obstructions of sight, hardly an overview (however spectacular the fighting scenes of the play may have been choreographed in earlier productions). Here as well the employment of technical media seems helpful to cope with the difficulty that, in Shakespeare, the people of the crowd don't really appear as such.[25]

The performance *Coriolan/us* does not take place in a conventional theatre building, but in a huge space without fixed boundaries between actors and spectators—an aircraft hangar at RAF St Athan in the Vale of Glamorgan, South Wales. Its siting in this location can be regarded as the most important decision made by Pearson and Brookes, enabling the audience to encounter the performance as an aesthetic-political 'event'.[26] This enabled the production to extend the experience of becoming part of a crowd, physically integrating the audience of the show into the often confusing situation of the moving people, thus allowing the spectators to embody the people of Rome (and also of

Corioli and Antium on the side of the Volscians). However, this embodiment means participation not in the direct sense of becoming Roman (that is, an act of pretence, of acting), but rather as a process of getting involved, being driven into something without the conscious effort to behave as someone else, and also without the illusion of really being a Roman or Volscian citizen or of being regarded as such. Instead of symbolically belonging to a played community and to a community of players, the spectators stay what they are: onlookers. However, their physical involvement into the space of action opens up a different experience, making them feel that spectatorship is not confined to a distanced and immobile, seemingly 'neutral' position as in the theatre spaces we are still used to regarding as normal.

For such an experiment, Shakespeare's *Coriolanus* provides particularly fruitful material, because, as argued previously, the play analyses and presents the public (appearing both as crowd and as an assembly of individual citizens) as performance and politics as theatre. The real spectators of the Pearson and Brookes performance become involved not by engaging in any histrionic action (playing someone or something), but by their very spectatorship, which is—in reversal—to be experienced not as something bound to theatre, but as our everyday life's basic condition. Therefore it is important to keep in mind that the decision for the experiment with the people (to use the spectators as spectators outside *and* inside of the play) went along with the idea to transmit pictures from within the crowd and from other scenes onto screens, where everyone could see from another perspective the various parts of the performance that often simultaneously developed in the space.

So, finally, what about the event itself, the spatial and technical organization of the experiment, the set-up? How did it look and sound? How did it feel to become involved as conscious spectator?[27] How did the concept work out practically? At least some background information about the team and the context will be helpful to understand the preconditions and the shape of this project. For the two directors, Mike Pearson, well known as former co-director of Brith Gof theatre company (also dramaturge of the performance),[28] and Mike Brookes, artist and designer (working in collaboration on this performance with scenographer Simon Banham), it was clear from their earlier co-productions that they would locate this work in a space with a unique size and atmosphere. The production team's last work, a new version of Aeschylus's tragedy *The Persians* (2010), also took place in an extraordinary setting—a military training ground from the Cold War era with a replica 'German village' in the Welsh Brecon Beacons national park. Having arrived by shuttle bus to this otherwise inaccessible area, the spectators were involved in a procession, with old cars and a funeral march for the former Persian King Darius. The tragedy about the historical defeat of the Persian army against a small Greek fleet was located in this fake village, mainly in a half-cut house for indoor combat training in front of a grandstand for army audiences. The event transformed the site at least temporarily into a theatre of memory, playing with a tacit knowledge of the place that could be experienced during the performance.[29]

As part of a whole season of location work, *The Persians* had been produced by the National Theatre of Wales (NTW), which invited the directors again for 2012 to produce a Shakespeare play, co-funded by the World Shakespeare Festival for the Cultural Olympiad, co-operating with the Royal Shakespeare Company. This context provided the directors with a large, professional apparatus that could cope with technical and organizational challenges even more demanding than in their former work. The choice of *Coriolanus* was not difficult, as Pearson had thought about it for a long time as offering a 'touchtone for physical theatre' (being aware of a certain interest in this play in fascist Germany and of Brecht's interpretation as well). After decades of site-specific performance work there was an ambition 'to look at it through all the techniques Mike and I have developed', in a contemporary perspective: 'not a show on the Arab Spring, although reflecting some political developments.'[30] For many reasons (their experience with performance in urban space, large-scale works and processions with crowds, and the practical reflection of surveillance technology in the public domain), Pearson and Brookes seemed well prepared to meet the particular challenges of the play, using it to develop their own politics of the appearance of a public in performance.

Thus Mike Pearson reflects the contemporaneity of the play, and Mike Brookes sees the 'publicness' of the space as one of the main impulses of this work:

> Why Coriolan/us? Because it is always unsettling: seeming to reflect the time in which we live without offering any easy solutions. Because it is always contemporary: ever challenging of our beliefs, demanding of us that we think politically, again.[31]
>
> In our imaginings, from the inception of this work, Coriolan/us was always going to unfold amongst a crowd, as it moved and flowed around the open public space of this event. Act following act, one thing leading another, the rolling consequences of our choices and reactions accumulating as they ripple on through the body and structure of a social forum constituted by all those present.[32]

Looking for an indoor location big enough to appear as 'public space', Pearson and Brookes first thought of a film studio. When this plan failed, they discovered the former military hangar of St Athan, which in fact seems even more appropriate for this project. Devised as a bunker for airplanes in the 1930s, with a curved roof construction and an area 90 metres long and 50 metres wide, this space conveys an atmosphere of technology and industrial warfare.

August 2012. After the big entrance gate has opened, a crowd of up to 300 spectators per night disperse in the front part of the hangar. This is Rome, while the back part of the hangar, less than a third of the area, is the territory of the Volscians, separated by a double wall of concrete blocks, with a wide passway in the middle. Suddenly a van drives into the crowd, beeping its horn, transporting two men of the people, the citizens (John Rowley and

Gerald Tyler). The spatial relations of this performance are condensed, resulting mainly from some fixed points of action: burned-out cars between the walls mark the zone of the civil wars; while the places of institutional power are confined to some empty caravans. As Pearson remarked, 'the most actual ideas of spaces came from the play itself': when he told Mike Brookes that for the domestic encounters of the play, they would need three enclosed spaces, his co-director just added 'or caravans', which turned out to be the best way of indicating private spaces within a public sphere.[33]

For instance, in the important 'close-up' scene with his family discussing appropriate behaviour in public, Coriolanus (Richard Lynch), his mother Volumnia (Rhian Morgan) and his wife Virgilia (Bethan Witcomb) can be seen by the spectators from outside through the windows of a small caravan (emptied of all interior fixtures, plastered and painted white, to provide enough light for the cameras and to maintain a certain neutrality of the atmosphere). The trial scene with the tribunes Junius Brutus (Chris Jared) and Sicinius Velutus (Nia Gwynne), takes place in the back of the van in which the citizens of the first scene have entered the space; and at the other end of the hangar, there is another little caravan housing Aufidius, general of the Volscians (Richard Harrington), playing silently with a model of the set during the long scenes where he is 'off stage'.

Some basic production decisions came out of necessity: because of the extreme echo in this place (more than 11 seconds) it was impossible to let the actors speak with their normal voices. A technical solution was found that strongly influenced the whole performance: the voice of the actors is transmitted via an equalizing

Figure 10.3 Richard Lynch and Jonny Glynn
Source: Mark Douet, National Theatre Wales

sound system and headphones to the spectators, who perceive them balanced and sometimes mixed with atmospheric music or background noises of the masses. For the actors it is difficult *not* to talk to all 300 people in the audience (as they would do normally), but only to their colleagues. For the spectators, the sound operates as an audioplay which enables them to follow the spoken lines without distraction even while moving around through the space. Another effect of mediation that balances the scale and allows the spectators to choose their position more freely is the use of video screens: with some hand cameras and two aerial cameras above the scene, the pictures of the actors within the moving crowd are constantly transferred to the two big monitors in the back part of the hangar above the playing zone. Pearson described the experience with the spectators' movements as something hard to imagine or plan in advance. A dispersed action would have caused dispersed attention: 'Incomprehensibility was a clue to the spatial organization, creating energy rather than perspective.'[34] Thus the spectators produced by themselves a specific distribution in space, different in each performance. This collective 'choreography' went along without any control, apart from some gestures by the citizens taking care that the cars could pass through the assembly of people. While the majority of the audience was rather strolling around, following the action, it was also possible to choose a position, even to take one of the folding chairs and to sit and just listen, or watch the screen images.

Being sometimes very close to the actors and yet listening to their voices through headphones produced a tension between a technically mediated and a physical experience, between distance and proximity or touch. In this regard, the audience of the play, for instance the people on the streets, was embodied by the spectators of the performance. The experiment with an embodied (and also *embedded*) audience[35] was based on this spatial and technical set-up ('Versuchsanordnung' in a Brechtian sense), and yet remained open to very different experiences due to the individual movement and the related perceptions of each spectator.

Relational theatre, audience in performance

After *The Persians*, and with respect to the context of the commission, it is no surprise that Pearson and Brookes have worked with a dramatic text again, challenging it with the methods of site-specific work. However, their new approach is neither text-based nor site-specific, but equally *text-related*, *site-related* and *audience-related*. The balance between these relations makes *Coriolan/us* paradigmatic for contemporary working methods beyond the post-dramatic theatre of the 1980s and 1990s.[36] It is not unlikely that the most advanced forms of experimental, devised and site-related performance will be able to generate a new kind of tradition for dramatic texts as well, reviving by change and transformation a different understanding of the drama as political *agon*.

Although there are many elements of postdramatic theatre aesthetics that could be analysed in this production, it is the use of space and technology

Figure 10.4 Richard Harrington
Source: Mark Douet, National Theatre Wales

that enables the audience to focus again on dialogue as the core element of dramatic texts. The whole audio sphere created by the performance, and the film technology with the tension between life film and projected action, reflect the structure of Shakespeare's play, which helps to realize its political impact. By integrating Brecht's approach to the performance of the public, the Pearson and Brookes production highlights not only the epic theatre in *Coriolanus*, but also some elements of the *learning play* ('Lehrstück'): the employment of mediation technology; the way in which the audience is 'used' beyond the traditional conventions of spectatorship; the confrontation of the citizens with the leader as an asocial individual; and the reflection of ritual behaviour, as in the manipulative strategies of the tribunes. When Coriolanus is exposed to the people who are testing his attitude towards them before giving him their voices (II/3), the political potential of rituals on stage becomes obvious, reflecting the ceremonial structure of trial, accusation and defence: as the hero is blindfolded,[37] the citizens are able to touch his skin, not so much to look for wounds and scars, but to inscribe a symbolic order physically onto the body of him who had always shown the greatest disgust and revulsion against the physical presence of the people.

The way in which the performance plays with the pathos of the conflict between the individual and the people is crucial to the political impact of this approach: it leaves just enough space to walk around, combining the elements of a process that thereby is freed from its tragic rigour. We may think here of Rancière's idea of an 'equal stage' for the mutual translation of stories and performances, but also of his notion of the shift between two tendencies of artistic practice in the second half of twentieth century. In the 1980s the *sublime* was discovered again as a quality of something incomprehensible, beyond representation and even beyond imagination, rejecting any direct comment on political contexts that had been so important for the arts in the decades before.[38] The main gesture for this tendency and its claim for a new kind of artistic politics had been the interruption of political engagement and debate in the traditional sense, in order to defend against the political instrumentalization of the realm of art, protecting it from becoming totally absorbed by the need to fulfil social and critical functions.[39] The other, more recent tendency appears as unspectacular, beyond the negativity in the aesthetics of the sublime, focusing more on context and relations, as the term *relational aesthetics* has been coined by Nicholas Bourriaud for some tendencies in the visual arts of the last decades.[40] Working collectively and the reflection of local and communal conflicts and resources have become a major issue for this kind of work.

Contemporary theatre, more or less based on texts and traditions of all kinds, is navigating between these two tendencies, in particular when it tries to redefine what might be (the) political (again) in theatre and performance, beyond all attempts to inform, educate and influence spectators to achieve a critical consciousness and attitude towards any regime of power. Pearson and Brookes's *Coriolan/us* balances the sublime elements of size, disruption, tragic pathos, failure and loss of control with rather playful and relational elements allowing for a certain sense of freedom in self-positioning as a spectator. In confronting the sublime elements of the text and the space with the interplay of individual movement and behaviour, the audience starts its own performance, crossing the space of dramatic conflict by participating in a casual and dispersed choreography. Thus the challenge of directing Shakespeare's *Coriolanus* after and with Brecht, which is, as Pearson puts it, one of 'finding a new role for the audience',[41] was realized by a politics of relation and 'distanced' participation. The production was worked through as an experiment with the people and for them, reflecting spectatorship as such, navigating between participation (moving with the crowd), voyeurism (watching the surveillance pictures, or the 'private' scenes in caravans and cars), and becoming a witness, perceiving close to one's body a particular event taking place: the performance of an audience in public.

Notes

1 Opinions about the play have been quite controversial, particularly in the twentieth century, as James E. Phillips has pointed out: 'The play has been both hailed and condemned as either propaganda for the totalitarian state or as a socialistic attack on the evils of dictatorship.' See his introduction to *Twentieth Century Interpretations of Coriolanus: A Collection of Critical Essays*, ed. James E. Phillips, Englewood Cliffs, NJ: Prentice Hall, 1970: 4. For an interpretation that reconsiders some of these controversies in a fruitful way see the chapter on Coriolanus in Jan Kott, *Shakespeare our Contemporary*, London: Methuen 1964: 179–210.

2 Cf. *Shakespeare's Plutarch: The Lives of Julius Caesar, Brutus, Marcus Antonius and Coriolanus*, trans. Sir Thomas North, ed. T.J.B. Spencer, Harmondsworth: Penguin, 1968: 296–362.
3 Cf. Oscar James Campbell, 'Shakespeare's Satire: Coriolanus', in *Twentieth Century Interpretations of Coriolanus: A Collection of Critical Essays*, ed. James E. Phillips, Englewood Cliffs, NJ: Prentice Hall, 1970: 25–36.
4 In his study on Shakespeare's stagecraft, following a methodological approach developed by Harley Granville-Barker, J.L. Styan gives some instructive comments on *Coriolanus* as well. See J.L. Styan, *Shakespeare's Stagecraft*, Cambridge: Cambridge University Press, 1991.
5 William Shakespeare, *The Tragedy of Coriolanus*, in *Coriolanus*, ed. Lee Bliss (The New Cambridge Shakespeare), Cambridge: Cambridge University Press 2000: 104–273. In the following, quotations from the play will be indicated in the text by numbers of act and scene.
6 Mike Pearson, 'Framing the Text', in National Theatre of Wales, in association with the Royal Shakespeare Company: CORIOLAN/US, performance programme, August 2012.
7 For a discussion of that 'stealing away' see Styan, *Shakespeare's Stagecraft*: 79f.
8 On the relevance of the kneeling gesture see Styan, *Shakespeare's Stagecraft*: 61f.
9 In regard of the comic elements in *Coriolanus* and how he is influenced by others, one might also think of Brecht's comedy *A Man is a Man* (*Mann ist Mann*) about a soldier whose identity is completely subjugated to the will of others. Walter Benjamin has analysed this changeable character as prototype of the 'untragic hero', as an 'empty stage on which the contradictions of our society are acted out': cf. Walter Benjamin, 'What is Epic Theatre?' (Second Version), in *Understanding Brecht*, trans. Anna Bostock, London: Verso, 1998: 15–22, at 17.
10 For a commentary on this point cf. the introduction to William Shakespeare, *The Tragedy of Coriolanus*, ed. R.B. Parker, Oxford: Oxford University Press, 1994: 115.
11 Regarding contemporary rebellions cf. *Shakespeare: Coriolanus*, in Bliss, *Coriolanus*: 17–33.
12 Pearson, 'Framing the Text'.
13 National Theatre Wales: From Shakespeare and Brecht, CORIOLAN/US. Directed by Mike Pearson and Mike Brookes, 8–18 August 2012 (unpublished production manuscript).
14 Bertolt Brecht, *Coriolanus*, in *Collected Plays, Vol. 9*, trans. and ed. Ralph Manheim and John Willett, New York: Vintage, 1972: 57–146.
15 For the writing process and also the performance history of Brecht's adaptation, see Anthony Tatlow, 'Coriolanus', in *Brecht Handbuch in 5 Bänden*, ed. Jan Knopf, Bd. 1: Stücke, Stuttgart: Metzler, 2001: 585–91.
16 Cf. Pearson, 'Framing the Text'.
17 Bertolt Brecht, [On Coriolanus], in *Werke*, Bd. 24: Texte zu Stücken, Berlin and Frankfurt/Main: Suhrkamp Verlag, 1991: 402.
18 Bertolt Brecht, 'Study on the First Scene of Shakespeare's "Coriolanus"', in *Brecht on Theatre. The Development of an Aesthetic*, ed. and trans. John Willett, London: Methuen 1994: 252–65, at 259. Translation partly revised by myself according to the original: 'Studium des ersten Auftritts in Shakespeares "Coriolan"', in *Werke*. Große kommentierte Berliner und Frankfurter Ausgabe, ed. Werner Hecht *et al.*, Bd. 23: Schriften, 1942–56: 386–402, at 395f.
19 It is unclear to what extent Brecht has used or altered the opinions of his collaborators in his report of the discussion. Cf. Brecht, *Werke*, editorial notes, 603, 581.
20 Jacques Rancière, 'The Emancipated Spectator', *Artforum International*, March 2007: 271–80, at 280.

21 Jean-Luc Nancy, *Being Singular Plural*, Stanford, CA: Stanford University Press, 2000: 1–100.
22 Brecht, 'Study on the First Scene of Shakespeare's "Coriolanus"': 264–65. Translation partly revised according to the original: 'Studium des ersten Auftritts in Shakespeares "Coriolan"', in *Werke*: 402.
23 Cf. Styan, *Shakespeare's Stagecraft*: 102.
24 Cf. Pearson, 'Framing the Text'.
25 Cf. Styan, *Shakespeare's Stagecraft*: 117; pointing to the change of the crowd between the first scene, rather individualized, and its later appearance as mob and 'rabble' (III/1).
26 For further discussion of theatre as event, and of this production in particular, see Adrian Kear, *Theatre and Event: Staging the European Century*, Basingstoke: Palgrave, 2013. A draft extract from this book, along with an earlier version of this paper, were shared by their respective authors in an Aberystwyth Politics and Performance research group symposium on *Coriolan/us* held on 26 November 2012.
27 I personally attended the performances on 15 and 16 August 2012. The atmosphere of the shows differed a lot, as has been mentioned by the production team and other spectators as well, who also agreed that these differences were mainly caused by the changing behaviour and energy of the audience (to be perceived much more than in other productions).
28 Mike Pearson is also Professor of Performance Studies, Department of Theatre, Film and Television Studies, Aberystwyth University and published widely on contemporary performance.
29 For a more detailed analysis of this production see Patrick Primavesi, 'Memories from a Theatre of War', *Performance Research* 17, no. 3: 50–56; and Adrian Kear, *Theatre and Event*.
30 These statements by Mike Pearson are part of an (unpublished) interview we conducted in Cardiff on 17 August 2012.
31 Cf. Pearson, 'Framing the Text'.
32 Mike Brookes, 'Shaping Coriolan/us', in National Theatre of Wales, in association with the Royal Shakespeare Company: CORIOLAN/US, performance programme, August 2012.
33 Pearson, (unpublished) interview.
34 Pearson, (unpublished) interview.
35 Cf. Patrick Primavesi, 'Embedded Audience. Wie Mike Pearson/Mike Brookes in Cardiff und die Wooster Group/Royal Shakespeare Company in Stratford die Funktion des Medialen im Krieg bearbeiten', *Theater der Zeit* 12 (December) 2012: 38–39.
36 Cf. Hans-Thies Lehmann, *Postdramatic Theatre*, London: Taylor & Francis, 2006.
37 The scene is a little reminiscent of the children's game Blind Man's Buff ('Blinde Kuh'), where a blindfolded player is surrounded by the others who would touch him and he has to figure out where, or sometimes who, they are.
38 Cf. Jacques Rancière, *Aesthetics and its Discontents*, Cambridge: Polity Press, 2009: 19–44.
39 This argument has been most extensively developed in Theodor W. Adorno, *Aesthetic Theory*, trans. Robert Hullot-Kentor, London: Continuum, 2004.
40 Nicholas Bourriaud, *Relational Aesthetics*, Dijon: Les Presses du reel, 1998.
41 Pearson, (unpublished) interview.

11 Bellies, wounds, infections, animals, territories

The political bodies of Shakespeare's *Coriolanus*

Stuart Elden

Introduction

This chapter examines Shakespeare's late tragedy *Coriolanus* in terms of the various political bodies that structure the narrative and its language.[1] The reading moves through a number of registers. First, and most obviously, the question of the body politic, which is recounted in a fable told to hungry citizens. It moves from this to discuss actual physical bodies and wounds, and then turns to the recurrent language of infection and infected bodies. This relates to the bodies of non-human animals, frequently mentioned as approbation or condemnation, particularly as this is played out in terms of the clash between the elite and the multitude, the singular and plural, and the understanding of the city as being both the people and the place. There are a number of examples of animals as the hunter and hunted, consumer and consumed. Finally, the chapter addresses the theme of banishment and the conquest of territories, in terms of bodily aspects in other political senses. In *Coriolanus* territory as the body of the state is only one aspect of its corporeal nature.

This chapter is part of a much wider project that reads a number of Shakespeare's plays to shed light on different aspects of the question of territory.[2] Territory, in my argument, is something that cannot be simply understood as a bounded space, but encompasses a variety of different, multiple and contested processes. I have suggested elsewhere that territory cannot be reduced to mere political and geographical questions, and that a range of economic, strategic, legal and technical issues are tangled up in the concept and practice.[3] To those different registers we might add the affective, emotional, physical and bio-physical aspects of territory, of bodies in places and places embodied. It is to those aspects that this reading most directly speaks.

Coriolanus has been described as Shakespeare's 'most political play',[4] and as 'hugely, indeed grotesquely, political'.[5] While set in ancient Rome, and based upon the life of the title character written by Plutarch, the resonances with Shakespeare's own time have often been remarked upon, especially in terms of the corn riots and resultant popular uprisings in the English

Midlands around the time he wrote the play, in 1607. The play has often been mined for its political leanings, particularly because it gives voice both to the common people and their rulers. It has polarized opinion in part because it presents different perspectives with such passion, leading William Hazlitt to suggest in the early nineteenth century that if it is studied it obviates the need to read Burke or Paine or listen to debates in the House of Commons.[6] Both T.S. Eliot and Bertolt Brecht, with very different political motives, attempted to adapt the play in the twentieth century.[7] Robin Headlam Wells suggests that the allusion to the corn riots in the opening scene would have had a strong contemporary resonance.[8] Yet Shakespeare took the corn riots from Plutarch's account of Coriolanus's life, which means it was not a gratuitous addition but part of the story itself.[9] However, as Philip Brockbank suggests, 'he could not have been unaware of their closeness to his own time',[10] and it is of course plausible that the parallels inspired Shakespeare to take up this story as the basis for his play. Brockbank notes that this is a recurrent theme in Shakespeare, as his 'theatrical engagement with popular risings began with the Cade scenes of 2 Henry VI, to be extended in Julius Caesar and Sir Thomas More and consummated in Coriolanus'.[11] Frank Kermode argues that while this link was certainly the immediate context, the political aspects of the play operate 'more abstractly' as:

> a study in the relationships between citizens within a body politic; the relationship of crowds to leaders and leaders to led, of rich to power. The polis has its troubles: dearth, external enemies, enmity between classes. The patricians have a ruthless but narrow and selfish code of honour. The people are represented by tribunes who are in their own way equally ruthless, scheming politicians. The monarchic phase of Roman history has recently ended, the kings replaced by an oligarchy tending to be oppressive, committed to warfare as the ultimate proof of valour and worth, and largely indifferent to social obligation.[12]

A brief plot summary may be in order. Caius Martius is a victorious Roman general, yet he is intensely disliked by the people as a whole because he is seen as one of the reasons behind their hunger while the grain stores are full. An encounter between the people and Caius goes badly, with Caius scornful of their claims. Caius leads a victorious army, defeating the Volscians at Corioli and fighting the Volscian commander Tullus Aufidius, who is dragged away by his soldiers. Caius returns to Rome as a conquering hero, taking the honorific *cognomen* (more properly an *agnomen*) of Coriolanus. He is persuaded by his mother to run for consul, and he is elected with the backing of the people. However, two tribunes, Junius Brutus and Sicinius Velutus, conspire against him, leading to a popular revolt. Coriolanus condemns the people, which means Brutus and Sicinius have him convicted of treason. He is condemned to execution by being thrown off a cliff, but banished as an alternative. Coriolanus goes to the Volscian city of Antium, initially to allow his enemy Aufidius to kill him to spite Rome. Instead they together plot the city's downfall. On hearing the two men are leading an army against them, Rome attempts to persuade Coriolanus against this course. While the soldier Cominius and the patrician Menenius fail, a delegation including Coriolanus's son, wife and mother Volumnia, succeeds. A pact is sealed with Rome, but Coriolanus is denounced as a traitor by the Volscians and killed by Aufidius and others.

The political questions in the play are thus not merely secondary aspects, but the very heart of the drama. Kermode has suggested that its plot is 'probably the most fiercely and ingeniously planned and expressed of all the tragedies'.[13] As Heller notes, 'Coriolanus is in my mind such a thoroughly political play that the politically uninteresting scenes (such as the introductory part of 2.1) also seem dramatically redundant'.[14] Among these many themes, I will focus on bodies.[15]

First, and most obviously, there is the question of the body politic. I move from this to discuss actual physical bodies and wounds, and then move to the recurrent language of infection and infected bodies. This leads to the bodies of non-human animals, particularly as this is played out in terms of the clash between the elite and the multitude and the understanding of the city, as being the people and the place, in its physical form. Finally, I examine the theme of banishment and the conquest of territories, in terms of the bodily aspects in another political sense. The aim here is to avoid the narrow, uninteresting political reading of the play that Stanley Cavell suggests 'is apt to become fairly predictable once you know whose side the reader is taking, that of the patricians or that of the plebeians'.[16]

The theme of bodies has, naturally, been discussed before. As Bristol notes:

> The image of the body is, of course, a familiar topic in the critical discussion of *Coriolanus*. The play is saturated with concrete situations in which the fate and condition of bodies is of paramount importance. Both literal and symbolic implications of the analogy between the private individual body and the body politic are elaborated in nearly every scene.[17]

Some of what I say here will, then, be familiar to students of the play. The discussion of bodies in a literal sense, particularly the fable of the belly in the opening scene, and the ideas of infection and contagion that run throughout the play, are relatively well known and examined. However, even here I think there are issues less commonly remarked upon, and I hope in terms of wounds, animals and territories that my reading goes beyond this. More broadly, this reading is an engagement with, and development of, some of the themes of literary geography.[18] It attempts to avoid some of the problems Nigel Thrift outlined in a letter to a journal he would later go on and edit.[19] It is informed, but not bound, by the kind of political approach to literary analysis for which Silk provided something of a manifesto.[20]

The most recent adaptation is Ralph Fiennes's film version.[21] This is undoubtedly a powerful piece of cinema, with a stellar cast, big-budget

182 *Stuart Elden*

production and striking cinematography. In this film version, the action is set in the contemporary moment. It was shot in Serbia and Montenegro, but the largely urban scenes of decay and despair could have been anywhere. The setting in the film is said to be 'a place calling itself Rome', having a 'border-dispute' with the Volscians.

Bellies

The initial complaint of the people is hunger in the face of dearth. They feel that the state has sufficient resources and does not release them. The patrician Menenius Agrippa tries to suggest that it is the gods that have created this situation, and that rather than carry arms against the Roman state, they should get on their knees to pray. He tries to explain the situation to the people by means of a corporeal parable that reverses this idea of grumbling bellies, something that is unfortunately cut from the recent Fiennes film version.

> MENENIUS: There was a time when all the body's members
> Rebell'ld against the belly; thus accus'd it:
> That only like a gulf it did remain
> I'th'midst o'th'body, idle and unactive,
> Still cupboarding the viand, never bearing
> Like labour with the rest; where th'other instruments
> Did see, and hear, devise, instruct, walk, feel,
> And, mutually participate, did minister
> Unto the appetite and affection common
> Of the whole body. The belly answer'd—
> FIRST CITIZEN: Well, sir, what answer made the belly?
> MENENIUS: Sir, I shall tell you. With a kind of smile,
> Which ne'er came from the lungs, but even thus—
> For look you, I may make the belly smile
> As well as speak—it tauntingly replied
> To th'discontented members, the mutinous parts
> That envied his receipt; even so most fitly
> As you malign our senators for that
> They are not such as you.
> FIRST CITIZEN: Your belly's answer—What?
> The kingly crowned head, the vigilant eye,
> The counsellor heart, the arm our soldier,
> Our steed the leg, the tongue our trumpeter,
> With other muniments and petty helps
> Is this our fabric … [22]

The sheer number of bodily parts is overwhelming. Menenius sets the other members of the body against the belly. It cupboards the viand, storing the food, but not distributing it to the other parts. Basic instincts—seeing, hearing, devising, instructing, walking, feeling, participating—are not served by the belly; the appetites and affections are not provided for. Menenius describes the complainants as 'discontented members, the mutinous parts', and notes that the belly is the root of this, not the lungs. One of the citizens replies by listing the parts of the entire body politic: the head, the eye, the heart, the arm, the leg, the tongue. The body politic is a recurrent theme in political theory. Perhaps the most important medieval example is found in John of Salisbury's twelfth-century *Policraticus*,[23] but the most striking early seventeenth-century example is Edward Forset's *Comparative Discourse of the Bodies Natural and Politique*.[24] Forset's work was published in 1606, shortly after his involvement in the prosecution of Guy Fawkes and his fellow conspirators. This play is Shakespeare's most thorough treatment of the idea.[25]

One of the things that is unusual is that he does not allow the fable of the belly (which has its root in Aesop before Plutarch) simply to stand as a metaphor of politics: the people to whom the story are told are actually hungry in Shakespeare's *Coriolanus*, while in Plutarch they are told the fable outside of the city walls where they are complaining about usury. Usury is mentioned only briefly in Shakespeare; in Plutarch the grain riots come later in the narrative. The exchange on the fable continues for some time, with the first citizen describing it as 'the cormorant belly',[26] trading on the idea that this is a voracious bird.[27] Menenius counters that 'your most grave belly was deliberate,/Not rash like his accusers', and that it acts as 'the storehouse and the shop/Of the whole body'.[28] What is stored there is distributed appropriately:

> I send it through the rivers of your blood,
> Even to the court, the heart, to th'seat o'th'brain;
> And, through the cranks and offices of man,
> The strongest nerves and small inferior veins
> From me receive that natural competency
> Whereby they live.[29]

It is clear what he intends, with the people getting the flour and only the bran being taken, though the crowd seem confused, so he makes it explicit:

> The senators of Rome are this good belly,
> And you the mutinous members; for, examine
> Their counsels and their cares, digest things rightly
> Touching the weal o'th'common, you shall find
> No public benefit which you receive
> But it proceeds or comes from them to you,
> And no way from yourselves. What do you think,
> You, the great toe of this assembly?[30]

The use of body parts to discuss the polity continues at other times in the play: 'the navel of the state' and 'the fundamental part of state';[31] 'lords and

184 *Stuart Elden*

heads o'th'state'.[32] Even the last, the well-known idea of a 'head' of state, follows from this basic idea. The bodily sustenance can be to disadvantage too, with Coriolanus claiming that whoever gave our stored corn freely 'nourish'd disobedience, fed/the ruin of the state'.[33]

Wounds

As Stanley Cavell has shown, ideas of hunger and cannibalism run through the narrative.[34] Yet the play is not concerned simply with the workings of the body, and the distribution of nourishment throughout it. As Zvi Jagendorf notes, 'the physical is inescapable in this most unerotic of plays; everywhere we encounter legs, arms, tongues, scabs, scratches, wounds, mouths, teeth, voices, bellies, and toes, together with such actions as eating, vomiting, starving, beating, scratching, wrestling, piercing, and undressing'.[35] It is worth dwelling a little on the wounds born by soldiers on behalf of the city.[36] Martius notes that 'I have some wounds upon me, and they smart/To hear themselves remember'd'.[37] Menenius and Volumnia wish him to come home from Corioli with wounds upon him. Menenius is pleased to receive a letter from Martius:

> A letter for me! it gives me an estate of seven
> years' health; in which time I will make a lip at
> the physician: the most sovereign prescription in
> Galen is but empiricutic, and, to this preservative,
> of no better report than a horse-drench. Is he
> not wounded? he was wont to come home wounded.[38]

Galen is of course a medical writer from antiquity who came after the action of the play, but the point is well made. ('Empiricutic' appears to be a combination of 'empiric' and 'pharmaceutic'.[39]) Volumnia learns news with which she is pleased: 'O, he is wounded; I thank the gods for't'; Menenius concurs: 'So do I too, if it be not too much: brings a'victory in his pocket? the wounds become him.'[40] They then have the following exchange:

> MENENIUS: ... Where is he
> wounded? [*To the Tribunes*] God save your good
> worships! Martius is coming home: he has more
> cause to be proud. [*To Volumnia*] Where is he
> wounded?
> VOLUMNIA: I'the shoulder and i'the left arm there will be
> large cicatrices to show the people, when he shall
> stand for his place. He received in the repulse of
> Tarquin seven hurts i'the body.
> MENENIUS: One i'the neck, and two i'the thigh,—there's
> nine that I know.
> VOLUMNIA: He had, before this last expedition, twenty-five

wounds upon him.
MENENIUS: Now it's twenty-seven: every gash was an enemy's grave.[41]

This passage enumerates the wounds, a calculus of pain from the battlefields that can be expended in the political marketplace.[42] However, breaking with custom, the newly named Coriolanus is unwilling to show his wounds to the crowd. Brutus is critical of this decision:

> I heard him swear,
> Were he to stand for consul, never would he
> Appear i'th'market-place, nor on him put
> The napless vesture of humility;
> Nor showing (as the manner is) his wounds
> To th'people, beg their stinking breaths.[43]

Coriolanus confirms this reluctance himself: 'Your honour's pardon:/I had rather have my wounds to heal again/Than hear say how I got them'.[44] And again:

> I do beseech you,
> Let me o'erleap that custom, for I cannot
> Put on the gown, stand naked and entreat them
> For my wounds'sake, to give their suffrage: please you
> That I may pass this doing.[45]

Siculus and Brutus see this failure to display the heroic body as an affront, as do the citizens.

> We have power in ourselves to do it, but it is a power that we have no power to do; for if he show us his wounds and tell us his deeds, we are to put our tongues into those wounds and speak for them; so, if he tell us his noble deeds, we must also tell him our noble acceptance of them. Ingratitude is monstrous, and for the multitude to be ingrateful were to make a monster of the multitude; of the which we being members should bring ourselves to be monstrous members.[46]

Coriolanus is reluctant simply to stand and tell the crowd of the wound he received, and outlines how he imagines it is desired he do:

> What must I say?
> 'I Pray, sir'—Plague upon't! I cannot bring
> My tongue to such a place:—'Look, sir, my wounds!
> I got them in my country's service, when
> Some certain of your brethren roar'd and ran
> From the noise of our own drums.'[47]

186 *Stuart Elden*

This is the contradiction: he does not wish his wounds to speak of his actions.[48] He later concedes that 'I have wounds to/show you, which shall be yours in private' to one citizen,[49] but refuses to confirm another's claim that 'You have received many wounds for your country' by replying that 'I will not seal your knowledge with showing them',[50] though he later boasts of 'wound two dozen odd; battles thrice six'.[51] Again there is the calculus, but he does not wish them visible, only known. The citizens later interpret this as disdain: 'He used us scornfully: he should have show'd us/His marks of merit, wounds received for's country'.[52] Instead of being part of a collective body, Martius/Coriolanus wishes to remain private, separate, his body to himself. He is later described as 'a carbuncle entire'.[53] This idea is returned to in Act III, when Menenius tells the crowd:

> The warlike service he has done, consider, think
> Upon the wounds his body bears, which show
> Like graves i'th'holy churchyard.
> Coriolanus: Scratches with briers,
> Scars to move laughter only.[54]

Infections

As well as the actual damage to a physical body, the play uses the recurrent theme of corruption, pollution and disease to the political body.[55] Something is rotten in the state, but the trope is also used to refer to different elements or characters. Following his earlier description of the crowd as making themselves scabs by 'rubbing the poor itch of your opinion',[56] Martius condemns the soldiers who are on the verge of defeat at Corioli in the following way:

> All the contagion of the south light on you,
> You shames of Rome! you herd of—boils and plagues
> Plaster you o'er, that you may be abhorr'd
> Farther than seen, and one infect another
> Against the wind a mile! You souls of geese
> That bear the shapes of men, how have you run
> From slaves that apes would beat! Pluto and hell![57]

Later, after being denied by the crowd, despite his sacrifices, he returns to taunt them.

> As for my country I have shed my blood,
> Not fearing outward force, so shall my lungs
> Coin words till their decay, against those measles
> Which we disdain should tetter us, yet sought
> The very way to catch them.[58]

Measles could be the modern disease, but could also be leprosy—the words have confused etymologies; while tetters are skin eruptions.[59] Later in the same scene he suggests that there is a need 'to jump a body with a dangerous physic/That's sure of death without it—at once pluck out/The multitudinous tongue: let them not lick/The sweet which is their poison'.[60] Yet how he describes them also is applied to him. He has already been labelled a 'poison';[61] now it is his turn to be described as a contagion:

> SICINIUS: He's a disease that must be cut away.
> MENENIUS: O, he's a limb that has but a disease:
> Mortal, to cut it off: to cure it, easy.
> What has he done to Rome that's worthy death?
> SICINIUS: The service of the foot,
> Being once gangren'd, is not then respected
> For what before it was.
> BRUTUS: We'll hear no more.
> Pursue him to his house and pluck him thence,
> Lest his infection, being of catching nature,
> Spread further.[62]

Sicinius and Brutus argue that his past deeds need to be forgotten, like a gangrenous foot is no use for its previous purpose, and that in order to prevent further infection he needs to be cut away. Menenius suggests that the loss of his blood in the service of Rome outweighs his current situation. Yet both use the same mode of language in their opposed views.

Animals

Throughout the play the people as a whole and particular characters are described as animals.[63] There are many beastly bodies. Coriolanus describes the people as a herd;[64] and Menenius talks of 'being the herdsmen of the beastly plebeians'.[65] The people are described as 'multiplying spawn' by Menenius,[66] and Coriolanus accuses Siculus of being the 'Triton of the minnows'.[67] There are other insults used of the crowd, such as Martius's evocative 'Go get you home, you fragments!'[68] which makes clear the collective nature of the crowd, sometimes described as the 'rabble'—often in stage directions as well as dialogue, which may indicate Shakespeare's own views.[69]

However, there is a veritable bestiary beyond this. Curs, lions and hares, foxes and geese all appear in Martius's first speech,[70] shortly after a contrast was drawn by Menenius between 'Rome and her rats'.[71] Coriolanus mocks the crowd's hunger and their use of proverbs such 'dogs must eat',[72] and links this to their unwillingness to fight with the lines 'The Volsces have much corn; take these rats hither/To gnaw their garners'.[73] Later exchanges bring in a 'fawning greyhound in the leash',[74] a cat and mouse,[75] mules, camels, dogs and sheep,[76] moths,[77] conies,[78] an 'old goat!'[79] and a hen.[80] The herd, 'souls of geese', and 'slaves that apes would beat' all appear in the condemnation of his soldiers.[81] He later claims he will 'never/Be such a gosling as to obey instinct'.[82] However the use of animals is sometimes rather lazy, with them simply listed and the auditor (or reader) having to do the work of embellishing the image. As Maxwell notes, a comparison with *Macbeth* is telling. In that play we find the evocative claim that 'A falcon, towering in her pride of place,/Was by mousing owl hawked at and killed'.[83]

One of the most striking things is how often the animals function as pairs, one the hunter and the other the hunted, one consumer and one consumed. The animals are frequently their bodies, meat.[84] When Menenius says that the people do not love Martius, Sicinius declares that 'nature teaches beasts to know their friends',[85] which generates an exchange where the crowd is compared to a wolf looking to devour a lamb, but Brutus notes that Martius sounds like a bear, to which Menenius replies that he's a bear who lives like a lamb.[86] The implication appears to be that in politics he is a lamb, ready to be devoured, while his true strength in is battle. This is confirmed by Coriolanus later referring to a 'wolvish toge': civilian dress covering his martial instincts.[87] He had earlier welcomed war as a 'means to vent/Our musty superfluity'.[88] What these contrasts mean is that while many of the terms are pejorative, there are also animals that evoke strength or nobility ('noble' is itself a recurrent theme throughout the play). It is very much not the case that no human should be like an animal.[89] Martius is described as a bear,[90] and he declares Aufidius 'a lion/That I am proud to hunt'.[91] That said, in their first encounter, Aufidius vows 'If I fly, Martius/Holloa me like a hare',[92] where the hare stands as a figure of timidity.[93] Later in the play, as he is sent into exile, Coriolanus complains that 'the beast with many heads butts me away',[94] and compares his fate 'to a lonely dragon that his fen/Makes fear'd and talk'd of more than seen'.[95] The multitude expels the individual. The dragon is echoed in Menenius's later description: 'There is difference between a grub and a butterfly; yet your butterfly was a grub. This Martius is grown from man to dragon; he has wings, he's more than a creeping thing.'[96] Menenius twice describes Coriolanus as a tiger, speaking of him having 'tiger-footed rage',[97] and saying there is 'no more mercy in him than there is milk in a male tiger'.[98]

Aufidius declares Coriolanus is ruled by animal instincts: 'I think he'll be to Rome/As is the osprey to the fish, who takes it/By sovereignty of nature'.[99] This relation of the osprey to the fish, a noble animal to prey, is found in other places in the play. It comes through in the idea that the people might have upset the natural balance of things, a reversal of power Coriolanus suggests would allow 'the crows to peck the eagles',[100] with the eagle a somewhat anachronistic imperial emblem. He later describes Rome as a 'city of kites and crows',[101] the kite being at Shakespeare's time a common sight scavenging in London. There are other times, however, where the power of the strong is clear, with the suggestion that the Volscian assault on Rome will be of soldiers following Coriolanus 'with no less confidence/Than boys pursuing summer butterflies,/Or butchers killing flies'.[102]

The animal imagery also is important in considering the relation of the people and the patricians to the city. In the opening scene Martius suggests that 'the rabble should have first unroof'd the city',[103] a claim that makes more sense in a later context.

> FIRST SENATOR: To unbuild the city, and to lay all flat.
> SICINIUS: What is the city but the people?
> PLEBEIANS: True,
> The people are the city ...
> COMINIUS: That is the way to lay the city flat,
> To bring the roof to the foundation,
> And bury all which yet distinctly ranges
> In heaps and piles of ruin.[104]

In distinction, Coriolanus sees them as in Rome but not Roman:

> I would they were barbarians—as they are
> Though in Rome litter'd; not Romans—as they are not,
> Though calved i'th'porch o'th'Capitol![105]

He wishes they were barbarians, so he could dispense with them as in a war: 'On fair ground/I could beat forty of them.'[106] There is an interesting structure to these lines with the wish followed by the 'as they are', and the negative description reinforced by the 'as they are not', with the two instances of 'though' used to qualify still further. There is also a use of terms that refer to their mere bodies. As Cantor notes, 'Coriolanus' use of terms for animal procreation, *litter'd* and *calved*, reveals his point: the plebians no more deserve to be called Romans than do the tame beasts who happen to be born every year within the city's walls'.[107]

However, the contrasts go deeper than this. The people believe they are the city, whereas the patricians clearly see a physicality to the city itself which is in danger of being destroyed.[108] The people care more about their own health, but Coriolanus, the Senator and Cominius talk of the destruction of the buildings, literally an 'unbuilding'; the city laid flat; a 'falling fabric'.[109] Sicinius re-enters, looking for Coriolanus in order to pass sentence:

> Where is this viper
> That would depopulate the city and
> Be every man himself?[110]

One of the citizens sees the enacting of the sentence as setting both the politics and the bodies in balance again. Thrown from the rock, 'he shall well know/The noble tribunes are the people's mouths/And we their hands'.[111]

190   *Stuart Elden*

When he goes into exile and seeks out Aufidius, Coriolanus addresses the city itself:

> A goodly city is this Antium. City,
> 'Tis I that made thy widows: many an heir
> Of these fair edifices 'fore my wars
> Have I heard grown, and drop. Then know me not;
> Lest that thy wives with spits, and boys with stones,
> In puny battle slay me.[112]

In the final scene, discovering his Coriolanus has been persuaded against the assault on Rome, Aufidius slurs him with the accusation of being a 'boy of tears', to which Coriolanus replies with the terrible lines that lead to his death:

> Cut me to pieces, Volsces; men and lads,
> Stain all your edges on me. Boy! False hound!
> If you have writ your annals true, 'tis there,
> That, like an eagle in a dove-cote, I
> Flutter'd your Volscians in Corioles.
> Alone I did it. Boy![113]

The description of himself as the eagle, the return to the scene of his greatest victory at Corioli, and the use of the animal descriptions of 'hound' and fluttering those in the 'dove-cote' returns to a number of key themes of the play. Coriolanus thus ends as he began, setting himself up alone against a crowd, with the people as a whole crying 'tear him to pieces' as a reply to his own 'cut me to pieces', before many blows rain down.[114] Recall the condemnation of the crowd as 'fragments' and a 'herd' in the first scene. The individual people only make sense as part of a whole; Coriolanus can himself be reduced to pieces. For Jagendorf, the manner of his death 'represents the number over singularity, of the limbs over the belly, of the spread of power over its concentration'.[115]

Territories

These bodies relate in a number of ways to the question of territory in a narrower, more specific sense. The key here is the expulsion of Coriolanus from the civil body, and the attack he then leads against it. When the tribunes rule him guilty of treason Sicinius notes that there are three options—'For death, for fine, or banishment'—and asks the Aedile to instruct the crowd to follow his lead.[116] Coriolanus is unrepentant:

> Let them pronounce the steep Tarpeian death,
> Vagabond exile, flaying, pent to linger

> But with a grain a day, I would not buy
> Their mercy at the price of one fair word,
> Nor check my courage for what they can give,
> To have't with saying 'Good morrow.'[117]

A few lines later Sicinius picks up the theme:

> That do distribute it—in the name o'th'people,
> And in the power of us the tribunes, we,
> Ev'n from this instant, banish him our city,
> In peril of precipitation
> From off the rock Tarpeian, never more
> To enter our Rome gates. I'th'people's name,
> I say it shall be so.[118]

The people reply enthusiastically 'It shall be so, it shall be so! Let him away!/ He's banish'd, and it shall be so'.[119] There is then the important exchange and reversal:

> BRUTUS: There's no more to be said, but he is banish'd,
> As enemy to the people and his country.
> It shall be so!
> PLEBEIANS: It shall be so, it shall be so!
> CORIOLANUS: You common cry of curs, whose breath I hate
> As reek o'th'rotten fens, whose loves I prize
> As the dead carcasses of unburied men
> That do corrupt my air: I banish you!
>   ... Despising
> For you the city, thus I turn my back.
> There is a world elsewhere![120]

The curs here, as they did in the first scene, invokes the dogs baiting the bear.[121] The Aedile claims 'the people's enemy is gone', to which the crowd replies that 'our enemy is banish'd, he is gone!'[122]

When he does leave, it is to the Volscian city of Antium. In the compressed dramatic action of the play, his journey is short and his arrival, disguised, follows quickly after. However, the recent film version captures this effectively in showing a lengthy journey the passage of time of which is tracked by the transformation in Fiennes's appearance. Shaven head and face become ever-lengthening hair and a thick beard. By the time he arrives in Antium, the transformation is such that stage devices such as a hooded cloak are unnecessary, but the geographical complications are shown in this version. The play is set by Shakespeare in early republican Rome, not long after the uprising against and expulsion of the Tarquin kings. The play is written in early seventeenth-century England. The film is set in a near-contemporary pseudo-Balkans, shot in Serbia and

Montenegro. The film, making effective use of newsreel and TV, shows that the Volscians are in close proximity to the 'place calling itself Rome'. The initial war footage, of the siege of the Volscian city of Corioli that gives Coriolanus his name, talks of a 'border dispute'. That implied a more proximate location, or at least, a contested front between the sides that appeared largely absent when he is making his way to Antium. The means used to mark the transition at other points in the film, where a motorway is punctuated by roadblocks, with a kind of no-man's land between them, was more effective. However, if this is so, and the two neighbours share a narrow, effectively modern border, a boundary, where does Coriolanus go when he moves into exile? Why does it take him so long to move between these places?

Yet, in republican Rome, it is indeed the case that there would have been areas outside of Rome that were not yet part of its neighbours: places that were not yet spaces; lands that were not yet cultivated, not yet territory. In the early seventeenth century, Shakespeare could effectively play this spatial politics. Exile was still a potential punishment, and features importantly in his history plays. The transportation of convicts to the new world or slavery were merely modern examples of an age-old practice. In the later seventeenth century John Locke would discuss the 'Indian who knows no Inclosure, and is still a Tenant in common', and yet still laid claim to private property and thus a nascent form of civil society[123]—Locke declaring that 'in the beginning, all the World was America'.[124] Not all places within Shakespeare's England were yet enclosed, much less if Scotland and Ireland were included.

However, in the late twentieth and early twenty-first centuries, and especially in the Balkan setting which is otherwise so effective in Fiennes's adaptation, the idea of a place *outside* territory is harder to grasp. Where *is* Coriolanus as he moves through that sequence of locations, sleeping rough and his hair growing ever longer? He could be in isolated locations. He is undoubtedly making his way through war-ravaged landscapes, contested places in the present or recent past, but given the modes of modern warfare and territorial settlements, he is either still within the 'place calling itself Rome', or behind enemy lines. It's hard to conceive of a no-man's land of such extent that the time could have passed in such a way. He is effectively either in one territory or another. It is hard to imagine him outside of territory, but for early Rome, or even in Shakespeare's England, it is not so difficult.

When Coriolanus arrives in Antium to talk to Aufidius he speaks of how the people were allowed by nobles to be cheered into exile, with the 'voice of slaves to be/Whoop'd out of Rome'.[125] (Whooped is a hunting term.[126]) Aufidius clearly sympathizes, recalling later how 'Being banish'd for't, he came unto my hearth,/Presented to my knife his throat; I took him,/Made him joint-servant with me'.[127] Back in Rome, Menenius condemns the crowd—'the clusters'[128]—for being those 'that made the air unwholesome when you case/Your stinking greasy caps in hooting at Coriolanus' exile'.[129] The citizens quickly claim that they agreed to banish him reluctantly: 'we willingly consented to his banishment, yet it was against our will.'[130] Later

Menenius suggests that those who sent him into exile should beg forgiveness: 'Go you that banish'd him;/A mile before his tent fall down, and knee/The way into his mercy.'[131] In his attempt to mediate, Menenius is criticized by the Antium guard:

> Can you, when you have pushed out your gates the very defender of them, and in a violent popular ignorance given your enemy your shield, think to front his revenges with the easy groans of old women, the virginal palms of your daughters, or with the palsied intercession of such a decayed dotant as you seem to be? Can you think to blow out the intended fire your city is ready to flame in with such weak breath as this? No, you are deceived; therefore back to Rome and prepare for your execution. You are condemned; our general has sworn you out of reprieve and pardon.[132]

Towards the end of the play, a Roman senator expresses a wish to 'Unshout the noise that banish'd Martius,/Repeal him with the welcome of his mother'.[133]

The play is also one of the few in the Shakespearean corpus to use the actual word 'territories'—still a rather rare word at the turn of the sixteenth and seventeenth centuries.[134] Only two plays by Shakespeare actually use the singular 'territory'.[135] Three passages are at stake in this play:

> AUFIDIUS: Worthy Martius,
> Had we no other quarrel else to Rome, but that
> Thou art thence banish'd, we would muster all
> From twelve to seventy, and, pouring war
> Into the bowels of ungrateful Rome,
> Like a bold flood o'erbear't. O come, go in,
> And take our friendly senators by'th'hands,
> Who now are here, taking their leaves of me
> Who am prepar'd against your territories,
> Though not for Rome itself.[136]

> AEDILE: There is a slave, whom we have put in prison,
> Reports the Volsces with several powers
> Are enter'd in the Roman territories,
> And with the deepest malice of the war
> Destroy what lies before 'em.[137]

> SECOND MESSENGER: You are sent for to the senate.
> A fearful army, led by Caius Martius,
> Associated with Aufidius, rages
> Upon our territories, and have already
> O'erborne their way, consum'd with fire and took
> What lay before them.[138]

All of these are in a single Act, when Coriolanus is mustering Volscian forces to attack Rome. It is Rome that has territories, and seemingly not its neighbours; Rome that has lands at risk. This only hints at the geographical complexities of Rome's rule, especially in the later Empire—there were lands currently part of its *imperium*, and those that could be at some point in the future. Rome did not see the political geographical status of its neighbours in the same terms.[139] Aufidius talks of the territories to attack; the functionaries of the threat at home. Yet these places are also related to bodies, and not simply Aufidius's description of 'the bowels of ungrateful Rome'.[140] Coriolanus is content to 'Let the Volsces/Plough Rome and harrow Italy'[141]—that is, to reduce it to a colony or *territorium*. An important moment in the founding of a new colony was the ploughing of the sacred boundary of the city walls, the *pomerium*. We hear about this from Cicero, Varro and Tacitus, for example, and in the early Middle Ages Isidore of Seville derives the etymology of the term territory from this practice: 'a *territorium* is so called as if it were a *tauritorium*, that is "broken by a plow" [*tritum aratro*] and by a team of oxen (c.f. *taurus*, "bull")—for the ancients used to designate the borders of their possessions and *territoria* by cutting a furrow'.[142] In this sense, even the 'geopolitics' of the play is figured as a body politics, if not always a bio-politics.

Finally, having been expelled and taken refuge in Antium, Coriolanus then returns to this language. He talks to Aufidius of his 'canker'd country with the spleen/Of all the under fiends'.[143] Aufidius continues the polluted body trope in the passage quoted above, suggesting that they 'muster all/From twelve to seventy, and pouring war/Into the bowels of ungrateful Rome,/Like a bold flood o'erbear't'.[144] Returning to this theme of cannibalism, the most powerful figure in the play, the most sufficient, the one who bore Coriolanus in her body and prevents his turning against the body of Rome, is Volumnia. It is she who utters the horrific line that 'Anger's my meat; I sup upon myself/And so shall starve with feeding'.[145] Finally she pleads with Coriolanus not to make 'the mother, wife and child to see/The son, the husband and the father, tearing/His country's bowels out'.[146] She then shifts the body to her own, suggesting that 'thou shalt no sooner/March to assault thy country than to tread—/Trust to't, thou shalt not—on thy mother's womb,/That brought thee to this world'.[147] Coriolanus has become Rome's other, its outside; his mother tells him not to tread on her womb, which gave him birth, but also on Rome itself, the site that made him possible.

Shakespeare was writing at a time when the modern conception of sovereign territory was emerging and so he helps us understand its variant aspects, tensions, ambiguities and limits. In *The Tempest* he explores what this might mean when Europe came into contact with its outside. In his own England the dominant form of political power was conducted in a space that was, by his time, relatively ordered and bordered, but its recent past—explored in the history plays—was anything but. We can see that, for example, in *Richard II*, which is a crucial play about the political economies of land and the politics of banishment. The earlier setting of *King Lear* shows a place that is historically distant and spatially disrupted. In that it is more similar to the Europe in which he set most of his tragedies and comedies. This was a space that was contested and fractured, both politically and spatially. We see that, especially, in *Coriolanus*. In *Coriolanus* territory as the body of the state is only one aspect of its corporeal nature. It is a play about the political body of the polity itself, its inside and outside, the aggressive wars to keep it safe externally, and its internal health and well-being. It also raises a range of questions about what it is to contribute to a political community, and who should rule. However, literally and figuratively these are often the physical bodies of its characters, with language invoking wounds, contagion, animals and a variety of body parts. Shakespeare helps us to understand what it means to be part of territory or outside territory, conceptually, historically and politically.

Notes

1 I have used the text in the Arden Shakespeare: *Coriolanus*, ed. Philip Brockbank, London: Routledge, 1976, though compared this to the RSC Shakespeare: *Coriolanus*, ed. Jonathan Bate and Eric Rasmussen, Houndmills: Macmillan, 2011. The edition of the text in the Third Series of the Arden edition (ed. Peter Holland, London: Bloomsbury, 2013) arrived too late to make use of its readings and apparatus. On the play generally, Adrian Poole, *Coriolanus*, New York: Harvester Wheatsheaf, 1988; and Jan H. Blits, *Spirit, Soul and City: Shakespeare's* Coriolanus, Lanham, MD: Lexington Books, 2006, are useful.
2 See also Stuart Elden, 'The Geopolitics of *King Lear*: Territory, Land, Earth', *Law and Literature* 25, no. 2 (2013) pp. 147–165.
3 Stuart Elden, *Terror and Territory: The Spatial Extent of Sovereignty*, Minnesota: University of Minnesota Press, 2009; 'Land, Terrain, Territory', *Progress in Human Geography* 34, no. 6 (2010): 799–817; *The Birth of Territory*, Chicago, IL: University of Chicago Press, 2013 pp. 147–165.
4 Robin Headlam Wells, *Shakespeare's Politics: A Contextual Introduction*, London: Continuum, 2009: 58; Frank Kermode, *Shakespeare's Language*, London: Penguin, 2000: 243.
5 Zvi Jagendorf, '*Coriolanus*: Body Politic and Private Parts', *Shakespeare Quarterly* 41, no. 4 (1990): 455–69: 457.
6 William Hazlitt, from *Characters of Shakespear's Plays*, excerpted in B.A. Brockman, ed., *Shakespeare: Coriolanus—A Casebook*, Houndmills: Macmillan, 1977: 26.
7 T.S. Eliot, 'Coriolan', in *Collected Poems 1909–1962*, London: Faber & Faber: 137–43; Bertolt Brecht, 'Coriolan', in *Collected Plays: Nine*, ed. and trans. Ralph Manheim and John Willett, New York: Vintage, 1972. See also Brecht's 'Study of the First Scene of Shakespeare's *Coriolanus*', in *Brecht on Theatre*, ed. and trans. John Willett, London: Methuen, 1964: 252–65.
8 Headlam Wells, *Shakespeare's Politics*: 58. On this see E.C. Pettet, 'Coriolanus and the Midlands Insurrection of 1607', *Shakespeare Survey* 3 (1950): 34–42.
9 Plutarch's text, in the North translation, appears in the Arden edition. On the relation, see Kwang-Ho Kim, 'Shakespeare's Treatment of the Source in *Coriolanus*', *English Studies* 7 (1983): 49–62; and David George, 'Plutarch, Insurrection and Dearth in *Coriolanus*', in *Shakespeare and Politics*, ed. Catherine M.S. Alexander, Cambridge: Cambridge University Press, 2004: 110–29; more generally see

Kenneth Muir, 'The Background of Coriolanus', *Shakespeare Quarterly* 10, no. 2 (1959): 137–45; and Anne Barton, 'Livy, Machiavelli and Shakespeare's *Coriolanus*', in *Shakespeare and Politics*, ed. Catherine M.S. Alexander, Cambridge: Cambridge University Press, 2004: 67–90.
10 Brockbank, 'Introduction', in *Coriolanus*: 26.
11 Brockbank, 'Introduction': 36.
12 Kermode, *Shakespeare's Language*: 243.
13 Kermode, *Shakespeare's Language*: 254.
14 Agnes Heller, *The Time is Out of Joint: Shakespeare as a Philosopher of History*, Lanham, MD: Rowman & Littlefield, 2002: 291. There is actually, *pace* Heller, quite a bit going on in the opening part of this scene that has political connotations. Nonetheless, chapter 12 of her study is helpful on *Coriolanus* generally.
15 On others, see G. Thomas Tanselle and Florence W. Dunbar, 'Legal Language in *Coriolanus*', *Shakespeare Quarterly* 13, no. 2 (1962): 231–38; Paul A. Cantor, *Shakespeare's Rome: Republic and Empire*, Ithaca: Cornell University Press, 1976: part I; W. Hutchings, 'Beast or God: The Coriolanus Controversy', *Critical Quarterly* 24, no. 2 (1982): 35–50; Charles Mitchell, 'Coriolanus: Power as Honor', *Shakespeare Studies* 1 (1965): 199–226; Alexander Leggatt, *Shakespeare's Political Drama: The History Plays and the Roman Plays*, London: Routledge, 1989: chapter 3; Alan Hager, *Shakespeare's Political Animal: Schema and Schemata in the Canon*, Newark: University of Delaware Press, 1990: chapter 4; Cathy Shrank, 'Civility and the City in *Coriolanus*', *Shakespeare Quarterly* 54, no. 1 (2003): 406–23; Brayton Polka, '*Coriolanus* and the Roman World of Contradiction: A Paradoxical World Elsewhere', *The European Legacy* 15, no. 2 (2010): 171–94.
16 Stanley Cavell, 'Who Does the Wolf Love? Reading *Coriolanus*', *Representations* 3 (1983): 1–20, at 2.
17 Michael D. Bristol, 'Lenten Butchery: Legitimation Crisis in *Coriolanus*', in *Shakespeare Reproduced: The Text in History and Ideology*, ed. Jean E. Howard and Marion F. O'Connor, New York: Methuen, 1987: 207–24, at 213.
18 For a helpful survey, see Sheila Hones, 'Text as it Happens: Literary Geography', *Geography Compass* 2, no. 5 (2008): 1301–17; and Angharad Saunders, 'Literary Geography: Reforging the Connections', *Progress in Human Geography* 34, no. 4 (2010): 436–52.
19 Nigel Thrift, 'Landscape and Literature', *Environment and Planning A* 10, no. 3 (1978): 347–49. See also his later 'Literature, the Production of Culture and the Politics of Place', *Antipode* 15, no. 1 (1983): 12–24.
20 J. Silk, 'Beyond Geography and Literature', *Environment and Planning D: Society and Space* 2, no. 2 (1984): 151–78.
21 For a discussion, see Slavoj Žižek, *The Year of Dreaming Dangerously*, London: Verso, 2012: 118–25.
22 *Coriolanus*, Act I, scene i: 95–118.
23 There is no complete English translation, but the best single edition is John of Salisbury, *Policraticus: On the Frivolities of Courtiers and the Footprints of Philosophers*, ed. and trans. by Cary J. Nederman, Cambridge: Cambridge University Press, 1990. The body politic is discussed in book V, chapter 2.
24 Edward Forset, *Comparative Discourse of the Bodies Natural and Politique*, London: Iohn Bill, 1606. On this, see Arthur Riss, 'The Belly Politic: *Coriolanus* and the Revolt of Language', *ELH: English Literary History* 59, no. 1 (1992): 53–75, 64–67; and Muir, 'The Background of Coriolanus', who notes that there is no direct evidence that Shakespeare knew Forset's work (page 141).
25 The literature on this is quite extensive. See, for example David G. Hale, '*Coriolanus*: The Death of a Political Metaphor', *Shakespeare Quarterly* 22, no. 3 (1971): 197–202; Andrew Gurr, '"Coriolanus" and the Body Politic', *Shakespeare Survey* 28 (1975): 63–69; James Holstun, 'Tragic Superfluity in *Coriolanus*', *ELH*:

English Literary History 50, no. 3 (1983): 485–507; Jagendorf, '*Coriolanus*'; and Riss, 'The Belly Politic'. For a contextual reading that puts it in conversation with other works from and the situation in the first years of James I's reign, see Alex Garganigo, *Studies in English Literature 1500–1900* 42, no. 2 (2002): 335–59. The classic work on the idea is Ernst H. Kantorowicz, *The King's Two Bodies: A Study in Mediaeval Political Theology*, Princeton, NJ: Princeton University Press, 1957. See Claire Rasmussen and Michael Brown, 'The Body Politic as Spatial Metaphor', *Citizenship Studies* 9, no. 5 (2005): 469–84.

26 *Coriolanus*, Act I, scene i: 120.
27 Brockbank, note to *Coriolanus*: 104.
28 *Coriolanus*, Act I, scene i: 127–28, 132–33.
29 *Coriolanus*, Act I, scene i: 134–39.
30 *Coriolanus*, Act I, scene i: 147–54.
31 *Coriolanus*, Act III, scene i: 150.
32 *Coriolanus*, Act V, scene vi: 91.
33 *Coriolanus*, Act III, scene i: 116–17.
34 Cavell, 'Who Does the Wolf Love?'
35 Jagendorf, '*Coriolanus*': 457–58.
36 See also Coppélia Kahn, *Roman Shakespeare: Warriors, Wounds, and Women*, London: Routledge, 1997: 152–54.
37 *Coriolanus*, Act I, scene ix: 28–29.
38 *Coriolanus*, Act II, scene i: 113–18.
39 Brockbank, note to *Coriolanus*: 158.
40 *Coriolanus*, Act II, scene i: 120, 121–22.
41 *Coriolanus*, Act II, scene i: 141–55.
42 See Jagendorf, '*Coriolanus*': 464.
43 *Coriolanus*, Act II, scene i: 229–34.
44 *Coriolanus*, Act II, scene ii: 68–70.
45 *Coriolanus*, Act II, scene ii: 135–39.
46 *Coriolanus*, Act II, scene iii: 4–13. The First Citizen's reply invokes 'the many-headed multitude' (16–17).
47 *Coriolanus*, Act II, scene iii: 51–56.
48 Jarrett Walker, 'Voiceless Bodies and Bodiless Voices: The Drama of Human Perception in *Coriolanus*', *Shakespeare Quarterly* 43, no. 2 (1992): 170–85, at 177.
49 *Coriolanus*, Act II, scene iii: 76–77.
50 *Coriolanus*, Act II, scene iii: 105, 106.
51 *Coriolanus*, Act II, scene iii: 127.
52 *Coriolanus*, Act II, scene iii: 160–62.
53 *Coriolanus*, Act I, scene iv: 55. This point is indebted to Rebecca Lemon, 'Arms and the Law in *Coriolanus*', in *The Law and Shakespeare*, ed. Constance Jordan and Karen Cunningham, Houndmills: Palgrave, 2010: 233–48, at 239. See also Riss, 'The Belly Politic': 55–56, although this overstretches the spatial resonances of Coriolanus's separation from the people.
54 *Coriolanus*, Act III, scene iii: 49–52.
55 More generally, see R.R. Simpson, *Shakespeare and Medicine*, Edinburgh: E. & S. Livingstone, 1959.
56 *Coriolanus*, Act I, scene i: 164–65.
57 *Coriolanus*, Act I, scene iv: 30–36.
58 *Coriolanus*, Act III, scene i: 75–79.
59 Brockbank, note in *Coriolanus*: 199.
60 *Coriolanus*, Act III, scene i: 153–56.
61 *Coriolanus*, Act III, scene i: 86.
62 *Coriolanus*, Act III, scene i: 292–308. There are parallels with *2 Henry IV*, Act III, scene i: 38–43 here. See Hale, '*Coriolanus*': 201.

63 On this theme see J.C. Maxwell, 'Animal Imagery in *Coriolanus*', *The Modern Language Review* 42, no. 4 (1947): 417–21; and Ineke Murakami, 'The "Bond and Privilege of Nature" in *Coriolanus*', *Religion & Literature* 38, no. 3 (2006): 121–36. There are some useful thoughts in the latter, but the application of Agamben seems a stretch. On animals in Shakespeare generally, though with no reference to *Coriolanus*, see Bruce Boehrer, *Shakespeare Among the Animals: Nature and Society in the Drama of Early Modern England*, New York: Palgrave, 2002.
64 *Coriolanus*, Act III, scene i: 32.
65 *Coriolanus*, Act II, scene i: 94–95; see also Act III, scene ii: 32.
66 *Coriolanus*, Act II, scene ii: 78.
67 *Coriolanus*, Act III, scene i: 88.
68 *Coriolanus*, Act I, scene i: 221. See also 'shreds' (Act I, scene i: 207).
69 See Annabel Patterson, *Shakespeare and the Popular Voice*, Basil Blackwell, 1989: chapter 6.
70 *Coriolanus*, Act I, scene i: 167–71.
71 *Coriolanus*, Act I, scene i: 161.
72 *Coriolanus*, Act I, scene i: 205.
73 *Coriolanus*, Act I, scene i: 248–49.
74 *Coriolanus*, Act I, scene vi: 38.
75 *Coriolanus*, Act I, scene vi: 44.
76 *Coriolanus*, Act II, scene i: 245, 249, 255.
77 *Coriolanus*, Act I, scene iii: 84.
78 *Coriolanus*, Act IV, scene v: 218.
79 *Coriolanus*, Act III, scene i: 175.
80 *Coriolanus*, Act V, scene iii: 162. For a near-complete list, see Maxwell, 'Animal Imagery in *Coriolanus*': 420.
81 *Coriolanus*, Act I, scene iv: 30–36.
82 *Coriolanus*, Act V, scene iii: 35.
83 *Macbeth*, Act II, scene iv: 12. See Maxwell, 'Animal Imagery in *Coriolanus*': 420.
84 See Gail Kern Pastor, 'To Starve with Feeding: the City in *Coriolanus*', *Shakespeare Studies* XI (1978): 123–44, at 135–36.
85 *Coriolanus*, Act II, scene i: 5.
86 *Coriolanus*, Act II, scene i: 6–11.
87 *Coriolanus*, Act II, scene iii: 114. Brockbank refuses to correct 'wolvish' to 'woolish', which other editors have suggested 'because the garb should be the sheep's; but it is the wolf's property and symbolizes his treacherous nature'. See also Andreas Höfele, *Stage, Stake and Scaffold: Humans and Animals in Shakespeare's Theatre*, Oxford: Oxford University Press, 2011: 111, who agrees with 'wolvish' and notes that 'toge' is itself an emendation of 'tongue' from the Folio, but claims this 'seems to me irrefutable' (page 111, n. 52).
88 Act I, scene i: 224–25. Holstun, 'Tragic Superfluity in *Coriolanus*': 488–89, notes that this evokes both the 'medical venting of excess humours and the commercial vending of excess stock'.
89 On this point more generally, see Höfele, *Stage, Stake and Scaffold*.
90 *Coriolanus*, Act I, scene iii: 31.
91 *Coriolanus*, Act I, scene i: 234–35.
92 *Coriolanus*, Act I, scene viii: 6–7.
93 Brockbank, note to *Coriolanus*: 141.
94 *Coriolanus*, Act IV, scene i: 1–2. He had earlier (Act III, scene i: 92) referred to a 'Hydra' but here the use of 'butts' seems to imply a rather more herd-like animal.
95 *Coriolanus*, Act IV, scene i: 30–31.
96 *Coriolanus*, Act V, scene iv: 11–14.
97 *Coriolanus*, Act III, scene i: 309.
98 *Coriolanus*, Act V, scene iv: 28–29.

99 *Coriolanus*, Act IV, scene vii: 33–35.
100 *Coriolanus*, Act III, scene i: 138.
101 *Coriolanus*, Act IV, scene v: 43.
102 *Coriolanus*, Act IV, scene vi: 94–96.
103 *Coriolanus*, Act I, scene i: 4–5.
104 *Coriolanus*, Act III, scene i: 196–205.
105 *Coriolanus*, Act III, scene i: 237–39.
106 *Coriolanus*, Act III, scene i: 240–41.
107 Cantor, *Shakespeare's Rome*: 82.
108 Pastor, 'To Starve with Feeding': 131. See, for example, the claim that 'if we lose the field,/We cannot keep the town' (Act I, scene vii: 4–5); and Robert S. Miola, *Shakespeare's Rome*, Cambridge: Cambridge University Press, 1983: 164: 'the constricted and constrictive city ... sharply defined by outlying battlefields, rival towns, and its own vividly realized topography—its walls, gates, Capitol, Tiber, Tarpeian rock, forum, private houses, and streets.'
109 *Coriolanus*, Act III, scene i: 245.
110 *Coriolanus*, Act III, scene i: 261–63. At 284 he describes him as a 'viperous traitor'.
111 *Coriolanus*, Act III, scene i: 268–70.
112 *Coriolanus*, Act IV, scene iv: 1–6.
113 *Coriolanus*, Act V, scene vi: 111–16.
114 *Coriolanus*, Act V, scene vi: 120.
115 Jagendorf, '*Coriolanus*': 467.
116 *Coriolanus*, Act III, scene iii: 15.
117 *Coriolanus*, Act III, scene iii: 88–92.
118 *Coriolanus*, Act III, scene iii: 99–105.
119 *Coriolanus*, Act III, scene iii: 105–6.
120 *Coriolanus*, Act III, scene iii: 117–35.
121 Höfele, *Stage, Stake and Scaffold*: 100.
122 *Coriolanus*, Act III, scene iii: 137–38.
123 John Locke, *Second Treatise*, in *Two Treatises of Government*, ed. Peter Laslett, Cambridge: Cambridge University Press, 1988 [1960]: V, 26.
124 Locke, *Second Treatise*: V, 49.
125 *Coriolanus*, Act IV, scene v: 78–79.
126 Brockbank, note to *Coriolanus*: 254.
127 *Coriolanus*, Act V, scene vi: 30–32.
128 *Coriolanus*, Act IV, scene vi: 129.
129 *Coriolanus*, Act IV, scene vi: 131–33.
130 *Coriolanus*, Act IV, scene vi: 145–46.
131 *Coriolanus*, Act V, scene i: 4–6.
132 *Coriolanus*, Act V, scene ii: 38–49.
133 *Coriolanus*, Act V, scene v: 4–5.
134 For a longer discussion, see Elden, *The Birth of Territory*, especially chapters 8 and 9.
135 See Elden, 'The Geopolitics of *King Lear*'.
136 *Coriolanus*, Act IV, scene v: 127–36.
137 *Coriolanus*, Act IV, scene vi: 38–42.
138 *Coriolanus*, Act IV, scene vi: 75–80.
139 See Elden, *The Birth of Territory*: chapter 2.
140 *Coriolanus*, Act IV, scene v: 131.
141 *Coriolanus*, Act V, scene iii: 33–34.
142 Isidore of Seville, *The Etymologies of Isidore of Seville*, trans. Steven A. Barney, W.J. Lewis, J.A. Beach and Oliver Berghof, Cambridge: Cambridge University Press, 2006: XVI, v, 22.
143 *Coriolanus*, Act IV, scene v: 92–93.

144 *Coriolanus*, Act IV, scene v: 129–32.
145 *Coriolanus*, Act IV, scene ii: 50–51. For a discussion, see Janet Adelman, '"Anger's my Meat": Feeding, Dependency, and Aggression in *Coriolanus*', in *Representing Shakespeare: New Psychoanalytic Essays*, ed. Murray M. Schwartz and Coppélia Kahn, Baltimore, MD: Johns Hopkins University Press, 1980: 129–49.
146 *Coriolanus*, Act V, scene iii: 101–3.
147 *Coriolanus*, Act V, scene iii: 122–25.

Part V
Dramaturgies of scenario and security

12 Power, security and antiquities

Christine Sylvester

Objects, no less than people, can be threatened and securitized in politically charged contexts. Architectures have fallen to dramatic wartime air attacks and acts of local vandalism.[1] Heritage sites have been damaged by military performances of security.[2] Artworks are regularly taken as war plunder; meanwhile, pieces of ancient pots disappear daily from the deserts of the American south-west—sometimes taken and sometimes saved by archaeologists.[3] This chapter explores threats to objects of antiquity that are usually associated with war looting but are also subject to quotidian threats from unexpected sources. It does so using literatures that do not usually link to the field of International Relations or its cognate of security studies: archaeological research on object acquisition, and new materialist philosophy about the power and agency of nonhuman objects.

Archaeologists have a broad conception of looting that includes the acquisition practices of esteemed museums and galleries, and of art collectors or everyday treasure hunters, all of whom feed a voracious market in antiquities. They have a narrower understanding, surprisingly, of the power of objects to attract the humans who loot them. While not addressing antiquity objects, political philosopher Jane Bennett argues that nonhuman things, operating with bodies and forces that are human and nonhuman, have power and agency. By combining insights from these disparate literatures, it becomes plausible to suggest that antiquity 'things' can, circumstantially, perform as actants, whose 'efficacy or agency always depends on the collaboration, cooperation, or interactive interference of many bodies and forces'.[4] Those bodies might include indigenous diggers, smugglers, crime syndicates, international organizations like UNESCO (the United Nations Educational, Scientific and Cultural Organization), militaries, museums and 'art' consumers, but it is important to realize that what actants do does not depend on the motivations or intentions of any of the humans involved. For that reason, the consequences of activities surrounding the taking of antiquities cannot be reduced to the usual use of the term 'looting', which has a motivational component, or spun into a security theory that assumes the centrality of human acts or intentions. The trajectory I follow maps antiquities onto new understandings of object–human relations, reveals object movements that link war, conflict and peacetime activities of museums, and frames a broader logic of the political performativity of security.

Thing power

When precious objects left the Iraq Museum, Baghdad during the 2003 war, people saw the looters on global media as well as the American tank forces standing by looking elsewhere for the 'real' war. Outrage surged through numerous countries, especially in the West, where the Middle East holds a privileged position as the cradle of (our) civilization. Few actual looters were identified and charged with stealing,[5] arguably because most such activities occur in the shadows cast by museums, criminal networks and the art market. That is to say, people seen running off with fabled figurines during moments of turmoil are small fry at the tail of an international money trail that earns admired institutions and individuals additions to holdings, status and income; it also can earn terrorist groups and autocratic leaders staying power. Issues of security, insecurity and agency lie along a twisted path in which pots have a performative role in their own fate, a phenomenon that cannot be appreciated when it is assumed that agency is strictly a human capacity.[6]

In *Vibrant Matter*, Jane Bennett presents students of political agency with the challenge of querying whether people have exclusive agency or whether they share agency with nonhuman things. For many art theorists and science historians, objects matter and important objects have power beyond or separate from the artist, viewer, or art institution.[7] Students of cultural studies know that nonhuman national flags have visual power—thus the waving of these in protest crowds. Books can be burned for the words they string into stories, and some subjects of the arts can be forbidden by certain religions. All of this can seem to show the symbolic power of material culture, but what if it is material agency of some kind?

In anthropocentric approaches, at issue would not be the agency of the material object but the agency of key individuals, movements, states or international organizations: the entities that make or breach security. Yet think of the Entartete Kunst (Degenerate Art) exhibitions staged by the Nazi state in the late 1930s. Assembled to show the degeneracy of modernist German arts compared to approved folk or genre art, the works nonetheless exerted an unexpected agency in tandem with, but in the opposite direction intended by, the people and ideological forces that staged the exhibitions. Some 2 million viewers thronged the shows, a far larger number than usually attended art exhibitions. One observer who saw the show in Munich several times recalls that spectators initially mocked the works loudly, as they were meant to do by the Nazi script. On a second visit, he says, 'there were only a few who talked, rather quietly, and it appeared that some of them had seen these works before or even liked them. They would stand in front of a work for longer periods of time than other visitors ... I remember hearing a whispered "Aren't they lovely?" ... '[8] The artworks powered as much if not more public interest in modernism in the arts than they deterred, which would suggest that the initial human-state aim was contravened or complicated by the performative power of the pieces themselves.

When Bennett raises questions about agency, she is not talking about the power of symbols, perception or representation, or the power of words, texts, language and interpretation, all of which follow paths back to the human as the instigator of knowledge and action. She is talking about the vitality, force and even political power of material things we assume to be inert in all ways: stones, tin cans, a bottle cap, a piece of clothing hanging in the closet. These things can produce effects in assemblages, which she understands as 'ad hoc groupings of diverse elements, of vibrant materials of all sorts. Assemblages are living, throbbing confederations that are able to function despite the persistent presence of energies that confound them from within ... Each member and proto-member of the assemblage has a certain vital force, but there is also an effectivity proper to the grouping as such: an agency *of* the assemblage'.[9]

Bennett's focus is ecology, not art, archaeology or museums. Following W.J.T. Mitchell, she eliminates known objects from her analysis of thing-power.[10] What we see and name and have expectations about are objects, e.g. a sardine can as a container for processed sardine fish. When something is unnamed, or when a named object does something seemingly impossible—'when the sardine can looks back', 'when the mute idol speaks'[11]—she calls that thing-power. Things, rather than objects, often escape human attention, or they can get kicked down the street, no longer seen as bona fide sardine cans. Humans assume that things are inert and acted upon, but Bennett provides evidence of things having moments of independent capaciousness belying human design and intention. One of her most illuminating examples is an electricity blackout that affected areas of the United States and Canada in 2003. She describes what happened as the:

> end point of a cascade—of voltage collapses, self-protective withdrawals from the grid, and human decisions and omissions ... what seems to have happened on that August day was that several initially unrelated generator withdrawals in Ohio and Michigan caused the electron flow pattern to change over the transmission lines, which led, after a series of events including one brush fire that burnt a transmission line and then several wire-tree encounters, to a successive overloading of other lines and a vortex of disconnects ... Investigators still do not understand why the cascade ever stopped itself ... [12]

In effect, they do know why unanticipated processes occurred that ran contrary to human design and control. Nonetheless it is clear that forces in the electrical swarm self-organized in a way that changed the electrical flows intended by human designers.

There is some slippage in Bennett's terminological distinction between things and objects that makes it reasonable, however, to map antiquities objects onto things and vice versa. Bennett is firm that nonhuman bodies can be actants while objects are named things humans imbue with an agentic presence that reflects our subjectivities and intersubjectivities. Humans, that is, can imbue animals with recognizable feelings and animate them as talkers; they can draw a zodiac and claim its impact on human lives. Those objects seem to act the way we expect because, in effect, we subjectively make them act. Things, by contrast, are beneath or outside human attention; they are not recorded as agents or even noticed much as entities. However, Bennett also talks of objects that 'appear as such because their becoming proceeds at a speed or a level below the threshold of human discernment'.[13] This means that they spend considerable time as 'things' that have no name or value at certain points in time but do have names and values at other times. Antiquities can lie buried in the ground for centuries, completely overlooked by humans walking above them; then, at a moment in time, they become valued in assemblages with humans and put in museums. Bennett also claims that 'thing-power gestures toward the strange ability of ordinary, man-made items to exceed their status as objects and to manifest traces of independence or aliveness, constituting the outside of our own experience';[14] it is 'an alternative to the object as a way of encountering the nonhuman world'.[15] Can objects be named, hold human expectations and also exceed those expectations at certain moments, as in ancient pots that come 'alive' and enter a new script after centuries, perhaps, of somnolence?

There are other such spaces of ambiguity surrounding things v. objects, actants v. recalcitrants. Bennett provides those spaces when she theorizes assemblages as:

> not governed by any central head: no one materiality or type of material has sufficient competence to determine consistently the trajectory or impact of the group. The effects generated by an assemblage are, rather, emergent properties, emergent in that their ability to make something happen (a newly inflected materialism, a blackout, a hurricane, a war on terror) is distinct from the sum of the vital force of each materiality considered alone.[16]

Those words resonate with art historian James Elkins's understanding of art objects as capable of staring back at viewers in a two-way interaction.[17] He calls it 'a "betweenness" (for lack of a better word): part of me is the object, and part of the object is me. There is no such thing as a pure self, or a pure object apart from that self'. The audience and the thing become dynamic.

Thing power and security

A human–nonhuman thing-power framework complicates the study of looting and brings up matters of security that have been neglected in security studies. Conventional security studies puts the state at the centre of a national security problematic of deterring or answering threats to core values. It has been known to err in the opposite direction, though, fetishizing nonhuman weapon systems as agents of deterrence or turning armed forces into figures slotted into war games.[18] Of course, weapons have been built by the human hand and exist at the beck and call of humans monitoring radar screens, so they start with human agency; it is still only in the realm of imagination and fear that a targeting computer—Hal in the film *2001: A Space Odyssey*—can go rogue and move beyond human control. Yet during the nuclear era of the Cold War, nuclear weapons commanded their own attention and budgets in the sense that they had the power to mask numerous options other than arms races. Today, the bigger threat is cast as actions of individual terrorists, politicized bodies that are at once fetishized as hyper-agents of national and personal insecurity, and assemblages of human body parts, evil intent and explosives. Many, many times the vibrant explosive matter in a terrorist assemblage fails to detonate. In such cases, the emphasis in the media is on the individual terrorist and our 'good luck' that something went wrong with his or her *intended* planning such that a catastrophe was averted, not on the unanticipated activity of vibrant matter overriding human intent.

Wars conducted in Iraq and Afghanistan using pilotless planes controlled by human operators in the United States set up another example of security-related issues surrounding the agency of things. Drones eclipse the power of the human controller by operating visually and actually in excess of human agency. The weapons become vital forces in assaults on the ground that seem to come out of nowhere and in negotiations at home for an increased defence budget. Drones are akin to DNA samples or, in a case Bennett mentions, to gunpowder residue on a human hand: 'Expert witnesses showed the sampler to the jury several times, and with each appearance, it exercised more force, until it became vital to the verdict.'[19]

At the opposite end of the spectrum, the human security stream of analysis identifies threats to well-being that imperil entire groups of people through poverty, illiteracy, poor governance, natural disasters, lack of potable water, inadequate health care, discrimination, war, rape and so on. Human security overlaps significantly with issues of development. Time and again reigning theories and practices of development fail to achieve human security, whether through modest projects to empower women in post-conflict situations[20] or through realization of Millennium Development Goals (MDGs) formulated by the UN.[21] Haroom Akram-Lohdi decries the fact that 'for all their florid rhetoric, the MDGs are not intellectually entrenched within a humane, democratic, alternative and socially embedded development paradigm that highlights the agency-led systematic changes necessary to achieve human security'.[22] Aid is often foregrounded as agentic, but how aid, local people, development goals, and politics actually perform together is often assumed rather than fully queried—with dire results.[23]

Yet do frameworks like Bennett's, which would broaden agency from people-centred locations to things + people-in-assemblages, negate the painstaking work on human agency conducted since the 1980s? Gayatri Spivak's postcolonial and literary query, 'can the subaltern speak?' was one among many concerns about agency that inspired greater inclusiveness and self-critical research on the Other, life on the margins, and people unheard over the din of Western certainties.[24] Post-structural analysis presented a new appreciation of language, representation, texts and discourse. Feminists moved women into spaces of agency they never held or many never saw them holding before. In the face of such hard-won achievement, though, Bennett wonders whether all this has also led to overly 'familiar fetishizations; the fetishization of the subject, the image, the word'.[25]

Bennett's insistence on the vitality of nonhuman things stands apart from a number of other strands of new materialist thought, including posthuman and material feminism,[26] and the neomaterialist writings in philosophy, cultural studies and science, technology and society studies.[27] In most such genres, the nonhuman is ultimately viewed through humanist lenses, or it is seen as acting in tandem with humans but not with vitality of its own. Bennett uses some of the accepted terminology of new materialism ('assemblages', 'actants') as she speaks of atoms or electrical circuits as well as corporeal assemblage and agentic power distributed in the 'swarm of vitalities at play'.[28] She says, however, 'the task becomes to identify the contours of the swarm and the kind of relations that obtain between its bits'.[29] Practically, this means that attempts to pinpoint 'the' source of something like the 'war on terror' miss the process and can lead to cycles of vengeful war or ecological disaster. As Bennett notes, 'there is nothing simple about materiality'.[30]

To say that is not to suggest that humans should stand by and shrug when watching the twin towers fall or development efforts that habitually fail to lift the living conditions of people in vulnerable situations. What her work signals, instead, is that agency must be shared: it includes humans but cannot be limited to them. Notions of agency distributed through assemblages of materialities lead to a more confederate and chastised understanding of the human self, which should put some brakes on the sense that everything can be controlled if we only send in the military or set up an electrical plant correctly.

Bennett's formulations are intriguing and compelling but do contain some worrisome points. If everything is an assemblage of vibrant matter, including the human body, then what type of politics follows? Does it matter if the subaltern can or cannot speak when 'she' is one of many cogs in many wheels and not an agent of her own destiny? Just as post-structuralism was accused of leaving policy makers with endless possibilities and no truth to uphold, an emphasis on forces in excess of human control can stymie action, hold up decisions and put societies seeking, say, to follow a greener path of production wondering if the issues are just too complicated to master. It could also feed back into the agency-of-the-constitution view of Tea Party politics in the United States.

As a political theorist, Bennett is not writing to affect public policy in any direct manner. Still, she offers this insight into a new politics based on awareness of vibrant matter:

> a heightened sensitivity to the agency of assemblages could translate into a national politics that was not so focused around a juridical model of moral responsibility, blame, and punishment. The hope is that the desire for scapegoats would be lessened as public recognition of the distributed nature of agency increased, and that politics would take on a less moralistic and a more pragmatic (in Dewey's sense of problem-solving) cast.[31]

Another way of putting it is that any sense that politics is down to a sovereign power to classify and reclassify others as security risks gives people exaggerated importance that can minimize complex confederations of power and agency.

Object looting: what takes what

Thinking about the power and potential agency of objects might help us to appreciate the complexities of securing antiquities, understood as object things that have some performative role in their own outcomes and cannot simply be securitized. The close association of looting with war and political turmoil would have to be expanded in meaning. Presently, war looting is amplified by media stories about extensive losses from the Iraq Museum in 2003, lesser incidents in the Egyptian Museum in Cairo in 2010, and instances of looting from museums and archaeological sites during the first Iraq War in 1991 and in the Croatia war of 1991.[32]

However, other cases do not quite fit the war context. The Entartete Kunst exhibitions can be thought of as looting the country's art museums by the Nazi state preliminary to the general plunder of art objects by all parties to World War II. Today, there is an ongoing heritage 'war' performed during peacetime in a number of countries, as police and archaeologists try to drive off diggers from using every tool available to them, including mechanical ploughing machinery, to unearth artefacts—Viking remnants from Gotland Sweden, Roman and Greek era pieces from Italy, ancient textiles from Peru, ceramics from Colombia, Anasazi pottery shards from northern Arizona and so on. Moreover, museums are identified by archaeologists as some of the biggest looters of the past and present. Looting antiquities *from* museums is tantamount to looting the looters; however, to say that is to suggest that antiquity objects are inert. They are not.

Museums as looters

Pots have been attracting pilferers for ages. How huge objects, such as the Assyrian reliefs, the Parthenon sculptures, and the Rosetta stone arrived at the British Museum and elsewhere in the West is not subject to much debate today among archaeologists and scholars of heritage studies.[33] The record is clear that in the mid-1800s, it was customary for adventurers and museum aficionados to travel to the Middle East and Mediterranean for the purpose of removing impressive sculptural pieces and hauling them back to London and other European capitals. The 'stones' or marbles were often said to be neglected in their sites and left to the elements. Removal would guarantee the very survival of deteriorating pieces; that was Elgin's argument for taking as much from the Parthenon as he could get to London: the pieces must be secured from human and environmental threats.

That type of justification can easily mask international power or colonial issues and result in local outrage. It also suggests, though, that the vital materialism of antiquity objects can be lost over time in their original places and regained in assemblages with entirely new audiences, who can even proceed to give the objects 'rights'. International relations has moved steadily away from the Westphalian tradition of protecting state sovereignty over nations and territory to protecting threatened groups and also objects and architectures. UNESCO's 1970 Convention on the Means of Prohibiting and Preventing the Illicit Import, Export and Transfer of Ownership of Cultural Property defines certain objects as having a rightful territorial place. The communitarian view imbedded in the Convention prohibits the transfer of cultural objects from countries that forbid or restrict such actions.

Italy has some of the most stringent laws on exporting antiquities. Marion True, Curator of Antiquities at the Getty Museum in California, was indicted by Italy and tried on the charge of knowingly ignoring national laws safeguarding forty-two antiquities that the Getty acquired between the 1970s and the 1990s. Italy's General Regulations for the Protection of Things of Historical and Artistic Interest holds that the state in effect owns all artefacts discovered after 1902 and does not allow the export of such items without a permit—and such permits are rare. The trial carried on for five years and then ended abruptly when the statute of limitations on the charges expired. It was a show trial that indicated to museums and assemblages of looters and gallerists what would happen if they acquired antiquities illegally or failed to return requested objects to Italy. It also aimed to disincentivize the massive antiquities digs that have taken place recently in Puglia and Sicily. In effect, the state, the Italian antiquities police and stolen or still-buried objects formed a working assemblage that had subpoena agency over important individuals and art institutions beyond Italy's shores.

Most British Museum holdings gained in the nineteenth century would be deemed illegally acquired if taken today. That argument has been used to try to pry key objects out of the Museum's hold to repositories in countries that claim them as cultural patrimony. Calls for repatriation of the Parthenon sculptures have been heard from their earliest days in England to the present day, heightened now that Athens has a state-of-the-art museum that awaits their eventual return. Such objects, it is argued, are central to local identity, pride and historical achievement, and should not be hoarded by institutions abroad, the only claim to the works of which is that they have them.[34] The other side of the argument, the cosmopolitan view embraced by major museums with antiquity holdings, is that there is rarely a rightful or essential national owner of antiquities; for instance, Greece is a recent state in an area that was under Ottoman (Turkish) control for 400 years. Those objects belong to the world now, say the cosmopolitans, and must be secured in countries that have stable political systems, up-to-date and well-run museums, and open societies that accept differences of ethnicity, religion, history and expression.[35] In each case, the museums speak for and on behalf of the objects and history of territories and entire populations, and yet it is the objects that attract the attention, that compel the arguments and justifications.

The British Museum is the standard-setter for the cosmopolitan argument. Its management maintains that the museum is the best in the world at displaying, conserving, comparing, securing and rendering accessible the heritage of all people.[36] That historically imperial museum now has a stringent policy on acquisitions: unless it can verify the provenance of an item offered for sale, as a gift, or as a bequeathal, the museum will not accept it. Other museums have been slow to reach that position. Staffan Lunden found Swedish gallery owners and curators astonishingly open about their own roles in networks of extraction and export that defy national and international laws.[37] His TV documentary 'On the Trail of Tomb Robbers (Heritage for Sale)'[38] shows them boasting about carrying small Asian artefacts in coat pockets or checked luggage, taking care not to include bronze items that can be detected by airport security machines. They admit hiring locals to procure and deliver larger objects to galleries abroad, where they are resold to Swedish collectors at low prices. A curator at the Mediterranean Museum of Antiquities Stockholm explains that museums must deal in smuggled objects if they are to fulfil state missions to build credible and admirable collections of antiquities. The director of the private Museum of Art and Far Eastern Antiquities at Ulricehamn (no longer open), ushers the Queen of Sweden around an exhibition, claiming all the while that the objects come from legitimate sales of 'old collections' in England, America and Sweden; later, he brags to interviewers that he personally smuggled many of the objects out of China.[39] Sweden has been nonplussed about smuggled or illicitly procured artefacts and has only been controlling the acquisition of antiquities since 2002.[40] Before then, its view was that the UNESCO convention prohibited only the exportation of illicitly procured objects, not their import into Sweden. It was not alone in this. Lunden argues that there was more grave robbing, clandestine digging and smuggling following the UNESCO convention than before it. That is to say, assemblages in Sweden (and Denmark, Norway and Switzerland until recently) tipped in the direction of powerful extraction networks, in which objects necessarily figured as co-actants of a different sort than in anti-looting assemblages with museums certain and antiquities police.

In both cases, the vitality of the objects is such that looters of all sorts—museums, collectors, local diggers, terrorist organizations and criminal networks—seek them and then try to secure them from other looters. Elkins maintains that objects and those who look at them act on one another in ways that change each a little bit, with impact and meaning flowing in both directions.[41] Antiquities that are moved about—for whatever reason, whatever the human intention—are vital parts of assemblages that re-form historical and contemporary identity and meaning. Bennett does not favour this kind of interpretation of thing-power. She sees it as an excursion into the '"historicity of objects", about the way the form and meaning of things change and detach from a social whole or become embedded in new relations with new things. (This is what the "social lives of objects" tradition in anthropology, sociology, and science studies does.)'[42] Yet she is keen on developing the imagination required to 'see' certain unseen or un-noted things as actants, whether those things are atoms or antiquities buried in the ground, both of which become vital materialities in certain circumstances and assemblages. Moreover, the electrical blackout Bennett describes is about changed relations between assemblage elements. It is reasonable to assume that following the blackout, the meanings electrical engineers attached to the forces they worked to channel more reliably changed under the impact of their new, unanticipated performance. Presumably the rogue flows of electricity also changed to some degree as a result of changes in operating procedures.

In assemblages of vibrant matter and designing humans, historicity will be inescapable but not necessarily predictable. The Entartete Kunst exhibitions illustrate this: modernist works that the Nazi state and cooperating museums intended to kill lived on in unintended ways by turning the heads of many viewers. The point is not that the way to save art is to exhibit it as atrocity! The point is to follow the logic of agentic actants to consequences that change the flows, meanings and agency of objects in assemblages of relocation. Not accounted for in most analyses of looting are the dynamics of everyday assemblages that are thick with actants and betweenness of objects, humans and art institutions. These can be more insecuring of antiquities over time than moments of looting during wars.

Looting during times of war and political turmoil

Consider: as coalition troops entered in Baghdad 2003, thousands of objects were looted or wilfully damaged at a number of institutions over an eight-day period. Little to no object protection was assembled until the US military on the ground received orders to secure museums and libraries—orders, in effect, to take the security of antiquities seriously in the war for Iraq.[43] In that case, media attention made it possible for distant observers to see objects being carted away and to interact virtually with them. Consider as well the socially destabilizing Taliban regime exploding the Bamiyan Valley Buddhas in 2001, because they encouraged performances of religious practices incompatible with newly Islamicist Afghanistan. That was a case of looting transhistory by trying to make it collapse into an everlasting present; however, the giant objects have not disappeared entirely—their agency appears physically outlined on each empty stone receptacle, giving the statues as a whole a dramatic afterlife that resists evisceration. Meanwhile, the ancient Hindu Preah Vihear temple on the Cambodia–Thailand border has been at the centre of a territorial dispute dating back to the withdrawal of France from Cambodia in the 1950s. The International Court of Justice ruled in 1962 that the structure was within Cambodia's territorial borders, and UNESCO listed it in 2008 as a World Heritage Site. Thailand launched five military exchanges in the intervening years and recently aimed artillery at Cambodian soldiers defending the temple as though it were a military fortification.[44] Just as the American and Polish military bases in Babylon brought serious damage to ancient ruins in 2003, efforts to secure Preah Vihear through regular military patrols of the area have already degraded the temple complex.[45] That is another way to loot history: militarize it, intentionally or otherwise. Still, ruins can be seen as changed objects that enter into new relations with succeeding generational assemblages of observers and users. Such objects have a vibrant presence at various historical moments sufficient to become centres of 'ruins cults' or of energetic projects of restoration.[46]

Each case reveals antiquities threatened by forces that fight over them, trample them in fighting, have political-religious disagreements with object meanings, or just want to have the objects. Looters are invisible in everyday forms of antiquities looting and they are equally so in war or regime change situations; TV media focus on shadowy figures in the fray and on the antiquities experts they interview. Sometimes the looted museum is secured by military as in the case of the Iraq Museum,[47] sometimes by civilian protesters as in Cairo.[48] Museum personnel make inventories of missing items, and Interpol and local police try to trace their movements. Conservationists zero in on damaged objects. Journalists and photographers on the ground investigate human interest issues—they are the ones, not security studies specialists, who note ancient vases, pots and candleholders scattered about an antiquities entrepreneur's makeshift shop—all recently brought in from diggers in southern Iraq. They are the ones who note shopkeeper comments: 'people have to make a living.'[49] Missing, however, are tales of interactions between antiquity objects and humans—trails of object-human assemblages that are simplistically reduced to 'looting'.

Roger MacGinty does present a typology of looting behaviours during war that includes looting from museums.[50] Usually described as an economic activity based on opportunistic circumstance and greed, MacGinty also suggests that affective considerations be taken into account, such as efforts to enhance individual esteem by taking fine objects, or the pleasure of owning and displaying them. MacGinty's interest in affective aspects of looting resonates with Judith Butler's very different writing on the politics of grieving in wartime,[51] and raises the question of whether some looting from museums could communicate meanings of grief, vulnerability and saving identity in situations where the built environment is being destroyed by air assaults or tanks are breaking apart Babylonian ruins.[52] It would be naive to think that greed or orders from metropolitan museums and auction houses for specific pieces would not be at play. Yet war is a sensory experience for people and for objects[53] and those who physically touch, remove or destroy objects are connecting the personal, the political, the sensory and the power of the object in a different kind of security script than one usually contemplates. At minimum, it makes sense to think of some such objects as 'companion[s] in life experience', as Sherry Turkle puts it in *Evocative Objects*.[54] It might also be the case that some objects are taken when their absence or destruction poses an existential threat that requires emergency measures, just as linking arms to protect the Egypt Museum from looters also suggests.[55] In that case, it would be important to note that ordinary people become involved in security operations in ways that reveal certain human security needs not yet named and addressed in studies of war.

Critical archaeology studies has been more attuned to such human security situations. David Matsuda, for one, discusses indigenous people who dig for artefacts in sites across Latin America for modest economic gain and to connect with the past of their ancestors and their own threatened future.[56] In their view, what some might call the museum-quality objects they unearth have meaning as gifts that real or mythological ancestors left for future generations of relatives to find. Any suggestion that they are looting is something these diggers reject. They claim to be saving and securing their heritage while selling some pieces for subsistence items—seeds, food, clothes and the like. It is the archaeological enterprise that encourages looting, some of these diggers attest, by setting up large excavation sites that attract outside thieves and land speculators, who take away land from subsistence farmers and then tear up the earth for objects to sell on the international market. Local militaries charged with working to conserve the jungle also steal its hidden objects for profit.

Matsuda refers to the agentic forces operating in such settings as class warfare. Those who are powerful decide everything is theirs, including the sites of indigenous culture. Those who are poor and disenfranchised dig. The objects? They are pivotal in all the contradictory assemblages, but their agency in tandem with humans remains unarticulated in this account, which means that the story leans on them vs. us thinking and not on mapped out security relations between pots and a variety of people. Similarly, Zahi Hawass, Egypt's then chief archaeologist, informed the global media that the invaders of the museum in Cairo did not appear to understand the value of the objects around them. 'I'm glad those people were idiots', Hawass told *Time Magazine*.[57] 'Thank God they thought that the museum shop was the museum.'[58] Is it idiotic to target the jewellery in the museum shop and not the antiquities of one's heritage?[59] Is the phenomenon as simple, and as stupid, as Hawass gloatingly asserts through his class bias? Or is that an old materialist way of masking relations or 'thickening significances', as Daston piquantly puts it, between object things and looters?[60]

Power, agency, objects, security, assemblages

Erik Nemeth argues that a new academic field is needed to integrate the insights of critical archaeology, International Relations and related studies of art and architecture security. He would call the new field cultural security and have as its raison d'être 'mitigating exploitation of cultural property as a pawn in foreign relations and as a tool in acts of political violence and terrorism'.[61] He would include in its purview acts of destruction and selective plunder of historic and religious monuments that draw international attention,[62] and looting by often interconnected terrorist groups and organized crime. While Nemeth makes a good point about 'factoring cultural property into the pursuit of international security',[63] security studies, a field he does not mention, is accommodating a variety of security issues today. What we should invite is attention to an object-people nexus that is too often simplified. We might state the task as identifying the swarm of vitalities involved in looting and other types of object-seeking practices in specific situations of conflict. Security would become a clearer problematic once elements of the swarm are known. It would not be an us vs. them approach or a task requiring that one group be designated as more deserving of the antiquities than others who also have relations with those objects. However, that is only one aspect of a security problematic around thing-power and antiquities. Very few specifics are known about looters of museums relative to museums as looters and other types of 'diggers'. Militarization as looting endangers antiquities and sites in order to secure a military mission; as a type of securitizing problematic, there are numerous object-people distributions of agency that require investigation.

I have two methodological/theoretical suggestions on how to proceed, which can only be touched on here. The first is to consider the object as an element of a collage that works with other elements framing it and with the attentive viewer.[64] The collage framework eschews the solace of artistic intentionality and flatly refuses the notion that every picture tells a story. Narrative paintings might tell a story or two but a collage, often called an assemblage, is a visual challenge to the comforts of known connections, optical competence, laws of physics, design convictions and common customs (would anyone ordinarily put violins and parsley together?). It is a juxtaposition of unexpected and seemingly unrelated objects in one frame, or as Max Ernst cannily put it, 'the meeting of two distant realities on a plane foreign to them both'.[65] Think of the tank facing outwards from the Children's Entrance to the National Museum of Iraq 2003. Think of fine Italianate vases painted with Grayson Perry's pornographic scenes. Think Guggenheim Bilbao. Collages mix things up, launch objects out of assigned places and into spots we least expect them to be, and disrupt coherent, causal storylines. These inanimate objects give nothing away, surrender to few laws of human logic, and compel those who view them to make something of the strange things they see, without any help. Collages cannot be fixed, controlled and definitively figured out. They are heterogeneous, active, and work in different ways in different situations and with different audiences. In some ways, collage-things are more in control than the people viewing them.

In 2005, I imagined a collage with the following elements:

> Paste a soft fabric tank onto the painted and sand-strewn steps of a columned building that has been set in the center of a large canvas. In the foreground, a ground scattered with cats eye marbles, glue shards of rounded clear glass to form a container. Fill that container halfway with water and place in it a representation of the Lady of Warka alabaster. She should appear as she does in life—a 20-centimeter face detached from a body, looking at us through hollow eyes and unsmiling lips. Her nose is chipped. Her hair is tightly curled. Her eyebrows join in the middle. The half of her head in water is clean; the other half is crusted with soil. Standing over her is a paper cutout of an Iraqi man and standing behind and over him is a British Museum culture soldier. A young American GI in combat dress looms over them all. In the upper left of the canvas a pair of figures moves away from the scene. One is clothed from head to foot in dark heavy fabric and the other, running unfettered towards the heavens, is painted wearing a white tee shirt with the word LIBERTY on the back; the painted figure looks anxiously over his shoulder at the scene below. Within the windows of the darkened building at the center of the frame, painted figures sit in featureless profile, all in identical white clinical jackets. They look down, look out, look up; they do not look at each other or at the Lady. The imagined collage is 'War Wards.'[66]

That is an imagined actant swarm, and at its centre is an antiquity from 3500 BC that was looted during the museum break-in in Baghdad and found half buried at a farm 40 miles north of the city. Which figure in the collage is the protagonist? Who is the looter or the audience? Who or what is in charge? Who should be blamed and punished, pursued, or congratulated? Where exactly is the security problematic located and of what does it consist? Is it about securing the Lady of Warka antiquity against the military invaders or the museum figures? Or is it about getting the identically dressed, featureless figures to look at the Lady of Warka and the assemblage around her as a security problem that straddles human, national and international meanings?

The second approach considers possible parallels between the agency and power of things like antiquities and the agency and power of things like images. Lene Hansen recently raised the question of whether images in the form of the infamous cartoons that appeared in Danish newspapers—one featured the Prophet Mohammad's head as a bomb—can speak security to us: 'speak' because one school of security thinking (the Copenhagen School) regards public speech acts as fundamental to the constitution of something as threatened or requiring defence.[67] Bennett and Hansen seem in unwitting dialogue with one another about the agency of 'thing power', with Hansen offering rules for when and how an image thing exerts agency in assemblages with other factors. She also identifies components, characteristics and genres of image/visual securitization that interact with speech acts to create a security problematic like the cartoon crisis. Using the post-structuralist concept of intertexuality to characterize the process, she presents a complex model that unsurprisingly privileges human language use and interpretation over the thing-power of the image. Hansen's order of events and rules can be rearranged and combined a bit, but they will always feature, she says, images, the immediate intertext, dominant policy discourses, and the linguistic texts that attribute meaning to images. The image-thing is there, but it ultimately relies on networks of human agency in order to 'speak'. Through Bennett's words I ask her, though: 'why are we so keen to distinguish the human self from the field?'[68]

At the end of the day, the researcher must make up his or her mind about how much power, or to use good social science terms, 'weight' to give the object looted versus the looter, whose identity can be interchangeable or defused by the power of objects. If, at the end of another day, the object returns to some of the institutions with a looting history, what has (whose) agency been about? Where does the object rest secure or where is it securest? Perhaps in the earth or at the bottom of the ocean, untouched for millennia, unseen and unsecuritized. That type of talk is anathema in cultural circles, but maybe for reasons not yet accepted, namely that the object has its own dramaturgy of travel and change, its own biography and security problematic as vibrant matter that is as interesting as those of humans, and just as precarious, as archaeologists know.[69]

Notes

1 Robert Bevan, *The Destruction of Memory: Architectures at War*, London: Reaktion Books, 2006.
2 Rory McCarthy and Maeev Kennedy, 'The Wrecking of Babylon: U.S.-Led Forces Leave a Trail of Destruction and Contamination in Architectural Site of World Importance', *The Guardian*, 15 January 2005: 1.
3 Wayne Sandholtz, *Prohibiting Plunder: How Norms Change*, New York: Oxford University Press, 2007; Craig Childs, *Finders Keepers: A Tale of Archaeological Plunder and Obsession*, New York: Little, Brown and Company, 2010.
4 Jane Bennett, *Vibrant Matter: A Political Ecology of Things*, Durham NC: Duke University Press, 2010: 22; see also Jane Bennett, 'The Force of Things: Steps Toward an Ecology of Matter', *Political Theory* 32, no. 3 (2004): 347–72.
5 One was an American who tried to smuggle a cylinder seal into the United States.
6 Roger MacGinty, 'Looting in the Context of Violent Conflict: A Conceptualization and Typology', *Third World Quarterly* 25, no. 5 (2004): 857–70; Erik Nemeth, 'Conflict Art: Scholars Develop the Tactical Value of Cultural Patrimony', *Cambridge Review of International Affairs* 23, no. 2 (2010): 299–323; Erik Nemeth, 'Cultural Security: The Evolving Role of Art in International Security', *Terrorism and Political Violence* 19, no. 1 (2007): 19–42.

7 Lorraine Daston, ed., *Things That Talk: Object Lessons from Art and Science*, New York: Zone Books, 2008; Joseph Leo Koerner, 'Bosch's Equipment', in *Things That Talk: Object Lessons from Art and Science*, ed. Lorraine Daston, New York: Zone Books, 2008: 27–66.
8 Peter Guenther, 'Three Days in Munich July 1937', in *'Degenerate Art': The Fate of the Avant-Garde in Nazi Germany*, ed. Stephanie Barron, Los Angeles, CA: Los Angeles County Museum of Art, 1991: 33–45, at 45.
9 Bennett, *Vibrant Matter*: 24, emphasis in original.
10 W.J.T. Mitchell, *What Do Pictures Want? The Lives and Loves of Images*, Chicago, IL: University of Chicago Press, 2005.
11 Bennett, *Vibrant Matter*: 2.
12 Bennett, *Vibrant Matter*: 25.
13 Bennett, *Vibrant Matter*: 58.
14 Bennett, *Vibrant Matter*: xvi.
15 Bennett, *Vibrant Matter*: xvii.
16 Bennett, *Vibrant Matter*: 24.
17 James Elkins, *The Object Stares Back: On the Nature of Seeing*, New York: Harcourt, 1996: 44.
18 James Der Derian, *Virtuous War*, New York: Routledge, 2001.
19 Bennett, *Vibrant Matter*: 9.
20 Megan MacKenzie, 'Ruling Exceptions: Female Soldiers and Everyday Experiences of Civil Conflict', in *Experiencing War*, ed. Christine Sylvester, London: Routledge, 2011: 64–78.
21 Jacqueline Leckie, ed., *Development in an Insecure and Gendered World*, Surrey: Ashgate, 2009.
22 Haroon A. Akram-Lohdi, 'The Macroeconomies of Human Insecurity: Why Gender Matters', in *Development in an Insecure and Gendered World*, ed. Jacqueline Leckie, Surrey: Ashgate, 2009: 71–90, at 76.
23 Dambisa Moyo, *Dead Aid: Why Aid is Not Working and How There is Another Way for Africa*, London: Penguin, 2009.
24 Gayatri Chakravorty Spivak, 'Can the Subaltern Speak?' in *Marxism and the Interpretation of Culture*, ed. Cary Nelson and Larry Grossberg, Chicago: University of Illinois Press, 1988: 271–313.
25 Bennett, *Vibrant Matter*, 19.
26 For example, Myra Hird, 'Feminist Engagements with Matter', *Feminist Studies* 35, no. 2 (2009): 329–46; Alaimo Stacy and Susan Hekman, eds, *Material Feminisms*, Bloomington: Indiana University Press, 2008; Donna Haraway, *When Species Meet*, Minneapolis: University of Minnesota, 2003; Karen Barad, *Meeting the Universe Halfway: Quantum Physics and the Entanglement of Matter and Meaning*, Durham, NC: Duke University Press, 2007.
27 For example, Bruno Latour, *We Have Never Been Modern*, trans. Catherine Porter, Cambridge, MA: Harvard University Press, 1993; Bruce Braun and Sarah Whatmore, eds, *Political Matter: Technoscience, Democracy, and Public Life*, Minneapolis: University of Minnesota Press, 2010; Gilles Deleuze and Felix Guattari, *A Thousand Plateaus: Capitalism and Schizophrenia*, trans. Brian Massumi, Minneapolis: University of Minnesota Press, 1987.
28 Bennett, *Vibrant Matter*: 32.
29 Bennett, *Vibrant Matter*: 32.
30 Philosophy in a Time of Error, 'Vibrant Matters: An Interview with Jane Bennett', April 2010, philosophyinatimeoferror.wordpress.com/2010/04/22/vibrant-matters-an-interview-with-jane-bennett/.
31 Philosophy in a Time of Error, 'Vibrant Matters'.
32 Marinka Fruk, *The Destruction of Museums and Galleries in Croatia During the 1991 War*, Zagreb: Ministry of Education and Culture, 1992.

33 Marjorie Caygill, *The Story of the British Museum*, 3rd edn, London: British Museum Press, 2003.
34 John Moustakas, 'Group Rights in Cultural Property', *Cornell Law Review* 74 (1989): 1179.
35 See discussion in Christine Sylvester, *Art/Museums: International Relations Where We Least Expect It*, Boulder, CO: Paradigm Publishers, 2009; Kwame Anthony Appiah, *Cosmopolitanism: Ethics in a World of Strangers*, New York: Norton, 2006; Michael Kimmelman, 'Is it All Loot? Tackling the Antiquities Problem', *The New York Times*, 29 March 2006.
36 Neil MacGregor, 'The Whole World in Our Hands', *Guardian Review*, 24 July 2004: 4–6.
37 Staffan Lunden, 'The Scholar and the Market: Swedish Scholarly Contributions to the Destruction of the World's Archaeological Heritage', in *Swedish Archaeologists on Ethics*, ed. Håkan Karlsson, Lindome: Bricoleur Press, 2004: 197–247.
38 Lunden explains: 'During the course of [my] investigation it became clear that the material gathered could (and should) be used for more than a strictly academic publication. Therefore in 1999 contact was made with the investigative journalists Johan Bråstad and Hannes Råstam at Sveriges Television … The result was the documentary … On the Trail of the Tomb Robbers … which was aired on February 29, 2000': Lunden, 'The Scholar and the Market': 199. The film won the 2000 Prix d'Italia.
39 Against this backdrop of slippage in museum ethics, an American museum survey found that visitors to museums of all kinds ranked them higher than government institutions as providers of trustworthy sources of objective information. James Cuno, ed., *Whose Muse? Art Museums and the Public Trust*, Princeton, NJ: Princeton University Press, 2004.
40 See also David Gill, 'Looting Matters for Classical Antiquities: Contemporary Issues in Archaeological Ethics', *Present Pasts* 1 (2009): 1–29; Neill Brodie and Colin Renfrew 'Looting and the World's Archaeological Heritage: The Inadequate Response', *Annual Review of Anthropology* 34 (2005): 343–61.
41 Elkins, *The Object Stares Back*: 43.
42 Bennett, *Vibrant Matter*: 57.
43 Sylvester, *Art/Museums*.
44 Tod Pittman, 'Historic Temple Caught in Cambodia-Thai Crossfire', Associated Press, 10 February 2011, news.yahoo.com/s/ap/20110210/ap_on_re_as/as_cambodia_thailand_frontline_temple.
45 In July 2011, the International Court of Justice responded to a case brought against Thailand by Cambodia with the decision that the area around the temple was to be demilitarized. Both countries have been directed to withdraw all their forces, thus securing the future of the temple before it reaches the stage of a ruin.
46 Simon Jenkins notes that the European romantics developed a particular relationship to ruins, 'celebrating not static humps of stone but active decay, the return of old buildings to the soil from which they sprung'. Simon Jenkins, 'The Cult of the Ruin Renders English Landscape Soulless', *The Guardian*, 14 April 2011, www.the-sheet.com/architecture-news/this-cult-of-the-ruin-renders-englands-landscape-soulless-better-to-rebuild-simon-jenkins.
47 Matthew Bogdanos, *Thieves of Baghdad*, London: Bloomsbury, 2005.
48 During the Arab Spring of 2011, one person emerged, through self-nomination and relieved acclamation, as the agent of the Cairo 'revolution'. Associated Press reports the Google Inc. executive Wael Ghonim claimed responsibility for drawing the crowds, owing to his call for action on internet networks. The media reported 'about 90,000 people have joined a Facebook group nominating Ghonim to be their spokesman': Hamza Hendawi and Maggie Michaely, 'Mubarek Forms Reform Committees', Yahoo News, Associated Press, 8

February 2011, news.yahoo.com/s/ap/20110208/ap_on_re_mi_ea/ml_egypt. In subsequent days, his singular agency was de-emphasized as a swarm of capable political representatives, including the Muslim Brotherhood, asserted their importance to democracy negotiations. Bennett might conclude that the distributive power of the crowd atomized, individualized, and reassembled with new emergent properties.
49 Matthew Campbell, 'Iraq's Culture Cops Go Hunting Looters', *The Guardian*, 11 January 2004: 29.
50 MacGinty, 'Looting in the Context of Violent Conflict'.
51 Judith Butler, *Precarious Life: The Powers of Mourning and Violence*, London: Verso, 2004.
52 Christine Sylvester, 'The Art of War/The War Question in (Feminist) International Relations', *Millennium: Journal of International Studies* 33, no. 3 (2005): 855–78.
53 Christine Sylvester, ed., *Experiencing War*, London: Routledge, 2011; Christine Sylvester, 'War, Sense, and Security', in *Gender and International Security: Feminist Perspectives*, ed. Laura Sjoberg, New York: Routledge, 2010: 24–37.
54 Sherry Turkle, ed., *Evocative Objects: Things We Think With*, Cambridge, MA: MIT Press, 2007: 5.
55 Of course, some looters vandalize museums and damage or destroy antiquities on their rampages, a subject that has also not been treated adequately in the literature.
56 David Matsuda, 'The Ethics of Archaeology, Subsistence Digging, and Artifact Looting in Latin America: Point, Muted Counterpoint', *International Journal of Cultural Property* 7 (1998): 87–97.
57 By 14 February 2011, however, Hawass was himself under attack by a legion of archaeology graduates, who claimed he preferred personal grandstanding to helping them find jobs working with antiquities. That he also agreed to be minister of antiquities, after the protests against the Mubarak government were well established, put him under suspicion as a Mubarak sympathizer.
58 Michael Sheridan and Corky Siemaszko, 'Protesters Defended Cairo's Egyptian Museum from Looters: Archeological Warehouses Raided', NYDaily News.com, 31 January 2011, www.nydailynews.com/news/world/2011/01/31/2011-01-31_protesters_defended_cairos_egyptian_museum_from_looters.html.
59 I thank Staffan Lunden for suggesting this 'unthinkable' possibility.
60 Daston, *Things That Talk*: 20.
61 Nemeth, 'Cultural Security': 20.
62 Nemeth refers to such acts as part of foreign relations or 'efforts to garner diplomatic attention' (Nemeth, 'Cultural Security': 22), but seems to mean international attention in general, including the global media.
63 Nemeth, 'Cultural Security': 36; also Nemeth, 'Conflict Art'.
64 Sylvester, *Art/Museums*.
65 Arthur Danto, *After the End of Art: Contemporary Art and the Pale of History*, Princeton, NJ: Princeton University Press, 1997: 21.
66 Sylvester, 'The Art of War': 864–65.
67 Lene Hansen, 'Theorizing the Image for Security Studies: Visual Securitization and the Muhammad Cartoon Crisis', *European Journal of International Relations* 17, no. 1 (2011): 51–74.
68 Bennett, *Vibrant Matter*: 121.
69 For a discussion of object biographies, see Igor Kopytoff, 'The Cultural Biography of Things: Commodification as Process', in *The Social Life of Things: Commodities in Cultural Perspective*, ed. Arjun Appadurai, Cambridge: Cambridge University Press, 1986: 64–94.

13 Staging war as cultural encounter

Maja Zehfuss

The destructiveness of warfare is an affront to liberal sensibilities.[1] Thus, in what is generally called the West, there has been a trend to make war less violent—gentler, if you will. Drawing lines between combatants and non-combatants and trying to keep the latter out of harm's way as much as possible has played a significant role in this endeavour. Roughly from the 1991 Gulf War until the end of the so-called first phase of the war in Iraq, this meant that the West's supreme capacity to blow up the right stuff with precision, that is without—or so the impression was created—hurting 'innocent civilians' played a significant role in the justification of war. Put differently, the West was seen to be 'better' at war on the grounds of its efficient use of high-tech weaponry. As I have argued elsewhere, this 'better' did not just refer to the West's greater capacity to win whatever conflict it might enter, but also to its doing so in a way seen as more ethical because, or so the argument goes, the West was killing fewer civilians.[2] Thus, technological superiority—and hence capacities derived from the natural sciences and engineering—provided not only the route to dominance but also the key to moral superiority.

The grossly misnamed 'war on terror' has not succeeded in shifting us out of this imaginary, but it has certainly managed to get a few serious scratches on the slick surface of these representations. The problem is at least twofold. First of all, when coalition troops, enemy fighters and civilians are not spatially separated, blowing up stuff becomes a rather less attractive proposition. Second, and probably more importantly, the very people who some of the cruder commentators have suggested only understand force have proven rather unwilling to do just that. That is, blowing up stuff has not led—and cannot lead—to any kind of meaningful victory in the ongoing conflicts; rather, if the West is to win, the people of Iraq and Afghanistan must be persuaded to put down arms and accept the new political order.

In this context an ability to understand the local population emerges as crucial to success; as Montgomery McFate observes, 'Winning hearts and minds requires understanding local culture'.[3] Hence, the culture of the countries to which militaries are being deployed has become of central interest. 'Cultural awareness' and 'cultural knowledge' have become significant to discussions in military circles. This means that militaries are now in need of expertise from the social sciences. This chapter explores the way in which this newfound interest in the social sciences stages war as a cultural encounter and thereby takes the production of war as gentle to an entirely new level: violence comes to appear as merely incidental to the practice of war.

The significance of cultural knowledge

Something did not go quite as planned with the invasion of Iraq by the United States and its allies. 'Shock and Awe' was meant to deliver a quick victory but spectacularly failed to do so. It was, as Thomas E. Ricks puts it, a 'fiasco'.[4] People were dying. The deaths especially of Iraqi civilians and coalition troops generated questions about the purpose, feasibility and conduct of the mission. Ricks sees the fiasco as enabled by an incompetent assessment both of the threat posed by Iraq and of the difficulties that would be associated with occupying the country.[5]

At the same time, this 'fiasco' was arguably part of a larger failure to prepare for the most likely operational environments. Put differently, the problem of the ill-advised and ill-prepared invasion was compounded, Ricks argues, by the military leadership's failure to prepare the forces for the sort of operation in which they would be engaged.[6] There was a 'disconnect' between the sort of war imagined on the basis of the so-called revolution in military affairs (RMA) and the reality of fighting protracted counterinsurgencies in Afghanistan and Iraq. *US News & World Report* observed in 2006 that '[a]fter three years of roadside bombs, midnight raids, and sectarian strife, one can safely say that Iraq is not the kind of war for which the National Training Center and the U.S. Army spent decades preparing. In fact, Iraq is the kind of fight that, after Vietnam, the Army hoped to avoid'.[7] Ricks further complains that the leadership of the US military had not only failed to prepare soldiers for the situation they would face in Iraq but then also 'wasted a year by using counterproductive tactics that were employed in unprofessional ignorance of the basic tenets of counterinsurgency warfare'.[8]

A central element of the rethinking, when it finally happened, involved the argument that the armed forces were in need of cultural knowledge in order to be able to complete their missions effectively. This view had been put forward for some time, not least by those who eventually drew up the 2006 US Army and Marine Corps *Counterinsurgency Manual*.[9] The manual is replete with references to the significance of such knowledge, which it declares to be 'essential to waging a successful counterinsurgency'.[10] It both explains why culture is quite so crucial and what that means, in practical terms, for a commander operating in a counterinsurgency environment. Because in a counterinsurgency operation military success is not in itself decisive, understanding the population in the area of operations is crucial. As the manual points out, 'American ideas of what is "normal" or "rational" are not universal'.[11] Linguistic and cultural skills are therefore of central importance.[12]

Some of the various cultural tidbits that soldiers deployed to Afghanistan and Iraq are told have become common knowledge: don't speak to women; never show the soles of your shoes; and the 'thumbs-up' gesture is rude. Some of this advice on do's and don'ts is handed out on so-called smartcards which also give basic sociocultural information about the country of deployment, such as the size of different faith groups. These smartcards are laminated and may be folded up like a map, making it easy for soldiers to carry them around in a pocket.[13] The *Counterinsurgency Manual*, however, envisages much more than an ability to communicate and to grasp some general insights about cultural specifics. Rather, '[c]ommanders and planners require insight into cultures, perceptions, values, beliefs, interests and decision-making processes of individuals and groups'.[14]

The manual also provides clear strategies for acquiring such insight. It proposes that in order 'to evaluate the people ... six sociocultural factors should be analyzed', namely society, social structure, culture, language, power and authority, and interests.[15] Each of these is defined, making chapter 3 of the manual sound more like over-simplified guidance for a basic social science project than a military manual. For example, a '*society* can be defined as a population whose members are subject to the same political authority, occupy a common territory, have a common culture, and share a sense of identity'.[16] The definitions appear rather crude. They lack the sense of complexity one would see in scholarly literature on such topics: after all, where are we to find a society with *one* common culture and shared identity? Yet the explanation of these sociocultural factors is quite detailed and includes illustrative examples. Commanders are, at any rate, asked to 'thoroughly' map out the culture. Once this has been accomplished,

> staffs should identify and analyze the culture of the society as a whole and of each major group within the society. Social structure comprises the relationships among groups, institutions, and individuals within a society; in contrast, culture (ideas, norms, rituals, codes of behavior) provides meaning to individuals within the society.[17]

All this is presented as though secure knowledge about *the* culture can be obtained, even if this may be a time-consuming and difficult process, and as though this knowledge will then provide significant access to the 'hearts and minds' of the population. In order to achieve the required insight into the culture, social network theory, explained in Appendix B to the manual, is presented as providing the right tool.

In fact, while much is oversimplified, the manual admits quite openly that all this is rather more complicated than the average soldier might like things to be. The example of 'culture' can usefully illustrate this. Since cultural knowledge is so central to counterinsurgency warfare, it is particularly important to know what is meant by the term. The manual invites us to think of culture as 'being the muscle on the bones' of social structure.[18] It is a "web of meaning" shared by members of a particular society or group within a society'.[19] As such, it involves a 'system of shared beliefs, values, customs, behaviors, and artifacts that members of a society use to cope with their world and with one another'; it is learnt, must be shared by several people, involves patterns and may change over time.

In other words, culture seems to be presented like a foreign language that can be learnt or perhaps like an opponent's strategic behaviour that may be different but that follows some logic that we may seek to grasp. This is certainly part of what is at stake. The reason why culture is of such interest to counterinsurgent forces is that it 'might also be described as an "operational code" that is valid for an entire group of people'.[20] That is, culture 'conditions the individual's range of action and ideas, including what to do and not to do, how to do or not to do it, and whom to do it with or not to do it with'.[21]

However, the manual also departs from the idea that these rules can simply be learnt, for crucially, while culture establishes the rules, it also affects when these can be treated flexibly or might even shift. What is not quite clear in this explanation is why whatever determines when rules might be broken or at least amended is not itself a rule. For the moment what matters, however, is that there are moments in the manual where it seems to push beyond the sort of understanding of culture that might have been common in the 1950s where culture is distilled into a sort of grammar book that would sum up the rules of a culture. The idea was that once you knew those rules, you were competent to operate in the culture.[22]

In places the manual uses the language of narrative rather than rule. That is, it informs us not only that the shared belief systems within a culture find their expression in cultural forms,[23] but also that the 'most important cultural form for counterinsurgents to understand is the narrative'.[24] The example of the Boston Tea Party is used to illustrate what a cultural narrative is and how it tells a group who they are and what they value. The manual even points out that this example also shows that 'narratives may not conform to historical facts or they may drastically simplify facts to more clearly express cultural values'.[25] Narratives, it explains, are significant for counterinsurgents as they give clues as to a society's core values and may also be used by insurgents to 'mobilize the population'.[26] Soldiers and Marines are further warned that culture is 'internalized' meaning, that it is 'habitual, taken for granted, and perceived as "natural" by people within the society', indeed that it is 'arbitrary' in the sense that they 'should make no assumptions regarding what a society considers right and wrong, good and bad'.[27]

What is interesting is that all this talk of other cultures as different, but following a logic of their own, stages war as a cultural encounter, with significant implications. Some of the manual in fact reminds me of the work I used to do preparing students who were going to live with a host family in a different country for a year for the challenges of inter-cultural communication.[28] These parts of the manual could easily be used to advise students going abroad:

observe and try to work out what the rules are. Remember that people might not know why they are doing something one way rather than another, and that this is quite all right. Don't assume that your view of the world is the only possible one or indeed superior. Remember that others may feel strongly about their values, even if you don't share them.

However, the manual is a manual for war; so the understanding of culture takes place not only within the context of violent conflict, but as part of its conduct. The manual talks of respecting the host nation population and says quite a lot about how understanding culture can help to reduce violent conflict. In order to mount a successful counterinsurgency, the manual argues, the source of grievances has to be understood. It explains that 'political stakes are often rooted in culture, ideology, societal tensions, and injustice'.[29] Because of this, the advice to soldiers and Marines is: 'Develop cultural intelligence ... Make every effort to learn as much about the environment as possible. Human dynamics tend to matter the most.'[30] This sounds benign: the idea of US forces striving to understand the culture of the country in which they are operating appears to be a world away from 'Shock and Awe'.

At the same time, the manual is less than coy about the ultimate purpose of 'learning' the culture. It instructs its readers to analyse the operation of power: 'Once they have mapped the social structure and understand the culture, staffs must determine how power is apportioned and used within a society.'[31] Power is defined as 'the probability that one actor within a social relationship will be in a position to carry out his or her own will despite resistance'. This dimension is significant, one presumes, because, as is pointed out, 'power is the key to manipulating the interests of groups within a society'.[32] Thus, while the manual notes the significance of understanding culture so as to not offend the population, here it becomes clear that the aim of such understanding is to extend control. In the wonderfully neutral words of the *Army Culture and Foreign Language Strategy*, cultural knowledge is to facilitate 'task accomplishment'.[33] Cultural ignorance, in contrast, gets in the way of mission accomplishment because it may create tension as well as leave US forces unable to impose their will. The willingness to be culturally attuned is therefore always determined and circumscribed by the needs of the mission. As Ricks reports, '"Be polite, be professional, but have a plan to kill everybody you meet" was one of the rules to live by that Maj. Gen. James Mattis gave his Marines'.[34] Or, as Mattis recounts himself having said to Iraqi military leaders after the invasion: 'I come in peace ... I didn't bring artillery. But I'm pleading with you, with tears in my eyes: If you fuck with me, I'll kill you all.'[35]

Cultural knowledge is thus portrayed as essential to achieving contemporary military missions. The point is unsurprisingly not to understand the other in order to empathise and make changes to the US military's courses of action so as to allow others to live as they wish, but rather to make operations go smoothly. The snag is, of course, that culture—even if reduced to a set of rules one might learn—is complicated.

The social sciences to the rescue: the Human Terrain System

It is, of course, one thing to say that military forces require cultural knowledge and quite another to make sure they have it. Although the *Counterinsurgency Manual* goes some way to addressing the issue, it leaves us with a set of instructions that more or less amount to saying that commanders need to complete a research project on the local culture before doing much of anything. It might be a good idea if they did this, but it does not seem likely.

Yet the US military appears to be taking the matter of cultural competence seriously. Both the Marine Corps and the US Army have set up training centres focused on culture with a view to promoting cultural awareness to soldiers across all ranks.[36] Keith Brown argues that the rhetoric on culture is matched by investment in infrastructure for related pre-deployment training. He mentions three elements of this infrastructure in particular: simulated 'Arab' villages; computer games to teach language and negotiation skills; and the establishment of military centres focusing on cultural issues.[37] There has, in other words, been an attempt to change training regimes across the board to reflect the new belief in the significance of culture. Soldiers must acquire 'cultural awareness'. However, while this may be of some help to ensure that they do not inadvertently cause offence and heighten tension, the strategies set out in the counterinsurgency manual seem to require much more advanced knowledge about the local culture and society. Cultural awareness is therefore not enough. As H.R. McMaster, now a US Army Brigadier General, points out, 'it is also important that leaders and units have access to cultural *expertise*'.[38]

This is where the social sciences are thought to be crucial. The most determined effort to make substantive expertise in cultural matters available to forces on deployment seems to be the design and implementation from summer 2005 of the so-called Human Terrain System (HTS) by the US Army. According to its mission statement, HTS:

> develops, trains, and integrates a social science based research and analysis capability to support operationally relevant decision-making, to develop a knowledge base, and to enable sociocultural understanding across the operational environment.[39]

HTS is meant to offer 'an organic capability to help understand and deal with "human terrain"—the social, ethnographic, cultural, economic, and political elements of the people among whom a force is operating', in order to 'address cultural awareness shortcomings at the operational and tactical levels'.[40] The idea is that deploying brigades would be 'culturally empowered' through HTS.[41]

HTS has created controversy, especially among anthropologists.[42] At the heart of this debate is the deployment of Human Terrain Teams (HTTs) that 'conduct social science research'.[43] In the original vision for HTS, these teams were envisaged to consist of 'experienced cultural advisors'.[44] The roles of HTT members were to be leader, cultural analyst, regional studies expert, human terrain research manager and human terrain analyst.[45] The intention was that the cultural analyst should be an anthropologist or sociologist fluent in the local language, while the regional studies analyst would have a similar background, but could be from any social science. Both analysts were meant to have an MA or PhD.[46] Recruiting to these specifications, however, has not proven straightforward and one observer points out that few individuals with the totality of the required skill set are likely to exist.[47] Current information on HTTs only highlights three roles, team leader, social scientist and research manager,[48] which seems to de-emphasise the element of regional or cultural expertise.

The unclassified *Human Terrain Team Handbook* describes in some detail what HTTs are meant to do. Their mission is to conduct:

> operationally-relevant, open-source social science research, and provide commanders and staffs ... with an embedded knowledge capability, to establish a coherent, analytic cultural framework for operational planning, decision-making, and assessment.[49]

The *Handbook* identifies three key points within this mission, the first of which is '*social science research*'.[50] The embedding of skilled field researchers is highlighted as a unique aspect of the programme. The 'required human terrain information' is to be acquired through the use of 'classic' anthropological and sociological research methods, involving both quantitative and qualitative methodologies.[51] The second key point is 'making the gathered data *operationally relevant*',[52] for if the information is not 'distributed and briefed in a relevant manner, it is worthless data'.[53] It is the team leader's job to 'couch' the information 'in terms familiar to a military audience, making it not significantly time-consuming, and insure it is operationally-relevant to the unit's operations and problem-set'.[54] Finally, the HTT must create an '*analytic cultural framework for operational planning, decision-making and assessment*'.[55]

It is claimed that the Social Scientist on the team is what makes HTS unique.[56] According to the *Handbook* issued to HTT members:

> The expertise for conducting research and analysis to provide valid and objective information on [the human dimension] are highly specialized in the social sciences. Social science research of a host nation's population produces a knowledge base that is referred to as the Human Terrain.[57]

It is the Social Scientist's job to create a 'Common Operating Picture in relation to the human terrain'.[58] This is to be achieved 'by using pattern analysis to detect underlying cultural assumptions about the world and using cultural operational knowledge to keep units away from mistaken policy and practice and prevent the misapplication of force'.[59]

The purpose of the HTT is, in other words, specifically to compensate for troops' lack of preparation for (and interest in) what is called non-kinetic aspects of the operation (that is, those not involving the use of force).[60] The Human Terrain Analyst's interpretation of the data should focus on the human terrain, defined as 'the entire spectrum of society and culture',[61] for, as the *Handbook* puts it without, I presume, any sense of irony, in 'non-kinetic roles, the population is the primary battlefield'.[62] The Human Terrain Analyst's job is to 'determine how to win the support of the local population'.[63] However, at the same time, the Human Terrain Analyst's job is defined by the needs of the mission: 'The HTA needs to bear in mind how their analysis and conclusions are relevant to the needs and success of their unit, and how their analysis and conclusions satisfy the tasking'.[64] Or, in the rather more candid words of a commander explaining what he expects from his HTT in a training scenario that involved them meeting a group of village elders: 'I need to know if I give them a handshake or a hand grenade.'[65]

Two points are worth drawing out. First of all, through HTS the problem of counterinsurgency is, again, set up as one of a cultural encounter. What is at issue in this problematization are, by and large, matters of communication and miscommunication. By improving communication, cultural experts are thought to be able to help the military to build more productive relationships with the host nation population. The expectation is that this will help overcome differences. In the words of the HTS *Handbook*, HTTs 'support the decision-making process by recommending options for the use of non-lethal effects to build trust, form partnerships and apply informed cultural knowledge to problem solving and building solutions'.[66] This intended focus on creating more positive relations with the people who live in what to the military is the area of operations also comes out in an explanation of the programme that Christopher King, who was deployed to Iraq as an HTS staff Social Scientist between July 2008 and March 2009 and who is now the HTS Social Science Directorate Director,[67] offers: namely, that it is to 'enable culturally astute decision-making', and that this 'allows commanders to consider the possible ramifications of their choices with consideration of local populations' perceptions, needs and interests'.[68] In this representation of the issues, the point clearly is to develop a better understanding of the people to facilitate getting along with them.

Second, this is so important because the deployment of cultural expertise through HTS will lead to a reduction in violence from both sides. McMaster suggests that such 'cultural expertise can help units distinguish between reconcilable and irreconcilable groups through an analysis of each group's fears and aspirations'.[69] The implication is that so-called reconcilable groups will be engaged in processes of negotiation. HTTs are, in fact, portrayed as promoting reconciliation, especially with 'actors previously viewed as irreconcilable'.[70] This is also highlighted in a recent job description for a social scientist which explains that the '[m]ission of the HTS program is to conduct field studies of cultures and work hand-in-hand with the Army to reduce violence and create peaceful relations with foreign countries'.[71] In this way of looking at the problem, violence appears to be merely a last resort within a larger activity called 'counterinsurgency'. In other words, violence is being portrayed as merely incidental to war.

This rolling back of violence is considered significant because any use of violence brings with it the risk of death. Thus, while there may be a range of uses for cultural knowledge, the most important reason for pursuing it is that, according to McFate, 'cultural ignorance can kill'.[72] HTTs are thought to achieve the reverse. By 'providing non-lethal options to the commander and his staff',[73] they are to reduce violence. There are indeed claims that, in this way, HTTs save lives.[74] Whatever saves lives is by definition a good thing.[75]

HTS is thus portrayed as more than a pragmatic tool for mission accomplishment. In McMaster's words, '[c]ultural expertise contributes to the *ethical* conduct of war by helping soldiers and units understand their environment and identify opportunities to resolve conflict short of using force'.[76] That is, the right kind of knowledge is portrayed as the key to resolving a situation that is recognized as problematic; it provides a new technological fix to the question of ethics, which always lurks close by in any discussion of war. Hence, in the end the appropriation of cultural expertise is not all that different to precision bombing, which is also considered to ameliorate the ethical dilemmas of war.[77]

This also begins to make some sense of why the so-called cultural knowledge needs of the military are being addressed by employing social scientists. After all, there is something peculiar about this. One might have hired anthropologists as consultants in order to, say, teach soldiers how to read cultural signs that might allow for the identification of insurgents or for advising on how to pursue a negotiation in a culturally acceptable way. One might also have brought these anthropologists along to the combat zone to act as experts in 'the culture', but that is not quite what HTS does. Instead, the military is employing social scientists to conduct *research*. *Prima facie*, it is difficult to see why employing academic researchers rather than individuals who would act as cultural advisers makes sense for the military. Clearly, HTS is actually not about buying in cultural expertise.

What is at issue is not the expertise—the substantive knowledge—but the method. Both the counterinsurgency manual and HTS *Handbook* make much of the capacity of social science methods to deliver objective information about the people and things they study. Ethnography and social network theory are mentioned time and again. Methodological expertise features prominently in descriptions of the function of HTS Social Scientists. It is, in other words, not about what these experts *know*, substantively, but about their skills as information gatherers.[78] As *Newsweek* pointed out in 2008, of '19 Human Terrain members operating in five teams in Iraq, fewer than a handful can be described loosely as Middle East experts, and only three speak Arabic. The rest are social scientists or former GIs who ... are transposing research skills from their unrelated fields at home'.[79] Processes of obtaining supposedly objective information are portrayed as techniques that can be learnt and then deployed to any context. This is why experts on Latin America, on Native Americans or indeed on the

United States' goth, punk and rave subcultures can be hired onto the programme.[80]

Crucially, the focus on research methods makes clear that HTS is not about what it claims to be about. It is not about respecting the other or even putting the human dimension centre stage (with or without any respect for it). Instead it is about making sure that the military is in possession of the latest technology—the technology of social science methodology—which enables it to control whatever environment they may find themselves in. That is, HTS is about erasing people and replacing them with a human terrain that can be manipulated by employing the right technologies. Put differently, HTS and the broader trend toward using cultural knowledge in the conduct of military operations creates something of an optical illusion: people become invisible through the very act of apparently putting them centre stage.

Conclusion

More broadly, the military's interest in cultural knowledge leaves us with two interrelated illusions. First of all, war is being staged as a cultural encounter and hence has been reduced to a problem of communication. I use the word 'reduced' with some hesitation here as one could certainly make an argument that war *is* about communicating or indeed that there is nothing reductionist about communication. What I mean is that war is produced as a sort of neutral communication process in which US forces are trying to understand and accommodate the other as much as possible, obscuring the ultimate aim of the violent imposition of control as well as the centrality of killing and destruction to the practice of war. This makes possible illusion number two: the idea of a gentler war enabled by cultural sensitivity. This idea moves beyond the obvious performative contradiction that was at the heart of what is often called liberal war when precision bombing was seen as rendering war less destructive and hence more palatable. To recall a 1960s slogan, 'bombing for peace is like fucking for virginity',[81] and this is so even if the bombs are now 'smart'. There is in contrast no such obvious contradiction between aspiring to peace and aiming to understand the culture of those whose peace is to be ensured. The violence of the project is obscured: violence appears to be nothing more than incidental to counterinsurgency and thus to the practice of war.

Notes

1 I would like to thank the participants of the discussion following my presentation in the Performance and Politics Research Group Distinguished Speaker Series at Aberystwyth University for their insightful comments and, more broadly, for an intellectually stimulating conversation. I am also grateful to Aggie Hirst for her research assistance on this project.
2 For more on this see Maja Zehfuss, 'Targeting: Precision and the Production of Ethics', *European Journal of International Relations* 17, no. 3 (2011): 543–56.

3 Montgomery McFate, 'Anthropology and Counterinsurgency: The Strange Story of their Curious Relationship', *Military Review* (March–April 2005): 25.
4 Thomas E. Ricks, *Fiasco: The American Military Adventure in Iraq*, London: Penguin Books 2007.
5 Ricks, *Fiasco*: 3–4.
6 Ricks, *Fiasco*: 4.
7 Julian E. Barnes, 'The Army is Rethinking how to Fight the Next War – and Win the Current One', *US News & World Report*, 17 March 2006, www.usnews.com/usnews/news/articles/060317/17military_print.htm.
8 Ricks, *Fiasco*: 4.
9 General David H. Petraeus and Lt General James F. Amos, 'Foreword', in *Counterinsurgency Field Manual*, The US Army/Marine Corps, Chicago: Chicago University Press, 2007: xlv.
10 US Army/Marine Corps, *Counterinsurgency Field Manual*: para. 1–80.
11 US Army/Marine Corps, *Counterinsurgency Field Manual*: para. 1–80.
12 US Army/Marine Corps, *Counterinsurgency Field Manual*: para. 1–125; see also 2–41.
13 See Josef Teboho Ansorge and Tarak Barkawi, 'Utile Forms: Power and Knowledge in Small War', *Review of International Studies* (FirstView 2013) for an interesting analysis of the function of smartcards.
14 US Army/Marine Corps, *Counterinsurgency Field Manual*: para. 3–2.
15 US Army/Marine Corps, *Counterinsurgency Field Manual*: para. 3–19.
16 US Army/Marine Corps, *Counterinsurgency Field Manual*: para. 3–20.
17 US Army/Marine Corps, *Counterinsurgency Field Manual*: para. 3–36.
18 US Army/Marine Corps, *Counterinsurgency Field Manual*: para. 3–36.
19 US Army/Marine Corps, *Counterinsurgency Field Manual*: para. 3–37.
20 US Army/Marine Corps, *Counterinsurgency Field Manual*: para. 3–38.
21 US Army/Marine Corps, *Counterinsurgency Field Manual*: para. 3–38.
22 Hugh Gusteron, in David Udris, James Der Derian and Michael Udris, *Human Terrain*, Providence, RI: Udris Film, Oxyopia Productions & Global Media Project, 2010.
23 US Army/Marine Corps, *Counterinsurgency Field Manual*: para. 3–49.
24 US Army/Marine Corps, *Counterinsurgency Field Manual*: para. 3–50.
25 US Army/Marine Corps, *Counterinsurgency Field Manual*: para. 3–50.
26 US Army/Marine Corps, *Counterinsurgency Field Manual*: para. 3–50.
27 US Army/Marine Corps, *Counterinsurgency Field Manual*: para. 3–37.
28 The Deutsches Youth for Understanding Komitee e.V. (www.yfu.de) was founded in 1957 by young Germans who had participated in an exchange scheme allowing them to spend a year in the United States. This was organized by the High Commission of Occupied Germany and was part of Re-education. When I was an exchange student Re-education was, of course, no longer the concern, though interestingly I benefited from a scholarship by the Bundestag under the Parlamentarisches Patenschafts-Programm, founded in 1983 to support transatlantic youth exchange. YFU in Germany remains a non-profit organization largely based on the work of volunteers who are alumni of its exchange schemes which now span the globe.
29 US Army/Marine Corps, *Counterinsurgency Field Manual*: para. 5–1.
30 US Army/Marine Corps, *Counterinsurgency Field Manual*: 166, table 5–2.
31 US Army/Marine Corps, *Counterinsurgency Field Manual*: para. 3–55.
32 US Army/Marine Corps, *Counterinsurgency Field Manual*: para. 3–55.
33 US Army, *Army Culture and Foreign Language Strategy*: ii. 1 December 2009
34 Ricks, *Fiasco*: 313.
35 Mattis quoted in Ricks, *Fiasco*: 314.
36 Remi Hajjar, 'The Army's New TRADOC Culture Center', *Military Review* (2006): 89.

37 Keith Brown, '"All They Understand is Force": Debating Culture in Operation Iraqi Freedom', *American Anthropologist* 110, no. 4 (2008): 444.
38 H.R. McMaster, 'Preserving Soldiers' Moral Character in Counterinsurgency Operations', in *Ethics Education for Irregular Warfare*, ed. Don Carrick, James Connelly and Paul Robinson, Farnham: Ashgate, 2009: 23, emphasis added.
39 See humanterrainsystem.army.mil (accessed 8 March 2013).
40 Jacob Kipp et al., 'The Human Terrain System: A CORDS for the 21st Century', *Military Review* (September–October 2006): 9.
41 Kipp et al., 'Human Terrain System': 15.
42 For more on HTS and the controversy surrounding it see Maja Zehfuss, 'Culturally Sensitive War? The Human Terrain System and the Seduction of Ethics', *Security Dialogue* 43, no. 2 (2012): 175–90.
43 See humanterrainsystem.army.mil.
44 Kipp et al., 'Human Terrain System': 12.
45 Kipp et al., 'Human Terrain System': 12.
46 Kipp et al., 'Human Terrain System': 13.
47 George R. Lucas, Jr, *Anthropologists in Arms: The Ethics of Military Anthropology*, Lanham, MD: AltaMira Press, 2009: 151–52.
48 See humanterrainsystem.army.mil.
49 Human Terrain System, *Human Terrain Team Handbook*: 4.
50 Human Terrain System, *Human Terrain Team Handbook*: 4, emphasis in original.
51 Human Terrain System, *Human Terrain Team Handbook*: 4.
52 Human Terrain System, *Human Terrain Team Handbook*: 4, emphasis in original.
53 Human Terrain System, *Human Terrain Team Handbook*: 4.
54 Human Terrain System, *Human Terrain Team Handbook*: 4.
55 Human Terrain System, *Human Terrain Team Handbook*: 4, emphasis in original.
56 Note, however, that the German Bundeswehr uses so-called Interkulturelle Einsatzberater (IEB), that is Intercultural Deployment Advisers, who are normally expected to hold a degree with a regional emphasis. Unlike with HTS, their background is not necessarily to be in a social science. Instead, the Bundeswehr highlights Middle Eastern Studies and Slavonic Studies alongside History and Political Science as desirable qualifications. See www.streitkraeftebasis.de/portal/a/streitkraeftebasis/!ut/p/c4/04_SB8K8xLLM9MSSzPy8xBz9CP3I5EyrpHK94uyk-ILMKr3SnNTM4hK9zNQk_YJsR0UAEMVL1g!!/.
57 Human Terrain System, *Human Terrain Team Handbook*: 3.
58 Human Terrain System, *Human Terrain Team Handbook*: 13.
59 Human Terrain System, *Human Terrain Team Handbook*: 13.
60 Human Terrain System, *Human Terrain Team Handbook*: 19.
61 Human Terrain System, *Human Terrain Team Handbook*: 19.
62 Human Terrain System, *Human Terrain Team Handbook*: 19.
63 Human Terrain System, *Human Terrain Team Handbook*: 19.
64 Human Terrain System, *Human Terrain Team Handbook*: 19.
65 Carol Burke, 'Combat Ethnography', in *Military Culture and Education*, ed. Douglas Higbee, Farnham: Ashgate, 2010: 29.
66 Human Terrain System, *Human Terrain Team Handbook*: 13.
67 See humanterrainsystem.army.mil/leadership.html.
68 Christopher King, 'Managing Ethical Conflict on a Human Terrain Team', *Anthropology News* 50, no. 6 (2009): 16.
69 McMaster, 'Preserving Soldiers' Moral Character': 23.
70 Human Terrain System, *Human Terrain Team Handbook*: 43.
71 Job description for a social scientist, Position ID J0213-0483, at cgi.njoyn.com/cgi/xweb/XWeb.asp?tbtoken=bVFRQVUSS21xE30FMVdJHCc6cnlddiIob11ZUVsRf2UrX0ppLEoaBmEGPApXVRVSSD5l&chk=dFlbQBJf&Page=JobDetails&Jobid=J0213-0483& brid=237527&sbdid=20464.

72 Montgomery McFate, 'The Military Utility of Understanding Adversary Culture', *Joint Forces Quarterly* 38 (2005): 44.
73 Human Terrain System, *Human Terrain Team Handbook*: 26.
74 Burke, 'Combat Ethnography': 33; Martin P. Schweitzer, 'Statement before the House Armed Services Committee', United States House of Representatives, 110th Congress, 2nd Session, 24 April 2008, science.house.gov/sites/republicans.science.house.gov/files/documents/hearings/042408_schweitzer.pdf.
75 I explore this point in more detail in 'Killing Civilians: Thinking the Practice of War', *British Journal of Politics and International Relations* 14, no. 3 (2012): 423–40.
76 McMaster, 'Preserving Soldiers' Moral Character': 23, emphasis added.
77 See Zehfuss, 'Targeting'.
78 My phrasing reflects representations of HTS. Needless to say, information is produced rather than gathered.
79 'A Gun in One Hand, A Pen in the Other', *Newsweek*, 12 April 2008.
80 'A Gun in One Hand, A Pen in the Other'; see also Hugh Gusterson, 'Human Terrain Teams and the Militarization of Anthropological Conscience: A Meditation on the Futility of Ethical Discourse', paper presented at the 2011 International Studies Conference, Montreal.
81 I would like to thank Jamie Johnson for reminding me of this slogan.

14 Lines of sight

On the visualization of unknown futures[1]

Louise Amoore

> We use this data to *focus on* behavior, not race and ethnicity. In fact, what it allows us to do is move beyond crude profiling based on prejudice, and *look at* conduct and communication and actual behavior as a way of determining who we need to take a *closer look at*.
>
> (US Secretary for Homeland Security Michael Chertoff)

> 'The thing about raster graphics,' Tariq was saying, 'is that you can precisely manipulate an image by altering a single dot at a time ... What they'd like to do with real people if they could. I work on bitmaps to make better pictures. That's raster graphics ... '

> She remembered what Tariq had said to her—how it was what they would like to do with real people if they could. But Tariq only changed images, dot by dot ... They were doing something far bolder: turning her from a woman into cartoons, headlines, opinions, fears, fate. They were morphing her pixel by pixel into what she wasn't, the unknown terrorist.
>
> (Richard Flanigan, *The Unknown Terrorist*: 76, 260)[2]

Introduction: making better pictures

Following the conviction and sentencing of the British 'fertilizer bombers' in May 2007, the US Secretary for Homeland Security, Michael Chertoff, spoke publicly about the need to create better pictures of unknown terrorists in advance of their arrival on US shores. In his lecture at Johns Hopkins University, Chertoff placed his emphasis on how to decide what to *focus* on, who to *look* at, which suspicious behaviour is deserving of *attention*. The significance of his comments far exceeds the specific context of airline passenger data that he is addressing here,[3] embodying a novel and politically significant move in the very visuality of the 'war on terror'. What do these data represent that they can be assumed so nearly to capture a picture of someone who has not yet been seen, who would not otherwise be recognized? If Chertoff is correct and these pixelated people are not seen through racial or other categories that are prejudicial, then what are the implications of living with a digital alter ego that, with the contemporary faith in techno-science, cannot be spurned?

The short answer is that the individuated items of data that have become the mainstay of the home front of the war on terror appear as the 'dots' that, if only they can be successfully joined up, are assumed to reveal a picture of an unknown terrorist. Most often derived from the residue of daily life left in the patterns of travel, financial and consumer transactions,[4] these abstracted items of data become the nodal points that, when joined in association with other items, are assumed to become an indisputable visualization of a person. It is not strictly, then, a picture or a snapshot of a person that is taken—an image from a specific and limited temporal standpoint; rather, it is a projected line of sight that seeks to capture the 'unknown unknowns'.[5] Just as the contemporary consumer is targeted via simulated or projected images of her dreams and desires in Richard Flanigan's startlingly observant novel *The Unknown Terrorist*, so the citizen who becomes a terrorist suspect finds her real self eclipsed by the projected picture of a dangerous and disturbed body, 'morphing pixel by pixel', 'becoming what she was not'. Like the screened visualizations of migrants and travellers that allow the 'border guard to become the last and not the first line of defence', or the London Underground pedestrian surveillance systems that 'mean you don't have to watch the screen all the time', how we see, who we see, to what we give our attention, takes on renewed significance.[6]

As decisions based on human lines of sight are integrated with computer encoded visualizations, authorities begin to claim that the calculated projections of a person could never be racialized or otherwise violent or prejudicial, and are no longer a matter of profiling. In fact, Chertoff's claims for the data visualizations of an air passenger were made in the context of a stark choice he presented between denying British citizens 'of Pakistani origin' the right to visa waiver—categorizing British citizenship into degrees of risk, singling out those 'potentially dangerous people' to whom 'we should pay greater attention'—and the acceptance of a system of data mining that already identifies past travel to Pakistan and specific name algorithms, among many other associations, as 'dangerous'.[7] The choice here, of course, is no choice at all, for the algorithmic calculation of who should be looked at more closely simply redraws the lines between those with entitlement (to visa, to cross a border, to be in a public place without disclosure of purpose) and those without. In short, the visa waiver effectively already is withdrawn from many British citizens by other means—via a picture 'based on behaviour not background'.[8]

The deployment in the war on terror of ways of life, broadly defined—conduct, behaviour, social custom, movement across a railway platform or airport terminal—is in many ways nothing new or significant. Recall in the aftermath of the terrorist attacks of 11 September 2001 (9/11) how the routines of daily life were called up as a source of resilience. 'We were told to shop,' says Susan Willis, 'shop to show we are patriotic Americans. Shop to show our resilience over death and destruction.'[9] The London bombings on 7 July 2005 (7/7) met with similar celebrations of the 'vibrant and resilient city, getting back to normal, going back to work, getting back on the Tube'. Yet, there is a need to be cautious with the treatment of culture in the practices of homeland security. Culture, Derek Gregory explains 'is never a mere mirror of the world', we can never simply hold up the looking glass of culture to shed new light on contemporary economy or society. Rather, 'culture involves the production, circulation and legitimation of meanings through representations, practices and performances that enter fully into the constitution of the world'.[10] In the specific and situated circumstances I am interested in here, culture embodies and advances an economy—a means of apportioning, segregating, singling out for our collective attentions. How do ways of life come to be known and recognized as such? How is a 'normal' way of life settled out, and how does it identify deviations from the norm? To what does the call to attentiveness to 'conduct' or 'behaviour' ask us to pay attention? How do we know to what it is that we should pay attention? As in contemporary profiling of consumers in the marketplace—where the as-yet-unencountered unknown consumer is the holy grail sought via fragments of data on their conduct and behaviour—so in today's homeland security practice, the unknown terrorist is rendered knowable through the fractured bits and bytes of a way of life.

In this chapter, I consider this economy of attention or attentiveness to the world, how it is that we come to focus on some elements of our way of life, establish them as normal and designate deviations from the norm. How does this attentiveness break up the visual field, 'pixelating' sensory data so that it can be reintegrated to build a picture of a person? Throughout, I am inspired by the work of art historian Jonathan Crary, whose careful and detailed genealogies of attention and its role in human subjectivity have urged us to consider that modern sensory stimuli are not primarily about making a subject *see*, but about 'strategies of isolation and separation'.[11] Understood in this way, lines of sight are not only about the vigilant modes of visual culture I have discussed elsewhere,[12] but they are also lines that segregate and divide— 'dividing practices' that render ways of life economic, make them amenable to management, trading, or exchange.

I begin by thinking through what it means to 'pay attention' in the context of calculable lines of sight that coalesce commercial and security practices. I then move to consider how individuated 'dots' of data become reintegrated into the visualization of a person, how it is precisely that the unknown risk comes to be perceived. Throughout, I am interested in how this mode of attentiveness targets, how it draws disparate elements of life into close association in order to designate the 'norm' and to project what is abnormal or out of the ordinary. Finally, I conclude by reflecting on the creative forms of attention that flourish even where the attentiveness of the consumer, the citizen, the border guard, the traveller, the migrant appears ever more directed and delimited. It is in these more creative modes of attention that we find one of the most important resources to contemporary political life—the capacity to question the 'better picture', to disrupt what we see as ordinary or out of the ordinary and confront the routines of our lives anew.

Because culture has an economy: are you paying attention?

Among the careful plastic-windowed advertising posters on the London Underground—'register for Oyster Card and get 10% off in London's museums and galleries'; 'enter an art competition and design a future Tube station'; 'download coupons to your mobile phone'—the Metropolitan Police Anti-terrorist hotline posters call us to attention: 'if you suspect it, report it'; 'look out for unusual or suspicious activity'; 'use all your senses'; 'you are that someone'. In so many ways already part of the prosaic and unnoticed sensory backdrop to the daily commute, the specific call for attention at the home front of the war on terror asks us to single out, from the cacophony of background noise in public spaces, that which demands a closer *look*, that which is out of the *ordinary*. How should we understand this mode of attentiveness? Indeed, is it of significance at all? As art historian Jonathan Crary has argued, the significance of attention and attentiveness to the world is not merely cultural, not confined in its implications to the histories of visual culture. Rather, modes of attention and attentiveness are also acutely material—central in modern times to the way that ways of life, culture and cultural difference are made governable. What we see, how we see, what is made visible, how visualization occurs—these are not simply the cultural dimensions of a material life, but instead they are the very essence of an economy of culture. That is to say, practices of attention themselves embody an economy—a means of representing and acting on the world such that it can be apportioned, segregated, annexed, exchanged or interchanged. As Crary writes on attentiveness, it is 'not primarily concerned with looking at images but rather with the construction of conditions that individuate, immobilize, and separate subjects, even within a world in which mobility and circulation are ubiquitous'.[13] In this sense, practices of attention are one specific means of instituting the dividing practices at the heart of contemporary techniques of government.[14]

As the contemporary global economy has sought to incorporate practices of attention, perception and affective judgement ever more closely into circuits of production and consumption—promoting touch-button 'interactivity', placing the screen in the palm of the hand, engaging playfully with the consumer—so, at the same time the state's security practices have sought to mobilize culture broadly defined—ways of life, looking out for the out of the ordinary, sifting the patterns of life left in transit or consumer transactions, providing hotlines for people's reported unease or suspicion. Thus, London Metropolitan police's 'if you suspect it' campaigns offer the transaction receipt as one fragment of a picture of a person that could be built; the mobile phone images and video clips from the 2005 London bombings are translated from 'careless cinema' into the data-driven analysis of actionable intelligence;[15] the flotsam residue of our travel bookings on global reservations databases are extradited to the US authorities.[16] Across these apparently disparate domains there is a resonance in ever more finite targeting of behaviours, conduct, the actions and inferred intentions of people. Someone as yet unknown is apparently identified and made visible, literally 'brought to attention', singled out and immobilized while all around him moves on.

Though the emergence of novel forms of attentiveness stretches across a spectrum of practices—from appeals to citizen 'readiness' and states of alert,[17] to the algorithmic calculations made on the screens of counter-terror 'hotlines', and the vast screening of prosaic daily transactions for the ever-attentive 'watch list'— there are a number of points of resonance that enter all of these different modes of attention. Contemporary forms of attentiveness are predominantly *screened* ways of perceiving and attending to the world. The interface of the screen— whether windscreen, mobile phone or PDA screen, computer screen, or security 'pre-screening'—has become an important site where sovereign decisions (who belongs to the nation, who is dangerous to 'us', what the 'other' looks like) are made. 'The screen,' writes Kaja Silverman, 'is the site at which social and historical difference enters the field of vision.'[18] It is not only that the screen becomes the mode of visual communication of difference, though of course this is important. Instead, the screen itself enters into the constitution and performance of difference. So, when the British government rejects the US move to deny visas to Britons of Pakistani 'origin', but accepts instead 'screening at their end, sharing intelligence with the Americans' and 'deporting Britons who failed screening once they arrived at an airport in the US',[19] they defer a decision based on racial categories into a screened calculation based on ever more finite classifications of difference. The computer screen, understood this way, as Anne Friedberg has shown, 'is both a "page" and a "window", at once opaque and transparent'. The flat surface of the screen, the 'page' that represents the calculation in this instance, is given depth by the layers and leaves of data, the multiple other screens and screenings that may appear transparent to the viewer but remain opaque to the person who is displayed there. The surface of the screen has, then, 'a deep virtual reach to archives and databases, indexed and accessible with barely the stroke of a finger'.[20]

The screened forms of attention that are dominating contemporary homeland security practice function through a process of 'screening out'. That is to say, they take large quantities of data, multiple sources of stimuli, and they sort and classify that which will appear on the surface. Inside the 34 'surface' items of airline passenger data in passenger name records, for example, are multiple layers of pieces of a person's life, integrated together via pre-screening programmes such as USVISIT, to produce a picture of a person's posed risk to security. It is, of course, only pixelated fragments that enter the visualization, vast quantities of data simultaneously fall out of the calculation, become 'background noise' and are screened out. In many ways this focusing of attention via the annulment of other sensory data is integral to the histories of practices of perception:

Whether it is how we behave in front of the luminous screen of a computer or how we experience a performance in an opera house, how we accomplish certain productive or creative tasks or how we more passively perform routine activities like driving a car or watching television, we are in a dimension of contemporary experience that requires that we effectively cancel out or exclude from consciousness much of our immediate environment.[21]

For Crary, the way that we have come to focus our attention on particular items, tasks or people cannot be understood without also acknowledging the processes that cancel out or exclude other stimuli. When we attend to one set of sensory data, in order to make it count we necessarily discount other sources. Crary identifies a critical turning point in the mid-nineteenth century, when scientific knowledge about how an embodied observer sees and perceives the world 'disclosed possible ways that vision was open to procedures of normalization'.[22] It is precisely this normalization within practices of attention that is at work in the visuality of homeland security. When the call is to look for that which is abnormal, out of the ordinary, or when the data on an individual is sorted according to patterns of normality and deviation, most of the detail behind the data is cancelled out. Conduct and behaviour that could, if attended to or seen differently, be an integral part of the 'norm', becomes part of the conduct and behaviour designated deviant from the norm and rendered suspicious. Thus, what might be expected to be 'normal' patterns of travel or financial transactions for a British citizen with family in Pakistan—travel to visit relatives, wire transfers of monetary gifts, telephone calls—will, within the screened attentiveness to passenger data, be designated suspicious. Like Richard Flanagan's protagonist, 'the Doll' in his novel *The Unknown Terrorist*, whose careful earnings from lap-dancing are hidden in her apartment—savings to buy a house, to find the security and prosperity that is promised to the prudent citizen—what would be the norm becomes deviant, the cash becomes evidence of 'a cell financing its activities through drug running and the sex industry'.[23]

In close association: attending to difference

In the immediate aftermath of 9/11, the homeland face of the war on terror identified an enemy whose probable future actions were already visible in the traces of life left in existing data. Giving evidence at a US Congressional hearing only five months after 9/11, IBM's federal business manager testified that 'in this war, our enemies are hiding in open and available information across a spectrum of databases'.[24] Technology consultants and IT providers such as IBM have made the generation of probabilistic association rules the forefront of homeland security practices. The idea is that locating regularities in large and disparate patterns of data can enable associations to be established between apparently 'suspicious' people, places, financial transactions, cargo shipments and so on.[25] Rules of association are produced by algorithms—models or 'decision trees' for a calculation.[26] In effect, algorithms precisely function as a means of directing and disciplining attention, focusing on specific points and cancelling out all other data, appearing to make it possible to translate *probable* associations between people or objects into *actionable* security decisions. In 2003, for example, a US joint inquiry concluded that 'on September 11, enough relevant data was resident in existing databases' that 'had the dots been connected', the events could have been 'exposed and stopped'.[27] It is precisely this 'connecting of dots' that is the work of the algorithm. By connecting the dots of probabilistic associations, the algorithm becomes a means of foreseeing or anticipating a course of events yet to take place:

> If we learned anything from September 11 2001, it is that we need to be better at *connecting the dots* of terrorist-related information. After September 11, we used credit card and telephone records to identify those linked with the hijackers. But wouldn't it be better to identify such connections before a hijacker boards a plane?[28]

The algorithm appears to make possible the conversion of *ex-post facto* evidence in the war on terror into a judgement made in advance of the event. The significant point here is that diverse data points or specified 'pixels' in a digital image are drawn together in association producing a recognizable whole. Though the visualized image may bear no resemblance to the actual way of life of the person depicted, this scarcely matters because the digital alter ego becomes the de facto person. As the US inspector general concluded in his survey of government applications of algorithmic techniques, 'association does not imply a direct causal connection', but instead it 'uncovers, interprets and displays relationships between persons, places and events'.[29] It is the specific visualization of threat, then, that marks out the algorithm as a distinctive mode of calculation—to be displayed on the screens of border guards, stored on subway travel cards, shared between multiple public and private agencies. In this sense, the algorithm produces a screened visualization of suspicion, on the basis of which 'other' people are intercepted, detained, stopped and searched.

The origins of algorithmic techniques for visualizing people lie, perhaps not surprisingly, in commercial techniques for imagining the consumer. In the early 1990s IBM mathematicians began to work on using bar code data on consumer purchases to project probabilistic judgements about the ways of life of the customer in a given scenario.[30] The point here was not to be able to *predict* future patterns on the basis of past data—indeed, the commercial clients categorically did not want predictability or to capture an already predictable customer. Instead, the dream was to visualize the impulse buyer, the capricious lifestyle of the unknown consumer who might be drawn into the targeting of the marketeers. Though the uncertainties of future patterns are not treated as strictly knowable, they are seen to be at least amenable to pre-emptive decision making based on the visualized person.

It is precisely this model of pre-emptive visualization of an unknown person that is now running through the logics of homeland security; indeed, IBM's same team is now leading the 'mathematical sciences role in homeland security',[31] with IBM prominent contractors on Heathrow Airport's MySense biometrics programme and on the trials for the UK's e-borders Semaphore and Iris programmes. Though programmes of this kind have attracted attention for their surveillant nature, with the implications for privacy and civil liberties this holds, I want to suggest that they are not primarily surveillant modes of seeing. Rather than strictly technologies that 'watch', taking a metaphorical snapshot or photograph in a specific spatio-temporal context, these are techniques of visualization. They project an image and they project it forward in time, displaying their mobility on the ubiquitous screen. As Friedrich Kittler has argued compellingly, projections are produced from fragments of visual data, from individually isolated characteristics that are then selected, differentiated and reintegrated into a visual whole.[32] Of course, gaps persist between the lines that join the pixilated dots.

These gaps, though, are filled with mobile and projected images that produce a seamless whole. Describing the illusion of a moving picture that is produced in the cinematic process of projecting still frames, Anne Friedberg suggests 'for motion to be reconstituted, its virtual rendition relies on a missing element, a perceptual process that depends on the darkness between the frames'.[33] To state my argument simply here, a visualized image of a person requires some gaps and invisibilities; these are simply filled in by the observer. The projected image, then, is extraordinarily difficult to challenge or expose—as Richard Flanigan's 'Doll' discovers, when the fragments of her life are reintegrated to project an unrecognizable whole: 'she becomes what she is not.'

It is important at this point to emphasize the ambiguity of practices of attention and attentiveness. It is not the case that these are wholly disciplinary practices that act on and through us and our lives. As Crary has argued, though industrialization and the market economy saw 'perception function in a way that insures a subject is productive, manageable, and predictable, able to be socially integrated and adaptive', simultaneously the management of attention reached limits characterized by more 'creative states of deep absorption and daydreaming'.[34] So, whilst the conduct of commerce and trade required particular attentive habits, it stimulated also the more creative and subjective ways of seeing that flourished in the arts.[35]

Arguably, in terms of attentiveness and the visualization of people, something interesting and politically challenging is also happening at the intersection of these 'productive' and 'creative' domains of attention. There can be little doubt that projected futures are experienced as both dangers and desires. As media theorist Jordan Crandall has argued:

> Being-seen is an ontological necessity; we strive to be accounted for within the dominant representational matrices of our time. We are not

only talking about a gaze that is intrusive and controlling. We are talking about a gaze that provides the condition for action—the gaze for which one acts.[36]

Consider, for example, the luxury fashion brand Prada and, specifically, the architecture of their New York flagship store. The glass-walled building, stretching one block and opening up inside with spaces to walk around, see and be seen, the store replaces displays of visible products with technologies that connect the consumer's sense of identity to future Prada projections of the person. The radio frequency identification (RFID) tags inside the clothing send radio signals to a screen in the fitting rooms, triggering images of the clothing as seen on the catwalk. The glass walls of the dressing room change in phases from transparent to opaque, and large video screens 'replace mirrors to show your back and side views live'.[37] The miniaturized sensor technologies embedded in the clothing and in store cards and credit cards provide focal points to be connected together in the visualization of the consumer. As these same RFID technologies are now inserted into passports and immigration documents, providing a route of identification into a visualized person, we see both commercial and security drives to become attentive to the element of surprise, the unpredictable or impulsive act.

In this sense, algorithmic techniques for making visible mobile people, and indeed products, goods and money, embody what Samuel Weber calls a 'target of opportunity', a competitive 'seizing' of 'targets that were not foreseen or planned'.[38] The targets of opportunity in the war on terror, then, involve the depiction of unknown and mobile enemies:

> However different the war on terror was going to be from traditional wars, with their relatively well-defined enemies, it would still involve one of the basic mechanisms of traditional hunting and combat, in however modified and modernized a form: namely 'targeting'. The enemy would have to be *identified* and *localized*, *named* and *depicted*, in order to be made into an accessible target ... None of this was, per se, entirely new. What *was*, however, was the mobility, indeterminate structure, and unpredictability of the spatio-temporal *medium* in which such targets had to be sited ... In theatres of conflict that had become highly mobile and changeable, 'targets' and 'opportunity' were linked as never before.[39]

Samuel Weber's key point of discussion is the theatre of war, though his argument sheds significant light on the modes of attentiveness that I depict here. The *identification*, *localization*, *naming* and *depiction* of mobile targets is, in this war by other means, conducted in and through daily life, in advance of any possible future strike or intervention. The targeting of unknown people is, put simply, becoming a matter of both positioning in the sights (targeting and identifying) and visualizing through a projected line of sight (pre-empting, making actionable). Just as Prada's customers are targeted via electronic tag identifiers and visualized via screened future images of their clothing, so the migrant or traveller is both targeted and anticipated—identified via their personal data and projected forward so that their digital shadow arrives at the border before they do. Algorithmic 'decision trees' draw even the most overloaded sensory domains into apparent management: the busy and noisy border crossing is stilled on the border guard's screened list of 'selectees' to single out for further attention; the crowded subway ticket hall quietly selects anomalous smartcard data and intercepts at the barrier; the RFID data from a football fan's swipe card transmits an automatic signal to the local police. From the visualization of a person is derived the possibility to act on that person. 'Ideally, I would like to know,' said Michael Chertoff, 'did Mohamed Atta get his ticket paid on the same credit card. That would be a huge thing. And I really would like to know that in advance, because that would allow us to identify an unknown terrorist.'[40]

In fact, of course, the algorithmic 'decision trees' do not take decisions at all; they merely defer decision into a calculation that is pre-programmed.[41] While they appear to visualize a picture of a person that is culturally nuanced—every minute and prosaic 'behaviour', every aspect of a way of life potentially becoming a part of the classification—they actually efface difference in their drive for identification. The logic of association rules appears to be peculiarly dependent on culture, yet it is a representation of culture that attends to (and makes us attentive to) some aspects of sameness and difference, whilst always failing to confront the agonistic difference at the heart of political life.[42] The claims that visualizations used in place of 'face-to-face' pictures avoid racial profiling and other prejudicial judgements cannot be upheld. It is always through the visualization of the identity of the 'other' that the sanctity of 'we the nation', 'we the people' is sustained. As Connolly puts it, the 'self reassurance of identity' is made 'through the construction and otherness' and this otherness is readily adopted as the 'definition of difference'.[43] The algorithmic attentiveness, then, becomes the 'multicultural'[44] society's technology of choice precisely because it gives the appearance of living alongside difference, of deciding without prejudice—'we are interested in behaviour not background'; 'this is not racial profiling'; 'we prefer screening to visa restrictions'; 'no more border guards taking decisions based on appearance'—when in fact it categorizes, isolates and annexes in ways that conceal the violence inside the glossy wrapper of techno-science.

There is an intensely important political problem here, then. We are faced with a technique of governing that makes humane, responsible or ethical ways of paying attention to the world extraordinarily difficult. Consider, for example, Waverly Cousin, former police officer and one of the 43,000 'screeners' employed by the US Transportation Security Administration to deploy the 'screening passengers by observation technique' (SPOT) at airports, ports and border crossings. 'The observation of human behaviour is probably the hardest thing to defeat,' explains Waverley, 'you just don't know what I am going to see.'[45] We do not know what he is going to see because the 'SPOT' calculation, while it engages all of the time in the visualization of what Dana Cuff calls an 'object of interest', is itself always invisible and never an object of interest.[46] Because in algorithmic modes of attention every ordinary everyday act becomes itself a means of settling out the norm and identifying the other that is anomalous, a responsible decision that, in Derrida's terms, 'advance[s] where it cannot see', is particularly elusive.[47] What becomes important politically, I want to suggest in my concluding section, is the capacity precisely to intervene in what we do not know in what we see, and to mobilize a different form of attentiveness that is perhaps always already co-present.

Attention in a state of distraction: what the artist saw

I have argued that theories of attention and attentiveness derived from histories of art are capable of revealing something significant about the contemporary economy of homeland security culture: that it is not primarily a way of seeing or surveilling the world, but rather a means of dividing, isolating, annexing in order to visualize what is 'unknown'. Yet, it is not only in concepts from the arts, but also in the *practices of artistic intervention* that we find a potentially valuable ethics and responsibility in how we pay attention to ourselves and other people. An 'absorbed attentiveness', writes Crary, is not only a 'necessary part of the individual's functioning within a modern world of economic facts and quantities', but is always also essential for the 'creative exceeding of the limits of individuality'.[48] Because relations of power inextricably contain the possibility of resistance, there could never be a fully efficient attentive subject whose attention to the world is entirely amenable to management. Indeed, as Crary has it, 'the more one investigated, the more attention was shown to contain within itself the condition for its own undoing'.[49]

Art theory and practice is all too readily overlooked as 'merely cultural' by the social sciences, accused of 'substituting a trivial form of politics' that focuses on 'transient events, practices and objects' in place of a 'serious' political economy of transformation.[50] I want to suggest here that even for those who wish to pursue what they see as 'serious' political economies of transformation—and I consider questions of culture to be among the most serious—artistic interventions in theory and practice are best placed to reflect on many aspects of an emergent economy of culture. The embedding of technologies into everyday objects; the visualization of unknown futures; the screened projection of mobile bodies; the economies of the mundane and the surprising in public space: these are not novel ideas to many contemporary artists. Indeed, far from focusing on trivial and transient events, innovative artistic practice engages in a deeply historical process of reflection on perspective, human subjectivity and cognition. Put simply, the 'resonances' that so many of our contemporary philosophers, social theorists and political economists are observing across science, technology, politics and culture, have long been at the heart of leading edge artistic interventions.[51] I will focus here on three areas where

I consider artist interventions to open up clear space for questions of ethical and political responsibility in the face of technical depoliticization.

Modes of attentiveness in contemporary homeland security practice, as I have argued, are particularly dependent on algorithmic logics that designate anomaly on the basis of a screening of the norm. The cultural practices of the visual arts precisely invert the logic of 'looking out for the out of the ordinary'—that which transgresses the norm—in order to identify danger, suggesting instead that the act of being surprised by the extraordinary can make us see the norm anew. Even in quite mainstream installations of temporary artworks in public spaces, there is an emphasis on surprise as a means of seeing daily life differently. In the spaces of the London Underground, for example, Platform for Art has confronted, to a degree, the post-7/7 fear of the unexpected, inviting international artists to install their work on the Piccadilly line stations, platforms and trains. In the Thin Cities project, the artist's installations were produced in 'unexpected places on the Tube network', offering new ways of seeing the daily commute, 'revealing new perspectives on London' and 'promoting greater understanding'.[52]

In this sense, artistic interventions have the capacity to call the norm into question, reminding us of what we do not pay attention to, creating what Tom Mitchell says 'looks like a picture of something we could never see'.[53] This is, argues Crary, 'experimental activity' that 'involves the creation of unanticipated spaces and environments in which our visual and intellectual habits are challenged and disrupted'.[54] In contrast to an attentiveness that tries to anticipate on the basis of the fragments that are seen, then, some installation artwork in public space offers us new ways of attending to the very images we had already screened out as normal. American artist Rozalinda Borcila's *Geography Lessons*, for example, seeks to 'intervene in apparently controlled spaces' that are 'policed through technologies of visualization and information management'.[55] Making 'counter-surveillance' videos of airport security and urban transport systems (and deported from the Netherlands when she video recorded Schipol Airport's security), Borcila projects her multi-screen films, rendering extraordinary what has become the ordinary practice of searching, removing shoes, interrogating, detaining.

The question of responsibility in attentive practices of security arises only in terms of the responsibility for vigilance, for paying attention and not becoming distracted. As I have argued, and following Derrida, there is an absence of responsibility in the sense that these forms of attentiveness seek to anticipate, to foresee an unknown future on the basis of an algorithmic calculation. If Derrida is correct, then a responsible decision would have to 'advance where it cannot see', confronting the difficulty and undecidability of all decisions, and recognizing that calculation cannot substitute for a judgement that may have to be made in the absence of pre-programmed information.[56] Artistic interventions, I want to suggest, embody the potential to confront the political difficulty of decision and to intervene in ways that are 'unanticipatory', advancing where they cannot see.

What is particularly interesting about artistic practices that engage with some of the emergent technologies of attention, is that they do not seek out a *resolution* to the political difficulties posed. Instead, they create a plural space for the articulation of difference, 'integrating technological tools into plural zones of creative activity' and providing ways of imaging the problem outside of narratives of security or consumption.[57] By way of example, consider New York artist Meghan Trainor, whose work integrates RFID tags—ubiquitous in the visualization of consumers and security 'threats'—into public installations and performances. The installation 'lets viewers encounter RFID tags in an application outside of its common commercial or surveillance context', explains Trainor, 'allowing for different reactions to its current and expanding ubiquity in our lives'.[58] Rather than seek to resolve the paradoxes and contradictions of these technological forms of attentiveness, then, the artworks function 'as catalyst' to the exposure of paradox and contradiction.[59] They remind us that within apparently disciplined and securitized modes of attention there are also interstitial spaces of 'inattention', 'enchantment' or 'reverie' that may work against prejudicial and individualized practices.[60] The background images and data that are discarded by security practices of visualization are potentially recovered by the changed perspectives of artistic interventions.

Finally, visionary work in artistic practice has, as its raison d'être, a form of critique that runs 'against the grain' of dominant knowledge about how we pay attention to the world. In Edward Said's last book before his death, he documents the 'late' work of visionary artists and musicians as not that which has 'harmony and resolution', but that which embodies 'intransigence, difficulty, and unresolved contradiction'.[61] In contrast to a line of sight that sees clearly and rationally, then, art against the grain is that which transgresses prevailing modes of thought in order to see the world differently. Thomas Keenan conjures a comparable alternative 'line' of sight against the grain when he speaks of politics 'on the bias', where there is 'a withdrawal of the rules or the knowledge on which we might rely to take our decisions for us'.[62]

In order for responsibility to be reintroduced to the decision, then, it is necessary for us to consider this diagonal line of sight that cuts across prevailing ways of attending to the world. A final example of such a cut across the grain can be seen in British artist Michael Landy's three-year project Break Down. Situating his work in a disused department store on London's Oxford Street, Landy made an inventory of his life—dismantling, weighing and cataloguing every item that he owned. Simulating the breaking up, classifying and profiling of individuals through their data, Landy stripped his pixelated profile down to nothing, publicly displaying the 7,000 disassembled objects on a moving production line. Because codified data can be used to visualize a person, no matter how absurd or tenuous, the artists who experiment with alternative ways to visualize a person do so against the grain, offering new modes of attention that attend also to the calculation that is made.

Conclusion: citizenship and unknown futures

In one reading of the implications of vigilant and anticipatory lines of sight for citizenship, a specific embodiment of the citizen is produced: an attentive, watchful and watched citizen whose actions and transactions in daily life are called up to secure the homeland security state. It is perhaps for this reason that so much attention has been paid in recent times, across the social sciences, to the surveillant practices of an apparently 'post 9/11 world'. Yet, as Foucault warned in his lectures on the emerging security apparatus, the panopticon is 'completely archaic', and 'the oldest dream of the oldest sovereign'.[63] In contrast to the 'exhaustive surveillance of individuals', a 'discipline' that 'concentrates, focuses and encloses', Foucault observes an 'apparatus of security' that 'opens up' to 'let things happen'.[64] Where disciplinary modes of surveillance produce particular pictures of people, drawn from the 'survey' in the conventional sense of 'surveiller', what I have depicted in this chapter is a projected picture of a person—one that pre-empts, visualizes and anticipates unknown futures. The citizen appears, then, not only as a *surveilled* picture of a way of life to be verified, checked against criteria and documentation, authenticated, but also and perhaps more importantly, as a *visualization of a potential person* who is never quite seen. In terms of material effects, the projected people who find themselves on selectee lists for secondary checks, or on no-fly lists, or with their assets frozen, are left confronting a digitized doppelgänger whose associations and profile have become more 'real' than even the conventions of passport or visa can attain.

There can be little doubt, at least in my sense of the emerging landscape, that much of contemporary security practice is assembling around a line of sight that conceals racialized and prejudicial judgements inside an apparently 'expert' and techno-scientific visualization. Indeed, as I have suggested, the processes of screening and projection precisely rely upon the gaps that are 'left out' of association analysis. We might even say that misidentification, so-called 'false positives' and false hits have become essential parts of the accidents that make citizenship and the denial of citizenship possible.[65] For the British citizens 'of Pakistani origin' who find themselves projected as as-yet-unknown terrorists, their visualization is achieved only via the constant and consistent screening out of other identity claims they could make. It is for this reason that I find artistic interventions particularly interesting in terms of recovering what is screened out, retrieving the lived detail and rendering it visible. One possible step to take in the political and ethical interventions in security visualizations, I have argued, is to expose the distractions and inattentiveness that make vigilant visualities possible.

Notes

1 This chapter originally appeared in *Citizenship Studies* 13, no. 1 (2009): 17–30, www.informaworld.com/smpp/content_db=all?content=10.1080/13621020802586 628. The author acknowledges the UK Economic and Social Research Council

(ESRC) funding of award RES 155 25 0087 'Contested Borders: Non-Governmental Public Action and the Technologies of the War on Terror'. Performance artists Rozalinda Borcila and Meghan Trainor have been much-valued collaborators and have given generously of their time and images.

2 Michael Chertoff, 'Remarks by Secretary Michael Chertoff to the Johns Hopkins University Paul H. Nitze School of Advanced International Studies', 3 May 2007, www.dhs.gov/xnews/speeches/sp_1178288606838.shtm; Richard Flanagan, *The Unknown Terrorist*, London: Atlantic Books, 2006: 76, 260.

3 In May 2006 the European Court of Justice ruled that the European Union–US agreement on the sharing of airline passenger data be annulled: Elspeth Guild and Evelien Brouwer, 'The Political Life of Data: The ECJ Decision on the PNR Agreement between the EU and the US', *CEPS Policy Brief* 109 (2006), www.libertysecurity.org/IMG/pdf/1363.pdf. The Passenger Name Record (PNR) agreement of 2004 required that airlines submit thirty-four items of data on each passenger (including, for example, credit card details, past travel data and in-flight meal choices, car hire, hotel bookings and other personal information) within 15 minutes of flight departure for the United States. The PNR data have become central to pre-emptive border controls, where risk ratings are assigned to individuals in advance of their arrival at a border: Louise Amoore, 'Biometric Borders: Governing Mobilities in the War on Terror', *Political Geography* 25 (2006): 336–51.

4 Louise Amoore and Marieke de Goede, 'Governance, Risk and Dataveillance in the War on Terror', *Crime, Law and Social Change* 43, no. 2 (2005): 149–73; Louise Amoore and Marieke de Goede, 'Introduction: Governing by Risk in the War on Terror', in *Risk and the War on Terror*, ed. Louise Amoore and Marieke de Goede, London: Routledge, 2008.

5 In a speech to the North Atlantic Treaty Organization (NATO) in 2002, Donald Rumsfeld pondered the importance of taking decisions on the basis of an absence of evidence, of taking into account the 'unknown unknowns': 'The message is that there are no "knowns". There are things we know that we know. There are known unknowns. That is to say there are things we know that we don't know. But there are also unknown unknowns. There are things we don't know we don't know ... There is another way to phrase that and that is the absence of evidence is not evidence of absence'. Hence, the sense that attention is to be paid to that which is not seen, has not been seen, but can nonetheless be 'projected': Donald Rumsfeld, 'Press conference by US Secretary of Defence Donald Rumsfeld', NATO, Brussels 6–7 June 2002, www.nato.int/docu/speech/2002/s020606g.htm.

6 Department of Homeland Security, 'Testimony of Secretary Tom Ridge before the Senate Budget Committee', 25 February 2004, US Senate: Washington DC; *New Scientist*, 'Smart Software Linked to CCTV Can Spot Dubious Behaviour', 11 July 2003.

7 Michael Chertoff, 'A Tool we Need to Stop the Next Airliner Plot', *Washington Post*, 29 August 2007: A15.

8 Chertoff, 'A Tool we Need': A15.

9 Susan Willis, 'Old Glory', in *Dissent from the Homeland*, ed. Frank Lentricchia and Stanley Hauerwas, Durham, NC: Duke University Press, 2003: 122.

10 Derek Gregory, *The Colonial Present*, Oxford: Blackwell, 2004: 11.

11 Jonathan Crary, *Suspensions of Perception: Attention, Spectacle, and Modern Culture*, Cambridge, MA: MIT Press, 1999: 3.

12 Louise Amoore, 'Vigilant Visualities: The Watchful Politics of the War on Terror', *Security Dialogue* 38, no. 2 (2007): 139–56.

13 Crary, *Suspensions of Perception*: 74.

14 In common with others who have sought to push economy 'beyond economism'—that is, beyond *the* economy as a pre-discursive, pre-political and self-evident

material reality—economy is used here to denote a field of intervention and a specific means of rendering political life governable: Marieke de Goede, 'Beyond Economism in International Political Economy', *Review of International Studies* 29 (2003): 79–97; Marieke de Goede, *Virtue, Fortune and Faith: A Genealogy of Finance*, Minneapolis: University of Minnesota Press, 2005; Peter Miller and Nikolas Rose, 'Governing Economic Life', *Economy & Society* 19, no. 1 (1990): 1–31. 'The art of government,' writes Foucault, 'is essentially concerned with answering the question of how to introduce economy—that is to say, the correct manner of managing individuals, goods and wealth within the family—how to introduce this ... into the management of the state': Michel Foucault, 'Governmentality', in *The Foucault Effect: Studies in Governmentality*, ed. Graham Burchell, Colin Gordon and Peter Miller, Chicago, IL: Chicago University Press, 1991: 92. Foucault finds in economy a continuity of the art of governing the state, such that the 'very essence of government' has come to mean 'the art of exercising power in the form of economy': Foucault, 'Governmentality': 93.
15 Iain Sinclair, 'The Theatre of the City', *The Guardian*, 14 July 2005.
16 Reservations databases Amadeus, Galileo and Sabre, used by the major airlines and hotel and other travel groups, are now the conduit for the routine submission of passenger data to the US authorities before a flight departs for the United States.
17 Engin Isin, 'The Neurotic Citizen', *Citizenship Studies* 8, no. 3 (2004): 217–35; James Hay and Mark Andrejevic, 'Toward an Analytics of Governmental Experiments in These Times: Homeland Security as Social Security', *Cultural Studies* 20, no. 4–5 (2006): 331–48.
18 Kaja Silverman, *The Threshold of the Visible World*, New York: Routledge, 1996: 135.
19 *The New York Times*, 'US Seeks Closing of Visa Loophole for Britons', 2 May 2007: 5.
20 Anne Friedberg, *The Virtual Window: From Alberti to Microsoft*, Cambridge, MA: MIT Press, 2007: 19.
21 Crary, *Suspensions of Perception*: 1.
22 Crary, *Suspensions of Perception*: 12; see also Jonathan Crary, *Techniques of the Observer: On Vision and Modernity in the 19th Century*, Cambridge MA: MIT Press, 1992.
23 Flanagan, *The Unknown Terrorist*: 231.
24 'For Want of a Nail', *Intelligent Enterprise* 5, no. 7 (2002): 8.
25 Richard Ericson, *Crime in an Insecure World*, Cambridge: Polity, 2007.
26 J.R. Quinlan, 'Induction of Decision Trees', *Machine Learning* 1 (1986): 81–106.
27 US Joint Enquiry, 'Report of the Joint Inquiry into the Terrorist Attacks of September 11, 2001', Washington, DC: House Permanent Select Committee on Intelligence (HPSCI) and the Senate Select Committee on Intelligence (SSCI), 2003: 14.
28 Chertoff, 'A Tool we Need': A15.
29 Department of Homeland Security, 'Survey of DHS Data Mining Activities', Washington, DC: Office of the Inspector General, 2006: 10.
30 Cf. Rakesh Agrawal, Tomasz Imielinski and Arun Swami, 'Mining Association Rules Between Sets of Items in Large Databases', *SIGMOD Proceedings* (1993): 914–25.
31 BMSA, *The Mathematical Sciences' Role in the War on Terror*, National Academies Press, 2004.
32 Friedrich Kittler, *Literature, Media, Information Systems: Essays*, Amsterdam: Arts Limited, 1997.
33 Friedberg, *The Virtual Window*: 92; see also Anne Friedberg, 'Urban Mobility and Cinematic Visuality', *Journal of Visual Culture* 1, no. 2 (August 2002): 183–204.
34 Crary, *Suspensions of Perception*: 4–5.
35 Crary, *Suspensions of Perception*: 52.

36 Jordan Crandall, 'Envisioning the Homefront: Militarization, Tracking and Security Culture', *Journal of Visual Culture* 4, no. 1 (2005): 17–38, at 20.
37 Jerry Kang and Dana Cuff, 'Pervasive Computing: Embedding the Public Sphere', *Public Law Research Paper Series* no. 04–23, Los Angeles: University of California, 2005: 121.
38 Sam Weber, *Targets of Opportunity: On the Militarization of Thinking*, New York: Fordham University Press, 2005: 4.
39 Weber, *Targets of Opportunity*: 3–4, emphasis in original.
40 *The New York Times*, 'Officials Seek Broader Access to Airline Data', 23 August 2006: 3.
41 For Jacques Derrida, a decision is not a decision if it simply redeploys calculative practices in order to decide. A decision cannot, in Derrida's reading, be determined by the acquisition of knowledge, for then it is not a decision but 'simply the application of a body of knowledge of, at the very least, a rule or norm': Jacques Derrida (in conversation with Richard Beardsworth), 'Nietzsche and the Machine', *Journal of Nietzsche Studies* 7 (1994): 7–65, at 37. An apparent decision taken on the basis of what is 'seen' evidentially, via the calculations of experts, or in the screened results of algorithmic visualization, is not a decision at all. 'The decision, if there is to be one', writes Derrida, 'must advance towards a future which is not known, which cannot be anticipated': Derrida, 'Nietzsche and the Machine': 37.
42 William Connolly, *Identity/Difference: Democratic Negotiations of Political Paradox*, Minneapolis: University of Minnesota Press, 1991: 170–71.
43 Connolly, *Identity/Difference*: 9.
44 As Slavoj Žižek has it, 'multiculturalism is a disavowed, inverted, self-referential form of racism, a "racism with a distance"—it respects the Other's identity, conceiving of the Other as a self-enclosed "authentic" community towards which he, the multiculturalist, maintains a distance rendered possible by his privileged universal position': Slavoj Žižek, *The Universal Exception*, London: Continuum, 2006: 171. Thus, the decision based on a visualized calculation is precisely a self-referential form of racism, a racism that disavows itself by stripping out its own role in identifying the Other that is threatening and dangerous.
45 *The New York Times*, 'Faces Too, are Searched at US Airports', 17 August 2006: 8.
46 Dana Cuff, 'Immanent Domain: Pervasive Computing and the Public Realm', *Journal of Architectural Education* 57 (2003): 43–49.
47 Derrida, 'Nietzsche and the Machine': 38.
48 Crary, *Suspensions of Perception*: 53.
49 Crary, *Suspensions of Perception*: 45–46.
50 Judith Butler, 'Merely Cultural', *New Left Review* 227 (January/February 1998).
51 William E. Connolly, *Pluralism*, Durham, NC: Duke University Press, 2005.
52 Platform for Art, *Thin Cities: 100 Years of the Piccadilly Line*, London: Platform for Art, 2006.
53 W.T.J. Mitchell, 'There are no Visual Media', *Journal of Visual Culture* 4, no. 2 (2005): 257–66, at 260.
54 Jonathan Crary, 'Foreword', in *Installation Art in the New Millennium: The Empire of the Senses*, ed. Nicolas de Oliveira, Nicola Oxley and Michael Perry, London: Thames and Hudson, 2003: 7.
55 Rozalinda Borcila, 'Geography Lessons', 2006, videos available at www.borcila.tk/geographie/index.html.
56 Jacques Derrida, 'Force of Law: The "Mystical Foundations of Authority"', in *Deconstruction and the Possibility of Justice*, ed. Drucilla Cornell, Michael Rosenfeld and David Gray Carlson, New York: Routledge, 1992; see also *On Cosmopolitanism and Forgiveness*, London: Routledge, 2001.
57 Crary, 'Foreword': 9.

58 Meghan Trainor, Exhibition notes accompanying RFID Project, part of the 2004 Winter Show of the Interactive Telecommunications Programme at the Tisch School of Art, NYU.
59 Nicolas de Oliveira, ed., *Installation Art in the New Millennium: The Empire of the Senses*, London: Thames and Hudson, 2003.
60 Jane Bennett, *The Enchantment of Modern Life: Attachments, Crossings, Ethics*, Princeton, NJ: Princeton University Press, 2001.
61 Edward Said, *On Late Style: Music and Literature Against the Grain*, London: Pantheon, 2006: 14.
62 Thomas Keenan, *Fables of Responsibility: Aberrations and Predicaments in Ethics and Politics*, Stanford, CA: Stanford University Press, 1997: 166.
63 Michel Foucault, *Security, Territory, Population: Lectures at the College de France, 1977–78*, trans. Graham Burchell, Basingstoke, Hampshire: Palgrave Macmillan, 2007: 66.
64 Foucault, *Security, Territory, Population*: 44–45.
65 Peter Nyers, 'The Accidental Citizen: Acts of Sovereignty and (Un)making Citizenship', *Economy & Society* 35, no. 1 (2006): 22–41.

Select bibliography

Abe, Kobo, *The Face of Another*, New York: Vintage Books, 2003.
Acquisti, Alessandro, Ralph Gross and Fred Stitzman, 'Faces of Facebook: Privacy in the Age of Augmented Reality', paper presented at BlackHat, Las Vegas, 4 August 2011, draft slides, www.heinz.cmu.edu/~acquisti/face … /acquisti-faces-BLACKHAT-draft.pdf; Face recognition study: FAQ: www.heinz.cmu.edu/~acquisti/face-recognition-study-FAQ/.
Adelman, Janet, '"Anger's my Meat": Feeding, Dependency, and Aggression in *Coriolanus*', in *Representing Shakespeare: New Psychoanalytic Essays*, ed. Murray M. Schwartz and Coppélia Kahn, Baltimore, MD: Johns Hopkins University Press, 1980: 129–49.
Adorno, Theodor W., *Mahler: A Musical Physiognomy*, Chicago, IL: Chicago University Press, 1996.
——*Aesthetic Theory*, trans. Robert Hullot-Kentor, London: Continuum, 2004.
——'The Pictorial World of *Der Freischütz*', in *Night Music: Essays on Music 1928–1962*, London: Seagull Books, 2009.
Agamben, Giorgio, *Homo Sacer: Sovereign Power and Bare Life*, trans. Daniel Heller-Roazen, Stanford, CA: Stanford University Press, 1998.
——*Means Without Ends: Notes on Politics*, trans. Vicenzo Binetti and Cesare Casarino, Minnesota: University of Minnesota Press, 2000.
——*The Open*, trans. Kevin Attell, Stanford, CA: Stanford University Press, 2004.
——*The State of Exception*, trans. Kevin Attell, Chicago, IL: Chicago University Press, 2005.
——*Profanations*, trans. Jeff Fort, New York: Zone Books, 2007.
——*What is an Apparatus?* trans. David Kishik and Stefan Pedatella, Stanford, CA: Stanford University Press, 2009.
——*Nudities*, trans. David Kishik and Stefan Pedatella, Stanford, CA: Stanford University Press, 2011.
Akram-Lohdi, Haroon A., 'The Macroeconomies of Human Insecurity: Why Gender Matters', in *Development in an Insecure and Gendered World*, ed. Jacqueline Leckie, Surrey: Ashgate, 2009: 71–90.
Alaimo, Stacy and Susan Hekman, eds, *Material Feminisms*, Bloomington: Indiana University Press, 2008.
Amin, Ash and Nigel Thrift, *Reimagining the Urban*, Malden, MA: Polity, 2002.
Amoore, Louise and Marieke de Goede, 'Governance, Risk and Dataveillance in the War on Terror', *Crime, Law and Social Change* 43, no. 2 (2005): 149–73.

Select bibliography

——'Introduction: Governing by Risk in the War on Terror', in *Risk and the War on Terror*, ed. Louise Amoore and Marieke de Goede, London: Routledge, 2008.

Amoore, Louise, 'Biometric Borders: Governing Mobilities in the War on Terror', *Political Geography* 25 (2006): 336–51.

——'Vigilant Visualities: The Watchful Politics of the War on Terror', *Security Dialogue* 38, no. 2 (2007): 139–56.

Ansorge, Josef Teboho and Tarak Barkawi, 'Utile Forms: Power and Knowledge in Small War', *Review of International Studies* (forthcoming).

Appadurai, Arjun, *Modernity at Large: Cultural Dimensions of Globalization*, Minneapolis; University of Minnesota Press, 1996.

Appiah, Kwame Anthony, *Cosmopolitanism: Ethics in a World of Strangers*, New York: Norton, 2006.

Arendt, Hannah, *The Human Condition*, Chicago, IL: University of Chicago Press, 1998.

Aristotle, *Poetics*, trans. Gerald F. Else, Ann Arbor: University of Michigan Press, 1973.

Ashley, Richard K., 'Living on Border Lines: Man, Poststructuralism and War', in *International/Intertextual Relations: Postmodern Readings of World Politics*, ed. James Der Derian and Michael J. Shapiro, Lexington, MA: Lexington Books, 1989.

Austin, J.L., *How to do Things with Words*, 2nd edn, Cambridge, MA: Harvard University Press, 1975.

Bacon, Francis, 'From *The Advancement of Learning*', in *Renaissance Debates on Rhetoric*, ed. Wayne A. Rebhorn, Ithaca, NY: Cornell University Press, 2000: 267–70.

Badiou, Alain, *Ethics: An Essay on the Understanding of Evil*, trans. Peter Hallward, London: Verso, 2001.

——*Being and Event*, trans. Oliver Feltham, New York and London: Continuum, 2005.

——*The Century*, trans. Alberto Toscano, Cambridge: Polity, 2007.

——'A Theater of Operations: A Discussion between Alain Badiou and Elie During, in *A Theater Without Theater*', ed. Manuel J. Borja-Villel *et al.*, Barcelona: Museu d'Art Contemporani de Barcelona, 2009.

——*The Rebirth of History: Times of Riots and Uprisings*, trans. Gregory Elliott, London: Verso, 2012.

Bailes, Sara Jane, *Performance, Theatre and the Poetics of Failure*, London and New York: Routledge, 2010.

Bakhtin, M.M. 'Forms of Time and Chronotope in the Novel', in *The Dialogic Imagination*, trans. Caryl Emerson and Michael Holquist, Austin: University of Texas Press, 1981.

——'Author and Hero in Aesthetic Activity', in *Art and Answerability*, trans. V. Liapunov, Austin: University of Texas Press, 1990.

Barad, Karen, *Meeting the Universe Halfway: Quantum Physics and the Entanglement of Matter and Meaning*, Durham, NC: Duke University Press, 2007.

Barthes, Roland, *Camera Lucida: Reflections on Photography*, trans. Richard Howard, London: Vintage, 1993.

Barton, Anne, 'Livy, Machiavelli and Shakespeare's *Coriolanus*', in *Shakespeare and Politics*, ed. C.M.S. Alexander, Cambridge: Cambridge University Press, 2004: 67–90.

Bassnett, Susan and Harish Trivedi, *Post-Colonial Translation: Theory and Practice*, London: Routledge, 1998.

Bauman, Zygmunt, 'The London Riots—On Consumerism Coming Home to Roost', *Social Europe Journal*, 9 August 2011, archive.is/h8pp.

Bayly, Simon, *A Pathognomy of Performance*, Houndmills: Palgrave Macmillan, 2011.

Beckett, Samuel, *Waiting for Godot*, London: Faber and Faber, 1959.
Benjamin, Walter, *Charles Baudelaire: A Lyric Poet in the Era of High Capitalism*, London: Verso Books, 1983.
—— 'Two Poems by Friedrich Holderin', trans. Stanley Corngold, in *Walter Benjamin: Selected Writing 1913–1926*, Cambridge, MA: Harvard University Press, 1996.
—— 'What is Epic Theatre?' 2nd edn, in *Understanding Brecht*, trans. Anna Bostock, London: Verso, 1998: 15–22.
—— 'On the Concept of History', trans. E. Jephcott, in *Walter Benjamin: Selected Writings 1938–1940*, Cambridge, MA: Harvard University Press, 2003.
Bennett, Jane, *The Enchantment of Modern Life: Attachments, Crossings, Ethics*, Princeton, NJ: Princeton University Press, 2001.
—— 'The Force of Things: Steps Toward an Ecology of Matter', *Political Theory* 32, no. 3 (2004): 347–72.
—— *Vibrant Matter: A Political Ecology of Things*, Durham, NC: Duke University Press, 2010.
Berger, John and Jean Mohr, *A Fortunate Man: The Story of a Country Doctor*, Harmondsworth: Penguin, 1967.
Bernardin, Susan, Melody Graulich, Lisa MacFarlane and Nicole Tonkovich, *Trading Gazes: Euro-American Women Photographers and Native North Americans*, New Brunswick: Rutgers University Press, 2003.
Berridge, G.R., *Notes on the Origins of the Diplomatic Corps: Constantinople in the 1620s*, Discussion Paper No. 92, Clingendale Netherlands Institute for International Relations, 2004.
—— 'Diplomacy After Death: The Rise of the Working Funeral', *Diplomacy & Statecraft* 4, no. 2 (2007): 217–34.
Bersani, Leo and Ulysse Dutoit, *Forms of Being*, London: BFI, 2004.
Besten, Michael Paul, 'Transformation and the Reconstitution of Khoe-San Identities: AAS le Fleur I, Griqua Identities and Post-apartheid Khoe-San Revivalism (1894–2004)', unpublished PhD dissertation, Leiden University, 2006, www.griquas.com/griquaphd.pdf.
Bevan, Robert, *The Destruction of Memory: Architectures at War*, London: Reaktion Books, 2006.
Bleeker, Maaike, *Visuality in the Theatre: The Locus of Looking*, Houndmills: Palgrave Macmillan, 2008.
Blits, Jan H., *Spirit, Soul and City: Shakespeare's* Coriolanus, Lanham, MD: Lexington Books, 2006.
Bloom, Clive, *Riot City: Protest and Rebellion in the City*, London: Palgrave, 2012.
BMSA *The Mathematical Sciences' Role in the War on Terror*, National Academies Press, 2004.
Boehrer, Bruce, *Shakespeare Among the Animals: Nature and Society in the Drama of Early Modern England*, New York: Palgrave, 2002.
Bogdanos, Matthew, *Thieves of Baghdad*, London: Bloomsbury, 2005.
Borcila, Rozalinda, 'Geography Lessons', 2006, videos available at www.borcila.tk/geographie/index.html.
Bottoms, Stephen, 'Putting the Document into Documentary: An Unwelcome Corrective?' *TDR: The Journal of Performance Studies* 50, no. 3 (2006): 56–68.
Bourriaud, Nicholas, *Relational Aesthetics*, Dijon: Les Presses du reel, 1998.
Brandstetter, Gabriele, 'The Virtuoso's Stage: A Theatrical Topos', *Theatre Research International* 32, no. 2 (2007): 178–95.

Braun, Bruce and Sarah Whatmore, eds, *Political Matter: Technoscience, Democracy, and Public Life*, Minneapolis: University of Minnesota Press, 2010.
Brecht, Bertolt, 'Coriolanus', in *Collected Plays, Vol. 9*, trans. and ed. Ralph Manheim and John Willett, New York: Vintage 1972: 57–146.
——[On Coriolanus], in *Werke*, Bd. 24: Texte zu Stücken, Berlin and Frankfurt/Main: Suhrkamp Verlag, 1991.
——'Study on the First Scene of Shakespeare's "Coriolanus"', in *Brecht on Theatre: The Development of an Aesthetic*, ed. and trans. John Willett, London: Methuen 1994: 252–65.
Bredekamp, Jatti, 'The Politics of Human Remains: The Case of Sarah Bartmann', in *Human Remains & Museum Practice*, ed. Jack Lohman and Katherine Goodnow, London: UNESCO and the Museum of London, 2006.
Brennan, Teresa, *The Transmission of Affect*, Ithaca: Cornell University Press, 2004.
Briggs, Daniel, ed., *The English Riots of 2011: A Summer of Discontent*, Hook, Hampshire: Waterside Press, 2012.
Bristol, Michael D., 'Lenten Butchery: Legitimation Crisis in *Coriolanus*', in *Shakespeare Reproduced: The Text in History and Ideology*, ed. Jean E. Howard and Marion F. O'Connor, New York: Methuen, 1987: 207–24.
Brockman, B.A., ed., *Shakespeare: Coriolanus—A Casebook*, Houndmills: Macmillan, 1977.
Brodie, Neill and Colin Renfrew 'Looting and the World's Archaeological Heritage: The Inadequate Response', *Annual Review of Anthropology* 34 (2005): 343–61.
Brookes, Mike, *Shaping Coriolan/us*, in National Theatre of Wales, in association with the Royal Shakespeare Company: CORIOLAN/US, performance programme, August 2012.
Brown, Keith, '"All they Understand is Force": Debating Culture in Operation Iraqi Freedom', *American Anthropologist* 110, no. 4 (2008): 443–53.
Burke, Carol, 'Combat Ethnography', in *Military Culture and Education*, ed. Douglas Higbee, Farnham: Ashgate, 2010: 29–38.
Burrows, Jonathan, *A Choreographer's Handbook*, London: Routledge, 2010.
Butler, Judith 'Merely Cultural', *New Left Review* I, no. 227 (January/February 1998): 33–44.
——*Precarious Life: The Powers of Mourning and Violence*, London: Verso, 2004.
——*Frames of War: When is Life Grievable*, London: Verso, 2009.
Campbell, Oscar James, 'Shakespeare's Satire: Coriolanus', in *Twentieth Century Interpretations of Coriolanus, A Collection of Critical Essays*, ed. James E. Phillips, Englewood Cliffs, NJ: Prentice Hall, 1970: 25–36.
Cantor, Paul A., *Shakespeare's Rome: Republic and Empire*, Ithaca, NY: Cornell University Press, 1976, Part I.
Carl, Andy and Sr. Lorraine Garasu, eds, *Accord #12: Weaving Consensus: The Papua New Guinea-Bougainville Peace Process*, London: Conciliation Resources, 2002.
Castells, Manuel, *Networks of Outrage and Hope: Social Movements in the Internet Age*, Cambridge: Polity, 2012.
Castellucci, Claudia, Romeo Castellucci, Chiara Guidi, Joe Kelleher and Nicholas Ridout, *The Theatre of Societas Raffaello Sanzio*, London: Routledge, 2007.
Cavell, Stanley, 'Who Does the Wolf Love? Reading *Coriolanus*', *Representations* 3 (1983): 1–20.
Caygill, Marjorie, *The Story of the British Museum*, 3rd edn, London: British Museum Press, 2003.

Césaire, Aimé, *Discourse on Colonialism*, trans. Joan Pinkham, New York: Monthly Review Press, 1972.

Chan, Janet, ed., *Reshaping Juvenile Justice: The NSW Young Offenders Act 1997*, Sydney: Institute of Criminology, 2005.

Childs, Craig, *Finders Keepers: A Tale of Archaeological Plunder and Obsession*, New York: Little, Brown and Company, 2010.

Clifford, James, 'Introduction: Partial Truths', in *Writing Culture: The Poetics and Politics of Ethnography*, ed. James Clifford and George Marcus, Berkeley: University of California Press, 1986: 1–26.

Collingwood, R.G., *The Idea of Nature*, Oxford: Oxford University Press, 1960.

——*The Idea of History*, Oxford: Oxford University Press, 1994.

——*Essay on Philosophical Method*, Oxford: Oxford University Press, 2008.

Connell, John, 'Compensation and Conflict: The Bougainville Copper Mine, Papua New Guinea', in *Mining and Indigenous Peoples in Australasia*, ed. John Connell and Richard Howitt, Sydney: Sydney University Press, 1991: 55–75.

Connolly, William E., *Identity/Difference: Democratic Negotiations of Political Paradox*, Minneapolis: University of Minnesota Press, 1991.

——*Pluralism*, Durham, NC: Duke University Press, 2005.

Conquergood, Dwight, 'Performing as a Moral Act: Ethical Dimensions of the Ethnography of Performance', *Literature in Performance* 5, no. 2 (1985): 1–13.

——'Rethinking Ethnography: Towards a Critical Cultural Politics', *Communication Monographs* 58, no. 2 (1991): 179–94.

Constantinou, Costas M., *On the Way to Diplomacy*, Minneapolis: University of Minnesota Press, 1996.

——'On Homo-diplomacy', *Space and Culture* 9, no. 4 (2006): 351–64.

Crais, Clifton and Pamela Scully, *Sara Baartman and the Hottentot Venus: A Ghost Story and a Biography*, Princeton, NJ: Princeton University Press, 2011.

Crandall, Jordan, 'Envisioning the Homefront: Militarization, Tracking and Security Culture', *Journal of Visual Culture* 4, no. 1 (2005): 17–38.

Crary, Jonathan, *Techniques of the Observer: On Vision and Modernity in the 19th Century*, Cambridge MA: MIT, 1992.

——*Suspensions of Perception: Attention, Spectacle, and Modern Culture*, Cambridge, MA: MIT Press, 1999.

——'Foreword', in *Installation Art in the New Millennium: The Empire of the Senses*, ed. Nicolas de Oliveira, Nicola Oxley and Michael Perry, London: Thames and Hudson, 2003.

Crawford, Peter Ian and David Turton, *Film as Ethnography*, Manchester: Manchester University in association with the Granada Centre for Visual Anthropology, 1992.

Critchley, Simon, 'On the Ethics of Alain Badiou', in *Alain Badiou: Philosophy and its Conditions*, ed. Gabriel Riera, New York: SUNY Press, 2005.

Cuff, Dana, 'Immanent Domain: Pervasive Computing and the Public Realm', *Journal of Architectural Education* 57 (2003): 43–49.

Cuneen, Chris, 'Restorative Justice and the Politics of Decolonization', in *Restorative Justice: Theoretical Foundations*, ed. Elamir Weitekamp and Hans-Jürgen Kerner, Cullompton, Devon: Willan Publishing, 2002: 32–49.

Cuno, James, ed., *Whose Muse? Art Museums and the Public Trust*, Princeton, NJ: Princeton University Press, 2004.

Daly, Kathleen, 'Conferencing in Australia and New Zealand: Variations, Research Findings, and Prospects', in *Restorative Justice for Juveniles: Conferencing,*

Mediation and Circles, ed. Allison Morris and Gabrielle Maxwell, Oxford: Hart Publishing, 2001: 59–83.
Danto, Arthur, *After the End of Art: Contemporary Art and the Pale of History*, Princeton, NJ: Princeton University Press, 1997.
Daston, Lorraine, ed., *Things That Talk: Object Lessons from Art and Science*, New York: Zone Books, 2008.
Debrix, Francois, 'Rituals of Mediation', in *Rituals of Mediation: International Politics and Social Meaning*, ed. Francois Debrix and Cynthia Weber, Minneapolis: University of Minnesota Press, 2003.
de Certeau, Michel, *Heterologies: Discourse on the Other*, trans. Brian Massumi, Minneapolis: University of Minnesota Press, 1986.
de Gay, Jane and Lizbeth Goodman, eds, *Routledge Reader in Politics and Performance*, London: Routledge, 2000.
de Goede, Marieke, 'Beyond Economism in International Political Economy', *Review of International Studies* 29 (2003): 79–97.
——*Virtue, Fortune and Faith: A Genealogy of Finance*, Minneapolis: University of Minnesota Press, 2005.
de Groof, Matthias, 'Statues Also Die—But their Death is not the Final Word', *Image & Narrative* 11, no. 1 (2010): 29–46.
Deleuze, Gilles *Spinoza, Practical Philosophy*, trans. Robert Hurley, San Francisco: City Lights Books, 1988.
——*Cinema 2: The Time Image*, trans. Hugh Tomlison and Robert Galeta, Minneapolis: University of Minnesota Press, 1989.
——*Expressionism in Philosophy: Spinoza*, trans. Martin Joughin, New York: Zone Books, 1990.
——*Bergsonism*, trans. Hugh Tomlinson and Barbara Habberjam, New York: Zone Books, 1991.
——'The Method of Dramatization', in *Desert Islands and Other Texts, 1953–1974*, ed. David Lapoujade, trans. Michael Taormina, New York: Semiotext(e), 2004: 94–116.
Deleuze, Gilles and Felix Guattari, 'Year Zero: Faciality', in Gilles Deleuze and Felix Guattari, *A Thousand Plateaus: Capitalism and Schizophrenia*, Vol. II, trans. Brian Massumi, Minneapolis: University of Minnesota Press, 1987: 167–91.
——*A Thousand Plateaus: Capitalism and Schizophrenia*, trans. Brian Massumi, London: Athlone Press, 1987.
——*What is Philosophy?* trans. H. Tomlinson and G. Burchell, New York: Columbia University Press, 1994.
Denzin, Norman, *Performance Ethnography: Critical Pedagogy and the Politics of Culture*, Thousand Oaks: Sage Publications, 2003.
de Oliveira, Nicolas, ed., *Installation Art in the New Millennium: The Empire of the Senses*, London: Thames and Hudson, 2003.
Der Derian, James, *On Diplomacy: A Genealogy of Western Estrangement*, New York: Basil Blackwell, 1987.
——*Virtuous War*, New York: Routledge, 2001.
Derrida, Jacques, 'Force of Law: The "Mystical Foundations of Authority"', in *Deconstruction and the Possibility of Justice*, ed. Drucilla Cornell, Michael Rosenfeld and David Gray Carlson, New York: Routledge, 1992.
——(in conversation with Richard Beardsworth) 'Nietzsche and the Machine', *Journal of Nietzsche Studies* 7 (1994): 7–65.

——*Archive Fever: A Freudian Impression*, trans. Eric Prenowitz, Chicago, IL: University of Chicago Press, 1995.
——*On Cosmopolitanism and Forgiveness*, London: Routledge, 2001.
Deutsche, Rosalyn, *Hiroshima After Iraq: Three Studies in Art and War*, New York: Columbia University Press, 2010.
Diamond, Elin, ed., *Performance and Cultural Politics*, New York: Routledge, 1996.
Diawara, Manthia, *African Cinema: Politics and Culture*, Bloomington and Indianapolis: Indiana University Press, 1992.
Didi-Huberman, Georges, *Confronting Images: Questioning the Ends of a Certain History of Art*, trans. John Goodman, University Park: Pennsylvania State University Press, 2009.
Dinnen, Sinclair, ed., *A Kind of Mending: Restorative Justice in the Pacific Islands*, Canberra: Pandanus Books, 2002.
Dorney, Sean, *The Sandline Affair: Politics and Mercenaries and the Bougainville Crisis*, Sydney: ABC Books, 1998: 44–45.
Düttmann, Alexander García, 'Life and Beauty: In the Middle, in the Extreme', *The New Centennial Review* 10, no. 3 (Winter 2010).
Dwyer, Paul, 'The Inner Lining of Political Discourse', *Australasian Drama Studies* 48 (April 2006): 130–35.
Edkins, Jenny, 'Legality with a Vengeance: Famines and Humanitarian Relief in "Complex Emergencies"', in *Poverty in World Politics: Whose Global Era?* ed. Sarah Owen Vandersluis and Paris Yeros, Basingstoke: Macmillan, 1999: 59–90.
——*Trauma and the Memory of Politics*, Cambridge: Cambridge University Press, 2003.
——*Missing: Persons and Politics*, Ithaca, NY: Cornell University Press, 2011.
——'Dismantling the Face: Landscape for Another Politics?' *Environment and Planning D: Society and Space* 31, no. 4 (2013): 538–553.
——'Still Face, Moving Face', *Journal for Cultural Research* 13, no. 4 (2013).
——'Politics and Personhood: Reflections on the Portrait Photograph', *Alternatives: Local, Global, Political* 32, no. 2 (2013): 139–154.
Edkins, Jenny and Véronique Pin-Fat, 'Through the Wire: Relations of Power and Relations of Violence', *Millennium: Journal of International Studies* 34, no. 1 (2005): 1–24.
Edwards, Elizabeth, *Raw Histories: Photographs, Anthropology and Museums*, Oxford: Berg, 2001: 152.
Edwards, Elizabeth and Janice Hart, eds, *Photographs Objects Histories: On the Materiality of Images*, London: Routledge, 2004.
Elden, Stuart, *Terror and Territory: The Spatial Extent of Sovereignty*, Minnesota: University of Minnesota Press, 2009.
——'Land, Terrain, Territory', *Progress in Human Geography* 34, no. 6 (2010): 799–817.
——'The Geopolitics of *King Lear*: Territory, Land, Earth', *Law and Literature* 25, no. 2 (2013).
——*The Birth of Territory*, Chicago, IL: University of Chicago Press, 2013.
Eliot, T.S., 'Coriolan', in *Collected Poems 1909–1962*, London: Faber & Faber, 2002: 137–43.
Elkins, James, *The Object Stares Back: On the Nature of Seeing*, New York: Harcourt, 1996.
Énard, Mathias, *Zone*, trans. Charlotte Mandell, Rochester, NY: Open Letter, 2010.
Ericson, Richard, *Crime in an Insecure World*, Cambridge: Polity, 2007.

Fabian, Johannes, *Out of Our Minds: Reason and Madness in the Exploration of Central Africa*, Berkley: University of California Press, 2000.
Fanon, Frantz, *Black Skin, White Masks*, trans. Charles Lam Markmann, London: Pluto, 1986.
Faris, James C., *Navajo and Photography: A Critical History of the Representation of an American People*, Albuquerque: University of New Mexico Press, 1996.
Fassin, Didier, 'Inequality of Lives, Hierarchies of Humanity: Moral Commitments and Ethical Dilemmas of Humanitarianism', in *In the Name of Humanity: The Government of Threat and Care*, ed. Ilana Feldman and Miriam Iris Ticktin, Durham, NC: Duke University Press, 2010: 238–55.
Felman, Shoshana, *The Juridical Unconscious: Trials and Traumas of the Twentieth Century*, Cambridge, MA: Harvard University Press, 2002.
Fenves, Peter, *The Messianic Reduction: Walter Benjamin and the Shape of Time*, Stanford, CA: Stanford University Press, 2011.
Ferrus, Diana, 'I've Come to Take You Home' (Tribute to Sarah Bartmann Written in Holland, June 1998), in *Black Venus 2010: They Called Her 'Hottentot'*, ed. Deborah Willis, Philadelphia, PA: Temple University Press, 2012: 213–14.
Fingleton, Wally, 'Bougainville: A Chronicle of Just Grievances', *New Guinea and Australia, the Pacific and South-East Asia* 5, no. 2 (1970): 13–20.
Finnegan, Cara A., *Picturing Poverty: Print Culture and FSA Photographs*, Washington, DC: Smithsonian Books, 2003.
Flanagan, Richard, *The Unknown Terrorist*, London: Atlantic Books, 2006.
Florensky, Pavel, *Iconostasis*, trans. Donald Sheehan and Oolga Andrejev, New York: St Vladimir's Seminary Press, 2000.
Forset, Edward, *Comparative Discourse of the Bodies Natural and Politique*, London: Iohn Bill, 1606.
Foucault, Michel, *The Archaeology of Knowledge*, trans. Alan Sheridan, New York: Pantheon, 1972.
——*Power/Knowledge: Selected Interviews and Other Writings, 1972–1977*, ed. and trans. Colin Gordon, Hemel Hempstead: Harvester Wheatsheaf, 1977.
——'The Confession of the Flesh', A Conversation, in *Power/Knowledge: Selected Interviews and Other Writings 1972–1977*, ed. Colin Gordon, trans. Colin Gordon *et al.*, New York: Pantheon, 1980.
——*Discipline and Punish: The Birth of the Prison*, trans. Alan Sheridan, London: Allen Lane, 1991.
——'Governmentality', in *The Foucault Effect: Studies in Governmentality*, ed. Graham Burchell, Colin Gordon and Peter Miller, Chicago, IL: Chicago University Press, 1991.
——*Security, Territory, Population: Lectures at the College de France, 1977–78*, trans. Graham Burchell, Basingstoke, Hampshire: Palgrave Macmillan, 2007.
——*Speech Begins After Death*, trans. Roberto Bonnono, Minneapolis: University of Minnesota Press, 2013.
France, Anatole, *Penguin Island*, New York: Modern Library, 1984.
Freud, Sigmund, 'Thoughts for the Times on War and Death', in *The Standard Edition of the Complete Psychological Works of Sigmund Freud, Volume XIV (1914–1916): On the History of the Psycho-Analytic Movement, Papers on Metapsychology and Other Works*, trans. and ed. James Strachey, London: Hogarth Press, 1957.
Friedberg, Anne, 'Urban Mobility and Cinematic Visuality', *Journal of Visual Culture* 1, no. 2 (2002): 183–204.

——— *The Virtual Window: From Alberti to Microsoft*, Cambridge, MA: MIT Press, 2007.
Fruk, Marinka, *The Destruction of Museums and Galleries in Croatia During the 1991 War*, Zagreb: Ministry of Education and Culture, 1992.
Garganigo, Alex, '*Coriolanus*, the Union Controversy, and Access to the Royal Person', *Studies in English Literature 1500–1900* 42, no. 2 (2002): 335–59.
Gates, Kelly A., *Our Biometric Future: Facial Recognition Technology and the Culture of Surveillance*, New York: New York University Press, 2011.
George, David, 'Plutarch, Insurrection and Dearth in *Coriolanus*', in *Shakespeare and Politics*, ed. Catherine M.S. Alexander, Cambridge: Cambridge University Press, 2004: 110–29.
Gill, David, 'Looting Matters for Classical Antiquities: Contemporary Issues in Archaeological Ethics', *Present Pasts* 1 (2009): 1–29.
Gilman, Sander L., 'Black Bodies, White Bodies: Toward an Iconography of Female Sexuality in Late Nineteenth-Century Art, Medicine, and Literature', *Critical Inquiry* 12, no. 1 (Autumn 1985): 204–42.
Gorman, Sarah, *The Theatre of Richard Maxwell and the New York City Players*, London and New York: Routledge, 2011.
Gould, Stephan Jay, 'The Hottentot Venus', in *The Flamingo's Smile: Reflections in Natural History*, ed. Stephan Jay Gould, New York: Norton, 1985: 291–305.
Gqola, Pumla Dineo, '"Crafting Epicentres of Agency": Sarah Bartmann and African Feminist Literary Imaginings', *QUEST: An African Journal of Philosophy / Revue Africaine de Philosophie* XX (2008): 45–76.
Gregory, Derek, *The Colonial Present: Afghanistan, Palestine, Iraq*, Malden, MA: Wiley-Blackwell, 2004.
Griffin, James, 'Bougainville: Secession or Just Sentiment?' *Current Affairs Bulletin* 48, no. 9 (1972): 258–80.
Grimshaw, Anna, *The Ethnographer's Eye: Ways of Seeing in Modern Anthropology*, Cambridge: Cambridge University Press, 2001.
Guenther, Peter, 'Three Days in Munich July 1937', in *'Degenerate Art': The Fate of the Avant-Garde in Nazi Germany*, ed. Stephanie Barron, Los Angeles: Los Angeles County Museum of Art, 1991: 33–45.
Guild, Elspeth and Evelien Brouwer, 'The Political Life of Data: The ECJ Decision on the PNR Agreement between the EU and the US', *CEPS Policy Brief* 109 (2006), www.libertysecurity.org/IMG/pdf/1363.pdf.
Gurr, Andrew, '"Coriolanus" and the Body Politic', *Shakespeare Survey* 28 (1975): 63–69.
Hager, Alan, *Shakespeare's Political Animal: Schema and Schemata in the Canon*, Newark: University of Delaware Press, 1990.
Hajjar, Remi, 'The Army's New TRADOC Culture Center', *Military Review* (2006): 89–92.
Hale, David G., '*Coriolanus*: The Death of a Political Metaphor', *Shakespeare Quarterly* 22, no. 3 (1971): 197–202.
Hall, Stuart, Chas Critcher, Tony Jefferson, John Clarke, and Brian Roberts, *Policing the Crisis: Mugging, the State, and Law and Order*, London: Macmillan, 1978.
Hamera, Judith, *Dancing Communities: Performance, Difference and Connection in the Global City*, Houndmills: Palgrave Macmillan, 2011.
Hamilton, Peter and Roger Hargreaves, *The Beautiful and the Damned: The Creation of Identity in Nineteenth-Century Photography*, Aldershot: Lund Humphries, in association with the National Portrait Gallery, London, 2001.

Hansen, Lene, 'Theorizing the Image for Security Studies: Visual Securitization and the Muhammad Cartoon Crisis', *European Journal of International Relations* 17, no. 1 (2011): 51–74.
Haraway, Donna, *When Species Meet*, Minneapolis: University of Minnesota, 2003.
Harris, Geoff, Naihuwo Ahai and Rebecca Spence, eds, *Building Peace in Bougainville* (National Research Institute Special Publication No. 27), Waigani: NRI, 1999.
Härting, H., 'Global Humanitarianism, Race, and the Spectacle of the African Corpse in Current Western Representations of the Rwandan Genocide', *Comparative Studies of South Asia, Africa and the Middle East* 28, no. 1 (2008): 61–77.
Harvey, David, 'Feral Capitalism Hits the Streets', *Reading Marx's Capital*, blog, posted 11 August 2011, climateandcapitalism.com/2011/08/11/david-harvey-on-english-riots-feral-capitalism-hits-the-streets/.
Havini, Marilyn Taleo, ed., 'A Compilation of Human Rights Abuses Against the People of Bougainville, 1989–95', Sydney: Bougainville Freedom Movement, 1995.
Hay, James and Mark Andrejevic, 'Toward an Analytics of Governmental Experiments in These Times: Homeland Security as Social Security', *Cultural Studies* 20, no. 4–5 (2006): 331–48.
Heidegger, Martin, *The Fundamental Concepts of Metaphysics: World, Fortitude, Solitude*, trans. William McNeill and Nicholas Walker, Bloomington and Indianapolis: Indiana University Press, 1995.
Heller, Agnes, *The Time is Out of Joint: Shakespeare as a Philosopher of History*, Lanham, MD: Rowman & Littlefield, 2002.
Hird, Myra, 'Feminist Engagements with Matter', *Feminist Studies* 35, no. 2 (2009): 329–46.
Hobson, Janell, 'The "Batty" Politic: Toward an Aesthetic of the Black Female Body', *Hypatia* 18, no. 4 (2003): 87–105.
Höfele, Andreas, *Stage, Stake and Scaffold: Humans and Animals in Shakespeare's Theatre*, Oxford: Oxford University Press, 2011.
Hölderlin, Friedrich, *The Death of Empedocles: A Mourning Play*, trans. David Farrell Krell, New York: SUNY Press, 2008.
Holstun, James, 'Tragic Superfluity in *Coriolanus*', *ELH: English Literary History* 50, no. 3 (1983): 485–507.
Hones, Sheila, 'Text as it Happens: Literary Geography', *Geography* Compass 2, no. 5 (2008): 1301–17.
Howley, Pat, *Breaking Spears and Mending Hearts: Peacemakers and Restorative Justice in Bougainville*, Sydney: Federation Press, 2002.
Hutchings, W., 'Beast or God: The Coriolanus Controversy', *Critical Quarterly* 24, no. 2 (1982): 35–50.
Isin, Engin, 'The Neurotic Citizen', *Citizenship Studies* 8, no. 3 (2004): 217–35.
Jaar, Alfredo, *Let There Be Light: The Rwanda Project, 1994–1998*, Barcelona: Actar, 1998.
——*Jaar SCL 2006*, Barcelona: Actar, 2006.
——*The Politics of Images*, Musée Cantonal des Beaux-Arts, Lausanne: JRP Ringier, 2007.
Jackson, Shannon, 'Just-in-Time: Performance and the Aesthetics of Precarity', *TDR: The Drama Review* 56, no. 4 (T216) (Winter 2012): 10–31.
Jagendorf, Zvi, '*Coriolanus*: Body Politic and Private Parts', *Shakespeare Quarterly* 4 (1990): 455–69.
Johannes, Fabian, *Time and the Other: How Anthropology Makes its Object*, New York: Columbia University Press, 1983.

Jonge, Ingrid Fischer, ed., *Geometry of the Face: Photographic Portraits*, Copenhagen: National Museum of Photography, 2003.
Kafka, Franz, 'The Truth about Sancho Panza', in *The Complete Stories*, trans. Willa and Edwin Muir, New York: Schocken, 1971.
Kahn, Coppélia, *Roman Shakespeare: Warriors, Wounds, and Women*, London: Routledge, 1997.
Kang, Jerry and Dana Cuff, 'Pervasive Computing: Embedding the Public Sphere', *Washington and Lee Law Review* 65 (2005); UCLA School of Law, Law-Econ Research Paper No. 04–23; UCLA School of Law Research Paper No. 626961, ssrn.com/abstract = 626961.
Kant, Immanuel, *Foundations of the Metaphysics of Morals* (1785), cited in Alphonso Lingis, *The Imperative*, Bloomington and Indianapolis: Indiana University Press, 1998.
——*Anthropology from a Pragmatic Point of View*, ed. Robert B. Louden, Cambridge: Cambridge University Press, 2006.
——*Groundwork of the Metaphysics of Morals*, ed. and trans. Mary Gregor and Jens Timmermann, Cambridge: Cambridge University Press, 2012.
Kantorowicz, Ernst H., *The King's Two Bodies: A Study in Mediaeval Political Theology*, Princeton, NJ: Princeton University Press, 1957.
Kaplan, Louis, *American Exposures: Photography and Community in the Twentieth Century*, Minneapolis: University of Minnesota Press, 2005.
Kear, Adrian, 'Intensities of Appearance', *Performance Research* 12, no. 4 (2008): 16–24.
——*Theatre and Event: Staging the European Century*, Basingstoke: Palgrave, 2013.
Kear, Adrian and Patrick Campbell, *Psychoanalysis and Performance*, London and New York: Routledge, 2001.
Kear, Adrian and Richard Gough, eds, *On Appearance Performance Research* Vol. 13, no. 4, London Routledge 2008.
Kear, Adrian and Deborah Lynn Steinberg, *Mourning Diana: Nation, Culture and the Performance of Grief*, London and New York: Routledge, 1999.
Keenan, Thomas, *Fables of Responsibility: Aberrations and Predicaments in Ethics and Politics*, Stanford CA: Stanford University Press, 1997.
Kelleher, Joe, *Theatre and Politics*, London: Palgrave, 2009.
Kermode, Frank, *Shakespeare's Language*, London: Penguin, 2000.
Kershaw, Baz, *The Politics of Performance*, London: Routledge, 1992.
Kim, Kwang-Ho, 'Shakespeare's Treatment of the Source in *Coriolanus*', *English Studies* 7 (1983): 49–62.
Kimmelman, Michael, 'Is it All Loot? Tackling the Antiquities Problem', *The New York Times*, 29 March 2006.
King, Christopher, 'Managing Ethical Conflict on a Human Terrain Team', *Anthropology News* 50, no. 6 (2009): 16.
Kipp, Jacob *et al.*, 'The Human Terrain System: A CORDS for the 21st Century', *Military Review* (September–October 2006): 9.
Kirsch, Stuart, *Reverse Anthropology: Indigenous Analysis of Social and Environmental Relations in New Guinea*, Stanford, CA: Stanford University Press, 2006.
Kittler, Friedrich, *Literature, Media, Information Systems: Essays*, Amsterdam: Arts Limited, 1997.
Koerner, Joseph Leo, 'Bosch's Equipment', in *Things That Talk: Object Lessons from Art and Science*, ed. Lorraine Daston, New York: Zone Books, 2008: 27–66.

Kopytoff, Igor, 'The Cultural Biography of Things: Commodification as Process', in *The Social Life of Things: Commodities in Cultural Perspective*, ed. Arjun Appadurai, Cambridge: Cambridge University Press, 1986: 64–94.

Kott, Jan, *Shakespeare our Contemporary*, London: Methuen, 1964: 179–210.

Krasznahorkai, Laszlo, *War & War*, trans. George Szirtes, New York: New Directions, 2006.

Kriel, Henery, 'Becoming Political', in *Teaching Political Science: The Professor and the Polity*, ed. Vernon van Dyke, Atlantic Highlands, NJ: Humanities Press, 1977.

Lacan, Jacques, 'Agressivity in Psychoanalysis', in *Écrits*, trans. Alan Sheridan, New York: Norton & Co., 1977.

Laracy, Hugh, *Marists and Melanesians: A History of Catholic Missions in the Solomon Islands*, Canberra: Australian National University Press, 1976.

Latour, Bruno, *We Have Never Been Modern*, trans. Catherine Porter, Cambridge, MA: Harvard University Press, 1993.

Lavine, Steven D. and Ivan Karp, 'Introduction: Museums and Multiculturalism', in *Exhibiting Cultures*, ed. Steven D. Lavine and Ivan Karp, Washington, DC: Smithsonian Institution Press, 1991: 1–9.

Leckie, Jacqueline, ed., *Development in an Insecure and Gendered World*, Surrey: Ashgate, 2009.

Leggatt, Alexander, *Shakespeare's Political Drama: The History Plays and the Roman Plays*, London: Routledge, 1989.

Lehmann, Hans-Thies, *Postdramatic Theatre*, London: Taylor & Francis, 2006.

Lemon, Rebecca, 'Arms and the Law in *Coriolanus*', in *The Law and Shakespeare*, ed. Constance Jordan and Karen Cunningham, Houndmills: Palgrave, 2010: 233–48.

Levinas, Emmanuel, *Totality and Infinity: An Essay on Exteriority*, trans. Alphonso Lingis, Pittsburgh, PA: Duquesne University Press, 1969.

Levi Strauss, David, 'The Sea of Griefs is not a Proscenium', in *Let There Be Light: The Rwanda Project, 1994–1998*, ed. Alfredo Jaar, Barcelona: Actar, 1998.

Lindqvist, Sven, '*Exterminate All the Brutes*', trans. Joan Tate, New York: The New Press, 1992.

Locke, John, 'Second Treatise', in *Two Treatises of Government*, ed. Peter Laslett, Cambridge: Cambridge University Press, 1988 [1960].

Lucas, George R. Jr, *Anthropologists in Arms: The Ethics of Military Anthropology*, Lanham, MD: AltaMira Press, 2009.

Ludden, David, 'Orientalism Empiricism: Transformations of Colonial Knowledge', in *Orientalism and the Postcolonial Predicament: Perspectives on South Asia*, ed. Carol A. Breckenridge and Peter van der Veer, Philadelphia: University of Pennsylvania Press, 1993.

Lunden, Staffan, 'The Scholar and the Market: Swedish Scholarly Contributions to the Destruction of the World's Archaeological Heritage', in *Swedish Archaeologists on Ethics*, ed. Håkan Karlsson, Lindome: Bricoleur Press, 2004: 197–247.

Lydon, Jane, *Eye Contact: Photographing Indigenous Australians*, Durham, NC: Duke University Press, 2005.

MacDougall, David, *Transcultural Cinema*, Princeton, NJ: Princeton University Press, 1998.

MacGinty, Roger, 'Looting in the Context of Violent Conflict: A Conceptualization and Typology', *Third World Quarterly* 25, no. 5 (2004): 857–70.

MacGregor, Neil, 'The Whole World in Our Hands', *Guardian Review*, 24 July 2004: 4–6.

MacKenzie, Megan, 'Ruling Exceptions: Female Soldiers and Everyday Experiences of Civil Conflict', in *Experiencing War*, ed. Christine Sylvester, London: Routledge, 2011: 64–78.

Malkki, Liisa H., 'Speechless Emissaries: Refugees, Humanitarianism, and Dehistoricization', *Cultural Anthropology* 11, no. 3 (1996): 377–404.

Manzo, Kate, 'Imaging Humanitarianism: NGO Identity and the Iconography of Childhood', Antipode 40, no. 4 (2008): 632–57.

Marcuse, Herbert, *An Essay on Liberation*, Boston, MA: Beacon Press, 1969.

Matsuda, David, 'The Ethics of Archaeology, Subsistence Digging, and Artifact Looting in Latin America: Point, Muted Counterpoint', *International Journal of Cultural Property* 7 (1998): 87–97.

Maxwell, Anne, *Colonial Photography and Exhibitions: Representations of the 'Native' and the Making of European Identities*, London: Leicester University Press, 1999.

Maxwell, J.C., 'Animal Imagery in *Coriolanus*', *The Modern Language Review* 42, no. 4 (1947): 417–21.

Mbembe, Achille, *On the Postcolony*, Berkeley: University of California Press, 2001.

McDonald, Matt, 'Securitization and the Construction of Security', *European Journal of International Relations* 14, no. 4 (2008): 563–87.

McFate, Montgomery, 'Anthropology and Counterinsurgency: The Strange Story of their Curious Relationship', *Military Review* (March–April 2005): 24–38.

——'The Military Utility of Understanding Adversary Culture', *Joint Forces Quarterly* 38 (2005): 42–48.

McMaster, H.R., '"Preserving Soldiers" Moral Character in Counterinsurgency Operations', in *Ethics Education for Irregular Warfare*, ed. Don Carrick, James Connelly and Paul Robinson, Farnham: Ashgate, 2009: 15–26.

Miller, Daniel, ed., *Materiality*, Durham, NC: Duke University Press, 2005.

Miller, Peter and Nikolas Rose, 'Governing Economic Life', *Economy & Society* 19, no. 1 (1990): 1–31.

Miola, Robert S., *Shakespeare's Rome*, Cambridge: Cambridge University Press, 1983.

Mitchell, Charles, 'Coriolanus: Power as Honor', *Shakespeare Studies* 1 (1965): 199–226.

Mitchell, W.T.J., 'There are no Visual Media', *Journal of Visual Culture* 4, no. 2 (2005): 257–66.

——*What Do Pictures Want? The Lives and Loves of Images*, Chicago, IL: University of Chicago Press, 2005.

Mitter, Partha, 'The Hottentot Venus and Western Man: Reflections on the Construction of Beauty in the West', in *Cultural Encounters: Representing Otherness*, ed. Elizabeth Hallam and Brian Street, London: Routledge, 2000: 35–50.

Monks, Aoife, 'Human Remains: Acting, Objects, and Belief in Performance', *Theatre Journal* 64 (2012): 355–71.

Mortensen, Mette, 'Photography in the Public Arena', in *Geometry of the Face: Photographic Portraits*, ed. Ingrid Fischer Jonge, Copenhagen: National Museum of Photography, 2003: 10–39.

Moustakas, John, 'Group Rights in Cultural Property', *Cornell Law Review* 74 (1989): 1179.

Moyo, Dambisa, *Dead Aid: Why Aid is Not Working and How There is Another Way for Africa*, London: Penguin, 2009.

Mudimbe, V.Y., *The Invention of Africa: Gnosis, Philosophy, and the Order of Knowledge*, Bloomington: Indiana University Press, 1988.

——*The Idea of Africa*, Bloomington: Indiana University Press, 1994.

Muir, Kenneth, 'The Background of Coriolanus', *Shakespeare Quarterly* 10, no. 2 (1959): 137–45.
Murakami, Ineke, 'The "Bond and Privilege of Nature" in *Coriolanus*', *Religion & Literature* 38, no. 3 (2006): 121–36.
Mussawir, Edward, *Jurisdiction in Deleuze: The Expression and Representation of the Law*, New York: Routledge, 2011.
Nancy, Jean-Luc, *The Inoperative Community*, ed. and trans. Peter Connor, Minneapolis: University of Minnesota Press, 1991.
——*Being Singular Plural*, trans. Robert D. Richardson and Anne E. O'Byrne, Stanford, CA: Stanford University Press, 2000.
——*Identité*, Paris: Galilée 2010.
Nemeth, Erik, 'Cultural Security: The Evolving Role of Art in International Security', *Terrorism and Political Violence* 19, no. 1 (2007): 19–42.
——'Conflict Art: Scholars Develop the Tactical Value of Cultural Patrimony', *Cambridge Review of International Affairs* 23, no. 2 (2010): 299–323.
Ngai, Sianne, *Ugly Feelings*, Cambridge, MA: Harvard University Press, 2005.
Nicolson, Harold, *Diplomacy*, Oxford: Oxford University Press, 1950.
Nutall, Sarah, ed., *Beautiful/Ugly: African and Diaspora Aesthetics*, Durham, NC: Duke University Press, 2006.
Nyers, Peter, 'The Accidental Citizen: Acts of Sovereignty and (Un)making Citizenship', *Economy & Society* 35, no. 1 (2006): 22–41.
O'Callaghan, Mary-Louise, *Enemies Within: Papua New Guinea, Australia, and the Sandline Crisis*, Sydney: Doubleday, 1999.
Oliver, Douglas, *A Solomon Island Society: Kinship and Leadership among the Siuai of Bougainville*, Boston: Beacon Press, 1955.
Opondo, Sam Okoth, 'Decolonizing Diplomacy: Reflections on African Estrangement and Exclusion', in *Sustainable Diplomacies*, ed. Costas Constantinou and James Der Derian, Basingstoke: Palgrave Macmillan, 2010: 109–27.
Paget, Derek, *True Stories? Documentary Drama on Radio, Screen and Stage*, Manchester: Manchester University Press, 1990.
Pastor, Gail Kern, 'To Starve with Feeding: the City in *Coriolanus*', *Shakespeare Studies* XI (1978): 123–44.
Patterson, Annabel, *Shakespeare and the Popular Voice*, Oxford: Basil Blackwell, 1989.
Pearson, Mike, *In Comes I*, Exeter: Exeter University Press, 2006.
——*Site-Specific Performance*, Basingstoke: Palgrave, 2010.
——'Framing the Text', in National Theatre of Wales, in association with the Royal Shakespeare Company: CORIOLAN/US, performance programme August 2012.
Pearson, Mike, Steve Daniels and Heike Roms, eds, *Fieldworks* (*Performance Research* 15, no. 4), London and New York: Routledge, 2010.
Pearson, Mike and Michael Shanks, *Theatre/Archaeology*, London and New York: Routledge, 2001.
Pettet, E.C., 'Coriolanus and the Midlands Insurrection of 1607', *Shakespeare Survey* 3 (1950): 34–42.
Phelan, Peggy, *Unmarked: The Politics of Performance*, London: Routledge, 1993.
Phillips, James E. (ed.), *Twentieth-Century Interpretations of Coriolanus: A Collection of Critical Essays*, Englewood Cliffs, NJ: Prentice Hall, 1970.
Pinney, Christopher, *Camera Indica: The Social Life of Indian Photographs*, Chicago, IL: University of Chicago Press, 1997.

——'Things Happen: Or, from Which Moment Does That Object Come?' in *Materiality*, ed. Daniel Miller, Durham, NC: Duke University Press, 2005: 256–72.

Platform for Art, *Thin Cities: 100 Years of the Piccadilly Line*, London: Platform for Art, 2006.

Polka, Brayton, '*Coriolanus* and the Roman World of Contradiction: A Paradoxical World Elsewhere', *The European Legacy* 15, no. 2 (2010): 171–94.

Pollock, Della, 'Marking New Directions in Performance Ethnography', *Text and Performance Quarterly* 26, no. 4 (2006): 325–29.

Pollock, Griselda, 'Not-Forgetting Africa: The Dialectics of Attention/Inattention, Seeing/Denying, and Knowing/Understanding in the Positioning of the Viewer by the Work of Alfredo Jaar', in *Alfredo Jaar: The Politics of Images*, Musée Cantonal des Beaux-Arts, Lausanne: JRP Ringier, 2007.

——'Photographing Atrocity: Becoming Iconic?' in *Picturing Atrocity: Photography in Crisis*, ed. Geoffrey Batchen *et al.*, Lonfon: Reaktion Books, 2012: 65–78.

Poole, Adrian, *Coriolanus*, New York: Harvester Wheatsheaf, 1988.

Poole, Deborah, *Vision, Race and Modernity: A Visual Economy of the Andean Image World*, Princeton, NJ: Princeton University Press, 1997.

Power, Nina and Alberto Toscano, '"Think, pig!" An Introduction to Badiou's Beckett', in *On Beckett*, ed. Alain Badiou, and trans. Nina Power and Alberto Toscano, Manchester: Clinamen Press, 2003.

Powys, John Cowper, *A Glastonbury Romance*, New York: The Overlook Press, 1996.

Primavesi, Patrick, 'Embedded Audience. Wie Mike Pearson/Mike Brookes in Cardiff und die Wooster Group/Royal Shakespeare Company in Stratford die Funktion des Medialen im Krieg bearbeiten', in *Theater der Zeit*, 12 (December 2012): 38–39.

Primavesi, Patrick, 'Memories from a Theatre of War', *Performance Research* 17, no. 3 (2012): 50–56.

Quodling, Paul, *Bougainville: The Mine and the People*, Sydney: Centre for Independent Studies, 1991.

Qureshi, Sadia, 'Displaying Sara Bartmann, the "Hottentot Venus"', *History of Science* 42 (2004): 233–57.

Rai, Shirin and Janelle Reinelt, *The Grammar of Performance and Politics*, London: Routledge, 2013.

Rainer, Yvonne, 'Some Retrospective Notes on a Dance for 10 People and 12 Mattresses Called "Parts of Some Sextets"', *Tulane Drama Review* 10, no. 2 (T30) (1965): 168–78.

Rancière, Jacques, *Disagreement: Politics and Philosophy*, trans. Julie Rose, Minneapolis: University of Minnesota Press, 1999.

——'Theater of Images', in *Alfredo Jaar—La Politique des Images* Exhibition catalogue, Musée Cantonal des Beaux—Arts, Lausanne, Zurich: JRP Ringier, 2002: 71–80.

——'Who is the Subject of the Rights of Man?' *South Atlantic Quarterly* 103 (2004): 297–310.

——*The Politics of Aesthetics: The Distribution of the Sensible*, trans. Gabriel Rockhill, London: Continuum, 2004.

——'Art of the Possible: Fluvia Carnevale and John Kelsey in Conversation with Jacques Rancière' in 'Regime Change: Jacques Rancière and Contemporary Art', *Artforum International* (March 2007): 252–85.

——'The Emancipated Spectator', *Artforum International* (March 2007): 271–80.

——*The Future of the Image*, trans. Gregory Elliott, London: Verso, 2007.

——*Aesthetics and its Discontents*, Cambridge: Polity Press, 2009.
——*The Emancipated Spectator*, trans. Gregory Elliott, London: Verso, 2009.
——*Dissensus: On Politics and Aesthetics*, trans. Steve Corcoran, New York: Continuum, 2010.
Rasmussen, Claire and Michael Brown, 'The Body Politic as Spatial Metaphor', *Citizenship Studies* 9, no. 5 (2005): 469–84.
Rassool, Ciraj, 'Human Remains, the Disciplines of the Dead and the South African Memorial Complex', paper presented at The Politics of Heritage, Museum Africa, Newtown, Johannesburg, 8–9 July 2011, sitemaker.umich.edu/politics.of.heritage/schedule_and_papers: 3–4.
Regan, Anthony and Helga Griffin, eds, *Bougainville Before the Conflict*, Canberra: Pandanus Books, 2005.
Regener, Susanne, 'Reading Faces: Photography and the Search for Expression', in *Geometry of the Face: Photographic Portraits*, ed. Ingrid Fischer Jonge, Copenhagen: National Museum of Photography, 2003.
Reguillo, Rossana, 'Sujetividad sitiada. Hacia una antropología de las pasiones contemporáneas', *E-misférica* 4, no. 1 (June 2007), (Issue entitled 'Passions, Performance, and Public Affects'), hemisphericinstitute.org/hemi/en/e-misferica-41/reguillo.
Ricks, Thomas E., *Fiasco: The American Military Adventure in Iraq*, London: Penguin Books 2007.
Ridout, Nicholas, 'On the Work of Things: Musical Production, Theatrical Labor, and the "General Intellect"', *Theatre Journal* 64 (2012): 389–408.
Riss, Arthur, 'The Belly Politic: *Coriolanus* and the Revolt of Language', *ELH: English Literary History* 59, no. 1 (1992): 53–75.
Ritter, Joachim, 'Landschaft. Zur Funktion des Ästhetischen in der modernen Gesellschaft', in *Subjektivität*, Frankfurt am Main: Suhrkamp, 1974.
Ryan, James R., *Picturing Empire: Photography and the Visualization of the British Empire*, Chicago, IL: University of Chicago Press, 1997.
Said, Edward, *On Late Style: Music and Literature Against the Grain*, London: Pantheon, 2006.
Salisbury, John of, *Policraticus: On the Frivolities of Courtiers and the Footprints of Philosophers*, ed. and trans. Cary J. Nederman, Cambridge: Cambridge University Press, 1990.
Sandholtz, Wayne, *Prohibiting Plunder: How Norms Change*, New York: Oxford University Press, 2007.
Saunders, Angharad, 'Literary Geography: Reforging the Connections', *Progress in Human Geography* 34, no. 4 (2010): 436–52.
Sekula, Allan, 'The Body and the Archive', in *The Contest of Meaning: Critical Histories of Photography*, ed. Richard Boulton, Cambridge, MA: MIT Press, 1989: 342–88.
Seville, Isidore of, *The Etymologies of Isidore of Seville*, trans. Steven A. Barney, W.J. Lewis, J.A. Beach and Oliver Berghof, Cambridge: Cambridge University Press, 2006.
Shakespeare, William, *Coriolanus*, ed. Philip Brockbank (Arden Shakespeare), London: Routledge, 1976.
——*The Tragedy of Coriolanus*, ed. R.B. Parker, Oxford: Oxford University Press, 1994.
——*The Tragedy of Coriolanus*, in: *Coriolanus*, ed. Lee Bliss (The New Cambridge Shakespeare), Cambridge: Cambridge University Press 2000: 104–273.

―― Coriolanus, ed. Jonathan Bate and Eric Rasmussen (RSC Shakespeare), Houndmills: Macmillan, 2011.
Shapiro, Michael J., *Studies in Trans-Disciplinary Method: After the Aesthetic Turn*, New York: Routledge, 2012.
Sharp, Naomi, 'Bougainville: Blood on Our Hands', Aid/Watch Report, Sydney, 1997.
Shrank, Cathy, 'Civility and the City in *Coriolanus*', *Shakespeare Quarterly* 54, no. 1 (2003): 406–23.
Silk, J., 'Beyond Geography and Literature', *Environment and Planning D: Society and Space* 2, no. 2 (1984): 151–78.
Silverman, Kaja, *The Threshold of the Visible World*, New York: Routledge, 1996.
Simmel, Georg, 'The Metropolis and Mental Life', in *The Sociology of Georg Simmel*, ed. Kurt Wolff, New York: The Free Press, 1950: 409–24.
Simpson, R.R., *Shakespeare and Medicine*, Edinburgh: E. & S. Livingstone, 1959.
Singer, Ben, 'Modernity, Hyperstimulus, and the Rise of Popular Sensationalism', in *Cinema and the Invention of Modern Life*, ed. Leo Charney and Vanessa R. Schwartz, Berkeley, CA: University of California Press, 1995.
Sirivi, Josephine Tankunani and Marilyn Taleo Havini, eds, *As Mothers of the Land: The Birth of the Bougainville Women for Peace and Freedom*, Canberra: Pandanus Books, 2004.
Sloterdijk, Peter, *The Art of Philosophy: Wisdom as Practice*, trans. Karen Margolis, New York: Columbia University Press, 2012.
Slovo, Gillian, *The Riots: From Spoken Evidence*, London: Oberon Books, 2011.
Smith, Lindsay, *Women, Children and Nineteenth-Century Photography*, Manchester: Manchester University Press, 1998.
Smith, Shawn Michelle, *Photography on the Colour Line: W.E.B. Du Bois, Race, and Visual Culture*, Durham, NC: Duke University Press, 2004.
Sobieszek, Robert A., *Ghost in the Shell: Photography and the Human Soul 1850–2000*, Los Angeles, CA: Los Angeles County Museum of Art; Cambridge, MA: MIT Press, 1999.
Spencer, T.J.B., *Shakespeare's Plutarch: The Lives of Julius Caesar, Brutus, Marcus Antonius and Coriolanus*, trans. Sir Thomas North, Harmondsworth: Penguin, 1968: 296–362.
Spivak, Gayatri Chakravorty, 'Can the Subaltern Speak?' in *Marxism and the Interpretation of Culture*, ed. Cary Nelson and Larry Grossberg, Chicago, IL: University of Illinois Press, 1988: 271–313.
Steichen, Edward, *The Family of Man*, New York: Museum of Modern Art, 1955.
Stengers, Isabelle, *Cosmopolitics I: I. The Science Wars. II. The Invention of Mechanics. III. Thermodynamics*, trans. R. Bononno, Minneapolis: University of Minnesota Press, 2010.
Stepan, Nancy Leys, *Picturing Tropical Nature*, London: Reaktion Books, 2001.
Styan, J.L., *Shakespeare's Stagecraft*, Cambridge: Cambridge University Press, 1991.
Sylvester, Christine, 'The Art of War/The War Question in (Feminist) International Relations', *Millennium: Journal of International Studies* 33, no. 3 (2005): 855–78.
―― *Art/Museums: International Relations Where We Least Expect It*, Boulder, CO: Paradigm Publishers, 2009.
―― 'War, Sense, and Security', in *Gender and International Security: Feminist Perspectives*, ed. Laura Sjoberg, New York: Routledge, 2010: 24–37.
―― ed., *Experiencing War*, London: Routledge, 2011.
Tagg, John, *The Burden of Representation: Essays on Photographies and Histories*, Basingstoke: Palgrave Macmillan, 1988.

Tanselle, G. Thomas and Florence W. Dunbar, 'Legal Language in *Coriolanus*', *Shakespeare Quarterly* 13, no. 2 (1962): 231–38.

Tatlow, Anthony, 'Coriolanus', in *Brecht Handbuch in 5 Bänden*, ed. Jan Knopf, Bd. 1: Stücke, Stuttgart: Metzler, 2001: 585–91.

Thomas, Nicholas, *Colonialism's Culture: Anthropology, Travel and Government*, London: Polity Press, 1994.

Thompson, James, *Digging Up Stories*, Manchester: Manchester University Press, 2005.

Thrift, Nigel, 'Landscape and Literature', *Environment and Planning A* 10, no. 3 (1978): 347–49.

——'Literature, the Production of Culture and the Politics of Place', *Antipode* 15, no. 1 (1983): 12–24.

Trainor, Meghan, 'Exhibition Notes Accompanying RFID Project', part of the 2004 Winter Show of the Interactive Telecommunications Programme at the Tisch School of Art, NYU.

Treadwell, James, Daniel Briggs, Simon Winlow and Steve Hall, 'Shopocalypse Now: Consumer Culture and the English Riots of 2011', *British Journal of Criminology* 53 (2013): 1–17.

Trimboli, Lily, *An Evaluation of the NSW Youth Justice Conferencing Scheme*, Sydney: NSW Bureau of Crime Statistics, 2000.

Turkle, Sherry, ed., *Evocative Objects: Things We Think With*, Cambridge, MA: MIT Press, 2007.

Tussing, Nicholas J., 'The Politics of Leo XIII's Opening of the Vatican Archives: The Ownership of the Past', *The American Archivist* 70 (Fall/Winter 2007): 364–86.

Udris, David, James Der Derian and Michael Udris, *Human Terrain*, Providence: Udris Film, Oxyopia Productions & Global Media Project 2010.

Ukadike, Nwachukwu Frank, *Black African Cinema*, Berkeley, Los Angeles: University of California Press, 1994.

Virno, Paolo, *A Grammar of the Multitude: For an Analysis of Contemporary Forms of Life*, trans. Isabella Bertoletti, James Cascaito and Andrea Casson, Los Angeles, CA: Semiotext(e), 2004.

Walker, Jarrett, 'Voiceless Bodies and Bodiless Voices: The Drama of Human Perception in *Coriolanus*', *Shakespeare Quarterly* 43, no. 2 (1992): 170–85.

Weber, Sam, *Targets of Opportunity: On the Militarization of Thinking*, New York: Fordham University Press, 2005.

Wellcome Collection, 'Identity: Eight Rooms, Nine Lives', London, 26 November 2009–6 April 2010, www.wellcomecollection.org/whats-on/exhibitions/identity.aspx.

Wells, Robin Headlam, *Shakespeare's Politics: A Contextual Introduction*, London: Continuum, 2009.

White, Hayden, 'Bodies and their Plots', in *Choreographing History*, ed. Susan Leigh Foster, Bloomington: Indiana University Press, 1995: 230–34.

Williams, William Carlos, 'Asphodel, That Greeny Flower' (1955), in *The Collected Poems of William Carlos Williams, Volume II, 1939–1962*, ed. Christopher MacGowan, New York: New Directions, 1992: 310–38.

Willis, Susan, 'Old Glory', in *Dissent from the Homeland*, ed. Frank Lentricchia and Stanley Hauerwas, Durham, NC: Duke University Press, 2003.

Winlow, Simon and Steve Hall, 'Gone Shopping: Inarticulate Politics in the English Riots of 2011', in *The English Riots of 2011: A Summer of Discontent*, ed. Daniel Briggs, Hook, Hampshire: Waterside Press, 2012: 149–67.

Zehfuss, Maja, 'Targeting: Precision and the Production of Ethics', *European Journal of International Relations* 17, no. 3 (2011): 543–56.
——'Culturally Sensitive War? The Human Terrain System and the Seduction of Ethics', *Security Dialogue* 43, no. 2 (2012): 175–90.
——'Killing Civilians: Thinking the Practice of War', *British Journal of Politics and International Relations* 14, no. 3 (2012): 423–40.

Žižek, Slavoj, *The Universal Exception*, London: Continuum, 2006.
——'Shoplifters of the World Unite', *London Review of Books*, 19 August 2011.
——*The Year of Dreaming Dangerously*, London: Verso, 2012.

Index

9/11 events 2, 6, 235, 239–40, 247
2001: A Space Odyssey 207

A Choreographers Handbook 96
A Fortunate Life: The Story of a Country Doctor 125
A Glastonbury Romance 9
Abe, Kobo 42
About, Nicolas 138
Acquisti, Alessandro 46
Adorno, Theodor W. 78, 80–82
Aeschylus 171
Aesop 183
aesthetic politics 8
Aesthetic Theory 82
aesthetic thinking 8
African National Congress (ANC) 138
Agamben, Giorgio 2, 4, 6–7, 30, 42–43, 132, 142
Akram-Lohdi, Haroom 207
Alsace-Lorraine 83
Amini, Abbas 2
An Heir (film) 9, 82
Anatomy of Melancholy 97
Andres Manuel Lopez Obrador (AMLO) 85–90, 92–93
'animatedness' 93
animating politics 84–94
Anthropology from a Pragmatic Point of View 7
aphanisis (disappearance of sexual desire) 33
Arab Spring 40, 84, 166, 172
Arendt, Hannah 104
Aristotle 103
Army Culture and Foreign Language Strategy 225
Ashley, April 50

Auschwitz 6
Austin, J. L. 86

Baartman, Saartjie (Sarah) 10, 48, 50, 133, 136–41, 143
Bacon, Francis 97
Badiou, Alan 2, 4, 8, 21, 27–31, 33, 40, 52–53
Bailes, Sara Jane 99
Bakhtin, M. M. 65
Balkans War 63
Bamiyan Valley Buddhas 212
Banham, Simon 9
Barrès, Maurice 83
Barthes, Roland 115, 126
Bastian, Adolf 135, 142
Baumann, Zygmunt 52
Bayly, Simon 99
Beautiful/Ugly 134
Beckett, Samuel 4
'Becoming Political' (essay) 150, 154
bellies, wounds, infections, animals, territories (political bodies of *Coriolanus*): animals 187–90; bellies 182–84; infections 186–87; introduction 179–82; territories 190–95; wounds 184–86
Benjamin, Walter 69, 72
Bennett, Jane 203, 204–9, 212, 217
Berger, John 125, 127
Bertillon, Alphonse 47
Blaškiš (character) 63
book summary 9–12
Borcila, Rozalinda 245
Boston Tea Party 224
Bougainville Photoplay Project 114–27
Bourriaud, Nicholas 176
Brandstetter, Gabriele 97–99, 101, 103–4

Index

Break Down project (Oxford Street, London) 246
Brecht, Bertolt 11, 93, 161, 166–70, 176, 180
Brennan, Teresa 84, 92
Briggs, Daniel 53
British citizens 'of Pakistani origin' 235, 247
Brith Gof theatre company 171
British Museum, London 210–11, 216
British Transport Police 45
Brockbank, Philip 180
Brookes, Mike 11, 40, 161–62, 166–68, 171–73, 175–76
Brown, Keith 226
Brutus (character in *Coriolanus*) 170
Burrows, Jonathan 96, 101
Burton, Richard 97
Butler, Judith 2, 133, 213

Caius Martius (character in *Coriolanus*) 162–63, 165, 169–70, 184, 186–89, 193
camera obscura 24
Cameron, David 40–41, 43–44, 52
Carnegie Mellon University (CMU) 45
Carter, Kevin (photographer) 23–25
Castellucci, Romeo 9, 102, 106
Castels, Manuel 84
Cavell, Stanley 181, 184
Chertoff, Michael 234, 243
Chirac, Jacques 138
citizenship and unknown futures 247
Clifford, James 119
Cloquet, Ghislain 130
Cold War 48, 171, 207
Collingwood, R. G. 150
Cominius (character in *Coriolanus*) 164, 181, 189
Comparative Discourse of the Bodies Natural and Politique 183
Conquergood, Dwight 119
Conrad, Joseph 73
Constantinou, Costas 133
Contempt (film) 70
Convention on the Means of Prohibiting and Preventing Illicit Import, Export and Transfer of Ownership of Cultural Property (UNESCO, 1970) 210
Copenhagen School (security) 216
Coriolan/us 170, 176
Coriolanus: production 11, 40: *see also* bellies ... ; performing audience

cosmopoetics 105–9
Cosmopolitics 107
'counter-surveillance' videos 245
Counterinsurgency Manual 222–23, 226
County Museum of Art, Los Angeles 50
Cousin, Waverly 243
Cowper Powys, John 80–81
Crandall, Jordan 241
Crary, Jonathan 236, 237, 239, 241, 244–45
Critchley, Simon 27
Cultural Olympiad, 2012 161

Das Lied von der Erde 82
de Cervantes, Miguel 64
de Lumley, Henry 138
Debord, Guy 105
Deleuze, Gilles 9, 42, 52, 64, 65–66, 72, 145
Der Freischütz (essay) 80
Derrida, Jacques 75, 244–45
Deutsche, Rosalyn 75
dissensus 26–31, 136
Distinguished Speaker Series 3
DNA samples 207
dOCUMENTA exhibition, Kassel, Germany 102
Dominguez, Ricardo 85
Don Quixote 64
Dreyfus, Alfred 74
drones (unmanned aircraft) 207
Du Bois, W. E. B. 49
Duchess du Barry Parisian ball (1829) 136
Duggan, Mark 40–41
Düttmann, Alexander Garcia 9
Dwyer, Allan 116

Edwards, Elizabeth 51
Egypt Museum 214
Elden, Stuart 1, 11
Elgin marbles 201
Eliot, T. S. 180
Elkins, James 206, 212
Embrace (exhibition) 34
'Emotional Geographies: What and Why?' 1
Énard, Mathias 63, 72–73
'energetic effects' 84
Engel, Erich 166
Entetarte Kunst (Degenerate Art) 204, 209, 212
Epilogue (exhibition) 33
Ernst, Max 215

ethic of singular truths 31
'ethical radicalism' 30
Ethics: An Essay on the Understanding of Evil 27
eudaemonia (happiness) 29
European Human Rights Act 43
Evocative Objects 214

Fabian, Johannes 119
Face of Another 42
Facewatch campaign 46
facing and defacing: face and physiognomy 46–51; introduction 40–43; returning the gaze 51–53; 'we have your face' 43–46
facingness 23
Family of Man 48
Fanon, Frantz 42
Fassin, Didier 142
Fawkes, Guy 183
Felipe, Liliana 92
Felman, Shoshana 72
Ferrus, Diana 138–39
Fiennes, Ralph 11, 166, 181–82, 191–92
Flanigan, Richard 234–35, 239, 241
Forset, Edward 183
Foucault, Michel 63, 247
Foundations of the Metaphysics of Morals 27
France, Anatole 74
Freire, Paulo 154
Freud, Sigmund 85
Friedberg, Anne 241

Gall, Franz Joseph 50
Galton, Francis 47, 50
Garasu, Lorraine 122
Gates, Bill 32
Gates, Kelly 44–46
General Regulations for the Protection of Things of Historical and Artistic Interest (Italy) 210
Geographical Conference of Brussels, 1876 135
Geography Lessons 245
Geography = War (exhibition) 22
Geometry of the Space (exhibition) 50
German Democratic Republic (GDR) 166
German Society for the Exploration of Equatorial Africa 135
Getty Museum, California 210
Getty, Paul 210
Ghost in the Shell (exhibition) 50

Godard, Jean-Luc 70
Goebbels, Heiner 102
golden surface (virtuosity and cosmopolitics): confusion and complicity 99–101; practice and cosmopoetics 105–9; rhetoric 96–98; virtuosity 101–5
Gopnik, Adam 74
Gordon, Dexter 152
Gorman, Sarah 99
Gould, Glenn 103
Goulish, Matthew 96
Grass, Günther 166
Gregory, Derek 236
Griqua National Conference, South Africa 138
Gross, Ralph 46
Group of Eight (G8) summit, Genoa 99
Guantanamo 2
Guattari, Félix 52
Guggenheim Museum, Bilbao 215
Guiliani, Carlo (protester) 9, 99–101
Gulf War 154

Hall, Steve 53
Hamera, Judith 97
Hansen, Lene 216–17
Harding, Jim 124
Harlem Globetrotters 131
Hawass, Zahi 214
Hawkins, Coleman 152
Hazlitt, William 180
Heathrow Airport, London 241
Hegel, Georg 150, 156–57
Heidegger, Martin 4–5
Hemingway, Ernest 73
Hinch, Charlotte and Emily (twins) 50
Hindu Preah Vihear temple (Cambodia–border) 213
Hiroshima after Iraq 75
Hiroshima Mon Amour 75
Hitler, Adolf 84
Hölderlin, Friedrich 72
the Holocaust 68
homo-diplomacy 133
Hottentot Venus 48, 136
Howley, Pat 113, 125
human rights 29
Human Terrain Analyst (HTA) 228
Human Terrain System (HTS) 226–30
Human Terrain Team Handbook 227–29
Human Terrain Teams (HTTs) 226

274   Index

Humanitarianism-Military-Industrial-Media-Entertainment network (H-MIME-NET) 143

IBM 239–41
'if you suspect it' campaign 237
impossibilities: generative misperformance and movements of teaching body: introduction – after end of world 150–51; misperformance 151–56; surprise 156–57
Indignados (Spain) 84
Introduction to a Distant World (video projection) 20–21, 31
Iraq Museum 204, 213
Iraq War 11, 212
Isidore of Seville 194
It is Difficult (exhibition) 10, 19–20, 23, 33, 37

Jaar, Alfredo 10, 19–23, 28, 31, 33, 37
J'Accuse 74
Jackson, Shannon 104–5
Jagendorf, Zvi 184, 190
Jeffreys, Alec 50
Johannesburg Mail and Guardian 23
John Crow (character) 80
John of Salisbury 183
Junius Brutus (character in *Coriolanus*) 173, 180, 185, 187, 188
justice and the archives: authorial invention 64–66; genre and temporality 72–75; introduction – a war crime *dispositif* 9, 63–64; Korin (character) 64–66, 67–72, 72–73; method of dramatization 66–67

Kafka, Franz 64–65
Kant, Immanuel 6–7, 27, 134
Kariel, Henry 150, 154
Kear, Adrian 12, 51
Kebono, Peter 115
Keenan,Thomas 246
Kermode, Frank 180–81
Khoisian Consultative Conference (NKOK) 138
King, Christopher 228
King Darius (character in *The Persians*) 171
King Lear 161, 194
Kittler, Friedrich 241
Kolbowski, Silvia 75
'*Kony 2012*' 143–44
Kony, Joseph 143

Korin, György (character) 64–66, 67–72, 73
Krasznahorkai, László 9, 64–67, 71, 73–74

Lady of Warka antiquity 216
Lament of the Images (1), (2) 2002 (exhibitions) 31–32
Landy, Michael 246
"*Le Mort saisit le vif*" 52
learning play ('Lehrstück') 175
Leopold II (Belgium) 135
Les Statues Meurent Aussi (Statues Also Die, essay/film) 10, 130–32, 134, 141
Let There Be Light (exhibition) 33
Levi, David 31
Levi, Primo 6
Leys Stepan, Nancy 47
Lindqvist, Sven 73
lines of sight (visualization of unknown futures): attention in a state of attraction – what the artist saw 244–46; close association – attending to difference 239–44; conclusions – citizenship and unknown futures 247; culture has an economy: are you paying attention? 237–39; introduction 234–37
Liobo, Samuel 124
'little cold breasts of an English girl', or art and identity 78–83
Locke, John 192
London bombings, July 2005 236
London riots, 2011 41, 53
London Underground 245
Lord Resistance Army 143
Lucas, Caroline 41
Lunden, Staffen 211
Lydon, Jane 51

Macbeth 188
McFate, Montgomery 221, 229
MacGinty, Roger 213
McMaster, H. R. 226, 228–29
Mahler (Jewish element) 82
Malkki, Liisa 143–44
Mandela, Nelson 32, 138
Marcuse, Herbert 91
Marian, Radu 100, 101, 104
Marker, Chris 10, 130–32
Markowicz, Mary (student) 154
Marx, Karl 52, 102–3, 150
Matsuda, David 214
Mattis, James 225

Mbeki, Thabo 140–41
Mediterranean Museum of Antiquities, Stockholm 211
Menenius Agrippa (character in *Coriolanus*) 162–63, 167, 169, 182, 184, 186–87, 192–93
Metropolitan Police, London 46, 237
Mexican politics 84–94
Millenium Development Goals (MDGs) 207
Mirković, Francis Servain (character) 63–64
misperformance (teaching): backpack and blue jeans 151; the blues come form Mali 155–56; body to body 151–52; the coup 154; faint praise 153; game theory 151; learning silence 153–54; love the one you're with 153; slacker's paradise 156; war! what is good for! 154–55
Mitchell, Tom 245
Mitchell, W. J. T. 205
Mitterand, François 138
Mohr, Jean 125, 127
Monks, Aoife 102
Monty Python 155
Mroué, Rabih 102–3
Mudimbe, V. Y. 134
Musée de l'Homme, Paris 130, 133, 138
Museum of Natural History, Paris 138
Mussawir, Edward 67
MySense biometrics programme 241

Nancy, Jean-Luc 2, 79, 168
National Museum of Iraq 215
National Portrait Gallery, London 50
National Theatre Wales (NTW) 172
Nemeth, Erik 215
New York Times 23
Ngai, Sianne 93
Nieto, Pena 93
Nietzsche 67
No Manifesto (No to Spectacle, No to Virtuosity) 105
North, Thomas 161
Nuttall, Sarah 134

'obstructionist politics' 93
Occupy Wall Street campaign 40, 84–85, 94
Oliver, Douglas 119
Orozco, Regina 89, 91
Out of Balance 22

Palizsch, Peter 167, 169
PAN party (Mexico) 88
Pangburn, Kara 156
Papua New Guinea (PNG) 113
Papua New Guinea Defence Force (PNGDF) 117–18, 123
Paris Exposition, 1900 49
Parthenon, Athens 209–10
pathognomy 47
Peace Foundation, Melanesia 113
Pearson, Mike 1, 11, 40, 161–62, 166–68, 171–73, 175–76
Peatewave village, Papua New Guinea 119–21, 123
Penguin Island 75
Pepys, Samuel 50
performing audience (*Coriolanus*, relation and participation): experimental set-up 170–74; play in public 161–65; political impact: ' ... then all power to the audience!' 165–70; relational theatre, audience in performance 174–76
Perry, Grayson 215
pharmakon (cure) 108
phrenology 47
physiognomy 47
plantón (Mexico) 89–91, 93
Platform for Art, London Underground 245
Plato 29, 67
Plutarch 180, 183
Policraticus 183
'political being-together' 3
Pond, Steve 154
Poole, Deborah 51
Pope Leo XIII 68
Pope Pius XII 68
'post-Fordist' capitalism 106
Pound, Ezra 73
power, security and antiquities: introduction 203–4; looting during wars and political turmoil 212–15; museums as looters 209–12; object looting: what takes what 209; power, agency, objects, security, assemblages 215–17; thing power 204–6, 217; thing power and security 206–9
Prada, New York 242
PRD party (Mexico) 93
Présence Africaine 131
PRI party (Mexico) 88
Prophet Mohammad 216

Qureshi, Sadia 137

radio frequency identification (RFID) 242–43, 246
Rainer, Yvonne 105
Rancière, Jacques 2–3, 8, 26–31, 36–37, 93, 144, 168
Rassol, Ciraj 139
redemptive dipositif 143
Reguillo, Rassana 84
relational aesthetics 176
Resnais, Alain 10, 130–32
revolution in military affairs (RMA) 222
Rice, Condoleezza 151
Richard II 194
Richter, Gerhard 80
Ricks, Thomas E. 222
Ridout, Nicholas 100, 102–3
Rio Tinto 117
Ritter, Joachim 82
Robinson, Sugar Ray 130–31
Rodriguez, Jesusa 89–92
Rosetta stone 209
Rovonana incident, Central Bougainville 117
Rülicke, Käthe 167, 169
Rwanda Project 1994–98 33–35
Ryan, James 48

Said, Edward 246
Sancho Panza (character) 64
Sanders, Pharoah 153
Saunders, Tanya 154
Schipol Airport, Amsterdam 245
Scottish Enlightenment 157
Sekula, Allan 49
Serra Palada, Brazil 20, 22
Shakespeare, William (*Coriolanus*) 161–62, 165–69, 171, 176, 179, 183, 187–88, 191–93, 195
Shapiro, Michael 7, 9
Shewan, Garry (chief constable) 43
'Shock and Awe' (US) 222, 225
'Shop a Looter' campaign 43
Sicinius Velutus (character in *Coriolanus*) 170, 173, 180, 187, 188, 190–91
Siculus (character in *Coriolanus*) 185, 187
Silverman, Kaja 238
Simmel, Georg 68–69
Sloterdijk, Peter 107
Slovo, Gillian 40
Smith, Adam 156

social distances 66
Societas Raffaello Sanzio (SRS) 99, 105
Society and Space (journal) 1
South African Heritage Resources Agency (SAHRA) 141
'SPOT' observation technique 243
stagecraft/statecraft/mancraft: beautiful/ugly: ethnological reasons and diplomatic body 134–36; conclusions 143–45; *dramatis personae*: Saartjie Baartman's dramatizing and racing of diplomatic/colonial body 136–41; necromancies and profanations: calling up/'recalling' postcolonial ontologies and apparatuses 141–43; poetics and histrionics of death and estrangement 130–34
staging war as cultural encounter (US): conclusions 230; cultural knowledge 223–25; introduction 221–22; social sciences to the rescue: Human Terrain System 226–30
Stanislavkian naturalism (acting) 102
Statues Also Die see *Les Statues Meurent Aussi*
Steichen, Edward 48
Stengers, Isabelle 107–8
Stifters Dinge (theatre work) 102
Stitzman, Fred 46
Straub, Jean-Marie 9, 82
Studies in Trans-disciplinary Method 7
'Survey of Jazz' (Cornell University) 155

Tagg, John 48–49, 51
Taliban 212
Tarlena Girls' High School Choir 121–22
Tenai, Lawrence 124–25
Tenschert, Joachim 167
'territories'/'territory' term in Shakespeare's works 193
The Art of Philosophy 107
The Beautiful and the Damned (exhibition) 50
The Death of Empedocles 78
The Emancipated Spectator 36
The Eyes of Guteta Emerita (exhibition) 34–37
The Fundamental Concepts of Metaphysics 4
The Jerusalem Post 74
'The Method of Dramatization' 9
The Persians 171–72, 174

The Pixelated Revolution (exhibition) 102
The Sound of Silence (exhibition) 23–25, 28, 31
The Tempest 194
'The Truth about Sancho Panza' 64
The Unknown Terrorist 234–35, 239
Theatre Journal 102
theatre as post-operative follow-up (Bougainville Photoplay Project): between ethnography and performance 118–25; introduction 113; photographs: standing before history 134–18; unfinished business 125–27
think, pig (Beckett, Samuel) 4–5
Thomas, Nicholas 120
Thrift, Nigel 1, 181
Thin Cities Project 245
Thucydides 156
Time Magazine 94, 214
Tobias, Philip 138–39
traces of presence: dissensus 26–31; illuminating the apparatus 31–37; presence and representation 19–26
Tragedia Endogonidia 99
Trainor, Meghan 246
Treadwell, James 53
Trotter, Andrew (chief constable) 45
True, Marion 210
Tullus Aufidius (character in *Coriolanus*) 164–65, 173, 180, 188, 190, 192, 194
Turkle, Sherry 214
Turning Turning (A Choreography of thoughts) 106

Ugly Feelings 93
Un hériter (An Heir, film) 9, 82
UNESCO (United Nations Educational, Scientific and Cultural Organization) 203, 210–11, 213
United Kingdom (UK): e-borders Semaphore and Iris Programmes 241; riots 40–42

United States (US): Army and Marine Corps 222–23; Defense Department 32; Farm Security Administration 48; security issues 207; Transport Security Administration 243: *see also* staging war as cultural encounter
unity of contradictions ('Einheit der Gegensätze') 167
US News 7
Verfremdungseffekt (estrangement) 119
Vibrant Matter 204
Virgila (character in *Coriolanus*) 173
Virno, Paolo 103–5, 106
visualization of unknown futures *see* lines of sight
Volumnia (character in *Coriolanus*) 164, 173, 181, 184, 194

Waiting for Godot 4
Walzer, Michael 154
War 67
Wellcome Collection, London 50
Wells, Robin Headlam 180
what is this? (question) 66–67
White, Hayden 97
Williams, William Carlos 19
Willis, Susan 235
Winlow, Simon 53
Wollaston, Sarah 44
World Shakespeare Festival, 2012 161

You Must Change Your Life! On Anthropotechnology 107

Zehfuss, Maja 1, 12
Žižek, Slavoj 2, 53, 94
Zócalo (Mexico City central square) 9, 85, 88–89
Zola, Emile 74
Zone 72
'Zones of Justice' 63